Under the Southern Cross

To all members of the U.S. Naval Reserve,
whose dedication and service to the defense
of our country goes often without notice
or acclaim, this work is thankfully dedicated

Under the Southern Cross

A Petty Officer's Chronicle of
the USS *Octans,* Banana Boat
Become World War II Supply Ship
for the Southern Pacific Fleet

by KENNETH G. OLIVER

McFarland & Company, Inc., Publishers
Jefferson, North Carolina, and London

Author's note: I have changed some of the names of my shipmates while relating certain specific incidents.

British Library Cataloguing-in-Publication data are available

Library of Congress Cataloguing-in-Publication Data

Oliver, Kenneth G.
   Under the Southern Cross : a petty officer's chronicle of the USS Octans, banana boat become World War II supply ship for the Southern Pacific Fleet / by Kenneth G. Oliver.
      p. cm.
   Includes bibliographical references and index.
   ISBN 0-89950-999-1 (sewn softcover : 50# alk. paper) ∞
   1. Oliver, Kenneth G.   2. World War, 1939–1945 — Food supply — Pacific Area.   3. Seamen — United States — Biography.   4. United States. Navy — Biography.   5. World War, 1939–1945 — Personal narratives, American.   6. Octans (Supply ship)   I. Title.
D769.75.045045   1995
940.54'26 — dc20   94-31153
                                                                        CIP

©1995 Kenneth G. Oliver. All rights reserved

Manufactured in the United States of America

McFarland & Company, Inc., Publishers
   Box 611, Jefferson, North Carolina 28640

Acknowledgments

Any chronicle with the scope of this one cannot be produced by one person working in a cocoon but must rely on the kind assistance of many other persons and organizations. I am deeply indebted to many who have provided data and encouragement, making this book possible. The following list is intended to be roughly in the order in which I applied for assistance, and not in any order of importance to the production of this book.

Naval Liaison Office, National Personnel Records Center, St. Louis, Missouri, for my service records.

John Campbell of United Brands Company, who referred me to Jeff Brown, through whom I got in touch with Richard W. Berry and Cornelius Maher, former officials of the United Fruit Company and United Brands Company.

Fall River Marine Museum, Fall River, Massachusetts, Mrs. Pontes and John Gosson.

National Archives, Military Reference Branch, Washington, D.C., Robert E. Richardson, James Cassedy, and Tod Butler.

U.S. Naval Institute, Annapolis, Maryland, Customer Service, and Paul Stillwell of the History Division.

U.S. Navy Office of Information, Washington, D.C., Judith V. Van Benthuysen, who put me in touch with several former crew members, among those listed below.

U.S. Navy Office of the Judge Advocate General, Cdr. R.N. Fiske.

U.S. Navy Historical Center, Washington, D.C., Bernard F. Cavalcante.

Acknowledgments

Department of Veterans Affairs, Records Processing Center, St. Louis, Missouri, Alice Hunter, who referred me to several former crew members among those listed below. (Rank or rating is given as it existed at the approximate time of service on the *Octans*.)

Royal New Zealand Hydrographic Office, Auckland, New Zealand.

John L.T. Butler, Director of Town Planning, Brisbane City Council, Brisbane, Australia.

Ralph Meilandt (lieutenant) and his Australian wife, who live in Alamo, California, both of whom were very helpful in checking technical details and in supplying me with stories from the wardroom.

Former crew members (with former ranks) who helped me immensely in furnishing details which give the narrative life and substance:

Spencer Batchelder, Fallbrook, California (bosun's mate)
Walter H. Costa, Lafayette, California (ensign)
Walter Dowgiewicz, Massachusetts (ship's cook)
Ben Crandall, Brighton, Iowa (chief watertender)
Joseph H. Forcier, San Diego, California (gunner's mate)
Hugh Foster, Otsego, Michigan (gunner's mate)
John Gager, Arlington, Virginia (ensign)
Marvin Huitt, Allegan, Michigan (coxswain)
Joseph Kuch, Cape Canaveral, Florida (cargo officer)
Donald Leonard, Attica, New York (electrician's mate)
James Lucid, Omaha, Nebraska (electrician's mate)
Walter Peplowski, Plains, Pennsylvania (shipfitter)
Dennis Rinaldi, Stroudsberg, Pennsylvania (watertender)
Mike Rosella, Old Bridge, New Jersey (chief electrician's mate)
Clarence Seagren, Dixon, Illinois (carpenter's mate)
Walter Setzco, Leominster, Massachusetts (carpenter's mate)
Lyle Stevens, St. Anthony, Minnesota (ship's cook)
J.W. Williams, San Marcos, California (radarman)
William W. Woodard, Garden City, South Carolina (chief yeoman)

Special thanks are due Mrs. Mary Melville, widow of John Melville, whose book *The Great White Fleet* supplied much of the data for the second chapter. Mention must also be made of the help of the various others, such as publishers, authors, librarians, public officials in the United States as well as New Zealand and Australia, known and unknown, too numerous to mention but important to the success of this story.

KENNETH G. OLIVER
August 1994

Contents

	Acknowledgments	v
	Preface	1
1	In the Beginning I: In Training	5
2	In the Beginning II: Bananas and SS *Ulua*	14
3	Transformation: SS *Ulua* to USS *Octans*	20
4	Supply Run #1: Shakedown I	34
5	Overhaul in Auckland, New Zealand	51
6	Supply Run #2: Shakedown II	74
7	Supply Run #3: To Australia	87
8	Supply Run #4: A Death at Sea	102
9	Supply Run #5: Aground!	120
10	Overhaul in Sydney in the Fall	136
11	Supply Run #6: To the Admiralty Islands	144
12	Supply Run #7: Stormy Weather	155
13	Supply Run #8: Fumigation	168
14	Supply Run #9: Scratch One Army Dock	179
15	Supply Run #10: To the Pits	189
16	Supply Run #11: Change of Command	198
17	Overhaul: Thirty Days in Sydney	209

18	Supply Run #12: Into the Fray	223
19	Supply Run #13: Tempting Fate	235
20	Supply Run #14: My Last Farewell	248
21	The Final Months	260
	Epilogue	273
	Notes	275
	Appendixes	
	A. Manning Complement, USS *Octans*	279
	B. Major Navy Abbreviations	281
	C. Refrigerated Stores Ships Operated by the U.S. Navy	283
	D. Ships of the U.S. Navy	285
	E. Australian English	289
	Bibliography	291
	Index	293
	Military History of Kenneth G. Oliver	303

Preface

The mighty carrier steaming at flank speed, escorted by one or more low, fast battleships, several cruisers, and out on the periphery the "small boys," all rushing to battle the enemy — radar screens rotating, spray from the sharp prows flying, signal lamps blinking, flags flying from the signal halyards, sailors in glistening white uniforms walking the decks in purposeful strides. That is the scene that average U.S. citizens think of when reading of the mighty exploits of their Navy. It is also the Navy that the brass in the Pentagon and the PR people in immaculate uniforms and proud postures instill in the hearts of Americans. This image is always at the forefront when there is a bill pending before Congress to fund another increment to the fleet or another dangerous year.

Then there is another Navy, known as the Auxiliary Fleet, that very few stalwart citizens have ever seen or read anything about. These are the ships that bear the letter A in front of their official designation, such as ARG, AO, or AF. They often go unnoticed and, when seen in the ports, usually at some obscure, commercial wharf, are often mistaken for one of the aging, obsolete Merchant Marine fleet. This aspect is promoted, perhaps not deliberately, by the Navy's refusing to place the big A in front of a ship's designation near the bow. The men that are seen on the decks of these nondescript vessels are dressed not in gleaming white uniforms, but usually in dirty dungarees and white hats, often dyed some shade of blue, that are bent out of shape and slammed on the head in any fashion, depending on how the wearer perceives his position on the ship, or what he thinks of it.

Probably the lowest of these are the heaps of rusting, gray metal known as yard oilers, with the letters *IX* before their number. These relics are usually to be found anchored in the bay at the far-flung American bases around the globe where so diligently is shown the flag.

As the armed forces built up in World War II's Pacific campaign, the U.S. Army Services of Supply found it necessary to expand rapidly to provide their forces with all of the necessary supplies. The U.S. Navy found it necessary to do the same, for in addition to those men aboard the fleet vessels, there were also a large number of Navy personnel on the many shore bases which were established in the Pacific islands. By the middle of 1944, the demand for food shipments alone to the forces in the Pacific totaled approximately 75,000 tons a month. Two-thirds of this consisted of what the Navy terms "dry stores," consisting of canned, bagged, and boxed foodstuffs not requiring refrigeration. The remaining 25,000 tons per month consisted of fresh and frozen foods, such as fruits, vegetables, and meat. The USS *Octans* accounted for about 36,000 tons total, in 17 supply runs for the refrigerated portion, plus over 5,000 military passengers, and an unknown amount of general cargo carried in the holds and on deck.

In addition to the ships commandeered by the U.S. Navy, the War Shipping Board also operated a large fleet of former Merchant Marine ships, both dry cargo types and refrigerated ships.

The public long ago became acquainted with one of the lower forms of this decrepit Navy, the "USS *Reluctant*," as described in the novel *Mr. Roberts*.[1] The present work is about an auxiliary ship which bore the name USS *Octans* (AF-26), somewhat above the level of the "USS *Reluctant*."

The USS *Octans* was one of a large number of merchant ships which were employed by the U.S. Navy Service Force, assigned to the 7th Fleet based in Hawaii during World War II. It was the old SS *Ulua* of the Great White Fleet belonging to the United Fruit Company and one of 35 such reefer vessels taken over from various commercial firms after December 7, 1941.

The U.S. Navy has a standard system for naming its ships, with all ships of the same service being named after a definite series, such as states, cities, places, people, battles, and so on. In the case of refrigerated food ships, or "reefers" as they are often called, the ships are usually named after constellations. The USS *Octans* was thus named after the constellation Octans. The constellation is a three-star pattern, one of which, Octantis, is almost directly over the south polar axis. It is very faint and requires at least a 5-inch telescope to capture sufficient illumination to permit finding it, let alone analyzing it.

During most of the life of the *Octans* in the war, we were constantly in view of the Southern Cross, a constellation which is circumpolar over most of Australia and appears on the flags for both Australia and New Zealand. The smallest of the constellations, its scientific name is Crux Australis. It appears something like the diagram (see facing page) and is located in the Milky Way on the southern edge of Centaurus.

Preface

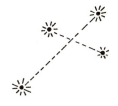

The Southern Cross (sketch by the author).

Thus we have the constellation Octans overlooking the Southern Cross, which in turn looks down upon the ship *Octans*. Could it be that someone, some time, sitting at a small desk in some remote nook of the Department of the Navy, who had been assigned the task of finding names for all of the various and sundry new ships being brought into service was just a little bit poetically inclined? Was it further possible that someone was aware of the future area of operation for our ship? I like to think that that was the case and that the namefinder felt he had done a good day's work when he hit upon *Octans* as the proper and fitting name for our ship.

There were many limitations which had to be contended with in the compiling of this chronicle, not the least of which was the fading memory of things which happened more than fifty years ago. My attempts to locate former personnel of the ship met with limited results, but these few did contribute a large amount of data and personal remembrances, for which I am deeply grateful. Added to this are the shortages in the deck log records available, as detailed at several places during this narrative, and the paucity of official correspondence of any value between Washington and the Mare Island Navy Yard during the conversion phase of the ship's history.

Often the incidents related to me by the many crew members contacted did not tie in to any entries in the ship's deck log. Also, the various reports on common incidents often only vaguely coincided with each other. It was necessary not only to attempt to place them in what appeared to be the proper point in the narrative, but also to try to provide details that had the greatest amount of congruence among the reports. Consequently, any reader who was directly involved may not completely agree with my telling of it. The incident took place, and that is the important part of the narration, I feel.

This, then, is the story of the USS *Octans* (AF-26), formerly the SS *Ulua*, as I saw it from the lowest point in the ship. There are places when my memory of events does not match the official record on the deck log, if, in fact there is any mention of it in the deck log. In some incidents, I have purposely changed the names of those involved. In some cases, the common nicknames or first names of the people involved is deemed necessary to make the story complete. After fifty years, of what purpose would it serve to lay blame or credit upon any person? We were all in the same boat — no pun intended. We were all doing our best as we saw the task, and we all made mistakes. Most, I trust, have profited by them. But, in the final analysis, the job was done, and the war was won.

May all ghosts rest in peace and not disturb our dreams.

Chapter 1

In the Beginning I: In Training

"Sorry, fella, but your eyesight doesn't quite make it."

With that pronouncement, the Navy medic dashed my hopes of joining the U.S. Navy. It was only temporary, however, as he looked at my crestfallen face and added, "Oh, hell, go on through!"

I wasted no more time but hurried to join the other naked recruits of the Bemidji, Minnesota, draft of October 13, 1942,* at the Wold Chamberlin Naval Recruiting Center at Minneapolis. The room was cold, the floor (it was still a floor to us landlubbers) was cold, and we were cold. I shivered throughout my whole body. In short order, we were sworn in, given travel vouchers and instructions, and told to report to the train station the next day for travel to the Great Lakes Naval Training Station for boot camp.

It was a happy day for me. I had thwarted the Army draft and was now an apprentice seaman, V-6, in the Naval Reserve, according to my enlistment record. Since my early ship modeling days at my home in Walker, Minnesota, I had always been interested in the sea and ships, an interest that carried on through the first four terms at engineering college. By the time I enlisted, I already had studied, in my spare time, the basics of marine engineering and dynamics of ship and yacht design. My library contained Audel's *New Marine Engineer's Guide*[2] and several books on ship and yacht design.

So now the Navy had me—age 20, weight 125 pounds, height 5 feet 8 inches, poor eyesight corrected with glasses to 20/20, and a physique

---

*Material for this chapter was mainly from the author's memory, with pertinent dates and data taken from his service record.

5

completely unfit for physical combat. What could the Navy do with such a sad specimen? I did not spend much time dwelling on the question, as I was their problem now. My problem was one of survival in the months ahead, reinforced with a desire to do the best I could to utilize my talents, such as they were.

Arrival at the Great Lakes Naval Training Station on October 16 was not an encouraging beginning. As soon as we stepped off the bus and lined up, still in our civies, we were greeted by the hoots and catcalls of those "Boots" parading by and such discouraging comments as: "You'll be sorrrry!" "Hey, Mac, watch out for the square needle in the left testicle!" "Wait till you taste the saltpeter in the chow!"

Not many weeks later, of course, we "Boots" would be making the same calls to the incoming new guys.

The barren drill grounds, the stark barracks, and the chilly air with the wind blowing off Lake Michigan would all have caused us to groan and gripe, except that we were kept too busy to give it much thought.

Our company consisted of a melange of male physical specimens from the Midwest area. The normal distribution curve indicated that there had to be at least one recruit who was just the opposite of me, and there was such an individual. Whereas I was about the lightest one in the company, he was the heaviest by far. Most of us felt sorry for him. He failed miserably in almost any physical activity to which we were subjected. Finally, he was transferred out of the company, I know not where.

The oldest man in the company was about 30, of average build and physical condition, who managed to perform as required. I noticed that many of the younger recruits treated him with some degree of respect, often masking it by throwing in some humorous banter. He survived boot camp.

We were taken under tow by a chief petty officer (CPO) with a gruff manner and a loud voice. He interspersed training lectures with friendly advice on getting along in the Navy and, especially, with the old Navy hands with whom we would come in contact; for example: "Some of the old Navy regulars have acquired some strange personal habits over their years in the Navy. My own personal advice to you is to keep your eyes and your thoughts to yourself, especially if you are in the head [shower and toilet rooms], or you may find yourself cold-cocked on the deck!" "Don't volunteer for a damned thing! If they wancha, they'll come and getcha!"

He also told us to feel free to ask him any questions we had concerning Navy life but warned us he was not our mother — he was not built that way.

There was one old geezer whose purpose we were never quite able to fathom — an antiquated CPO with a chest full of campaign ribbons and a sleeve covered with hash marks. It was obvious that he and his uniform had gone into moth balls together and had come out together. His accent and manner of speaking were so comical that any advice he had to offer during his brief visits to our barracks was missed entirely. He no doubt meant well, but we looked at him as a much-needed comic relief in our lives.

We had calisthenics at any time of the day or night, and once, we lined up for our shots in both arms directly after a long hike. There was drilling, drilling, and more drilling on the cold, wind-swept parade ground to the harsh calls of the squad drillmaster. To boost our patriotic fighting spirit, and to help us keep in step, the drillmaster would break into a song or a cadence chant around which we were expected to rally. One of the most-heard songs on the parade grounds was "Remember Pearl Harbor."[3] It often got to be quite a sight when the parade ground was completely covered with the various companies, each practicing their marching and singing prowess at the same time, while attempting to stay clear of each other. Interspersed through it all would be the shouted command of the drillmaster, calling cadence and giving maneuvering orders. It not only was inspiring, but also kept us warm and helped us forget the biting winter wind coming off the lake and any other gripes we may have been harboring.

Our sleeping arrangements consisted of the old Navy hammocks, slung between pipe rails about three feet from the deck, with just enough space between hammocks to permit us to sleep without bumping our neighbors, providing we had slung the hammock in the prescribed Navy fashion. Those of us who understood the instructions had little trouble sleeping through the night without rolling out onto the deck. But those who insisted that the most comfortable way was to sprawl over it like they had done in their backyard at home were the ones that went THUMP! in the night, accompanied by cursing and groans. They soon learned that the barracks' deck was much harder than their backyard lawn. The trick was simply to curl up inside the hammock, with the mattress and the sides around you, not just under you. The problem was getting into and out of it, but that was soon mastered by most of us.

Fortunately, we managed to escape the long, early hours of that old hated chore of basic training, kitchen police (KP). Instead, our company drew battalion work parties consisting of painting for the station facilities. For one solid week, we painted loose boards—two coats, both sides— which were destined for use on the parade ground bleachers. I learned how to properly hold a paintbrush during that week, and that is all that I can truthfully admit to. Except for that, the week was a total loss.

The Navy had quite a battery of training films to which we were often subjected; mandatory, of course. Among them were films on Navy life, health, and hygiene. Among the latter were the inevitable films on how to comport ourselves off base and among civilian life. The main worry seemed to be that we would not know how to prevent getting a nasty case of that old devil, venereal disease (VD). The gist of the message was that if we got to her, we could be sure that some other sailor, serviceman, or 4-F got to her first! The main remedy available from the pharmacists on duty at Navy sick bay was a small, single-application tube of prophylactic, or "Pro's" in Navy lingo. All sick bays were amply supplied with them, and they were available free, no questions asked. Dirty, leering looks, maybe, but no questions.

An attempt was made at teaching us how to handle and row the Navy whaleboat, and that was a fiasco. It only lasted about two hours and was dropped, either from lack of time or because it was considered a lost cause.

Swimming tests resulted in a few men having to take lessons. I managed to swim the required 100 yards but was one of the last to finish. This was followed by training in staying afloat in the water using only our clothes, pillow cover, and mattress cover as floats. Fortunately, I never had to put that training into practice.

We all griped among ourselves about almost everything. The chief assured us that it was expected of us, as long as it did not get personal or militant. Most of the men griped continually about the chow. I am not sure they were used to better meals back home, considering the recent economic Depression.

Personally, I managed to thrive quite well on Navy chow, and that was true through my entire career of 39 months. At times, I didn't especially care for beans for breakfast, but I ate them. When we got in the chow line for breakfast and the message "Hebrews 13.8" was passed back from the front of the line, we knew there were beans again that morning. To this day, I can eat almost anything put before me. In addition to beans, there was a nondescript concoction called, in Navy lingo, "Shit on a Shingle," consisting of slightly creamed beef bits on a piece of toast. Then there was scrapple, a fried chunk of meat scraps mixed in with what appeared to be cornmeal mush. It didn't taste bad at all, as it was usually smothered in thin syrup. (I can guarantee you that no one in the chow line bothered to ask the Navy chef for the recipe!) I have never seen, smelled, or heard of anything like it since, missing nothing as a result.

As I was probably the only one in the battalion who had any college courses behind me, the aptitude tests put me at the top of the battalion with a score of 94.4. This gave me my choice of service schools. I chose Navy quartermaster school, with a second choice being the engineering department, commonly known as the Black Gang aboard ship. My poor eyesight ruled me out of the first choice, so I ended up in machinist's mate school.

With four weeks of boot camp completed, with a fireman third class rating, and with a short home leave behind me, I reported back to the Great Lakes Naval Training Station (GLNTS), machinist's mate school, on November 26, 1942. We had the same type of barracks, but now we were sleeping in bunks, two high.

We all went on liberty quite often in Chicago and Waukegan, Illinois, and in Kenosha and Milwaukee, Wisconsin. In spite of the miserable climate of that area, we managed to enjoy ourselves quite well.

The daily routine was similar to boot camp, with the exception that the emphasis was on shop time and classroom work, with "homework" to be performed in the barracks during our spare time. There were still housekeeping chores to be done in the barracks, such as steelwooling the deck, cleaning windows, regular policing of the barracks, watchstanding, and those damned inspections.

Speaking of inspections, we were lined up periodically while in service school and told to drop our pants and pass in review before the battery of pharmacist's mates in what is known as Short Arm inspection. Ostensibly, they were looking for any signs of venereal disease, but we rather suspected that some of the "chancre mechanics" were simply taking unfair advantage of Navy procedure to get their kicks. The scuttlebutt around the barracks informed us that the women in the service were subjected to the same procedure, except they called it "Foxhole Inspection."

Each and every Sunday morning in boot camp, as well as in service school, we were marched off to the church service of our listed denomination. In boot camp, before the first such service, the chief explained to us that throughout the history of our country, the Navy has always had a religious base, observed whenever and wherever practical. All services ended with the singing of the "Navy Hymn," which was a very thoughtful and sobering reminder to all sailors of the dangers and pitfalls inherent in our chosen profession.

When Christmas came, there was a special treat in store for us. We were marched off to the gymnasium, which had been converted to an auditorium for the occasion. There was no Bob Hope, Francis Langford, or big band, but a Bing Crosby Christmas movie. First, there were a number of Christmas songs played over the speaker system. The audience was very quiet during the renditions of "I'll Be Home for Christmas"[4] and "I'm Dreaming of a White Christmas."[5] A feeling of good old-fashioned homesickness hit many of the men gathered there that night. There were even a few sobs detected when the songs were over. There was no singing that night when we marched back to the barracks in the bone-chilling wind coming off the lake.

Drilling consisted mostly of marching to and from classes and chow lines. Oh, there were occasional drilling sessions assigned as punishment for some breach in regulations, and usually at importune times, such as midnight.

The battalion I was in was made up mostly of men from Massachusetts, with about a dozen of us from Minnesota. This made for some good-hearted rivalry between the two groups. With over a hundred of the "Bawston" men lined up against us, we were hard-pressed to hold our own, but we managed. As might be expected, there was one "Bawstonian" who was more aggressive than the rest. Even his own friends from Skolley Square had trouble with him and often had to restrain him. He was a heavy gambler (yes, there was some of that in the barracks), and as a result, when the school was over after 16 weeks and the entire battalion was going on leave, he did not have enough money to buy his train fare home. Some of his colleagues made the rounds of the barracks asking for donations to permit him to go home on leave. As I recall, he did not get very much from the Minnesota contingent; nothing, in fact, from me, as we were the butt of most of his insults.

Class work consisted mostly of basic mathematics, trigonometry, shipboard arrangements of the machinery spaces, fire fighting systems, and basic theory of boilers, steam turbines, propulsion and auxiliary machinery. My previous college courses, along with my interest in ships as a hobby, helped me immensely. Many of the budding machinist's mates had difficulty with the algebra and trigonometry problems. As I had already had several courses in both, in high school as well as college, I soon found myself holding impromptu classes.

Finally, our schooling was completed, and the battalion chief was notified that I was to graduate as Honor Man of the class of 525 students, with a final score of 94.63. My rating was to be machinist's mate second class, along with many others. The graduating ceremony was held on March 22, 1943, in the gymnasium at the base. Prior to this, my picture was taken with the base commandant, and it, along with the PR blurb, was circulated to the news media. This included my hometown newspaper, which my family had owned for years. My father proudly ran the article in the family paper.

Schooling was not over for many of the graduates, as many were assigned to several advanced courses of training available throughout the country. Among those, 16 of us were assigned to an additional four weeks of training in refrigeration at the Carrier Corporation, in Syracuse, New York, following a short home leave.

Home leave over, I reported for training at Syracuse and commenced

1. In the Beginning I: In Training

The author, 1943.

school with the other graduates of GLNTS on April 3. Living accommodations consisted of rooming at various private homes in the city and taking our meals at restaurants as best we could. We received a per diem allowance of $2.75, which was almost sufficient. Eating our lunches at the Carrier Corporation cafeteria helped.

The four weeks was a continual daytime cram course, but it was well organized and taught. We learned the theory of refrigeration, the practical aspects of operating the Carrier equipment which was installed on many Navy ships, and troubleshooting.

Evenings and weekends were free, and we made the most of them. We thought that since Syracuse was an inland city, there would be no problem in getting dates with the local girls. For the most part, that was

1. In the Beginning I: In Training 13

true, and the local ice skating rink was a popular hangout for many of us. It was there that I managed to get acquainted with a cute little Italian girl. We went to several movies together, and I walked her home after each date — until, that is, the evening when we were standing and talking outside her front door and her father roared down for her to come in at once. It was just my luck, of course, to be dating the daughter of a World War I Navy man who did not want his daughter associating with a sailor.

Graduation ceremonies on May 1, 1943, were brief and consisted mostly of a class picture being taken, with all members identified, and copies of the picture being sent to our homes.

Just prior to this, however, we gathered in the classroom to sort out the berthing assignments available in the fleet for refrigeration machinists. Most of the class were anxious for active sea duty, and the fighting ships were quickly snapped up. However, there were four of us who were a little reluctant to volunteer for heavy fighting duty, so we accepted assignment to the USS *Octans* (AF-26), a refrigerated food supply ship.

Our training period was over. Transportation drafts were assigned, and I was put in charge of the four of us for the train ride to commissioning and fitting out duty for the ship of our choice in the yards of the United Engineering Company at Alameda, California, under the direction of the Mare Island Navy Yard.

All of the horror stories told about wartime travel on the nation's trains were true, as I can verify. Our travel vouchers stated that we were to travel by sleeper, but there were none available, and our vouchers did not contain any type of priority. All attempts to cajole, bribe, and plead with the porter were futile. He simply pointed out that we could see for ourselves what the conditions were. And he was right, of course, as there were servicemen sleeping in the overhead baggage racks. So we had to sleep sitting up as best we could in our seats, lucky to have even those.

Reporting into the receiving station at San Francisco, we were given our instructions, told where to catch the ferry to the Alameda dockyards, placed on per diem again, and were left up to our own decisions as to where to stay from a list of available accommodations. I chose the local YMCA, as it was the closest to the ferry landing.

Opposite: Carrier Corporation Refrigeration school class of May 1, 1943. The author is pictured center of back row (author's collection).

Chapter 2

In the Beginning II: Bananas and SS *Ulua**

When Columbus took possession of the West Indies in the name of Spain, that country was quick to establish her domain over the area. In about 1516, the banana was introduced from the Canary Islands into what was at the time known as Hispaniola. The man generally credited with bringing the first bananas into the western hemisphere was a Spanish Franciscan, Friar Tomas de Berlanga. From there, it spread slowly into neighboring islands and became well established on Jamaica.[6] This was the Cavendish variety, small, thin-skinned, and easily bruised. The Central American variety is known as the Gros Michel and originated in Africa. It is larger, thicker skinned, and the one with which we are most acquainted in this country. It was the one chosen by the United Fruit Company to cultivate in large tracts throughout the other Caribbean countries.

When the banana import business was young, it was usual for a ship to travel from one grower to another, taking on board whatever was available and loading and stowing the bananas mostly by manual labor. This was no problem because local labor was cheap and plentiful and even included native women. In those cases where no wharf was provided, the bananas often had to be carried through the surf and loaded into surfboats outside the surf line. The surfboats then went alongside the ship, and the bananas were handed to men on temporary staging slung from the bulwarks, who then placed them into the holds, either through cargo doors or through the hatches on deck.

Much of the material for this chapter was provided in the book The Great White Fleet *by John Melville (1976), Vantage Press, Inc. The author is deeply indebted to his widow, Mary Melville, for her kind approval of the use of information contained in that book.*

Loading from a wharf was much simpler. Each workman would carry a bunch of bananas on his shoulder, bring it alongside the ship tied up at the wharf, and then pass his load up to the deck loaders, who would then take it into the hold. There it would be stacked wherever the foreman directed.

Those procedures were typical, but there were several varieties of the process, depending upon the loading facilities. In all cases, it was necessary for the bunches of bananas to be counted, and this was done by the tallyman, who tallied each bunch as it was loaded and handed a "counter" to the bearer to claim his pay at day's end.

During those early days, when the banana cultivation and shipping was steadily expanding, the crop provided one of the major sources of income to the developing Central American and Caribbean economies, as it still does.

Bananas required ventilation and or refrigeration throughout the holds to regulate the rate of ripening in order to insure proper condition when they arrived at their destination in the states. For this reason, the bananas were green when loaded into the ship and usually yellow with a tinge of green when they reached the grocer's premises.

There were natural catastrophes, of course, which caused temporary disruptions. The growers were sometimes faced with the loss of an entire crop, either from tropical storms and hurricanes or from banana wilt, also called the Panama Disease.

The native workmen who loaded the bananas into the ships developed their particular versions of the work songs reflecting their history and that of the Caribbean. Many of the songs were variations of the old sea chanties, a hand-me-down from the days when the sloops and schooners plied their trade among the islands of the Caribbean. Even to this day, the romance of the banana trade is still being kept alive in calypso music from Jamaica. Who hasn't stopped whatever he was doing and listened to the singing and unique rhythm and romance in calypso songs like "Day-O"?[7]

Of such was the work and sweat — and the romantic appeal — of the early days of the banana trade.

On May 19, 1871, Captain Lorenzo Dow Baker brought his two-masted schooner, *Telegraph* into Long Wharf, Boston Harbor. The produce merchants crowded around to see what he had brought, as he was noted for bringing exotic fruits and other items from the Caribbean and, notably, Jamaica. His cargo consisted mostly of coconuts and some strange fruit clustered on stems, known as bananas. The merchants had heard of bananas, but no one among the Boston produce merchants wanted to risk selling them to their customers — no one, that is, except one

Andrew W. Preston, who was employed by Severns & Company produce brokers and who talked his employers into letting him try his skill with the strange fruit. He sold all of them, and at a fair profit; and thus the banana trade was introduced into Boston.

Captain Baker gradually increased his banana imports over the next 14 years; then in 1885, he joined with Andrew Preston to found the Boston Fruit Company. The fruit business prospered steadily, and more sailing vessels were added as the demand for their exotic fruits increased, each vessel larger than the previous ones. Soon, steam replaced sail, and another cycle of evolution was started.

The business was doing so well that toward the end of the nineteenth century, several steps were taken to expand their business even further. One bold step was taken to acquire and prepare for cultivation a large number of coastal areas around the Caribbean and Central America. During this time, also, several mergers were accomplished, culminating in the United Fruit Company, capitalized at $11,230,000,[8] making it one of the largest conglomerates of the period.

The turn of the century brought more progress in the shipping of bananas, starting with the advent of mechanical refrigeration for the holds. This required that the holds be insulated, and considerable experimentation was performed to determine the ultimate temperature for ripening the bananas during their voyage. Finally, it was determined that 50 to 53 degrees Fahrenheit (F) was the best range, and that has held fairly well to this day.

The firm added its own staff of naval architects and marine engineers, and for two decades they kept the firm of Workman Clark & Co., of Belfast, Ireland, very busy. Ships were being launched rapidly, all designed to carry passengers in addition to bananas and other cargo. The first three vessels were delivered in 1904, three more in 1908, seven in 1909, three in 1911, and three in 1913. These last three were the largest, each with a length of 470 feet. All of them were coal burning, with mechanical refrigeration, and accommodations for passengers.

During this period, ship-to-shore radio communication was perfected and adopted in the marine shipping industry, with the United Fruit Company being among the leaders. They were quick to see the advantages of being in constant communication with the ships in the fleet and with their banana plantation station houses. This produced a large network of radio stations, ashore and afloat, completely equipped and manned by trained operators. In 1913, a subsidiary of the company was formed and called the Tropical Radio Telegraph Company.

While Workman Clark & Co. were busy turning out ships for their American customer, a short distance to the east of Belfast two cousins were engaging in a dangerous game of one-upmanship. King George V of England and Kaiser Wilhelm II of Germany were drawing heavily on their country's resources to see which one could build the largest and most deadly battleships, with all of the personnel and auxiliary ships necessary to their operation. As might be expected, the race came to its ultimate end when war broke out in August 1914. Politicians, historians, and military analysts have constantly attempted to explain what happened, but happen it did, and we will not go into that subject here.

We now come to the SS *Ulua,* the subject of this narrative. In that same year, 1914, the United Fruit Company (UFC) had placed an order with Workman Clark & Co. for three more combination cargo and passenger ships to add to their fleet of banana boats.* Delivery was scheduled for 1917, and work on them proceeded on schedule, in spite of some shortages of material. Ireland at the time was, as usual, at odds with Great Britain and refused to cooperate or to take an active part of any kind in her argument with Germany.

The three ships were sturdy vessels, 440 feet long, 54 feet in beam, with a capacity of 55,000 bunches of bananas and 131 passengers. They were powered with twin reciprocating engines for a total of about 6,400 horsepower, giving a top designed speed of 14½ knots. They were oil-fired and forced-draft, although there was a strong indication that the design had been hastily changed from a typical coal-fired natural-draft forerunner.

The British shipbuilding industry was centered in Belfast, Northern Ireland, and in Scotland on the River Clyde. Both spots had established an excellent reputation in the shipbuilding industry, and to have a ship in service bearing the builder's bronze identification plaque with a hull number from a yard in either location meant that the ship was "Clyde Built." The *Ulua* and her two sister ships were thus part of a long and illustrious heritage. Such ships were often called upon to perform far beyond their designer's original intentions, and the *Ulua* was to prove to be capable of just that, as we shall soon see. In addition to other new innovations, these were the first UFC hulls to be built with watertight bulkheads between the four holds.

As the war continued and developed into a meat grinder on the western front, England soon became short of troop transports and cargo vessels, due mostly to ravages of the German U-boat campaign and also to lack of foresight, which constantly plagues peace-loving nations. It was only natural that the British government should look to the shipyards in Belfast for possible additions. They must have had their eyes on the Workman

---

To the landsman any vessel which carries passengers is usually called a "boat," and that term will often be used here in regards to the "three war babies." When the Ulua *becomes the USS* Octans, *it will be termed a "ship," in true Navy fashion.*

SS *Ulua* in Peacetime Service (D. Rinaldi, WT).

Clark & Co. ways for months, watching development of the three ships. The first was launched on March 1, 1917. On November 29, 1917, two months after her launching and seven months after the United States had entered the war, the *Ulua* was turned over to the British government as His Majesty's Transport *Ulua* at her launch site in Belfast. Her actual construction cost was $1,400,503.[9]

When the American troops were finally ready to be sent to France, the *Ulua* was on hand to oblige, and many of our Doughboys, as they were called, had the distinction of being carried over there on this future addition to the Great White Fleet — now painted gray.

Upon signing of the Armistice on November 11, 1918, the flow of American troops went into reverse, from east to west, back home for our surviving Doughboys and the *Ulua* was again in the vanguard.

Her duty as a troopship completed, and still under British control, she was then sent to Archangel and Murmansk, Russia, in September of 1919 to remove the British General Staff just ahead of the advancing Bolshevik army. This ended her World War I service, after she discharged the General Staff in Scotland in October 1919. She then proceeded to the Workman Clark & Co. yard at Belfast where she was restored to her original designed condition for service with the United Fruit Company. Her cost on the company's books was then $2,099,895.[10]

Still under British registry, but owned and controlled by the United

Fruit Company, the *Ulua* went into regular service as a banana and passenger boat between New York and the Caribbean. At some time in the 1920s, the *Ulua* was removed from British registry and transferred to U.S. registry.

Finally, as it must to all ships, the time came when faster ships were built to replace her and others of her age on the New York-Caribbean run. She was placed in storage in the Erie Basin, New York, in 1932. It looked as if this was the end of her career, as she languished in retirement. Eventually, she was reactivated for service on the New Orleans-Caribbean run and remained in this run until World War II commenced for the United States.

The coming of hostilities in the days after December 7, 1941, found the United States in the same spot in which it and England had been in 1917 — woefully short of marine transport bottoms. Another bureaucracy, known as the War Shipping Administration, was added to the burgeoning masses congregating in Washington to solve the dilemma. The *Ulua* was taken over by this bureau and placed under its control. She was transferred to the Navy in April 1943.

Chapter 3

Transformation: SS *Ulua* to USS *Octans*

Months before the attack on Pearl Harbor, the Navy had commenced building up its auxiliary fleet, including refrigerated storeships. The first one was acquired in December 1940. Seven months later, the first United Fruit Company ships were taken over. After the start of hostilities, this pattern was continued as the Navy expanded its vast network of overseas fleets and bases. In all, 11 ships formerly owned by the United Fruit Company were taken over by the Navy.[11] The War Shipping Administration had taken over the operation of all merchant ships after Pearl Harbor's devastation.

Near the end of April 1943, the SS *Ulua* was homeward bound from Hawaii, having just completed one of her trips under the direction of the War Shipping Administration. With her normal Merchant Marine crew and officers aboard, she entered the approach to the Golden Gate Bridge. As she passed under it, she was met by a Coast Guard cutter and was signaled to heave to and throw out the sea ladder for boarders. The crew complied and watched as several officers in U.S. Navy uniforms came aboard, carrying briefcases. These men went up to the bridge and took possession of the ship in the name of the U.S. Navy. Not only that, they inducted several of the ship's officers into the Navy. They had with them all of the required papers and documentation to make it legal. The ship's officers were now under Navy discipline and were told to continue the voyage, but they were to deliver themselves and the empty ship to Pier 56 in San Francisco.

That incident was the culmination of weeks of a game of three-cornered tag. The Navy had already completed the necessary preparations for taking over the *Ulua* but was now attempting to snag the ship with its

3. Transformation: SS Ulua to USS Octans

Merchant Marine officers. The ship was no good to the Navy without a core of experienced officers to run her, as there was an extreme shortage of such men. The Navy induction (impressment?) team finally got wise to the game. The port captain was in constant radio communication with the ships. The officers were simply hitting the dock as soon as the ship was close enough for them to do so, and they were then doing a fast disappearing act. The answer to the Navy was obvious: Board the ship before it hit the docks. It worked.

The *Ulua* was the last vessel of the United Fruit Company Great White Fleet to be taken over. There were to be two more former banana boats to be acquired by the Navy before the fleet of new construction of reefers was launched and delivered to the Navy. By the end of hostilities, there were 35 reefers under operation by the U.S. Navy.

Loading bananas at the various pickup points in the Caribbean was often done through the cargo ports located along the sides of the ship, just above the waterline. The *Ulua* had eight of these on each side. These were covered by heavy, substantial steel doors, hinged, gasketed, and closed tight by means of heavy latching dogs. In addition to loading cargo through these ports, the normal operating supplies, such as food for the crew's mess, machinery parts, and supplies, were also loaded by this means.

The Navy apparently did not like these cargo ports, and for some reason or other, those on the *Ulua* were ordered welded shut during the preliminary conversion phase at Pier 56. In retrospect, I can see their concern. There was a possible problem with them in case the ship was torpedoed. Could the doors be blown off, hastening the sinking of the ship? Against the advice of one former UFC officer, the yard welders proceeded to weld the doors shut, after removing the rubber gasketing, relying on the ability of the welders to assure the final integrity of the hull. This was a mistake, as would be found out later, with much embarrassment.

The day that the four of us "reefer men" checked into the Navy Receiving Station at San Francisco, May 5, 1943, the ship entered the yard of the United Engineering Company in Alameda, California, which is across the bay from San Francisco. The Navy had issued a cost and materiels contract to that firm for conversion work, under Project Order Number 1788/IRMV (C&M), and they wasted no time in tearing into the ship and converting her to the new owner's requirements.[12] When we first came into the yard and saw the ship, it was a shock. The workmen were removing all excess piping, tubing, wood and metal bulkheads, and old United Fruit Company fixtures that did not meet the Navy's requirements.

From that day until June 11, we took the ferry from San Francisco across to Alameda, then walked the short distance to the yard. For me, it was a very easy walk from the YMCA down to the ferry landing at the foot of Embarcadero Street. I ate breakfast at the YMCA cafeteria and dinner out at any of the small cafes for which the city is noted.

The BuShips in Washington had specified that the ship be delivered in a bareboat condition. Delivery was to be complete in all respects, "as is" (without any changes), both hull and machinery, including all consumable stores, fuel, lubricating oil, and water on board at the time of delivery, but excluding leased equipment, liquor bar stock, subsistence stores, slop chest stores, perishable supplies, and any articles of no value to the Navy, as specified by the Navy Yard Commandant at Mare Island. All available spare parts and equipment on board required by the American Bureau of Shipping were to remain on board. The BuShips had issued a list of things they felt should be done, but it was much too long for the 37 days available. Consequently, much did not get accomplished. Not on the list, conspicuous by its absence, was any mention of repair or reconditioning of the mechanical equipment and machinery.

Except for signing in and out each day, there was almost a complete lack of supervision over us. We were left to roam and inspect the ship at our own pace and discretion. Of course, there had as yet been no duty station assignments made, but it seems as if some attempt should have been made to direct us green swabbies as to what was expected of us, other than an admonition not to interfere with the civilian workmen. There were several regular Navy petty officers in the group, and they were of little help. I did watch them at frequent intervals, but for the most part we prowled and roamed the ship at will, mostly in the engineering spaces.

One of the first operations performed by the yard workmen was to start removing the wood decking on the weather deck. When the wood decking was torn off in the first available location, there was nothing underneath but a thick layer of rust, which peeled off easily with the fingers. A consultation was held with the Navy, the wood decking was replaced, and no more was torn up in areas exposed to the weather. The wood decking on the main deck throughout the center deckhouse, containing the mess hall, crew's quarters, sick bay, and similar facilities, was removed, however, and replaced with the standard linoleum, troweled in place. The steel deck plates under the wood were not as rusty.

It was impossible to expect that such things as bottom scraping and final painting would be performed. However, there was some chipping. I recall inspecting some of the paint chips being removed from the deck fittings. The chips were about a quarter of an inch thick, and I could count the number of paint jobs the ship had received. Some chips I examined showed a couple of coats of dark gray as a base coat, followed by

3. Transformation: SS Ulua to USS Octans

many coats of the famous Great White Fleet paint, and finally a couple of coats of gray; the ship's history in microcosm.

The first pass at providing a manning schedule for the ship was rejected by the captain, as it included too few hands for the amount of work involved in running and maintaining a ship of this size. The first list submitted had a total complement of 129 enlisted personnel. The captain pointed out to the chief of Navy personnel that the size and purpose of the ship were such as to require much more. He submitted his list of 220, which was then approved.[13]

Considering that only 37 days were available to convert the ship to Navy use, the Navy Yard at Mare Island and the contractor worked what is almost a miracle. From the correspondence—about 350 pages, which I pored over—it is surprising that the ship was actually able to load up and leave on schedule. There were over 150 pages of materiel and equipment allowances which were requisitioned, reviewed, and approved, of which about 40 percent did not make it on board before we left.

While we were getting acquainted with the ship, the contractor's men were rushing through the conversion from SS *Ulua* to USS *Octans*. The major items which were carried to reasonable completion will be given here, with the understanding that it is not complete.[14] There were many other changes made not given here.

The Navy furnished two motor whaleboats and two motor launches, and the yard constructed supports for them on board, with upgrading of the cargo booms for handling them. The Navy also furnished a new Mark 28 Rangefinder, which the yard mounted over the bridge near the forward 20mm guns (item 33, p. 24). Included in the Navy-supplied materiel was a new Sperry Gyrocompass, with several repeaters at various locations throughout the ship. The old 4-inch/50 caliber gun on the poop deck was replaced with a 5-inch/51 caliber gun (item 25). Four 3-inch/50 caliber double-purpose guns were added in tubs, elevated above the deck, two forward over the fo'c'sle (item 28) and two aft over the poop deck (item 27). Eight 20mm guns on four mounts were installed, four forward over the navigating bridge and four on the after end of the boat deck (item 33). All ammunition storage and handling facilities were included, such as magazines in the holds, handling equipment, ventilation, lighting, emergency flooding, sprinklers, and ready boxes at each tub. The 20mm stations had cooling tubes for the barrels and a forward and after clipping room for the ammunition, with fittings.

Major changes were made on the main deck, in the center deckhouse. The area forward was supplied with a ship's store, crew's mess hall (item 45) and galley (item 38) enlarged to accommodate the larger complement of men. In the center, on the port side, three-tier bunks were installed for the crew, with lockers (items 31, 38). On the starboard side, the CPO's

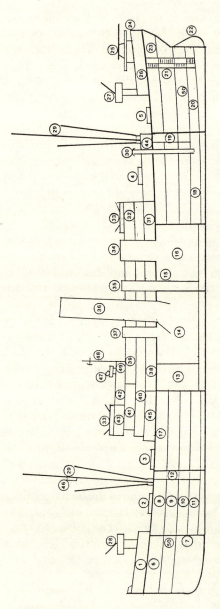

Longitudinal Section, USS *Octans* (AF-26) (sketch by the author). Legend for locations on cross section of the ship: 1. Fo'c'sle; Shipfitter's department, painter's locker, Bosun's locker; 2. Hatch, #1 hold; 3. Hatch, #2 hold; 4. Hatch, #3 hold; 5. Hatch, #4 hold; 6. Chain locker; 7. Watertight bulkheads, typical, four locations; 8. Upper 'tween deck, typical for all holds; 9. Lower 'tween deck, typical for all holds; 10. Orlop deck, typical for all holds; 11. Lower hold, typical for holds #1 and #2 only; 12. Fan and brine coil rooms for cooling holds; 13. Fuel oil bunkers; 14. Fireroom, boilers 1, 2, 3, and 4; 15. Fan room and combustion air plenum; 16. Engine room; 17. Main deck; 18. Ice machine compartment; 19. Fan and brine coil rooms for cooling holds; 20. Shaft alley; 21. Companionway; ladder from poop deck to shaft alley and ice machine; 22. Rudder; 23. Steering engine compartment; 24. Poop deck; 25. 5-inch gun and platform over the poop; 26. Passage to companionway on port side, brig on starboard side; 27. After 3-inch AA gun, tub, and ready boxes; 28. Forward 3-inch gun, tub, and ready boxes; 29. Mast and derrick booms, two booms per hatch; 30. Ventilating shaft/escape hatch from ice machine compartment; 31. Crew's quarters, port; crew's head, amidships; CPO's quarters and laundry, starboard; 32. Geedunk stand, barber shop; 33. 20mm guns, total of eight; 34. Engine room skylight, ventilation shaft and fidley (note: fidlies are open spaces above the engine room and fireroom); 35. Combustion air intake for the boilers; 36. Stack; 37. fireroom skylight, ventilation shaft and fidley; 38. Crew's quarters, port; galley, starboard; 39. Officers' quarters, forward; officer-passengers, amidships; 40. Officer-passenger's quarters forward; enlisted-passengers aft; 41. Officers' wardroom and pantry; 42. Captain's quarters; 43. Navigating bridge; 44. Sick bay; 45. Crew's mess hall; 46. Crow's nest lookout station; 47. Searchlight platform; 48. SF2 radar, surface search; 49. Radar room; 50. Ammunition magazine.

quarters were installed. In between the CPO's quarters and the crew's quarters were the heads for both, the master-at-arms shack and the auxiliary gang machine shop (item 31). Aft of the crew's quarters were the sick bay and hospital.

Air and surface search radar was supposed to have been furnished by the Navy, with support mast and radar room (items 48, 49). The radar equipment was never installed, but the room for it was piped with all necessary signal ducting. Located just aft of the captain's quarters, the radar room was occupied by one of the deck officers during this first cruise. This was just as well because there were no radarmen on board this first cruise, not even a radarman striker. Also on the boat deck, a trash burner with spark arrestor and smoke head were installed and two 12-inch and two 24-inch searchlights (item 47).

Someone high up in the BuShips apparently thought the *Octans* would make a good stand-in as a mine sweeper, for the ship was supplied with four complete sets of paravanes, with all rigging, tackle, special fittings, and tools, all installed on the main deck forward of the mess hall. In the 24 months I was on the ship, I never saw them broken out and rigged. That is just as well—with our draft of 20 to 26 feet, we would probably have gone through the minefield rather than over it.

On the platform above the main starboard engine (item 16), a compartment was provided for a new freshwater evaporator, rated at 12,000 gallons a day. The piping system was capable of discharging the water to any of the ship's freshwater tanks. Ventilation was furnished, but it proved to be inadequate for the equatorial runs.

A towing bridle was attached to the fantail. So, not only were we to serve as a reefer ship, a military passenger liner, and a minesweeper, but perhaps also as a tug.

All wooden doors opening to the weather deck were changed to regulation-style steel watertight doors. All portholes and other openings were altered to permit complete darkening of the ship.

On the aft end of the promenade deck, overlooking #3 hatch and the after well deck, a new crew's lounge was installed (item 32). This included the geedunk stand (soda fountain) and the barber shop. Many happy hours were spent by those off watch, sitting at the tables in the lounge, enjoying the pleasures of the back-home drugstore soda fountain, exchanging liberty stories, discussing the latest scuttlebutt and scandal on the ship, and comparing notes on girl friends, or lack of same. Occasionally, the current war situation found its way into the conversation, from the news posted on the nearby bulletin board. Here, also, could be found excess reading material, well-worn and dog-eared, with pages missing from the magazines. This meant that someone's locker door was probably graced with the latest pinup.

There were a number of changes made in various compartments throughout the ship, such as storerooms, chart room, and hold access trunks. Changes included lighting and ventilation of some of these spaces. Peloruses were installed on each navigation wing, next to the gyrocompass repeaters, for taking bearings relative to the ship's centerline.

The degaussing system was checked and found in working order. This consisted of a large electrical cable circling the inside of the ship, which counteracted and cancelled the magnetic lines of force usually surrounding the ship from the electrical equipment on board. This was a protection against magnetic mines and torpedoes.

A complete Navy-type intercom system, using sound powered telephones, was installed throughout various important points of the ship, such as the gun mounts. Fire control for the guns was purely local and basic, with each gun platform being under local control from a gun captain, in telephone contact with the bridge. The only orders received from the bridge were "commence firing" and "cease firing." In the case of drills, the order also stipulated the number of total rounds for the 3-inch and the 5-inch guns. The 20mm guns were strictly under the sole control of the men seated behind the gun, for the training, pointing, and trigger work. For firing the 3-inch and the 5-inch guns, the old method of range and bracketing firing was used for surface targets as directed by the gun captain. For aircraft targets, the gun captain estimated the range and called out the fuse settings, in seconds, to the gun crew, where the fuse settings were made just before ramming the shell into the open breech. The rest was up to the skill and training of the men at the gun.

The 5-inch gun was notorious for being a filthy station because, when it fired, the surrounding area was spattered with burning and unburned gunpowder, leaving a black residue over everything and everyone. It was only good for surface targets, and that was subject to much speculation. Also, as the scuttlebutt reported, every time the 5-inch gun was fired, rivets were heard to pop off at various locations throughout the ship.

The new Rangefinder never really had a chance to prove its usefulness, as it was only good for slow-moving surface targets, which we never encountered, fortunately. It turned out to be mostly a toy for some of the officers.

As a final step, calculations were made to determine what effect the addition of all the extra equipment, which was mostly above the waterline, had on the center of gravity of the ship, and thus what effect it would have on the stability of the ship. As a result, 288 tons of concrete were added to the lower hold in #2 hold and 31 tons in the shaft alley. An inclining test was made while at dockside to check the results. It was accepted that the change in the center of gravity of the ship was within allowable limits, and the ship's stability at sea was not appreciably impaired, while loaded.

The test reports included the ship in both a loaded and unloaded condition and apparently overlooked the potential stability problem indicated in the unloaded condition. This would surface very soon, as we shall see.

As the ship was built in British shipyards, everything on board was originally to British standards. This meant that all screw threads, pipe threads, and valve operations were just the reverse of American standards, which resulted in a constant source of trouble and bewilderment. With the age of the many valves on board, some valve stems were broken by applying leverage to open or close a valve in the wrong direction. Of course, all work accomplished at the Alameda yards was to American standards, which greatly complicated our later repair efforts. More than once, we in the engineering division cursed the situation very strongly. The men in the auxiliary gang machine shop must have had some interesting problems to solve as a result of the mixture. Their shop was known as "The Pigeon Roost," and one of the machinist's mates was soon dubbed "Pidge."

By the time commissioning day had arrived, most of us on duty for the past few weeks had staked out our claims for the best bunking location. It was established that the engineering division would be bunked in the after part of the berthing area. I had my eye on a middle bunk, outboard, next to a porthole, and that is where I threw my gear when the day of moving on board came. My weekends of visiting with friends and relatives in the bay area were about over. There were 22 officers and 133 enlisted men, myself included, signed in that day, June 11, 1943. Soon after settling in, the call came: "All hands lay forward on the well deck for commissioning!"

We lined up in ranks, parallel to the ships bulwarks, while the officers lined up on the #2 hatch cover. The captain read his letter of authorization, gave a short speech, then directed that the commissioning pennant and the ensign be hoisted. The former SS *Ulua* was now officially the USS *Octans*, reefer supply vessel, military passenger vessel, U.S. mail ship, floating Brink's delivery service (as it later developed), as well as possible minesweeper and tug boat.

The next few days were hectic, with supplies coming on board, more enlisted personnel arriving and signing in, establishing their own space in the crew's berthing area, all accompanied with the usual noisy comments, griping, and swearing. From then until June 21, more crew members came on board in small drafts, until the muster roll consisted of about 220 men.

During that period (I do not recall the exact date), we took the ship for a run around the bay area. From the maneuvering, I suspect the ship was going through compass calibration and the Navy's degaussing range at Yerba Buena Island during this mini trial run. The final assignments had not yet been posted for the engineering division, and three of us from the refrigeration school were in the engine room, mostly serving as oilers. The engine room was a shambles, with the CPO and the first class machinist's mates giving directions and attending to the engine room telegraph, throttles, and ahead-astern gear during the maneuvering, with the rest of us keeping the main and auxiliary engines lubricated and operating. Practically every piece of rotating and reciprocating machinery was of an ancient and venerable design heritage, but simple and highly visible in operation.

Following that brief trial run around the bay, Watch and Station bills were posted, listing the personnel manning for the various duties throughout the ship. As I scanned the bill, I found that I was the only one from refrigeration school assigned to the ice machine. One of the others was placed in the fireroom, one in the engine room, and one in the auxiliary gang. The other two watches in the ice machine gang were headed by Leo, MM2c, and Henry, MM3c. We each had a fireman assigned as assistant and oiler for our watches.

At no time did anyone in authority ever tell me that I was to be the lead petty officer of the ice machine gang. However, as my name was listed first for the gang on the Watch and Station Bill and I was the only one in the gang with refrigeration training, I assumed that I was in that position. It was evident from the beginning that that assumption was correct, as everyone treated me as such, especially as time went on and changes took place both in the gang's personnel and operation of the department.

Before going any further into the chronicle of the *Octans*, let us take a look at the ship, then the ice machine and hold cooling arrangements. The figure on the top of page 29 is a Navy photograph of the ship taken broadside from the port side, and the figure on the bottom of page 29 is a close-up view taken off the starboard bow.

The figure on page 30 is a schematic drawing of the carbon dioxide refrigeration system for the cargo holds. It was a very basic design, dating back to about 1900. According to the UFC correspondence to the Navy, it was rated at 62 tons of refrigeration. When the UFC transmitted that data, they did not specify the speed of the steam engine driver required to produce that amount of refrigeration. Later, when I had sufficient data to keep a check on the output, I was able to estimate the speed to produce that output to be about 60 revolutions of the flywheel per minute. That may have been sufficient for carrying bananas, but, for our purposes, we

3. Transformation: SS Ulua to USS Octans

Top: USS *Octans* (AF-26) (National Archives). *Bottom:* USS *Octans* (AF-26) (Author's collection).

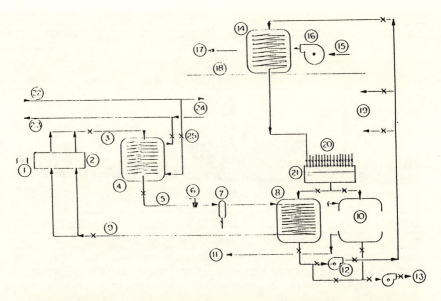

Cargo Spaces Cooling Systems, USS *Octans* (AF-26) (sketch by the author). Legend for USS *Octans* (AF-26) Cargo Spaces Cooling Systems: 1. Compressor rod packing gland; 2. Carbon dioxide compressor, port side; 3. Hot-gas discharge line; 4. Carbon dioxide condenser; 5. Liquid carbon dioxide line; 6. Expansion valve, hand operated (the warm high-pressure carbon dioxide liquid is reduced in pressure and temperature, about 15°F below desired brine temperature, when going through this valve, some gas is formed in the process); 7. Oil separator; 8. Evaporator for cooling the calcium chloride brine (the cold liquid absorbs heat from the brine, forming carbon dioxide gas, thus cooling the brine); 9. Carbon dioxide vapor return line; 10. Evaporator for the starboard compressor system; 11. Carbon dioxide vapor return line to starboard compressor; 12. Cold brine circulating pump for holds #3 and #4; 13. Cold-brine circulating pump for holds #1 and #2; 14. Brine coil bank for cooling the holds; 15. Return air from the hold space; 16. Circulating fan; 17. Cold air to the hold space; 18. Upper 'tween deck; 19. Cold brine supply to the lower 'tween deck and orlop deck systems; 20. Brine flow control station, all systems; 21. Brine catch and mixing tank; 22. Sea water supply to condensers, from main injection system; 23. Condenser water overboard line (the overboard line carries all of the heat removed from the cold storage holds, the work of the compressor, and the heat from the steam condenser); 24. Condenser water supply and return for ice machine engine condenser; 25. Isolation valves, typical throughout.

found it necessary to speed up the machine considerably to carry our reefer and frozen cargoes.

There were two cylinders on the compressor end (item 2), each bored out of solid steel forgings about 14 inches wide, 18 inches deep, and 36 inches long. Power came from a double expansion reciprocating steam engine, horizontal, with the high-pressure steam cylinder driving the port compressor and the low-pressure steam cylinder driving the starboard one. The opposite end of the steam cylinders drove a flywheel about 1 foot thick and 6 feet in diameter through a crankshaft. The entire machine was mounted on a cast-iron base about 8 feet wide and 15 feet long. The steam pressure was about 190 pounds per square inch (psi), exhausting from the low pressure cylinder to a vacuum condenser, mounted athwartship under the steam cylinders, cooled with water from the main seawater injection system in the engine room (item 24). The figure on page 30 only shows the port compressor cylinder system. The compressor rods were packed with metallic packing (item 30), lubricated by small hydraulic reservoirs mounted beside each cylinder (item 2). These reservoirs had to be kept full of oil by a hand pump, which required pumping at intervals of a few minutes to about 30 minutes.

Many of the nuts used on our machinery required two hands just to place them and screw them down to the final take-up point. To tighten them required a large, short-handled slugging wrench. Using this wrench required one man to hold the wrench in place and another man wielding an 8- or 10-pound hammer on the handle of the slugging wrench. This operation was difficult and dangerous enough in a calm sea or moored to a dock, but in a seaway with the ship rolling and pitching, it was a real challenge.

Much of the machinery in the engine room was of equally unwieldy dimensions. There are cases listed in the deck log of engine room men being treated for lacerations and bruises during their maintenance operations. The engineering spaces were provided with checkerboard pattern floor plates, which were supposed to provide a fairly firm and safe footing. However, when these floor plates became covered with spilled oil, as they often did, this made it a challenge to perform some normal maintenance operations.

The main engines were triple expansion, three cylinder, vertical reciprocating engines, using steam at full broiler pressure, about 195 psi, and exhausting to a condenser cooled by seawater. All auxiliary pumps were driven by old style reciprocating steam engines, as were also the electric generator and the stand-by driver for the forced draft fan for the boilers.

The boilers were of the Scotch Marine style, oil fired, with two boilers being double ended (they were long enough to take oil burners on each end) and two being single ended. The design maximum steam pressure was 200 psi. The forced draft fan was mounted on one through shaft, normally driven by an electric motor. The boilers were in rather poor condition, due to their age and to the dubious quality of the freshwater which was taken on board at various ports of call in the Caribbean while in the service of the UFC.

Communication between the engineering spaces was by telephone, and access was by steel ladders (stairs) from the main deck. In the case of the ice machine room, the ladder was in a trunk from the main deck in the poop, as shown in the figure on page 24 (item 21). In addition, there was a ventilating shaft from the ice machine room, going up to the deck beside the #3 hatch (item 30). It also had rungs inside for emergency use. It was supplied with a door in the side where it ended out on deck. In the hood over the top, there was an eyebolt inside for the use of a hoist up the shaft. We used this method for removing the empty carbon dioxide cylinders and for lowering the full ones into the ice machine room. The hoisting line was fed through a block from the eyebolt and over to the port deck winch wildcat. One of the regular chores when we hit port was to remove the empties and to lower the refilled cylinders when they came back on the dock alongside. Every time we performed this task, there was a small pile of rust deposited on the deck in the ice machine room, knocked off the ladder and the shaft. No one ever attempted to test the emergency use of the shaft by climbing up it, and it was a constant source of speculation as to its worthiness if the time ever came that it was needed.

The four watertight bulkheads (item 7, page 24) had watertight doors between the engine room (item 16) and the ice machine room (item 18), and in the bulkhead isolating the shaft alley (item 20). They were closed at sea, with the exception of the one between our department and the shaft alley, which was always open. In addition, there was a manway in the bulkhead between the engine room and our department, hinged and dogged, through which we could climb. Opening and closing those watertight doors was a chore, as they had not been regularly used prior to the Navy's acquisition of the ship.

Immediately after assignments were made, it was necessary to start work in the ice machine room. The calcium chloride brine system had to be brought up to strength in the catch tank (item 21, page 30). The compressor systems had to be charged with carbon dioxide from the cylinders stored in the shaft alley. The lubrication systems had to be put into service, then the ice machine started up, slowly, and speeded up gradually. Fortunately, the assistant engineering officer, who had experience with the UFC on this type of equipment, was on hand to direct the start-up.

We finally managed to get the system operating, the brine circulating, the air circulating fans (item 16) in the holds in operation, and the hold temperatures to come down. Those were hectic days, and they went fast. We were quickly indoctrinated into the schedules and procedures we were to follow for the rest of our life on board.

There were thermometers in the air passages in the holds, and we had to log the readings from them once each watch, along with other data from the system. The brine flow had to be controlled at the catch tank to regulate the hold temperatures. The catch tank (item 21 in the figure on page 30), was located on the orlop deck directly above the brine cooling evaporators (items 9 and 10). The brine flow control station (item 20), was directly above the top of the catch tank. We attempted to hold the #1 and #2 holds at about 45 degrees (Fahrenheit) and holds #3 and #4 at about 20 degrees.

I do not know what the conditions were in the rest of the engineering spaces, but from indications of what we were experiencing, it must have been equally as fast and furious. The general ship condition was about on the par with that in the ice machine room, except that the temperatures in the fireroom and the engine room must have been much more severe.

About June 21, we pulled up to the cold storage loading dock at the Naval Supply Center at Oakland to load our first cargo. We were the first ship to be serviced by this new facility. During the ensuing months, the harbor at Oakland would see a heavy string of traffic at the center as the demand for food and other supplies built up rapidly to meet the requirements of the fleet in the Pacific.

Our stateside days were fading fast as the food flowed into the holds.

Chapter 4

Supply Run #1: Shakedown I

Navy ship routine is governed basically by what are known as Conditions of Readiness. Each ship sets its own manning schedule to meet these conditions. As practiced on the *Octans*, the following will describe the five conditions, as I saw them.

Condition 1: General quarters, all hands at battle stations. Ship is in imminent danger of attack. Initiated by piping over the loud speaker: "General quarters! All hands man your battle stations! Set Condition, affirm!"

Condition 2: Modified general quarters. Ship is in a moderate danger zone. On the *Octans,* guns were manned with skeleton crews, while the normal watch schedule was changed to four hours on and four hours off watch.

Condition 3: Normal cruising, a third of the crew on watch, the remainder off watch or doing routine maintenance chores. Thus, watches were four hours on and eight hours off.

Condition 4: In port, with only enough steam up to maintain the auxiliary services. A skeleton crew on watch. In the engineering division, this is the auxiliary watch. When in a liberty port, one half of the crew rates liberty each day or evening.

Condition 5: Ship without power of its own, getting all power and services from the shore. Ship is probably undergoing repairs. Crew performing minimum cleaning and maintenance duties.

The loading of fresh and frozen provisions into the holds took place fairly fast, too fast, while we were rushed into getting acquainted with the general routine to be followed for the months ahead. We were on regular Condition 3 watch schedule, and the watches were labeled thus:

First Watch	2000 to 2400 (same as 0000)
Mid Watch	0000 to 0400
Morning Watch	0400 to 0800
Forenoon Watch	0800 to 1200
Afternoon Watch	1200 to 1600
Dog Watch	1600 to 2000 (Saturday on *Octans*)

Each man had the same watch for the entire week. On Saturday, the Dog Watch was split into First Dog Watch, 1600 to 1800, and Second Dog Watch, 1800 to 2000. Then at 1800 on Saturday, the man on First Dog Watch would be relieved by the man who had been on the First Watch for the past week and who would have the 1600 to 2000 Watch for the coming week. By splitting the 1600 to 2000 watch into two short ones, each man's watch moved forward one watch from his previous one. "Dogging the watch," as it was called, broke up the monotony and gave everyone an equal break.

Not all men stood the regular watches just described. There were quite a number of the crew who had the duty during the day only. However, such duty included being available any time that their services were required. The CPOs never stood regular watches but were considered to be available on 24-hour call for their particular specialty. This was true also for some of the officers. Deck officers stood regular watches at their assigned stations. The division master-at-arms was expected to know where each man in his division bunked, for it was often his job to roust the man out when ordered.

The standard uniform of the day for the enlisted men on board the *Octans* was the regulation dungaree pants and blue cotton shirt. The hat was the typical Navy hat, but often dyed blue in varying shades, ostensibly to make it less conspicuous at night on deck. All of these items were very soon turned into a multitude of shades of blue by the ship's laundering process. The combination served very well as our work uniform.

Each sailor had at least one dress blue uniform and one white uniform. The regulation dress blues were wool, dark blue with the familiar white striping, rather loose fitting, with only a slight hint of a flare at the cuffs. The white uniform was of the same cut, cotton, with the colors reversed from that of the dress blues.

Most sailors, myself included, as soon as possible went to a tailor ashore and ordered a tailor-made set of dress blues. This was generally permitted during wartime, but during peacetime, it was often prohibited by the ship's dress code. The tailor-made blues were much tighter fitting, of lighter weight wool, and with a very large flare at the cuffs to produce the bell bottoms so well known. I ordered a set at Auckland, at a cost of about $60 as I recall.

The main thing we all found wanting in the dress uniforms was pockets. There was only one, a small one on the left breast of the jumper. Money and ID cards were usually carried in a thin, single fold wallet, draped over the top edge of the pants, in the small of the back, under the jumper. Not the best arrangement, but it worked for most.

Normally, when a ship has just been commissioned and fitted out or when it has undergone extensive modifications and overhaul, before it is deemed advisable to send her on a full-scale voyage, it takes what is known as a "Shakedown cruise." But in our case, there was not enough time for such a luxury, and so the ship was being loaded as fast as possible in an attempt to get us out of the states and on our assigned duty. Consequently, it came as no surprise that we would experience a considerable amount of annoyances from glitches in the machinery, the boilers, and the hull and some personnel problems. Many of the crew had never seen a ship before, so this was a totally new experience. The Navy relies on its experienced officers, chief petty officers, petty officers from the regular Navy, and a sprinkling of other experienced hands to train the raw recruits. Much of the sharp edges are usually knocked off in boot camp, but since the start of hostilities, the boot camp schedule had been reduced to the barest essentials.

Before the ship had been commissioned, the freon refrigeration system for the crew's mess was started up to bring the cold storage boxes down to holding temperatures. Fresh and frozen provisions and the normal complement of canned goods, dry stores, and other food supplies had been brought on board in readiness for the arrival of the crew on June 11. On June 21 the following general mess stores were taken on board:

Ice cream	144 gal	French bread	150 lbs	White bread	300 lbs
Carrots	400 lbs	Cabbage	300 lbs	Cauliflower	332 lbs
Corn	340 lbs	Garlic	281 lbs	Grapefruit	524 lbs
Oranges	370 lbs	Onions	400 lbs	Potatoes	2,000 lbs
Lettuce	310 lbs	Avocados	104 lbs	Asparagus	116 lbs
Celery	452 lbs	Cucumbers	211 lbs	Squash	279 lbs
Turnips	423 lbs				

Just before sailing on June 25, the cold storage boxes for the general mess were topped off with the following frozen foods:

Cod steaks	990 lbs	Peas	200 pkgs	Cherries	75 lbs
Oysters	288 lbs	Corn, cobbed	500 ears	Corn, cut	200 pkgs
Sole fillets	500 lbs	Strawberries	25 pkgs	Broccoli	200 pkgs
Halibut	500 lbs	Lima beans	100 pkgs	Mixed fruit	140 pkgs
Ice Cream	250 gal				

The provisions we carried were generally for the surface fleet and the Navy's shore bases. The submarine fleet required a better, more compact supply of fruit, vegetables, and meats, frozen and packaged especially for them. It was a general practice that all reefer ships leaving the states would be required to carry a consignment of such special cargo. We took on our lot while the ship was being loaded at Oakland, and it was stowed in the general mess freezer boxes, so as not to get it mixed up with the general cargo and to permit the supply officer to keep a close watch on it, as it was premium merchandise. Our lot of this special cargo was destined for New Caledonia.

When the frozen and preserved meat was being loaded into the holds, a few of the ship's crew stationed themselves in the holds, watching for the more choice items being stowed. They had already determined the best location to retrieve some of the cargo for use during those long, hungry night watches. When a net containing the right items, such as hams, came down the hatch into the hold, they would indicate to the stevedores where to place them, taking into account access from the fan rooms. This diversion would had to have been done with the connivance of the storekeeper in the hold, whose job it was to direct the stowage of the cargo according to a sketched plan in his possession. (Just another indication of that inherent Yankee ingenuity for which the American serviceman is known. As will be shown later, there would be plenty of that in the coming months.)

By noon on June 25, the holds were full, the deck hands were closing up the hatches, the fireroom was getting steam up in all boilers, and the engine room was warming up the main engines and auxiliaries in preparation for getting under way. The mooring lines were singled up, the tug came alongside, and the pilot came aboard. Finally, we were under way, under the Oakland Bay Bridge, past the Treasure Island Naval Station, past Alcatraz, and under the Golden Gate Bridge. Those of us not on watch were topside, getting that final look at the underside of the bridge as we passed under it, saying our farewells to all and sundry who might be watching. To the Bay area residents driving across the bridge, we were probably just another ship on its way to war someplace in the Pacific.

As we left the Golden Gate behind, we hit the Pacific swells, coming in from the sea. Immediately, the first effects of seasickness hit some of the crew. I was standing on the after-well deck, and felt some lightheadedness for about 30 minutes; then it passed. By the time of evening chow, I had no further trouble, my giddiness was over. After that, I can truthfully say that I never again suffered any effects of the ship's rolling or pitching—with one exception.

Going on watch at midnight, I took the flashlight and the cold weather coat (government issue) and went up to check the fan and coil rooms and take the temperatures in the holds. I had no problem with holds #3 and #4, but to get into holds #1 and #2, it was necessary to go through the crew's mess hall. The door from the mess hall was dogged shut in the usual Navy fashion. I was having trouble with the last of six dogs and was using the flashlight to help in my struggle with it. Just as I got it loose, the ship rolled to port and the door swung open, my flashlight shining wildly out on deck. There was a roar from the bridge, ordering me to douse that light and get up there immediately, which I did, to receive a thorough chastisement, followed by confinement to the gyro room. The bridge arranged for another man on my gang to take over the remaining portion of my watch, while I sat in that gyro room, listening to the gyrocompass, scared as I had never been before and cussing my stupidity. Soon after dawn, the captain came in to see me. I explained what had happened; he gave me a harsh lecture and then released me. The humiliation from the remarks of the crew was worse than the captain's tongue-lashing. It did not last long—there were so many other infringements the first few days out of port that mine was soon forgotten.

Our destination was the South Pacific area of operations, as one element of the 7th Fleet Service Force. But at that time, we didn't know where or for how long we would be steaming. In fact, the captain probably only had a general idea as to our future operational area, for he received his orders from the Service Force Headquarters as the area requirements developed.

To add some perspective to this story, it is well to take a look at what was happening to the war effort, concentrating on that theatre of operations to which we were to add our small, but important, bit.

By the time we were ready to leave Oakland, the buildup of our forces in New Zealand and Australia was sufficient to insure some expectations of success when we took the offensive. The initial ventures were taken months before, when the 1st Marine Division from New Zealand fought their epic battles in taking Guadalcanal and Tulagi from the enemy, so that by the time of our departure from Oakland, that area had been fairly well stabilized. About the beginning of 1943, those Allied forces available in the area were embarked on a training regimen in New Caledonia and New Zealand in preparation for the amphibious landings necessary to start MacArthur's island hopping to retake the Philippines.[15]

4. Supply Run #1: Shakedown I

On June 22, 1943, while we had been in the final stages of preparation for our present voyage, U.S. forces landed and secured the island of Woodlark, off the northeast coast of New Guinea. The next day, the same operation was performed on Kiriwina Island, just east of Woodlark, and air bases were constructed in short order on both. Next, on June 30, came simultaneous invasions on the New Guinea coast at Nassau Bay and on Rendova Island in New Georgia in the Solomons. Throughout the month of July, determined resistance from the enemy was steadily overcome, and the beaches were enlarged and secured until Munda Airfield was taken on August 5, 1943.[16]

Soon after we headed southwestward and the ship had settled into her regular pattern of rolling and pitching to the seas, water was discovered sloshing around in the port cargo spaces. The bridge, wardroom, and forward deck force all went into emergency operation, and it was some time before they had settled down to handle the inflow of water by forming a modern version of the time-tested bucket brigade to bail the seawater out of the cargo spaces.

Investigation pinned the problem to the cargo ports which had been welded shut at Pier 56 in San Francisco. The cargo doors no longer were able to permit the hull to slide beneath them to relieve the stresses concentrating at the port openings in the side strakes of the ship's skin. The stresses were concentrating at the welds, which apparently were not strong enough to resist the stresses and so some of them were cracking. It seemed that the lower edges of the doors were submerged on the roll of the ship, and water was coming in through the cracks between the doors and the hull.

Needless to say, there were some embarrassed and angry officers over this predicament. This is one goof they could not blame on each other or the crew, as the blame was with the BuShips or the Mare Island Navy Yard, whoever gave the order to weld the cargo doors shut. The Navy's welding foreman and inspector bear some responsibility for this fiasco.

According to a former UFC deck officer, the ship was consistently loaded deeper than had been the practice when the ship was a banana boat. In fact, when the ship was being loaded at Oakland for this first trip down to the islands, that same deck officer had protested to the Naval authorities that the ship was being greatly overloaded, far beyond the normal practice when she was operated by the UFC. He was ignored.

Data supplied by the UFC indicated that in this period the ship had a Load Line set at 26 feet 2 inches, which was considered to be a safe maximum draft. Several times during this first cruise out of the States, the ship sailed with a mean draft of about 26 feet 2 inches, or very close to it.

From the photo on page 29, it is obvious that with a mean draft of even close to 26 feet 2 inches, the cargo doors on the side of the ship would be partially below the water. This would, of course, lead to flooding of the ship's cargo spaces if the cargo doors were not properly sealed.

Of course, the added weight of the military hardware, such as the guns, magazines, ammunition, steel structures, and the 319 tons[17] of concrete ballast poured into the ship's bottoms all brought the ship down deeper than she had ever sailed while with the United Fruit Company or the War Shipping Administration.

The third day out of San Francisco, the results of the greenness of the crew were further evidenced when the captain held report mast, with three cases of infractions, one each on a seaman, a fireman, and a steward's mate. Each received varying amounts of extra duty.

Ah, yes, there, but for the grace of God and the captain, . . . !

Soon after leaving the Golden Gate behind, we attempted to settle down to a long voyage of about 6,500 statute miles, which was to take 21 days before we dropped anchor in Noumea, New Caledonia. The time for our gang went fairly fast, due to the many difficulties encountered. I am sure the fireroom and engine room gangs also had more than enough to keep them hopping. Their troubles were visible in our department, from the frequent slow-downs of the propeller shafts and even some complete stops. One time we traveled on a single engine for several hours.

A letter of April 29, 1943, from the United Fruit Company Marine Department to the Brooklyn Navy Yard assured the Navy that we could operate the two after holds at 18 to 20 degrees, providing that the cargo was delivered to the holds already frozen. The War Shipping Administration had been operating the ship for some months prior to the Navy commandeering it, and supposedly, at least some of the holds had been utilized at those low temperatures.

When the Navy received the ship, there was some of the required lubricating oil on board for the ship's machinery, including the ice machine. For the first couple of weeks, we were using that oil in the ice machine and had no particular difficulties from that source. We had other problems, some of undetermined origin, which continued to plague us.

About the time we entered the South Pacific area, with the warmer days and seas, we had used up the old oil left us from the previous operations and began using the oil furnished us by the Mare Island Navy Yard. We ran into more extreme difficulties immediately, right at the time when the cooling load on the ice machine was increasing due to the rising air and seawater temperatures. At least part of the problem was finally diagnosed as coming from the new oil being of the wrong specification for our service. We were stuck, with no alternate source available for thousands of miles, so we had to make do with the existing situation. The oil tended to congeal in the carbon dioxide lines in the evaporator coils, plugging the lines, and causing the compressor cylinders to build up a high discharge pressure. This could only be cured by opening up the expansion valves, permitting the brine temperature to rise.

When the station assignments were made, a fireman was put in charge of the seawater evaporators, installed to maintain our freshwater supply. As mentioned previously, the station was over the starboard engine, and the compartment was inadequately ventilated. He protested immensely and asked several times to be reassigned, due to the heat. All requests were refused. About three days into the voyage, he accidently opened the wrong valve and ran seawater into several of our freshwater tanks. He was immediately taken off the job, and the crew went on short water rationing for the washrooms and showers. His new assignment was down in the ice machine gang as my oiler. I never knew which of us was being punished.

Short water rations on the *Octans* simply meant that the washroom for the crew was open for only short periods at specified times of the day, and no running water for the showers. In place of taking showers, each man coming off watch could draw one bucket of hot water, with which he could stand in one of the shower stalls, and with a bar of soap and a wash cloth give himself a bath in whatever manner he chose. This entire water rationing process was administered by Pappy, our congenial master-at-arms, who had the keys and, more importantly, the authority. It lasted about two weeks.

In the meantime, the ship's evaporator was turning out replenishment freshwater under the management of a new, more congenial "Water King." He came around into the ice machine room about once a day, on his regular sounding runs, taking the soundings of the tanks, some of which were in the ice machine room and the shaft alley.

One of the leisure time hobbies going on at the time was the making of knives. Those engaged in this hobby were competing in a small way to see who could make the most vicious looking one. My new fireman oiler was no exception, and he soon was working on his knife while on watch. One day, we were sitting on the bench beside the compressor, taking care of our duties, and in between trips away from the bench, he was attempting to put a point on his knife. He asked me to see what I could do, as he was not having much luck. I declined. After a few minutes of further working on it, I asked him what he intended doing with the knife. He held the knife up, looked at me, and said, "In case we get torpedoed, this tells who goes up the ladder first!"

Very early in the voyage, the chief engineer decided that all machinist's mates were to run what is known as an indicator test on one of the main engines to measure the horsepower output of the engine. The device for running the test permitted calculation of the horsepower being produced by each cylinder, and it also indicated the valve setting for the cylinders. The device used springs, each of which had a spring value in pounds per inch measured vertically on the indicator card tracing, with an alternative scale value for use with the metric system.

We all took cards on the cylinders of one engine, then proceeded to calculate the horsepower, from the spring values given us by the chief. My calculations did not make sense, and it was obvious that the numbers he gave us for the springs were in error. I went to him and pointed this out. He checked the box for the instrument and discovered that he had mistakenly given us the metric values. Alongside was the English measurement values, which coincided very closely to my results. Applying the correct values to my cards gave a total indicated horsepower for each engine of about 3,200, which was close to the rated value.

One of my duties was the servicing of the many small refrigeration units on board, such as the geedunk stand's carbonated drink dispenser and several scuttlebutts (drinking fountains) around the ship. There were no tools, gauges, gas, or spare parts for any of them. I had to borrow tools and a pressure gauge from the auxiliary gang's machine shop, and the end result was that the units were not operating too well. Fortunately, the several larger refrigerators on board, such as in the galley, sick bay, and wardroom pantry, did not require any servicing. The refrigeration machine for the crew's mess stores did not give any trouble, other than needing a cleanout of the condenser tubes occasionally. That was the one unit on board which we had studied at the Carrier school.

As we approached the warmer latitudes, the brine coils in #3 and #4 holds began to frost up. Soon they were solid ice. There was a method designed into the brine circulating system to permit isolating one coil bank at a time and using hot brine to defrost the coils. The equipment was so old and rusty that we did not trust it, so we resorted to taking a fire hose from on deck, snaking it down the companionway into the coil rooms, and using it to defrost the coils. It was a cold, wet job, even with foul weather gear on. The water was supposed to flow into the drains in the coil rooms, then down to the bilges for pumping out. There were so many loose cork granules from the insulation leaking on the decks that the drains soon became clogged. Gradually, we got all of the cork swept up and the drains cleared, so we were then able to defrost the coils without further problems.

As we approached the equator, the frost was again building up so fast that the engineering ensign talked the chief engineer into letting him try using the defrosting system, and the chief agreed. For some reason or other, the ensign soon had the entire brine system warmed up, and before he got it under control, both #3 and #4 holds were above freezing. At this same time, we were having trouble with the oil in the compressor cylinders down below and could not stop the rise in brine temperature. By the time everything was coming down to temperature, a large portion of the meat and most of the fish in the holds had thawed out and began to drip blood and stink. Even when working properly, the refrigeration system was not intended to freeze cargo, merely hold it at temperature. Consequently, much of the frozen cargo spoiled.

This episode caused pandemonium in officer country, with round-robin finger pointing in an attempt to fix the blame, with threats of court martialing being thrown around. In the end, the only result that we saw down below was the ensign being reassigned and the assistant engineer being put directly over us. This suited us very well as he was knowledgeable and had a very low-key approach. It was very interesting to discuss things with him. We got along fine. He was an ex–United Fruit Company man, one of those shanghaied into the Navy when the ship was taken over.

Each member of the crew was issued a "Mae West" life jacket, with his name stenciled on it and a small orange flashlight attached. This was supposed to permit search-and-rescue personnel to spot a man in the water. The jackets got filthy after a few weeks, and they could not be washed; the filling would not take the washing. They were to be kept handy at all times and were to be worn when at any of the drills. They made very good pillows when we slept out on deck, which we often did when it was too hot in the bunks. Yes, there were comments about sleeping with Mae West!

I and another machinist's mate had general quarters stations in the ice machine room, along with the assistant engineer, who had a .45 service automatic, which took precedence over any fireman's knife. Fortunately, the opportunity for a showdown never came.

On July 6, we crossed the equator, just east of Jarvis Island.[18] No ceremony was held, due to the wartime exigencies. Personally, I couldn't have cared less. We had our hands full with the problems from the refrigeration equipment, and the thought of any highjinks did not appeal to me at all.

Several days later, we passed by the Samoan Islands, then crossed the international date line, just south of Fiji on July 13, where we skipped Tuesday and went from Monday to Wednesday. All during these trying days, the captain held regular report masts, and more steward's mates saw the inside of our brig while on P & P (piss & punk for bread and water). On July 14, the executive officer held a summary court martial to try two men, one of whom was the fireman who contaminated our freshwater tanks. The result was not published by the time we entered Noumea, New Caledonia.

A favorite spot for bull sessions was on the fantail, under the 5-inch gun platform, where we could talk in comparative solitude and evaluate the helmsman's skill by watching the ship's wake astern. On one of these sessions, there was a young seaman second class present, who had the attention of all of us. He was extolling the virtues of patriotism and how he felt it his duty to serve his country. He was still talking when I heard the speaker announce time to relieve the watch, so I left and went below. I mention this because we shall hear more about him later (in Chapter 20).

As mentioned in Chapter 3, the library was located in the geedunk stand. Very popular were the special issues of novels of the time, printed in small pocket-sized editions, measuring about four inches by six inches long, on the wartime rough beige paper, not intended to hold up over the ravages of time. The library was well utilized, and I read many of the current novels being supplied to the library. Also available were the armed forces editions of magazines, such as *Reader's Digest,* and others.

When the ship was in peacetime service for the UFC, there was a recreation lounge on the main deck, starboard side, just aft of the galley. This room was still in place and being used for the crew members off watch and with leisure time to spare. It was unofficially taken over by "Snake Eyes," who had available most of the gaming and gambling equipment necessary to satisfy the urge of those crew members who loved to gamble. This, of course, is against Navy regulations. The fact that such things went on without becoming known by the officers may be credited partly to that Yankee ingenuity mentioned earlier. There is another reason, and that is the reluctance of the officers to invade the privacy of the crew's domain, except during the normal inspections, drill stations, and so on, which are announced in advance. Maintaining discipline of the crew, cleanliness, performance, and off-duty activities, for example, are left in the hands of the warrant officers, CPOs, leading petty officers, and the master-at-arms. As a result, only the flagrant infractions were ever sent to captain's report mast.

As might be expected, the recreation room did not last forever. At the Auckland overhaul period, major changes in that portion of the midship house were made, and the room was incorporated into the CPO quarters. In exchange, another lounge and the library were provided on the next deck up, in the area of the geedunk stand. The lounge was then more visible to passing officers.

The weather was warm, sometimes hot and clear, as we sailed from summer in San Francisco to winter south of the equator. The further south we got, the more changes we noted in the stars and the constellations in the night skies. At some point on this leg of the trip to Noumea, we saw the first appearance of the Southern Cross as it rose over the southern horizon. It was to be our constant companion for months to come, a reassuring guide each evening when we came out on deck, either to go below on watch, coming off watch, or simply to see what was happening among the men gathered on the after-well deck exchanging gossip (or scuttlebutt, in Navy lingo). Often the group would include "Pappy," our master-at-arms, who knew his way around the ship, and usually had the "straight dope" on what was happening above the main deck. He was older than the rest of us and was liked, in spite of his job of keeping the peace and carrying out the orders of the bridge when disciplining the men. He had a rare form of dry, or droll, humor and was a stabilizing influence to most of us. Generally, he was quiet and seldom became aroused or perturbed. Every ship in the Navy of any size has at least one MAA, and many have a chief over them, as did we. It was Pappy's job to escort the recalcitrants into and out of the brig, bring them their chow or P & P, and to round them up for appearance at captain's mast, or court martial.

When we crossed the international date line, we turned due west for a straight shot into Noumea, New Caledonia, arriving on July 17. We were directed to tie up at a pontoon dock which had been constructed by the Navy SeaBees. The SeaBees came aboard to work the cargo, unloading it at a fast pace, in between air raid alerts from the shore. They were very agile at coming out of the holds when the alarm came, so I gather they had a bit of experience at this game. Much of the cargo was unloaded here, and the Navy doctor ashore came aboard to inspect the meat which had thawed out. He condemned most of the cargo in holds #3 and #4. Also, quite a few crates of tomatoes in hold #1 were spoiled and had to be deep-sixed (thrown overboard).

While at Noumea, the submarine provisions in the general mess freezer boxes were off-loaded and placed into the storage facilities ashore for further distribution to the submarine fleet. As the crates and cartons went over the side, the supply officer watched them go, breathing a sigh of relief with each parcel. For most of the trip down from Oakland, the executive officer, who had a craving for strawberries, had been badgering him to release some of them for use in the officer's mess. The supply officer held his ground, and came out ahead in the game of nerves. By so doing, one fact was made clear to the wardroom — the loud, boisterous, threatening executive officer was a big bluffer. Unfortunately, very few aboard ever really recognized this fact, and most of the crew and a few of the officers were intimidated by his threats, rantings, and ravings. It was obvious that life on board under him was going to be, at the least, interesting and lively.

Our orders next called for us to go to Espiritu Santo, which took us north through the area known as "Torpedo Junction." First, as we left the harbor at Noumea, the deck force had to deep-six the condemned meat and tomatoes, throwing it over the side as we left. I can remember standing on the fantail, under the 5-inch gun platform, watching the many carcasses and crates floating away astern of us, while I shook my head at the waste.

During the weeks following the attack on Pearl Harbor, Washington was a whirling maelstrom of big wheel bureaucrats, making decisions — any decisions — so long as something was accomplished. Out of this came a few good ideas, and one of them was the decision to send as many troops as possible as fast as possible down to New Zealand and Australia. To do this, the convoy route had to be protected, and the best places to establish our advance bases as a protection from the enemy just happened to be two groups of islands belonging to the Fighting Free French. Luckily, they were in exactly the right location to serve the purpose, being just to the southeast of the advancing Japanese and between our proposed convoy routing and the enemy. Posthaste, the necessary negotiations were entered into and permission received to place our bases on New Caledonia and New Hebrides.[19] We wasted no time in doing so, and the French assisted in choosing the right spots, one of which was near Noumea, the capital of New Caledonia. The other ones were on the islands of Efate, on the south fringes of New Hebrides, and on Espiritu Santo, on the northern end of the archipelago.

Prior to the battle of Midway, the Japanese Imperial General Staff had, rather optimistically, included New Caledonia, Samoa, Fiji, and New Hebrides in their plans for occupation, in addition to their campaign to subjugate New Guinea and Australia, which was already underway. As a result of the defeat at Midway, the plans were quickly altered, and Lt. Gen. Tomitaro Horii at Rabaul was ordered to mount an all-out offensive on Port Moresby, via a land assault near Buna, on July 21, 1942. Thus, a major portion of the South Pacific area was saved from assault, another welcome side effect of the battle of Midway. Our supply routes from the States to Australia and New Zealand were secured, except for the Solomons.[20]

The usual procedure for handling the cargo was well established. Our deck force was in charge of opening and closing the hatches, directed by one of the bos'uns, usually referred to as "Boats." Our storekeepers kept tabs on the cargo as it left the ship, tallying it and entering it into the records, which, unfortunately, have not survived. The entire operation was under the watchful eye of our cargo officer.

Cargo handling in most cases was done by the Navy SeaBees' Special Battalion, consisting of stevedores and dock workers, recruited from the country's seaports. By the time we arrived on the scene, they were well established at the various bases where we were directed to anchor or dock. They were ready and willing as soon as our hatches were open and lighters, pontoon barges, or other means of bulk transhipment were lined up to get their allotment of goodies. The pontoon barge, which was found in quantity at nearly every port of call, consisted of modules of watertight steel boxes bolted together to form a floating platform. At the rear was mounted one or two special boxes containing an outboard motor. This motor was huge, something not seen in civilian life very often before the war.

If the SeaBees were not available, then the job was done by local Army work parties or work parties from the ships being serviced. Whoever did the job, it was always fascinating to watch them operate. They were experienced professionals, and it amazed me that they had a very low accident rate during the entire life of the ship in this service, as judged from the records available in the deck log.

At some locations, the unloading was done in part by local natives, known as Bushmen. They were short, strong, and willing to work for extremely low wages, not even starvation wages by our standards. Their hair was usually dyed in bright colors, the selection or purpose of which I do not know. It did not take them long to determine that we treated them much better than the enemy, in those areas in which the two cultures clashed, Bushmen versus Japanese military.

After a week at Segund Channel at the southeast tip of Espiritu Santo, unloading the last of the cargo, we received orders to go to Auckland, New Zealand, for needed repairs and alterations. We wasted no time and headed due east at full throttle, wide open, for about 24 hours and then turned straight south toward Auckland. The engines were pounding, the spring bearings were running hot, and we made excellent time, all at the expense of the driving machinery. I made several trips from the ice machine room into the engine room, to watch the accumulation of small attachments being thrown off the engines, consisting of grease fittings, lengths of oil tubing, small cocks and valves, and so on.

Shortly after the start of this dash south, the stern packing gland for the port propeller began to leak excessively, filling the bilges in the shaft alley. A full bale of packing material was brought down to the shaft alley, and pound after pound of it was rammed into the inboard end of the gland, until the leak was brought partially under control. Two portable pumps, together with the existing ship's bilge pumping system, were able to handle the inflow, in spite of the ground cork and other crud plugging the intake strainers.

During the eastward run at high speed, the officers on the bridge noticed that the ship was behaving in a dangerous manner. It was obvious that the unloading had placed the ship in an unstable condition, evidenced by the slow, sluggish rolling. They were greatly worried, as well they should be, for it was plain that we were in danger of capsizing, as the unloading had raised the center of gravity of the ship to a dangerous point. Seventh Fleet Service Headquarters were contacted immediately, and the only answer was to get to Auckland as soon as possible. So the course was due south, flank ahead both engines.

We were not doing too badly on this southerly leg, until, just about east of Norfolk Island, we began to get buffeting wind and waves coming from the Tasman Sea to the west. The ship developed a port list and continued to wallow sluggishly and eerily. This situation existed for two days until we gained the protection of the north tip of New Zealand, and the ship rode a little easier.

During this entire ordeal, very few of us below decks were aware of the danger. It was probably just as well; we had enough to occupy our minds. About half of the crew were confined to their bunks, seasick. The officers did not escape this malady, either, with some of those who were old hands being laid up also.

There was one compensating factor, however, for those who were able to perform their duties and had to stand double watches at times. The galley cooks did not reduce their output sufficiently to handle the reduced demand for chow, so those of us who were still on our feet had extra chow to gorge on.

The reason for our predicament was the apparent ignoring of the stability dynamics in an unloaded condition (as mentioned in Chapter 3). It was still causing trouble, because of all the changes in armament, crew accommodations, and insufficient ballasting. This dash brought us into Huaraki Gulf, at the entrance to Auckland, then it was southwest for a turn past Rangitoto Island, hard right past North Head, and into Waitemata Harbor, August 7. Leaking, reeking and dangerously rolling!

The tally of captain's report mast is as follows for the shakedown cruise period, June 21 to July 25.

6 Steward's mates   2 Electrician's mates
5 Seamen   1 Coxwain
3 Firemen   1 Officer's cook

During this period, there were only 11 steward's mates on board, and of those who came before captain's report mast, four were given brig time on P & P, one was fined $30 and confined to the ship for 30 days, and one was given extra duty to be performed. This tended to be the pattern for some time to come, with the steward's mates, the only blacks in the Navy, constantly in trouble. Of course, they were in an unenviable position, in close daily contact with the officers. The steward's mates had no buffers between them and the officers they were there to serve, whereas the general body of the crew had warrant officers, CPOs, and the master-at-arms to serve as buffers.

The executive officer of a ship is responsible for the operation of the ship and management of the crew, so his personality and management manner are highly visible, and any bad traits he may have would immediately be noticeable in the confines of the ship.

Conditions among the officers during this shakedown were not good, either. In fact, there was a general atmosphere of fear throughout officer's country. The executive officer appeared to be the center and cause of most of it, and the confines of the wardroom and the bridge tended to bring out the worst in some officers.

Of the 22 officers on board during this period, 15 of them were reserves, most of whom were inducted into the Navy from their Merchant Marine service without benefit of any formal Naval training or indoctrination courses normally given to young officers being trained for service in the fleet. However, discipline among Merchant Marine officers was much more relaxed than among Naval officers. In the Navy, more rigid rules of responsibility, behavior and, authority are placed in the rank, represented by the amount of gold braid shown. The threat of court martial bears heavily on the Naval officer's shoulders but also carries with it more power over those below him.

The behavioral infringements by the enlisted men were handled by the captain at report mast, and only the more severe cases were assigned to the deck or summary court martial level, both of which were presided over by the executive officer. The executive officer had a tendency to hand down multiple sentences. The ones given here were the final results, as many times the executive officer would add confinement to the ship for a certain period, only to have the captain rescind it, retaining only the lesser sentence. This made the executive officer the "bad guy" and the captain the "good guy." As a result, there was a widespread fear of the executive officer among the crew. There were very seldom any hard words passed around about the captain, even though he handed out brig time on P & P quite often. What mattered to the crew in the final analysis was liberty time. Brig time was usually served while at sea, whereas confinement to the ship cut into liberty time ashore.

There was to be a slight delay in docking because the port authorities did not know what to do with us. We were directed to anchor out in the stream and stand by to await instructions. The morning of August 8, we were told to get up steam; a tug appeared and nudged us into Prince's Wharf. Almost immediately, we were visited by several men, consisting of a mix of New Zealand and USN personnel, all there to assess the requirements and to help in making the arrangements to correct the deficiencies which had developed and make the ship useful and shipshape.

Chapter 5

Overhaul in Auckland, New Zealand

Those of us off watch crowded the bulwarks and railings, eagerly watching all the activities going on as the ship's utilities were hooked up to the wharf and officials came and went between the wharf, the city, and the ship. Prince's Wharf is right at the foot of Hobson Street, which starts at Quay Street and from which the eager sailor could soon find himself right in the heart of the city. In true Navy fashion, rumors were rampant regarding our future in this new playground. Hopes and spirits were high, and that afternoon, the long-awaited word was passed over the ship's speakers: "Now hear this! Liberty will commence for the port section at 1630, to end at 0100!"

About noon the next day, we moved to Export Wharf, which was to be our permanent berth until October 13.

Liberty was granted two nights out of three, as the ship's mechanical departments were all secured for the general overhaul which had been decided when the ship tied up at the dock. As none of us had ever been to New Zealand before, we were completely unprepared for this new experience. We had only the vaguest idea of what New Zealanders would be like, but that didn't cause us any undue concern. On our first liberty, we simply took everything for granted, full of spirit and anxious to see what types of entertainment the place had to offer.

The crew's berthing area was a complete shambles that first afternoon in Auckland, with the men scurrying around, showering, shaving, and dressing in their best, all in preparation for this first night ashore. The comments, the braggadocio, the formation of cliques and buddies, all combined to give the place a festive atmosphere.

One of the loudest was Sharecropper, sometimes known as the

Rebel, who, above all the rest, made the statement, "If my wife only knew what I have in mind for tonight!" This was followed by one of the other men saying, "What makes you think she doesn't?"

It took the crew about a week to really get the feel of the city and to learn their way around. By this, I mean they had to find the best places to hang out for beer, liquor, and women. Then, things began to get rough and interesting.

Off Queen Street, up the hill from the wharves, near Victoria Street, is a short street called Darby Street. On this street, there was a private club, known as the Lonely Hearts Club. Soon after our arrival in Auckland, several of the officers managed to get access to its services and became frequent callers there. The very first evening, they made the acquaintance of Paula, a young girl who frequented the club quite often; a very friendly girl who loved to associate with officers. Our executive officer soon fell for her, completely. In spite of the entreaties of his fellow officers and the fact that he had a wife and family back home, he insisted that he was going to marry her. The more he thought about it and the drunker he became, the more insistent he became. Soon the girl's parents came into the picture and thwarted his plans, assisted by the Naval authorities, who refused permission for him to marry her.

One evening soon after this, on the way back to the ship, complete depression set in. He threatened to jump off the gangplank because he couldn't marry her. He had to be restrained by the OOD (officer of the deck) and some other officers, who put him in his bunk to sleep it off. It wasn't long before some of the officers decided that if they were going to enjoy themselves, it was best not to go ashore in the company of the executive officer.

We were not the first Yanks to come to New Zealand. The U.S. 1st Marine Division had been in Wellington since June 15, 1942, and the 3rd Marines had come to Auckland just a few months later.[21] New Zealand was being used as a training and staging area in preparation for the coming amphibious actions in the islands north of New Zealand.

New Zealand has a high degree of self-government granted by Great Britain in what is known as Commonwealth status. During World War I and, in fact, in all of England's wars since about 1890, New Zealand had supplied a substantial draft of troops for the British Army and Navy. When we came to their country in 1942, there were very few men left in the country, and they felt somewhat threatened by the advance of the Japanese, although their land was so far south and beyond the general reach of the first onslaught. They were rather ambivalent in their acceptance of the Yanks but felt it was necessary if for no reason than that it was helping England and her battles for the Empire. Also it was good for

5. Overhaul in Auckland, New Zealand

Queen Street, Auckland, N.Z., ca. 1930s (H. Foster, GM).

business, which was booming, and it was comforting having friendly troops occupying their land.

None of this, of course, concerned us at the time, and we had only a superficial idea of what their background was or their reasons for either resentment or gratitude that we were there. Here we were, and our ship was going to be here for three months, so we were going to see what the city was like for liberty.

During this initial exploratory period, we learned to catch the tram on the left side of the street, not the right side. After nearly getting clobbered several times, we soon caught on to the fact that when stepping off the curb to cross the street, you looked first to the right, and not to the left. It didn't take us long to get used to the change in the monetary system, and we were soon able to mentally make the transition, so that on liberties we could hand out the correct amount in American change. But very quickly we were handling only New Zealand coin of the realm, and transactions came much faster and smoother. Like all Yanks overseas, we were free with the tips and probably raised havoc with the local economy, but that didn't even enter our minds, except as only a fleeting thought. Then we were on to more pressing thoughts, like where was the closest pub, and where did the girls congregate.

On one of the very first liberties, several of us were on a tram, which had stopped at a traffic light. Looking out the window, standing next to the tram, we saw two other sailors from the ship, a bos'un's mate and a machinist's mate. Both were regular Navy, old hands, been around the Horn, and so on. They were dressed in their custom tailored blues, tight fitting, with white hats drawn down in rakish fashion and with a cherubic look on their tough, bronzed, scarred face. In their hands, they each clutched a bouquet of flowers. We all hooted and hollered at them, and they just stood there foolishly grinning and blushing.

Because of the war, petrol (gasoline) was in short supply and expensive, so New Zealanders had devised at least two ingenious alternative fuels. One of these was a rack on top of the cars, especially taxi cabs, with a large fabric bag mounted on it. This held a supply of the local heating and cooking gas, which was in fairly good supply; the engines had been altered to handle it. The supply in those bags was not very great, and the driver had to watch his mileage and the condition of the bag very carefully, or he could be caught in an embarrassing situation. More than once, we sailors had to help the driver push his cab to the nearest replenishment point. We were young, and to us this was only part of the adventure of liberty in a foreign port.

Another substitute quite often seen was a coal-burning gas convertor on the car, usually in the normal trunk space, but exposed. It converted coal, which was glowing and smoldering, into coal gas, which served as the fuel for the engine. Not the safest arrangement, to be sure, but it worked and unfortunately polluted the air enormously.

The pubs were open only from 1000 to 1800 and closed on Sundays; it was not possible to purchase beer or anything stronger and remove it from the pub. It was served only over the bar or to tables on the premises. They were modeled after the English system, in that there was also a private lounge in connection with the pub, where you could sit and drink and where women were allowed. Women were not allowed in the pub area. This arrangement worked very well for most of the Yanks, but there were some who did not like to be restricted in their source of supply and who then sought other sources. Those sources were the local bootleggers, known as Slygroggers, who worked out of their homes. Any cab driver knew at least one and was probably getting his share of the profits by referring those rich Yanks to the right address.

The ship's liquor lovers soon located one house, owned and run by a woman they called "Ma," who had a daughter, about 25 years old. Also in the house was a little girl around six or seven years old, who was probably the granddaughter. I don't know if there was a "man of the house" or not, but there were usually several Yanks hanging around.

Albert Park lies just off the civic center in Auckland. When the Japanese started their plundering into the South Pacific, the Auckland city fathers, believing that their citizens could be in danger, decided to take some minimal measures, just in case. One measure was the digging of trenches at vital spots to permit some resistance against invaders. A series of trenches in Albert Park were dug flanking what was thought to be a natural route for the invaders to rush inland through the park.

Just to the south of Albert Park, in the street marking its southern boundary, there was an old gentlemen's club. When the *Octans* came into port, the club management extended an invitation to the officers to make use of their facilities, which included a bar, restaurant, lounge, showers, and so on. One rainy evening, a group of *Octans* officers decided to make use of the offer. Among them was Neils, the first lieutenant, a former Merchant Marine officer, who was born in Sweden and spoke the typical mixture of Swedish and English. They gathered at the bar, had a few drinks, and then decided to go into the restaurant for dinner. Neils, however, decided to go back to the ship and started down the path through the park. He stumbled into one of the trenches, filled with weeds and mud from the rain. He was a complete shambles—thoroughly scratched, torn, and soaked—but managed to find his way back to the ship.

When the other officers heard what had happened, they immediately saw the humor in the incident and made the most of it. The supply officer, somewhat poetically inclined, composed a short ditty to commemorate the event:

> When it rains again in Albert Park,
>   That'll be the day.
> That will be a Friday night—
>   That's all I've got to say.
> Our man will come out again
>   To wrestle in the dark—
> Digging ditches in the rain
>   In beautiful Albert Park.

The song's author sang it to the entire wardroom a few nights later after dinner. Neils was not favorably impressed. His comments went something like: "Gawdammit, you guys yoost don't undertand vhat happened. I vasn't drunk—I yoost got lost in the Gawdam park!"

The ship was required to furnish a contingent of shore patrol men to help keep the peace. Every evening at about 1800, up to five petty officers were sent ashore to report to shore patrol headquarters for duty. The men would split up, with one sailor patroling with one marine. The marine had usually been there for some time and knew the hot spots to be watched. The men would return at about 0100 the next morning.

On August 11, the captain held report mast, with seven cases to be tried. One of these was a member of the fireroom gang, a rather loud, boisterous regular Navy man, with a large tattoo on his chest, featuring a goat and the words "Hogan's Goat" emblazoned on it. On the previous evening, he left the ship, broadcasting to all who would listen what he was going to do. He was AOL (absent over liberty) the next morning for almost nine hours. He said that he got drunk and passed out. When he came to, he was in the gutter on a side street alongside one of the main streets of the city, in an area containing mostly native New Zealanders, known as Maoris. He was minus his wallet and ID card; his uniform was a mess; and he had to be helped back to the ship by the shore patrol. The captain assigned him to a summary court martial. A couple of weeks, later he was fined $60, and the street where he had been found was dubbed "Hogan's Gulch" by his shipmates in the engineering division.

During my first liberties, I scouted out the book stores and found two books on refrigeration, one to assist me in repairing the small units on board and one that gave some information on the obsolete system in the ice machine room. Also, as I did not have sufficient tools, I went to an ironmonger's shop and bought a set of Snap-on socket wrenches, small size, for use in my work.

I knew that sooner or later I would be given shore patrol (SP) duty, and I didn't care for the idea at all. It finally came, my first trick; I was duly put on patrol with a marine, who knew his way around. I felt very insecure next to him, what with my weight at about 130 pounds. All I had was the club assigned to each of us to back up the authority implied in our SP armbands. We commenced our patrol, and the marine explained the pattern to me. First, we stopped off at one of the pubs, where it was obvious that he was well known by the bartender. The marine ordered up two straight shots of Scotch whiskey. He passed one to me, said "Bottoms up!" and downed his drink in one gulp. I was not going to let him show me up, so I did likewise. It burned and I nearly gagged; but I held it down and attempted to hide the shuddering it caused in my body. If this was meant to be a test, I don't know if I passed it or not, and I didn't really care. All I knew was that I never wanted to repeat the test and decided then and there that straight Scotch whiskey was not for me.

As we walked the beat, he described various things to watch for as we passed through the crowds in the pubs and on the streets. He told me that if there was any trouble, to let him handle it, and for me to stand aside and protect his back. I agreed, hoping that it would never happen. He probably was of the same mind. Dinner came and went, consisting of the usual "styke and eyggs." By this time in our stay in New Zealand, I had given up trying to swallow their coffee, as it consisted mostly of chicory, I was told. I switched to tea and had no problem with it.

The evening was without any major incidents, fortunately, and midnight came none too soon. Just before time to turn in our gear, there was one minor incident, somewhat of a comical nature. The U.S. military maintained what were known as "Pro Stations," which were there for the sole purpose of dispensing prophylactics in a tube to our servicemen who were "exposed" to VD (venereal disease). The applicant had to sign a sheet, giving the name of the girl and the time of "exposure." Although of questionable value, the purpose of signing was an attempt to identify the worst sources of VD. As the marine and I were walking along toward the SP station, an obviously nervous young sailor of about 17 years old came walking up to us and asked, "Hey, Mac, can you tell me where the Pro Station is, huh?"

After telling him how to get to it and after the shaking kid had left, we both had a good laugh. The marine mentioned that this happened quite frequently.

Work on board the *Octans* was proceeding at a slow but steady pace. The New Zealand workmen were methodical but slow. We often made jokes about it, although we weren't interested in the job getting done too fast — we were beginning to enjoy our liberties. The workmen in the ice machine room loved to stop and talk, and I became quite friendly with some of them. There was an elderly man, Bert Early, who claimed to be the uncle of Stephen J. Early, President Roosevelt's press secretary. I also became on good talking terms with Ken Moberly, who traveled among the sailing people of Auckland. He invited me out to his home for dinner, which I gladly accepted. He gave me instructions for getting there, and I had no problem finding his house. I was immediately introduced to his wife and their six-year-old daughter. She was shy at first, but soon warmed up, and since there was still some time before dinner would be ready, she asked her mother if we could go for a walk on the beach, which was very close to the house. Her mother consented, and off we went, hand in hand, walking along the beach, talking and looking for seashells. We soon came to a bluff overlooking the beach, and on top of the bluff was a walkway. As luck would have it, walking along that bluff were two sailors from the ship with a girl. They saw me and started to hoot and holler, accusing me of robbing the cradle. When I got back to the ship that night, I was met with some ribbing.

The dinner was similar to a New England boiled dinner and was delicious. There was only minimal food rationing in New Zealand. The country was one of the chief sources of food for the Allied forces in the Pacific during the war. After dinner, Ken proposed that he and I go over to visit a home where the owner was building a sailboat in his basement. I asked Ken how that could be; I could not envision how the owner could get it out of the basement when it was finished. Ken laughed and said to wait and see. The host was only too glad to take us down into the basement and show us his work. It was obvious as soon as I saw the set-up how he was going to get it out of the basement. The house was built on a slope, with the back wall of the basement facing the downhill side, completely exposed. The boat was facing that wall, and the wall, of concrete blocks, only had to be partially demolished to permit rolling the boat into the backyard.

The New Zealanders are great yachtsmen and take the sport seriously, mostly for the joy of it. They detested the Aussies, who turn any sport into a gambling shambles, they claim. The New Zealanders are well known for piling on as much sail as a boat will take and taking aboard extra crew as ballast, simply to hold the boat from capsizing.

Getting back to one of the purposes of our stay in Auckland, there was quite a list of things to be remedied and changes to be made. I do not have the original list, but from memory and from what had to be done, it is possible to arrive at a fair estimate of what was expected to be accomplished during our three months in Auckland.

The stern tubes were inspected and repacked; both propellers were inspected for nicks and dents; and corrections were made as required. The zinc sacrificial plates bolted to the stern on either side of the rudder were replaced with new plates, ready to resume protection of the bronze propellers and bushings.

One of the first high priority items to be done was the reballasting of the ship to correct the poor stability dynamics which was almost our undoing on the high-speed run down from Espiritu Santo. This took much of the time during the early stages of the overhaul. Those leaky cargo doors along the side of the ship were all rewelded where inspection indicated there was a problem or a potential one. We had no further trouble from them after that was done.

In the ice machine system, the brine coolers were dismantled sufficiently to permit removing the carbon dioxide coils through the #3 orlop deck, slide them over to the hatch, and lift them out with a crane. They were then trucked over to the contractor's yard and dismantled; and for several days it was the task of our gang to chip and scrape the enormous amount of scale off the coils.

The ice machine was partially dismantled, and the steam pistons, rods, and bearings were taken into the shop for working over. The compressor blocks were not removed, but the pistons and rods were taken into the shop also. New babbitt metal was poured into the shells of the major bearings while in the shop. They were then brought back aboard, and the constant scraping to make them fit was started. It was never really completed, and they were a constant source of noise and irritation to us. New packing was made and installed for the compressor rods. We opened up the carbon dioxide condensers and cleaned the tubes. The machine was put back together, after lining up all components.

In the engine room, the main bearings on both engines were taken into the shop and rebabbitted and then scraped in. The cylinders were rebored, and new piston rings were fitted. Similar treatment was given to some of the auxiliaries. The condenser tubes were cleaned, checked for leaks, and replaced where necessary. The alignment of both main engines was checked and adjusted in an attempt to solve the problem of misalignment, particularly in the port engine. The job was not quite done correctly, so trouble persisted for some months.

There was much to be done in the fireroom, due to the age and poor condition of the four Scotch marine boilers. The main problem was failure of a number of staybolts and rivets, which had to be replaced. Caulking of them had to be done, and the results tested. The boiler tubes had to be cleaned and checked for corrosion and repairs made. Burnt and missing refractories had to be replaced. The fuel oil system needed cleaning and overhauling, as did also the forced draft fan system and drivers.

There were some drastic changes made in the crew's quarters, including removal of some more of the old staterooms, installation of more bunks, laundry improvements, showers, and washrooms for the crew and for the CPOs.

The yard workmen remodeled much of the electrical installations and brought them up to an approximation of Navy standards. Much of the existing wiring and fixtures were antiquated and unsafe. Some of the electric motors also came in for a share of the overhaul budget.

In #3 hold, the trunk around the hatch was enclosed with removable bulkheads on the lower levels, permitting working one deck at a time without exposing the other decks to warm air.

There were probably many more changes and repairs made in other parts of the ship, but memory and lack of surviving records do not disclose them.

By the end of August, we had settled down to a regular routine of two liberties out of three. During the day, we turned-to in our departments, taking care of those items within our capability. The ice machine gang stood nighttime cold standby watches in the engine room and ice machine room, the watertight door between the two rooms being open.

Among the ship's crew were several boxers of various abilities and experience, which often lead to impromptu matches, sparring bouts, and just plain horsing around. Hugh, a gunner's mate, was one of the boxers, and he quite often was seen exchanging punches with one of the seamen. In time, the seaman became fairly proficient, so much so that the time came when he felt he could take on one of the bos'un's mates who had become a thorn in his side. So he waited until the right moment came while ashore on liberty with the intended victim, then pounced on him, and managed to come out the better of the two. When it was over, he realized what he had done, panicked, and ran away as fast as he could. In so doing, he ran into a tram and suffered a fair amount of bruises.

At several places in the deck log during this cruise, there are accounts of men coming back from liberty appearing as if they had been in a fight, with nothing said in the log about the cause of the damages. One wonders if perhaps the boxing lessons gained aboard ship may have had something to do with those instances.

There were the usual cases coming before the captain's report mast, which was held as cases accumulated—a few AOL cases, some instances of standing an improper sentry watch, losing ID card, and so on. There was a case just a few weeks after our arrival of an officer's cook being brought back aboard by the shore patrol who charged him with threatening a woman with a loaded pistol. Another time, two of the five shore patrol men sent ashore for duty were returned a few hours later under arrest for being drunk and for improper performance of their duty. Obviously, they went far beyond just one shot of Scotch whiskey.

It was at about this time, while the ship was still at the Export Wharf, that another episode took place, confirming the general impression that our executive officer was a maudlin, guilt-ridden drunk and was to be avoided when in this condition, evidenced by a deep depression.

One evening, a gunner's mate was dispatched with one of the ship's boats to the Auckland wharves to pick up several officers who were returning from a night on the town. When he got there, many of them were in various stages of intoxication, with the executive officer one of the worst. Almost from the moment they got into the boat, trouble was encountered with him. He finally got to the stage, which they all knew he would, when he was determined to jump overboard. The consensus on the boat was that they should let him, as they knew he could swim and it might sober him up. No one made a move to stop him, and he slithered off the gunwale into Waitemata Harbor. He could indeed swim, and he proceeded to thrash around, swearing at those in the boat, but doing a fine job of staying afloat. The boat circled around him for several minutes. When it was decided that he had had enough, the boat pulled alongside him. He was pulled aboard — soaked and dripping, but almost sober and somewhat subdued.

About the time we hit Auckland, the Navy changed its policy regarding men who came down with VD. The previous policy stipulated that their allotment home was stopped while they were in the hospital for treatment. This was changed so that those on the home front were not aware of any playing around by a husband or a son. The main purpose, however, was to insure that the sailor would be more willing to report to sick bay for treatment.

On August 28, the captain held report mast again, another five cases of various infractions, with all receiving sentences of loss of liberty in varying amounts. On August 31, three men from the previous captain's mast were sent to the Receiving Barracks ashore for general court martial. On September 2, one of the men sent ashore for shore patrol duty was returned by the shore patrol, intoxicated and unfit for duty. He was placed in the brig to sober up.

On September 3, four men were caught gambling on board and came up before captain's report mast. Sentence was loss of ten liberties each. At the same time, a steward's mate was given a summary court martial for striking his superior officer. Also that same day, another man was sent to the Naval hospital for treatment for VD, and an officer was struck by one of the local cars while on liberty. The medical officer examined him and found he had a bruised chest.

The men who frequented Ma's house were always bragging about the wonderful times they were having on liberty at her place. So one afternoon, two other men and I decided to check the place out, just to satisfy our curiosity as to what was going on. When we got there, the "party" had been going for some time. The place was a madhouse, with a couple of extra girls present. Soon after we arrived, Sharecropper came barging in with a bouquet of flowers in his hand. He glared at the daughter and said, "A fine thing! I brung ya flowers, and I find ya loving up some other sailor!" He flung the bouquet in her lap, turned to Ma, and said, "What da ya got to drink, Ma?"

It was spring in New Zealand, the days were getting longer and warmer, and it was an excellent time of the year to be getting liberty in Auckland. For the earliest part of our overhaul there, we had enough money in our pockets to assure having a good time ashore. There were the normal spring rains at times, but that didn't bother us much. There were the usual captain's report mast sessions, with the usual petty and not so petty infractions. One man in particular began to follow a pattern which boded no good for himself. He appeared to be deliberately fouling up to force the officers to give him a transfer or to get him out of the Navy. He was not the only one, but he was the first to exhibit this behavior during this cruise out of San Francisco.

One at a time, the cases of VD continued to appear. During our three months at overhaul, a total of 11 men were sent to the hospital ashore for VD treatment. They were always brought back aboard, of course, after their treatment was declared complete. This usually took about three weeks.

Meanwhile, on the northern battle front, conditions were hot, humid, and dangerous. On New Georgia Island, Munda was taken about August 5, and Vella Lavella was invaded on August 15. For the remainder of August and into September, our forces gained ground steadily on the island. Around the end of September, Kilombangara was evacuated by the enemy, and by October 10, the entire area of New Georgia was in our control.[22]

In further consolidation of our control over the Solomons, Mono Island, a part of the Treasury Island group, just off the southern tip of Bougainville, was occupied on October 27. The next day, our forces occupied Choiseul Island, just across the famous "Slot" to the east.[23]

The ship's officers by this time had become acquainted with enough women of Auckland that the decision was made to hold a formal dinner dance on board in the wardroom. One of the lieutenants had become friendly with a lovely young woman who was a member of the Royal New Zealand Navy and was the cox'un of the Admiral's barge at the Naval base across the harbor. She and the other women all came in their finest formal evening dresses, and it was quite a successful party. When it came time for the lieutenant to take his date back to the Naval base where she was stationed, the ship's motor whaleboat was called, they got in, and our cox'un and the boat engineer started across the harbor. As they approached the landing, the sea was running very high and the cox'un had difficulty maneuvering the boat into the landing against the tide and the waves. Finally, the lieutenant's date asked if she could try it. The cox'un was dubious, but the lieutenant assured him that she was well qualified, so she took over the tiller. Standing in the stern sheets, her gown billowing in the wind, giving instructions to the boat engineer, she deftly brought the boat up to the landing, where the cox'un snagged the dock with the boat hook. The lieutenant helped his date off the boat and onto the dock. They said goodbye; she thanked him for a smashing evening and departed. The boat's crew were amazed and loud in their praise.

Soon it was my time to go on shore patrol again, only this time I did not dread it as much. It followed the same pattern as before, with the marine telling me to simply protect his back if trouble came. This time, there was no Scotch whiskey. We had a fairly routine, quiet patrol during the first part of the evening, with the usual "styke and eyggs" for dinner; then it was time for things to get lively—it was Saturday evening.

The main street of Auckland is Queen Street, which starts near the Queen's Wharf in the harbor and runs uphill away from the docks. Near the top of the hill there is a major cross street called Karangahape Road. The marines, in true Yankee fashion, had dubbed it "Slap-Happy Road," due to the number of dance halls, pubs, and clubs along its length. There were one or two dances in progress, which we casually meandered through, just to show the colors, so to speak. We stopped to watch the dancing, which was nothing like we had ever seen in the States. They loved their Round Dance, in which the couples danced side by side, holding hands and facing the backs of the next couple in a large circle around the dance floor. This dance took a lot of floor space, and the couples did not touch each other, except for holding hands at a respectful distance. The dance would proceed around the circle in one direction, then after a few dances, the rotation would be reversed and they would go around in the opposite direction for a few dances. Many of our men thought it was ridiculous. As for me, I couldn't have cared less, not being a dancer.

After assuring ourselves that there were no rowdy Yanks about to cause trouble, we then went to one of the clubs and found an entirely different condition. This club was down in the basement of a pub, and it had a bad reputation, both among the local populace and among the military. It was dark, smoky, and noisy. The dance band didn't help any, and the net result was that it was difficult to carry on a normal conversation. But then, it was obvious that there weren't very many normal conversations taking place. The marine reminded me of the plan in which I was to protect his back, and perhaps if I thought I could handle it, I might attempt to separate the women from the men in any fight he was trying to break up.

We had been there only a few minutes when one young girl, who could not have been more than 17 or 18, obviously well along to becoming completely inebriated, came up to me and said "You watch me! Before this bloody night is over, I am going to start a fight!" And she did. Not one fight, but five of them.

Fortunately, she wasn't too hard to handle when the fighting started. She did not fight back when I separated her from the sailors who were fighting over her. She enjoyed the spectacle, just watching them fight while I held her back and later held her so she wouldn't collapse while the fighting was being broken up by my marine partner. That was some night, and I was glad when it was time to check in at shore patrol headquarters, turn in my armband and club, sign out, and return to the ship with the rest of the contingent for the evening. The girl was known by the shore patrol and worked at a milk bar, which was their equivalent of our soda fountain, at the foot of Queen Street. My next liberty, out of curiosity, I stopped by and asked if she remembered us breaking up the fights she had started. All she answered was, "I don't remember it."

The New Zealand workmen enjoyed their tea breaks and would heat up the water for tea on deck; then they would all sit around and tell stories and poke fun at each other, as men often do in such situations. The second division bos'un's mate soon became on good terms with them, and often they shared their tea with him. He became friendly with one about his own age, who was the son of the owner of a contracting firm doing some of the work on board. He had recently bought a used American Chevrolet and was just dying to drive it around and show it off to his lady friends. The only problem was lack of petrol for it.

When the *Octans* left Oakland, two drums of aviation gas were placed on board. The reason was obscure, but there it was, lashed on the fantail, under the 5-inch gun platform. The bos'un's mate, in a friendly gesture, told his new friend he could help himself to the gasoline in the drums on the fantail. This he did, bringing on board two five-gallon cans, filling them up, then sneaking them off the ship. He invited the bos'un's mate to come to his house, and they would drive around, pick up a couple of girls he knew, and have some fun. The bos'un's mate accepted, and they had a good time with the girls and the car to drive around in. The invitation for the petrol supply was extended, and there were several more raids on the two drums on the fantail.

Several weeks later, the man was complaining about his wonderful car losing power, and he just could not figure it out. The bos'un's mate did not tell him that the problem was no doubt burned-out valves from the rich gasoline for which the engine was not designed.

The harbor at Auckland has a great many scenic spots, suitable for outings and general recreation. The officers on the ship arranged for a daytime picnic on one of the islands a short distance from the wharves.

5. Overhaul in Auckland, New Zealand   65

They used the two ship's motor launches, picked up the girls who had been recruited for the event, and had their picnic, complete with liquid refreshments. When the day was over and it was time to end it, everyone was more or less drunk. The girls were put in one boat and dispatched to the point where they had been picked up. The officers got in the other boat and headed back to the ship.

Very soon on the return trip, the executive officer began to show signs of depression, raving and moaning about no one liking him, especially his fellow officers, which was basically true. It got steadily worse, and no one aboard the boat was paying any heed, some even wishing he would make good his threats to jump overboard. Finally, when he started to crawl over the gunwhale, two of the warrant officers decided they had better act. They took hold of him, quieted him down by assuring him that they cared about him and that he had two friends on board. That mollified him, and he behaved for the remainder of the trip.

The spring rains continued intermittently. Normally, we paid little attention to such mundane and inconsequential things. I was standing the morning watch, 0400 to 0800, in the engine room and ice machine room, when the rain started. The engine room fidley ran continuously up to the boat deck and ended in a skylight that was designed to give light and ventilation to the men down on the engine room floors. When the rain started, I did not know what to do, other than move all paperwork from the top of the watch desk and into the drawer beneath it. The rain came down into the engine room and fell on the bearings, machine parts, tools, and so on, which were spread out on the floor plates for the civilian workmen to continue on in the morning.

Muster that morning was held on station, and soon after that, while we were working in the ice machine room, the warrant officer from E division came back to see me, asking me why I hadn't placed the tarpaulin over the skylight when the rain started. I simply had no real answer, other than that I did not know the procedure, as no one had informed me that the tarp even existed. He smirked, gave me a dirty look, and left.

The rains started early again the next morning. After about an hour of turn-to time, one of the machinist's mates from the engine room came back to see me, laughing and having a hilarious time. He told me that when the rain started again, the man on watch had gone up to the boat deck and had stretched the tarp over the skylight in the prescribed manner. The civilian workmen gathered at 0830 to start work and were working away on the machinery in the center of the engine room floors. The rain continued and had built up on top of the tarp, causing it to sag in the center of the open skylight. It was an old tarp, and when it became full of water, it suddenly split down the middle, and the whole avalanche of water came down the trunk, soaking the workmen, the parts they were working on, and the floors.

Somehow that made me feel a little better about my dereliction of duty and the dirty look I got for it.

Liberty started early on Saturdays and Sundays, commencing at 1000 those two days. On one of the Saturday liberties, another man and I decided to go to the race track, the first time for both of us. We managed to find our way there, got some help in betting procedure from one of the touts at the entrance, and became thoroughly indoctrinated, or so we thought. The problem, and we soon recognized it, was that neither of us knew a thing about picking the horses, so we ended up just making wild guesses. It would be nice to be able to say we had beginner's luck, but it didn't happen that way. Instead, we had sucker's luck. We lost on every bet, and finally gave up betting and just watched the horses run, trying to make some sense out of what was going on. I have never been a gambler.

Liberties for me in Auckland for the most part were quiet and pleasant. The hours allotted for liberty were not conducive to any extended trips from the city, and the local laws reflected the English conservative hours for business. Many hours were spent in simply walking around, from one gathering spot to the next. There were movies, the amusement park, and the many scenic spots to visit and admire. The local transportation was good, after we got used to the schedules and the routes.

It was here that we became acquainted with the favorite meal mentioned earlier, available in the restaurants, "styke and eyggs," or steak and eggs, served with chips (french fries). The price was very reasonable, about the equivalent of 65 cents as I recall. Ice cream was almost unheard of in the milk bars and restaurants, as also were cold beverages. At the milk bars, you could get lemonade, fruit drinks of all types, and what they called milk shakes. These were nothing but milk with flavoring added and skaken up to achieve the mixing.

The city of Auckland is located in a very beautiful spot, with many vistas available from the various lookout places. With the many harbors and bays, it is no wonder that the inhabitants are sea-sports oriented.

As I have indicated earlier, Auckland did have its wilder side, and there were men on board who were expert in locating it without losing any time. With the early end of liberty while there, it isn't any surprise that some of the crew were often lax in getting back aboard before the end of the liberty.

During the first two days of September 1943, Eleanor Roosevelt visited Auckland while on a tour of the South Pacific bases. She was accorded a very warm welcome by the New Zealanders. Generally speaking, our own troops paid very little heed to her visit, with the exception of those recuperating in the hospitals, where she was well received.

While on our walk up from the ship into the city, we saw a large announcement out front of the Auckland Town Hall, stating that Mrs. Roosevelt was appearing there that evening at a dance with Artie Shaw's Navy band. We stopped off at a pub across the street, and the pubkeeper (called a publican) asked if we were going to join the festivities that night. He was shocked when we told him we had no interest in her or her travels. He obviously thought that she was more than just the president's wife, perhaps even coming close to the position of a princess consort. We explained that she did not have nearly that position in our country. She was simply known as the "First Lady."

The average middle-aged New Zealander had mixed feelings about the Yanks in their land. They were mostly a reserved people, similar to their British and Scottish ancestors. One got the feeling that they tolerated us and would be glad to see us leave when the war was over. That was understandable, of course. They were simply careful about making friends with the Yanks. When they found one they could relate to, they were very hospitable, as I found out and related earlier in this chapter.

As another example, Lyle, a friend of mine who was with the 3rd Marines in Auckland earlier in the war, had an experience which illustrates their attitude very well. He became acquainted with one of the New Zealand men, a middle-aged civilian, who decided to invite Lyle to his home for dinner. They got on the train and were riding along, talking, when his host recognized a man sitting directly ahead. He reached over, tapped the man on the shoulder, and said, "Meet Lyle. I'm taking him home to meet my wife and daughter."

The man glanced back at Lyle, then turned to Lyle's host, and said, "Do ya think ya can trust him?" End of conversation.

There was very little trouble meeting the girls and young women in the city. Most of them were not quite as reserved as the acquaintance of Lyle's host. Some, in fact, later married some of our servicemen stationed in New Zealand and were brought back to America.

Many of the crew members became friendly with the workers on board, with results similar to my experiences related earlier. Quite often, men from the ship would be invited to go sailing on weekends and reported back very favorably. At times, the sail took the form of a party, held usually after the sailing. An invitation to dinner at the host's home often went with it. In general, we Yanks were very well treated by the people of Auckland. Another pastime enjoyed by the crew was swimming at one of the many public beaches in the area. This could be as a result of an invitation from one of the workers on the ship or by a group of shipmates getting together and heading for the closest beach. Of course, the beaches were also an excellent place to meet girls.

Mike and Don, from E division, were invited to a party by one of the workers on board, and permission was obtained for them to stay ashore overnight; the worker assured the captain that they could stay at his house. They ended up at a house owned by a woman whose husband was stationed overseas. The party progressed in the usual fashion, and, at some point during the festivities, the woman of the house decided to sit on Mike's lap, which she did, very forcibly. The impact sent the chair, with both occupants, backward into the front of a china cabinet, smashing it considerably.

Work below decks continued steadily, but slowly. The evaporator coils were reassembled, brought back aboard ship, dropped into the #3 hold down to the orlop deck, skidded over to the open top of the evaporator shells, and dropped into place. They had already been tested and found to be tight, with no leaks.

The right specification lubricating oil for the compressor had been ordered and delivered aboard in five-gallon cans. We stored it in the shaft alley and pondered the best way to make the change when the time came to start up the system again. There was still quite a lot of the old oil in the piping, and we did not relish the thought of dismantling the entire system to get rid of it. Finally, it was decided that the best way was to introduce the new oil into the lubricators from start-up and to discard the drainage from the separators until the compressor behavior indicated that there were no more plugging problems from bad oil.

Life aboard continued in a steady routine, so much so that the two nights liberty out of three began to tell. It was not uncommon for a man to forego a jaunt ashore when he rated it, either from pure boredom or most usually from the lack of money. It soon reached the point where those who were more careful of their finances were being approached for loans. This brought out the Yankee ingenuity again in the form of the "Walking Pawnshop." Several members of the crew entered into the business of buying and selling wristwatches. Pappy, our master-at-arms, was one of them and was often seen with his arms adorned with his stock in trade, walking among the crew, offering to buy, sell, or trade.

Fresh milk and ice cream came aboard daily, and fresh food to replenish our larder came aboard as needed. All of it was inspected by the medical officer and the OOD before being accepted. Muster was held every morning, either at quarters on the promenade deck for the engineering division or on regular duty stations and the shore patrol contingent left the ship daily about 1630 or 1000 coinciding with start of liberty, returning at about midnight or 0100.

5. Overhaul in Auckland, New Zealand

After the first few weeks in Auckland, the crew settled down to a behavioral pattern which was fairly steady but with some foul-ups. There were a few dribbles of men being transferred, some replacements coming aboard, and some cases of AOL, some so minor that only a warning was issued. The more drastic cases of misbehavior were dealt with severely, some even being transferred to the Naval base ashore for handling of the captain's report mast punishments. There were a couple of cases which indicated that we had some misfits on board, and they would have to be dealt with sooner or later. On October 3, we had a case of an officer being disciplined for open criticism of the captain. He was a lieutenant (jg) and was suspended from duty for five days. In Chapter 4, I told of the fireman who caused the freshwater supply to be contaminated with seawater. On October 5, his sentence was finally rendered. He was fined $30. One of the minor repair items accomplished at overhaul were changes in the fire main and the freshwater system, designed to eliminate the possibility of any more "accidents" which had contaminated our freshwater system on the voyage down from San Francisco.

One of the foul-ups appearing regularly before the captain's report mast was an electrician, who just could not stay sober, even while on shore patrol. He came back aboard once while we were in Auckland without part of his uniform, his pants held in his hands, and a deep gash in his buttocks. When taken down to sick bay for treatment, he very forcefully told everyone present to mind their own damn business when asked how he got the gash. He had fouled up so many times that the captain finally decided the man was just not reliable and was unworthy of any more attempts to rehabilitate him. On October 7, the result of the last of his summary court martial trials was published—loss of pay of $120 and a bad conduct discharge. The last part was modified by the authorities ashore, placing him on probation in the care of the captain for six months. If he fouled up during that time, the captain had the option of initiating his discharge.

That very night, October 7, he went ashore and was brought back aboard the next morning by the shore patrol, drunk and almost eight hours AOL. That was the final straw. He was taken, bag, baggage, hammock, and papers, to the local Navy Receiving Barracks for execution of his sentence.

The ship's service officers decided that the morale of the crew would best be served with a ship's dance before our next supply run. As there were Naval regulations to be met, requiring that while a ship was in commission, it must be adequately manned at all times, it followed that two dances were necessary, which is the usual procedure for U.S. Navy vessels, one dance each for the port and starboard liberty sections.

Arrangements were made with the Farmers Tea Rooms in Auckland for the nights of Tuesday, October 12, and Wednesday, October 13. Invitations were printed and distributed to the officers and crew, a dance band was engaged, liquid refreshments and food were ordered, and everyone looked forward to the happy times ahead.

The executive officer had declared that the drink for the evening was to be punch, without alcohol. This, of course, was simply unheard of in the eyes of some of the crew and the officers; so several men decided the situation called for quick and drastic action. Consequently, when the punch had been mixed and set next to the refreshment table, just before the event was to start, a couple of men brought a quart of pure alcohol, obtained from some remote hiding place on the ship, and dumped it into the punch. Before they could mix it up, they were warned that the officers, including the exec, were coming.

The officers approached the entrance to the convention hall, and the exec took one look at the huge sign over the door, "OCTANS," and exploded. He tore the sign down and declared that someone should be court martialed for breaking the secrecy code. This, after the ship had been in the harbor for overhaul for two months. Then they entered the hall, and he insisted that he be the first to sample the punch. His sample consisted of a very potent mix of punch and alcohol, as it had not been thoroughly mixed. He was sent reeling from the effects and immediately accused the other officers of setting him up.

During the festivities, one of the electrician's mates (EM) had in his jumper pocket, a package of cigarettes with a folded $20 bill behind it. One of the girls at the party reached over, grabbed the package of cigarettes, and removed it. Soon after that, the EM noticed that the $20 bill was also gone. He searched the floor, with no results, and so surmised that it had gone with the cigarettes. He mentioned it to a bos'un's mate, noted for his size and strength, who grabbed the girl by the ankles and dangled her out the window, four flights up, until she admitted she had the money.

From entries in the log, there is no evidence of extreme measures being taken to police the entertainment. A contingent of five shore patrolmen were assigned both nights, and their main function was to quietly return the overly intoxicated men to the ship. At 0800 muster the mornings after each dance, there were no absentees and no mention of anyone being AOL. The report masts for the subsequent days gave no indication that any of the cases were a direct result of the dances.

One thing is certain, however. The New Zealanders would remember it for some time to come, for ship's dances are usually notable for their noise, drinking, eating, and general carousing, although the latter is often restrained somewhat by the presence of officers. However, as our contin-

5. Overhaul in Auckland, New Zealand

> *You are cordially invited to attend a Dance sponsored by the Officers and Crew of a vessel of the U. S. Navy the night of October 12, 1943, at the Farmers Tea Rooms.*
>
> DANCING, 8 - 11.45 P.M.

Invitation to the ship's dance (R. Meilandt, Lt.).

gent of officers were mostly former Merchant Marine officers, I rather doubt that their presence dampened the enthusiasm of the crew.

On October 13, the dock utilities were removed, and the ship was eased away from the dock with a tug. The tug and the pilot then took us west in the channel and into position alongside one of the repair facilities at the Western Wharf. There, cranes and machine shop facilities were available to continue work laid out for the contractors, with the ship's utilities again connected to the dock. It was obvious that the repairs were winding down at that stage of our visit in Auckland when, on October 19, we took the ship for a sea trial lasting several hours and then returned to the Western Wharf for more adjustments and work yet to be performed.

The civilian workmen often took a few minutes off to tell us about the past history of their country and to answer many questions we had. They gave me two books that told much of the history not only of the country, but also of the Maoris, who were on the land when it was explored and colonized. There are several estimates of when the Maoris arrived in New Zealand, including the verbal stories passed down through generations by the Maoris themselves. They were reputed to have come from an island far to the north, called Hawaikii, in seven large canoes.

The Maori men are noted for their strong, military bearing and are often married to white women in New Zealand. This is an accepted fact of life there. The Maori women are typical for the mix of Polynesian and Melanesian ancestry from which they came. The Maoris and the New

Zealanders have, over the years, mixed to a great extent, and this is accepted by most white New Zealanders. The Maoris have managed, in spite of the mixing of the races, to maintain much of their culture and heritage, and most of the New Zealanders are proud of the result.

By the end of October, the results of captain's report mast began to show signs of a few more repeaters who continued to plague the system. One at a time, they were either transferred in the normal routine manner or simply sent to the Naval Receiving Barracks for completion of their deck or summary court martial.

Also about this time, there occurred an unfortunate incident involving one of the oilers in my gang, a fireman. He was a tough, black Irishman, very mild mannered and a good worker. He regularly went to Ma's house on liberty with some of the other men. On one of his liberties, Ma found him in the bedroom of the little girl, with a dazed look on his face, drunk with the product of the house, and his flap unbuttoned. The girl was terrified; Ma immediately jumped to conclusions, and called the shore patrol. He was brought back aboard ship, and there was a considerable amount of discussion as to what to do about it. Ma soon dropped charges and wanted to quash the whole thing; but our executive officer wanted to press charges. He was one sad Irishman for days but still performed his duties on board. His explanation was that as far as he could remember what happened, he was looking for the bathroom and got confused as to which door it was. According to the deck log, he was packed up and sent to the Naval Receiving Barracks ashore. There was no mention in the log of any action against him. We never heard a thing about him after that.

As October waned, the machinery was being put back together. There was some trouble lining up the steam engine driver and the compressor blocks on the ice machine. The day came when the burners were lit off in the boilers, steam was slowly raised, the steam mains feeding the engines and the rest of the ship were warmed up; then the main steam stop valves opened. Following this, the engine cylinders were warmed up, the drains all closed, and it was time, October 23, to perform another trial. A few hours spent maneuvering around Hauraki Gulf disclosed a few glitches still to be remedied. The ship stopped overnight at the Calliope Wharf across the harbor and then went to King's Wharf, near the center of the harbor, for final adjustments.

On October 25, the ship was again put through a few hours' test run around the Gulf, with some improvements noted. Our allotted overhaul time was over, and we had to accept what we had. We would continue to be plagued with some of the same problems which had existed since we left San Francisco. Mostly, our problems were with the bearings, the equipment being out of alignment, and leaking boilers. Added to this, of course, was the general aging of the machinery and boilers, from stem to stern.

The ice machine was turned over slowly at first to give the new bearings and the reworked portions of the steam driver and the compressors time to work in for awhile before applying full load. While this was happening, the brine system had to be replenished, the brine circulating pumps started, and the brine coolers vented of any entrapped air. The lubricators were fed the new oil, and the mixture of the old and new oil was drained and discarded. This latter process went on for weeks before we were sure all of the old oil had been purged out of the system.

It was then time to speed up the compressor and to commence cooling the holds for loading. This required more carbon dioxide to be charged into both systems, as they were practically void of gas. We went on our regular steaming routine in the ice machine room, with the exception that half our gang still rated liberty each evening.

When the final trial run was complete on October 25, the ship returned to King's Wharf and commenced loading for Supply Run #2.

Chapter 6

Supply Run #2: Shakedown II

As the only records available from the National Archives for this period are Administrative Remarks, and not the ship's deck log, parts of this run are estimated. The Administrative Remarks contain only the results of captain's report mast, crew transfers and replacements, passengers carried, the ship's shore patrol activities, and provisions taken on board for the general mess. However, several former shipmates supplied the ports of call, arrival and departure dates, and the incidents related in this chapter. Other details given herein are my estimates, based on later trips through the same area and routes. The validity of the history should not be lessened by this mixture of fact and conjecture.

Those two short jaunts around Hauraki Gulf in no way could be considered as shakedown cruises, so again, as we did in leaving Oakland, we had to fill our holds with food for the fleet and accept this first run out of Auckland as another shakedown. This became obvious when we continued to have problems with the ship's machinery and boilers, although not quite as bad as when we left Oakland on that first supply run.

With most of the work orders signed off, all tests run to determine the results, the ship commenced taking on her cargo for the next run up north. The easy, lazy days of liberty two nights out of three were a thing of the past. For some, who had long ago used up their stash of cash and were existing from day to day on borrowed funds from sympathetic shipmates, getting back into the old routine was a welcome relief, although a sad one. Auckland was a lovely, lovely liberty port. The ship continued to provide its complement of men for the daily shore patrol. The ship was refueled from the dock, and down below in the fireroom, the Black Gang were standing auxiliary watch, hoping that the repairs to the boiler would prove satisfactory. The engine room watch was keeping a close eye on the machinery which had undergone extensive overhaul. In the ice machine room, we were tending the compressors very carefully. We were anxious to see how the system would perform, now that the evaporators were clean, the condensers flushed out, and the proper oil provided. When the compressor came up to speed, the brine's temperature started coming down. With the air-circulating fans on, the hold temperatures started to drop steadily. The dock crew was ready to load our next cargo of reefers and frozen foods, and they pitched in with the usual routine, around the clock, with frequent breaks for hot tea from their billies.

The immediate results of the overhaul on operation of the ice machine were disappointing, as the bearings still gave out with the usual THUMP, THUMP. There was some improvement in the output, as a result of the work on the evaporators and the condensers. We had hoped there would be more improvements in the bearings, but it was not to be. We did not expect an immediate change in the periodic plugging of the carbon dioxide lines, as there was still a considerable quantity of the old off-spec oil in the system. With patience, however, this problem steadily improved, until another problem developed which produced about the same results; that will be covered later.

With all of the ships operating out of New Zealand, Australia, and other allied countries, the question arises as to who was paying for all of this food. The Lend-Lease Act of January 1941 was signed into law in March of that year and opened the door for our bureaucrats in Washington to tack on any number of programs. In September 1942, the Lend-Lease in Reverse program was started, with agreements made with allied countries in which our armed forces were stationed, that those countries would help support them. This was to include food, supplies, land, and services to the extent of their capabilities, all of which we on the *Octans* were getting during our operations in the Pacific, with port space in place of land. It was all a bookkeeping transaction, with, presumably, a final accounting to be made after the war was over.[24]

On October 30, 1943, the special sea detail was set, and preparations were made for getting underway. The pilot came aboard, the tug snuggled alongside the starboard quarter, and we got underway for Espiritu Santo in the Hebrides. All four boilers were on the line, the pilot was discharged over the side outside the harbor, the tug cast off, and standard speed was set at 10½ knots. The degaussing coils were energized (just in case the Japanese had mined the harbor under the New Zealand Coast Guard's noses) and Condition 3 watch was set throughout the ship. We threaded the prescribed course in getting to the open sea, through the channel marked as cleared by the minesweepers, then changed standard speed to 12 knots. Once in the open sea, we commenced zigzagging on our base course and then secured the degaussing coils. We were free and running, following the regular daily routine. To keep us on our toes, the usual round of drills were held, general quarters, abandon ship, and fire drills.

At 1000 on November 2, the captain held report mast to deal with a couple of recalcitrant men who had fouled up the last day in liberty port, a fireman who was one of the ship's frequent foul-ups and a yeoman. Both were AOL for several hours, and both received sentences of loss of several liberties the next time in liberty port.

On November 4, we approached Espiritu Santo Island, ceased zigzagging, set special sea detail, stopped engines, and took on the pilot. Standard speed was resumed, passing through the antisubmarine boom and entering Segund Channel, on the southeast tip of the island, where we anchored and secured the steering engine and degaussing system. We discharged two of our passengers and unloaded the general cargo from on top of #1 and #2 hatches, which had been loaded at Auckland. We then loaded more cargo on top of the same hatches, destined for further transit.

At about 1200 on November 5, the word went out that a beach party was being organized for those off watch. About 20 men answered the call, and they walked down the gangplank and into the motor launch. They went first to the flagship USS *Wright* (AV-1), seaplane tender to pick up chits for beer. On the way, the officer with them got seasick from the rough ride. One of the men, Jim, went up the gangplank to the deck and inquired as to where he could get chits for the beer. The OOD asked how many were in the party, and Jim told him about 40. The OOD looked over the side to count for himself, but the launch was bounding around so much that he had difficulty getting a count. He wasn't helped any by getting seasick from the effort; he accepted the count of 40 men. Jim bought the 80 chits at 10 cents each, then returned to the launch. The beach party then went to pick up the beer and found that the SeaBees had given nostalgic names to the various buildings, such as Yankee Stadium, Ebbetts Field, and Duffy's Tavern. The men lined up and got their allotted two cans of beer apiece, with Jim holding the extra chits, and they started for the assigned beach area, anticipating an afternoon of fun and games in the hot sun, with the cold beer. But it wasn't to be quite like that.

Exheavyweight champion Gene Tunney was in charge of the base facilities, and his CMAA (chief master-at-arms) ordered all of the party to line up for calisthenics. These lasted for about an hour, while the beer sat in the sun and got hot, almost as hot as the men were after the exercises. Fortunately, the second round of beer came as a welcome relief. In addition, a chancre mechanic with the party had brought along a couple of quarts of alcohol from the sick bay, which further fortified the cold beer. As was to be expected, several of the party got quite loaded and had to be helped aboard the ship when the launch returned. With the condition of the men and the existing rough seas, one wonders what the launch was like when it reached the ship.

Overnight, the warm weather turned wet and miserable, as foretold by the rising seas the previous afternoon. Early that morning, the captain received orders to accept on board a shipment of bottled beer to be delivered to the shore base at Guadalcanal. It arrived on board a lighter, manned by an Army working party. The beer was on pallets, which were hoisted aboard alongside the #1 hatch. The beer had to be stowed in #1 hold, forward in an isolated spot, one case at a time.

Knowing the tendency of the ship's crew to help themselves to anything which could be eaten or drank, a trusted storekeeper was stationed at the stowage spot in the hold, to count the cases as they were placed. When the last case had been stowed, the final counts were compared; 1,000 had arrived on deck; about 900 had entered the hold. The word was passed that if the missing beer did not turn up when the beer was unloaded at Guadalcanal, there would be no liberty at the next civilized port of call.

When the beer was brought up from the hold at Guadalcanal and placed on the pallets on deck and counted, strangely enough, there were only a few cases missing. A cursory walk around the ship did not disclose any hidden or visible empty beer bottles. No doubt there was a string of them floating all the way back to Espiritu Santo.

About noon on November 6, we got underway from the anchorage in Segund Channel, stood out to sea enroute to Guadalcanal, all boilers on the line, standard speed 11½ knots, degaussing coils energized, then passed through the antisubmarine boom. Condition 2 watches were set, and we joined up with a small convoy. With three escorts screening, the columns were 600 yards apart, and the ships in each column maintained intervals of 600 yards, with the convoy zigzagging at standard speed of 10 knots.

One of the three escort vessels was an odd looking type of cargo ship flying the Free French flag. She had been seen at the Mare Island yards just previous to entrance of the *Ulua* into Alameda. The French Navy officers had been circulating freely among the U.S. Navy officers ashore but never gave out any hint as to their purpose or that of the odd looking ship.

When a safe distance from the harbor choke point and with sufficient depth below our keel, the degaussing coils were secured. The next two days were fairly routine for this area, with the convoy zigzagging on the base course. The escort vessels were continually patrolling their assigned area, lookouts always on the alert and the sonar pinging the underwater surrounds for any lurking enemy submarine. When one appeared on the screen, the convoy was alerted, an emergency turn away from the contact was made, and a patrol vessel went off in hot pursuit of the enemy submarine. Usually it proved false, and the patrol vessel would signal the convoy commander to resume base course and zigzag pattern, while it returned to its patrol beat.

The first time general quarters was sounded as a result of a submarine contact, the odd-ball Free French ship became transformed from a nondescript cargo ship to a bristling raider, known as a Q ship. All of her camouflage came down, her 8-inch gun amidships became active, and she sped off to hunt down the enemy submarine. She was completely equipped for this action, having Y guns for depth charges, 40mm gun mounts, and high-speed engines. It was really quite a show, as she went into action, circling, making high-speed runs over a contact, and throwing depth charges to both sides.

When it was all over, results unknown, she resumed her slow, plodding place in the convoy screen, and replaced her movable camouflage. The men on the bridge of the *Octans* felt a little more relaxed and reassured knowing that we had such an escort.

If the lookouts on the patrol vessels and the convoy leader spotted an unidentified ship or object on the horizon, all efforts were made to make identification as soon as possible. If it proved to be a ship, recognition signals were exchanged. If it was a bit of flotsam, the patrol vessel would investigate, always alert for a submarine periscope or floating life rafts, lifeboats, or bodies. We were on the southeast edge of the war zone and pushing our luck.

Before leaving the convoy and entering the harbor at Guadalcanal, we shall take this time to look at how the Pacific War was going directly northwest in our path. With the landings on Treasury, Vella Lavella, and Choiseul Islands fairly well secured, Admiral Halsey's next move was to establish a base at Empress Augusta Bay, on Bougainville, bringing our air force closer to Rabaul, the thorn in the plans to march towards the islands of Japan. The enemy had established an enormous base there, and Halsey decided that it had to be neutralized. First, of course, Bougainville and Empress Augusta Bay had to be taken. Halsey directed that our forces attack at three places, widely scattered, to throw the enemy off base. It worked, and on November 1, 1943, the 3rd Marine Division landed in the bay and commenced fighting their way inland.

A powerful enemy force from Rabaul was immediately dispatched to drive our forces off the island, but Admiral Merrill's Task Force 39 repelled them. To cinch the security of our landing at Empress Augusta Bay, Halsey ordered a carrier task force to attack Rabaul, which they did on November 5. General Kenney's 5th Air Force followed this up by repeated B-17 bomber raids, forcing the Japanese to evacuate their naval forces up to their base at Truk.[25]

Major elements of our 37th Infantry Division landed on November 8, 1943, to assist the Marines and SeaBees in building an air field in the swamp on Bougainville, inland from Empress Augusta Bay. The enemy refused to give up without a determined fight and continued to attack from the other side of the island. Sporadic skirmishes, both by land and by sea, lasted for weeks, finally ending about the end of the year.

On that same November 8, we were detached from the convoy to proceed to Guadalcanal alone. We secured from Condition 2 watches, passed through the antisubmarine net, and took on the pilot, who guided us to dockside at Lunga Point. The degaussing and steering engines were secured, and the engine room placed on 30-minute notice. Almost immediately, the deck cargo was removed from the hatch tops. Next, the crews came on board to work the cargo from the holds. The ice machine gang was kept rather busy, changing the fans and regulating the hold temperatures for the next several days while the cargo was removed first from one set of holds and deck, to others, as the local demand required and the ability to carry it away permitted.

When a red alert sounded ashore, the ship went to general quarters. The crews in the holds clambered up the ladders in smart fashion, and dispersed, either on shore or on board, waiting for the alert to end. When the all clear sounded, they were back again, working the holds. We were amazed at how fast they could get up out of those holds when the alert sounded.

During this period, from November 8 to 19, we were constantly being shifted around between Guadalcanal, Tulagi, and Florida Islands. At times, we were moored to one of the docks, when available, but more often anchored in the harbor. We saw much of the tropical island shorelines as hot, humid, and unappealing. We were thankful to be on board the ship, where we enjoyed showers and a clean place to eat and sleep. The bronzed, healthy, and Atabrine (the antimalarial drug) tinted speciments of American GIs were a stark contrast to us pallid sailors. We knew we were destined to be in a liberty port within a couple of weeks, while those poor souls working the cargo were doomed to an indefinite sentence on these pestilent islands. We were happy to be able to provide anything possible to help them in their miserable existence.

At one of the island stops, while discharging our precious cargo to a string of small craft alongside, an accident happened involving the winches on #4 hold. Those two winches were equipped with a two-speed arrangement, similar to the automobile manual transmission. One control system could handle light loads at high speed, and the other system could handle heavy loads at low speed. That particular time, the bos'un's mate in charge of unloading #4 hatch had elected to use the slow-speed system because the cargo consisted of heavy loads of frozen meat. The executive officer ordered him to switch over to the high speed, as the unloading was going too slow for him. The bos'un's mate didn't trust the order but went along with it. He then alerted the men on the boat alongside, who were aware of what was going on between the executive officer and the bos'un's mate; so they scampered out of the way. The winches strained and labored, bringing the loaded net out of the hold, then slung it outboard. When over the hold of the boat alongside, the outboard winch slipped in some way, as it could not handle the load. The load dropped down, wiping out part of the superstructure of the boat, and causing considerable other damage. The boat managed to limp back to its destination.

While there, on November 12, we were introduced for the first time to the use of amphibious trucks for unloading cargo. The trucks were capable of receiving the cargo from alongside the ship and carrying it directly to the ships anchored in the harbor or to cold storage warehouses on shore. They could not carry much, but they kept up a steady stream; and as each one left the ship for its delivery, another came alongside in rapid order. It was a fast, neat, orderly, and efficient operation — also a fascinating one to watch from the deck of the ship.

Another function of the *Octans* surfaced here — a minor function, but one for which the men stationed in these forward areas were thankful. These men had been without any of the ordinary "comforts" of home, such as any form of alcoholic beverages stronger than the occasional ration of the regulation 3.2 percent beer. True to Yankee ingenuity, they had their own methods of devising workable substitutes from raw materials at hand, but none of it was equal to the genuine stuff. The U.S. Navy had been officially dry for years, but the medical departments were allowed to have small stocks on hand of good, stateside liquor, for medicinal purposes only. More than once, a member of the crew, standing around on deck, would be approached by one of the men working the holds and barges or trucks alongside, seeking help in locating a little of the "good stuff." The crewman usually quietly pointed in the right direction, thus doing his good deed for the day by helping a thirsty fellow serviceman. I was privy to this trade only once and do not know how much of it went on, but it makes sense, as we carried almost anything else imaginable. After all, it was well known that the Air Force, when shuttling planes back and forth between bases, often carried more than just men, mail, and money—especially if their flight was connected on one end to civilized society.

Our "dry" Navy harks back to the reign of one Josephus Daniels, who was appointed by President Wilson to be the secretary of the navy in 1913. He was a newspaper editor and a very active member of the Democratic Party.[26] There were two major changes in the U.S. Navy during his tenure in office. One, as already mentioned, was the attempted abolishment of all alcoholic beverages in the Navy. The other one was the attempt to eliminate the terms *port* and *starboard* in Naval procedures, substituting the normal landlubber terms of *left* and *right*. In the latter case, he managed to succeed only in changing the directions to the helmsman, and that has persisted to this day. The helmsman gets his orders as in these examples: "Come right ten degrees," or "Hard left rudder." Undoubtedly, this is for the good—the helmsman then does not have to make the mental switch, for instance, from *port* to *left* (or is it right?) before he acts.

The abolishment of alcohol, however, was only partially successful. There are several uses of alcohol on board ships of the Navy. One has already been mentioned, along with an implied side effect. Another use is for the floating compass rose in the standard Navy compass, of which there are probably thousands in use. Also, most torpedoes are driven with miniature steam plants, fueled with alcohol, known as torpedo juice. The *Octans*, of course, did not have torpedoes on board, but we did have a fair number of standard compasses which had to be serviced from time to time; so someone on board had to be in charge of storage of this alcohol. Whether he volunteered or was simply appointed by the captain, the chief engineer found himself with several gallons of the "hot" stuff in his cabin.

Among the crew of any Naval vessel, there are always a few who have the ability and the initiative to smell out the hiding places for the torpedo juice, and the *Octans* was no exception. Two regular Navy petty officers, a bos'un's mate and a watertender, eyed the chief engineer's cabin with larceny in mind. They waited until the coast was clear and the chief was in the wardroom eating lunch, then struck. They went into his cabin and helped themselves to about a gallon of the precious stuff.

For some time thereafter, there were many a glow in the bos'un's locker in the fo'c'sle added to those in the furnaces in the fireroom.

One afternoon, while the SeaBees were unloading the holds into the barges alongside, I stood for a few minutes on the fantail, in the shade under the 5-inch gun platform, and watched the activities ashore. Just astern of us, there were several barges moored to a pier, all with outboard motors on one end. I noticed on one of the barges a pile of rags mixed with a bloody pulp. I asked one of the SeaBees working the cargo what it was, and he told me it was the remains of one of the SeaBees who had fallen off the barge earlier in the day, and gotten tangled up in the propeller. They stopped the barge and retrieved what was left of the poor guy before the sharks got to him, and they were going to bury him later in the day.

On November 13, it was up anchor again, and we were underway, with the degaussing coils energized, and escorted by one of the numerous small Navy escort vessels fairly common in these forward bases. This time it was to be new territory, another hot, festery area, Tulagi and Florida Islands, just about two hours easy run north of Guadalcanal. Our forces there were also hungry and glad to see us drop anchor. This was to be a six-day stopover, almost a repeat of the call made at Guadalcanal. Immediately we commenced discharging cargo to barges and lighters alongside.

A welcome break in the rigors of working and standing watches in the tropics came on the afternoon of November 15 while the ship was anchored at Purvis Bay and discharging cargo. The ship's PA system blared out the message: "Now hear this! A swimming party will be held at 1415 at the Army Personnel Depot! All those interested will assemble on the quarterdeck for transportation. Those on watch will be ready at 1600!"

The beach was hot, the water was warm but inviting, and many of the crew took advantage of the opportunity to work off the sweat and grime of the ship and replace it with the salt from the ocean and the burning of the skin. If nothing else was accomplished, the break in the routine of shipboard life was worth the effort.

The executive officer appeared to be riding certain members of the crew, rightly or wrongly, and strong resentment was building up in the affected crew members. Conditions finally reached the point around this time in the cruise that it was rumored one of the steward's mates was prowling the decks in officer country at night, carrying a short length of pipe, looking for an opportunity to finish off the executive officer. The other officers must have been aware of the situation because it would be impossible for it to be kept quiet for long. It was possibly the reason behind some of the transfers which took place about this time.

In the back recesses of the officer's pantry one of the steward's mates usually had a batch of wine fermenting which he shared with other "oppressed" crew members. He and, it was thought, other steward's mates, whenever they had the chance, would contaminate the officers' food and drink, especially that of the executive officer, by such tricks as spitting in it.

6. Supply Run #2: Shakedown II

Cargo handling was often interrupted by a red alert sounded ashore, signaling a possible air raid. The ship went to general quarters, men from holds erupted forth and stood on the deck, with no place to go, since we were anchored in the bay. They stood around, watching for the enemy, ready to duck, if necessary, while the barges and lighters alongside backed off and dispersed as well as they could. After about 30 minutes of this seriocomical standoff, the all clear sounded, the crew secured from general quarters, and all hands and cargo handlers resumed unloading the cargo.

There was a flurry of excitement throughout the ship the morning of November 19 when our cargo booms for #3 hatch were swung over the side to pick up the wreckage of a Japanese plane. It was a model 97 Mitsubishi, larger than the famed Zero. It was not a complete wreck, but badly damaged. We watched as it was slowly snaked through the rigging and past the liferafts, then lowered onto the hatch cover. The deck force carefully chocked it in place and lashed it down to prevent it from working adrift in any storm we might encounter. They then installed a manila line around it, apparently as a gesture to indicate someone was telling the crew to keep hands off. They certainly were being naive, if that was the intent. Within hours, there were scraps of duralumin sheets floating around in the crew's quarters and work spaces. It was easy to work with and filled a void in the various hobby crafts going on among the crew. Watchbands were a favorite, and I even tried making one for my wristwatch. It worked fine, but within days the salty perspiration from my arm had eaten away a large portion of it, disappearing in a white powder. I went back to my original stainless steel band.

There were a few rumors circulating about the plane, about the American manufacturer's signature on some of the plane's accessories, such as the Goodyear tires. The major portion of the wreckage did reach its assigned destination. After all, it is rather difficult to remove a plane's engines and squirrel them away aboard ship. The plane was unloaded when we pulled into Auckland.

"Now hear this! Set special sea detail, make all preparations for getting underway for a swimming party!" This came at about 1415, November 19.

You can be sure the ship was underway, in record time. At about 1435, we anchored just off the beach in Purvis Bay. Some of the ship's boats were lowered, shark watches were set, and the off-duty watch dove in for a good time. A lot of surplus energy was discharged during the next two and a half hours.

At about 1530, those due to go on watch at 1600 were called out of the water, and shortly the next watch dove in, happy to be able to get rid of the sweat and dirt of the past few days. Some of the swimmers were skilled enough or brave enough to dive off the ship, and many simply used the boats as temporary resting supports, while they swam around and dove to their heart's content.

As might be expected, the event was not without its shocking moments, at least for one unlucky sailor. There were no shark alerts, but one man did get tangled up in a Portuguese man-of-war. These are a form of jellyfish, common to the warmer seas. They float and sail about on the surface and dangle numerous tentacles deep underneath. Some of these tentacles are covered with minute stingers, which kill small sea life for other tentacles to grab and digest. When these tentacles wrap around a human being, the result is similar to being whipped with a cat o' nine tails. The man who was unfortunate enough to tangle with one was taken in hand by the duty chancre mechanic and the doctor and treated with salve and bandages. It was a very painful time for him for several days thereafter.

On the evening of November 19, the last of the provender had left the hold; the hatches were closed up; the tarps spread over them and battened down for sea. This phase of the supply run was always a happy one. It meant that very soon we would be in a liberty port, that haven of all sailors. A few hours later, with the crew at Condition 2 stations, we passed through the antisubmarine nets and commenced maneuvering to take our assigned position in a convoy. The trip down through the lower Solomons, past the Torres islands, for a brief stop at Espiritu Santo was the usual convoy routine. We would steam on base course for a few hours, then switch to a standard zigzag pattern along the base course, then switch back to base course again. The routine was punctuated by the occasional false submarine contact, with the escort leaving the convoy to check it out, then resuming position. There were sightings of other ships, all of which had to be checked out with recognition signals exchanged.

Earlier in this chapter, I mentioned the confusion which could result from instructions to the helmsman being misunderstood or misinterpreted. A case of this came to light during this trip south in convoy. The helmsman, a signalman, turned the ship to port when the order was to starboard. The ship caused complete havoc in the convoy. The other ships were turning away in an attempt to avoid collision, while at the same time blowing their whistles and joining in the rush of signal lights flashed to the ship's bridge. It took several minutes for the helmsman, guided by the watch officer, to jockey the ship back into some semblance of order in the convoy.

When it was all over, there still was no response from the captain, who had remained completely out of it during the entire fiasco. Lady luck was with us that day, as well as with the helmsman.

That was not the only time that happened: During a night trick at the helm while in another convoy, the helmsman, a seaman first class this time, mistook something he heard in a conversation between two officers on the bridge and applied 30 degrees, right rudder. The lieutenant on watch immediately detected the change and ordered the helmsman back on course. Again, no harm done, except to the pride of those on the bridge.

Manning the helm can be a very boring duty at times, especially after the procedures and skills have been mastered. To prevent accidents, standard Navy procedure calls for the helmsman to repeat the change in course order verbatim in a loud and clear manner, before executing the order. Also, to prevent boredom, the helmsman is often relieved by another helmsman on duty during the watch, for boredom can cause the mind to wander far away from the task at hand.

Somewhere in the vicinity of New Caledonia, we were detached from the convoy to proceed independently to our destination. This took us off Condition 2 and back to normal steaming on Condition 3, but we went to general quarters to watch the sun rise off the port beam.

We were steaming alone, unhindered by slower merchant ships, with standard speed at 13½ knots, and on the prescribed zigzagging pattern for about a day. Then it was straight down into Auckland, relaxed and happy, counting our accumulated cash, and making plans for the coming liberties.

In the ice machine room, we had a few days of "down time," which gave us a chance to work over any of the deficiencies which had cropped up on the trip north. The overhaul in Auckland had done a fairly good job in most cases, but there were some things the mechanics simply could not accomplish in the time allotted. We were still attempting to work all of the old oil out of the line. The flywheel bearings were still rough and pounded too much to our liking; so they had to be opened up and checked for clearances. There wasn't time to do much scraping on the bearings before we had to put them back in place and start up the compressor to get the holds cold for reloading in Auckland.

Another problem we continued to have was with the quality of the wiping materials furnished us. Machinery of the type we had on board requires constant wiping with hand rags, and our hands also took their share of wiping while we were running and maintaining the equipment.

This required cloth rags, but we were supplied with bales of cotton waste, shreds from the textile industry. This waste deposited fine threads over everything and got into the oil passages and feeders. We spent many hours dismantling the oil feed systems and cleaning them out. This was a problem not only with the ice machine, but also with the spring bearings on the propeller shafts. The engine room had the same difficulties.

Finally, as we passed the northern tip of North Island, New Zealand, we had the compressor going at speed, the holds were coming down, and our department was in full operation, getting ready to take on cargo.

The morning of November 30, we tied up at Prince's Wharf. That afternoon over the loud speaker came the welcome call: "Set Condition 4 all departments. Liberty for the port watch will commence at 1630."

The engine room and the fireroom were on Condition 4, but we were on a stripped down Condition 3 watch, meaning that we only had one man on watch from 1600 to 0800 the next morning while in port. The ice machine was in full steaming operation, keeping the holds cold while they were being loaded.

Ah yes, a tough life, but we managed.

Chapter 7

Supply Run #3: To Australia

From this point on, the National Archives records of the ship's deck log are fairly complete. This run is the first which contains a decent record of the ship's activities. The early part will be covered in fairly complete detail, sufficient to give a reasonable picture of how we operated for the good of the service and the country. Later runs will not be covered in such detail but will still be complete enough to portray our life, both on board and on liberty.

December 1, 1943: The first lot of shore patrolmen returned to the ship, having left for duty ashore the evening before. The engine room and fireroom were on Condition 4, with boiler #1 on the line. Freshwater and telephone service was provided from the dock. The ice machine gang had hoisted the empty carbon dioxide (CO_2) cylinders up on deck and over the side unto the dock. At 0800 muster, a seaman first class was missing, AOL from liberty. At 1245, the evening shore patrol contingent left the ship, and at 1600, 30 men reported aboard for duty, all seamen second class.

December 2: The ship's shore patrol contingent returned aboard at 0100. At 0800 muster, the seaman first class was still AOL. At 1152, the oil barge came alongside, and 265,000 gallons of fuel oil were taken into our tanks. The ship's shore patrolmen left the ship at 1258, and at 1312, a signalman first class was transferred to the mobile hospital ashore for treatment for VD.

In the Navy, rumors are known as "scuttlebutt," a term descending from the days of wooden ships, when drinking water for the crew was dispensed from a wooden cask, called a scuttlebutt, with a spigot on it.

Like their counterparts in civilian business life, the men tended to congregate around the scuttlebutt and exchange news, stories, and gossip. On board ship, the news from the bridge and the quarterdeck usually reached the crew by means of those enlisted men who circulated back and forth between the lower decks and the bridge. On the *Octans,* therefore, our main source of information—or scuttlebutt—was from the signalmen, radiomen, yeomen, quartermasters, chancre mechanics, and Pappy, the master-at-arms. Whenever a group of us would gather for bull sessions, we could usually count on Pappy sauntering by, offering the latest "straight dope," as he termed it, from the upper decks.

December 3: The men on shore patrol the previous evening returned aboard at the usual time of 0100. Muster at 0800 disclosed that the seaman first class was still AOL. At 0915, the first of our cargo was lowered into the holds. This activity would continue around the clock until the ship was ready to depart for the islands, as would the tea breaks by the stevedores. About noon, the #3 boiler was lit off, for auxiliary steaming, being brought up to pressure slowly, so as not to overstress the pressure shell. It was cut in on the line at 1620, and #1 was removed from the line and secured. At 1430, a Navy lieutenant reported aboard for temporary duty. The evening's shore patrol contingent left the ship at 1500, and at 1540, a gunner's mate third class was transferred ashore to the mobile hospital for treatment of VD.

December 4: Our shore patrolmen returned aboard at 0115. The seaman first class was still AOL at 0800 muster. At 1448, the evening's shore patrolmen left the ship.

December 5: Practically the same as for December 4.

December 6: Shore patrol activity about the same as for previous two days. The seaman first class was still AOL at 0800 muster. Down in the engine room, where they were working over a bad bearing, a fireman third class dropped the upper half of one of them on his toe, badly damaging the toe. At 1530, we took on board 251 RNZAF (Royal New Zealand Air Force) personnel for transportation to the islands, the first large contingent, but by far not the last, that we would be carrying before the war came to a close. Finally, at 1745, all hope for the AOL seaman was abandoned and his baggage, records, and transfer papers were sent to the Navy base ashore. A machinist's mate second class reported aboard for duty at 2035, assigned to the engine room crew.

Earlier in the afternoon of that day, a truckload of refilled carbon dioxide cylinders was deposited on the dock alongside the #3 hold. This called for the ice machine gang to turn to, man the cargo winches, lower the cylinders down the escape hatch, and lug them into the shaft alley for stowage.

7. Supply Run #3: To Australia

December 7: All four boilers were made ready in preparation for getting underway, and the shore patrolmen came aboard at 0100. At 0230, the manhole gasket on #2 boiler blew out, the steam pressure was released by manually lifting the safety valve, and repairs were commenced. Special sea detail was set at 0800, and the crew was mustered while on their stations, with no absentees. The ship got underway at 0834 for Espiritu Santo, with the pilot conning the ship and the captain, executive officer, and navigator on the bridge. With standard speed at 10½ knots, on three boilers, and Condition 3 watch schedule, we passed through Rangitoto Channel, then through the antisubmarine net, and energized the degaussing coils. After the pilot left the ship, and still on three boilers, we threaded our way toward the open sea. At 1150, the #2 boiler was lit off, having been repaired, and the steam pressure in the boiler was sufficient to permit cutting it in on the line at 1415, with the fireroom gang keeping their fingers crossed. At 1900, the standard speed was boosted to 12 knots, and at 2000, we were free enough of the approaches to start zigzagging on our base course north, after securing the degaussing coils.

December 8: Steaming alone, still zigzagging, with ship on Condition 3. At 0410, the crew went to morning general quarters, and we were secured from general quarters at 0517, resuming Condition 3 watches. More trouble developed in the fireroom when the forced draft fan failed at 0817, causing the ship to come to "slow ahead both engines." The trouble was solved quickly, and at 0836, the engine room telegraph signalled "all ahead full."

At 1400 came the inevitable captain's report mast, with four cases to be heard. The result was two warnings, one loss of ten liberties, and one deck court martial.

Our activities at the various ports of call during this run were typical of our routine throughout the cruise. To avoid repetition for the remainder of this narrative, the following items will seldom be mentioned again.

Normal refueling from whatever source available
Exchange of passengers
Trips for the mail by Flags, our mail clerk
Activation and deactivation of the degaussing system
Passage through the antisubmarine nets guarding the harbor
Minor captain's report mast cases
Morning and evening general quarters

Anything out of the ordinary pertaining to the listed activities will be given; otherwise, the reader can assume that the activities were carried out, where applicable for the particular port.

December 9: Steaming as before, with standard speed now 11½ knots. The clocks were set back one hour at 0200 due to a change in time zone from zone − 12 to zone − 11, with Greenwich Mean Time as a base of 0. The speed was changed several times during the day, for various reasons. At 1450, the emergency generator was tested for 15 minutes. The duty generator was of ancient vintage, probably original equipment with the ship's launching in 1917. It was so old that the Navy Yard at Mare Island decided it was useless to attempt to obtain spare parts for it.

December 11: More trouble reported below from the fireroom when a slug of water came through the oil lines feeding the burners, which resulted in a slight reduction in speed for a few minutes. At 0637, the USS *Daring* (AM-87) took position ahead to escort us. She was a minesweeper, which were often assigned to this duty. The executive officer convened the deck court martial at 1500 to try three cases pending from December 10, results to be announced later. We passed Efate Island to starboard at 1650, distance about five miles.

Just a year before, following the earlier victories along the lower portion of the northern New Guinea coast, there still remained some pockets which were in enemy hands and were still a threat to MacArthur's march towards the Philippines. The Aussie troops retook Gona from the enemy on December 9, 1942, after some very bitter fighting, as the Japanese defenders were under strict orders to hold the area to the death.[27] This opened the way for advancement along the coast towards Sanananda.

Australian and United States forces wrested Buna village from the enemy on December 14, 1943. The next day, our forces landed on the northwestern coast of New Britain, at Arawe, opposite New Guinea. Cape Gloucester, on the extreme western tip of New Britain, was occupied by allied forces on December 26.[28] The New Year was celebrated in fine fashion when allied forces occupied Buna Mission on January 2, 1944, and also Saidor, near Sarawak Bay, about 100 miles northwest of Finschafen, on the northern New Guinea coast.[29] We were now on the offensive, and the enemy was retreating steadily. But there were many more miles to steam and many more battles to be fought; so our services as part of the 7th Fleet Service Force were still very much in demand.

Because we usually learn to walk on a surface which is level and steady, it takes some time and practice before the subconscious mind learns to automatically adjust to the rolling and pitching of a ship. By this time, most of us former landlubbers were beginning to get our "sea legs" as a result of this process. The change was subtle, and few of us were ever really aware of it.

December 12: We passed Ambrym Island, about five miles off the

7. Supply Run #3: To Australia

starboard beam at 0110. Special sea details were set at 0656; we ceased zigzagging and took aboard the pilot at 0708, who guided the ship past Bogacio Island port to anchor in Segund Channel, Espiritu Santo, New Hebrides Islands, at 0807. A USNR lieutenant reported aboard for duty at 1125, who later became the captain of the ship. General cargo was loaded on hatches #1 and #3, starting at 1550, finishing at 1830.

It was about this time that a situation developed which would later result in a mystery over a possible death on board which was not entered into the deck log. However, several reports received from various former crew members indicate that it happened. It is given here with the understanding that it almost certainly happened, but there is no tangible or documented proof that it did.

While the ship was at sea, a seaman was always stationed in the crow's nest, located about 55 feet above the deck on the foremast, as part of the regular steaming lookout schedule. To enter this crow's nest, it was necessary to climb an exposed ladder on the mast. One of the men assigned to this duty suffered from vertigo, brought on by a fear of high places. He complained several times and requested to be assigned to other duties. John, the C division ensign, remonstrated with the executive officer in an attempt to prevent the seaman having an accident. The executive officer insisted that all men must follow orders and perform their assigned tasks; he refused to reassign the seaman.

John was transferred off the ship December 18, 1943, at Tulagi. He kept in touch with the ship's doctor by letter. Shortly after John boarded his new ship, he received a letter from the doctor, informing him that the seaman had finally fallen to the deck and was killed. He died July 31, 1952; they buried him at sea. The doctor would be the one officer on board who would know of its happening; he would have served as the coroner on board.

There is absolutely no mention of this or any similar incident in the deck log copy which was supplied by the National Archives. Did it actually happen? If so, was it as described here? Perhaps someone reading this will be able to add some enlightenment. Several crew members have said they remember a burial taking place at sea but did not remember any of the facts surrounding it.

During this first cruise, from June 11, 1943, to May 15, 1945, when we pulled into San Francisco Bay, there was only one acknowledged death on board. That one, which is described in the next chapter, was fully documented in the deck log.

December 13: Anchored as before, with all four boilers hot, the engine room on 30-minute standby notice, and receiving cargo on top of #4 hatch. We got underway at 1335 for Florida Island, under Condition 2 watches, forming into a convoy in single column as follows: USS *Crater* (AK-70), USS *Octans* (AF-26), SS *Junipero Serra,* SS *Albert Nicholson,* USS *Chestnut* (AN-11), and screened by USS *McConnell* (DE-163) and USS *Daring* (AM-87). At 1640, the convoy passed Malekula Island abeam to port and formed into two columns, at 600 yards between columns and 600 yards from bow to stern. Commenced zigzagging at 1730 on base course.

December 14: Steaming as before, all hands at Condition 2. At 1400, the captain held report mast and issued punishments for two cases, one to lose five liberties, the other confined on bread and water for three days. At 2215, the commander of the task unit signalled an emergency turn of 45 degrees to starboard. The new course was followed for 15 minutes, and then the original course was resumed. The reason for the maneuver was not given, possibly just an exercise to check the response of the various captains.

December 15: Steaming as before in convoy. We met two small convoys, traveling southeast, and two friendly planes. Also passed San Cristobal, Ulawa, Malaulalo, and Aliiti Islands in the Solomons.

December 16: At 0550, we formed into a single column, passed Taivu Point, Guadalcanal Island, at 0710. Then at 0800, we were detached from the convoy to proceed to Purvis Bay, Florida Island, under escort of USS *McConnell* (DE-163), anchoring at 0945.

At 1132, we got underway enroute to Tulagi Harbor, taking on the pilot, and then tying up at the dock. At 1730, commenced unloading cargo from #1 hold and completed unloading deck cargo from the top of #2 hatch. At 1855, we got underway to shift berths, anchored out in the harbor, and at 2000, commenced working deck cargo from #3 hatch and mail from the mail room.

On November 30, while loading at Auckland, the ship had acquired a new warrant bos'un ("Boats"), a regular Navy veteran of many years in the service. He was short, tough, knew his job very well, and cared nothing for some of the Navy spit and polish routines, including daily attire on board ship. Consequently, he and the executive officer were often at loggerheads. The new bos'un was very quick to see that the executive officer was mostly a bluff in dealing with his fellow officers, and he lost no time in taking full advantage of it.

The ship was equipped with a heavy lift boom on #2 hold, known as a jumbo boom. We had no use for it, but apparently others did; about this time in the run, we received orders to be prepared to transfer the boom onto a barge at Guadalcanal. The new warrant bos'un, Boats, was the logical person to supervise the transfer. Boats proceeded to make the necessary measurements and calculations on the forward-well deck to perform the task, dressed in his uniquely casual, hot weather manner, completely out of uniform. Not only did this, of course, bring down from the bridge invectives on the proper attire for a Naval officer, but, which was worse, the executive officer presumed to know more about the task at hand than did Boats. After a few minutes of this, Boats straightened up to his full height, looked up at the bridge, and said, "Mr. Exec! Pipe down! I'm rigging these booms!"

Surprisingly, the exec did as he was told. Boats had taken the wind out of his sails completely.

There were many hands watching as the jumbo boom was unshipped from the king post, using all of the forward booms. It was laid down on the well deck, while the tackle was adjusted to permit snaking the boom over the side and onto cradles on the barge alongside. Considering the size and weight of the jumbo boom, and the limitations of the rigging, it was a remarkable feat and one which gained much respect for the bos'un.

When the project was completed, Boats looked up at the bridge; then, with his prideful best, he stalked off the well deck and up to the wardroom to pour a cup of coffee. No one clapped, but there were many smirks and smiles on the onlookers as Boats performed his exit.

December 17: Anchored in Tulagi Harbor, ship at Condition 4, unloading general cargo from #3 hold, and engines on 60-minute standby. At 0530, the ship got underway, enroute for Lunga Point, escorted by HMNZS *Kiwi*; and with the crew at condition 1, then Condition 2, we anchored off Lunga Point at 0805. The crew went to Condition 4 next, with engines on 10-minute standby, and at 0948, we commenced discharging cargo to amphibious trucks.

December 18: Anchored as before, discharging cargo, with ship darkened at night according to port regulations, with all four boilers simmering. All holds were worked intermittently until 1547, at which time we got underway to shift berths to Koli Point, anchoring there at 1646. We immediately commenced working cargo from the holds. This day three ensigns and a lieutenant were transferred from the ship, ordered to duty on other ships; so we were now short of officers—not that the crew were aware of it or would mind one bit.

December 19, 1208: "Now hear this! Fire in hold #3! Set fire quarters, set condition, affirm! This is not a drill!" The one thing that mariners fear the most, next to sinking by enemy action, had occurred. The constant drilling really paid off, as the first stream was released on the fire two minutes after the alarm, and it was declared extinguished 34 minutes later. The fire was probably started by a cigarette from one of the cargo workers from shore. There was some slight damage to the insulation material and the hatch boards, and some of the frozen cargo was ruined from saltwater. This damaged cargo was isolated and marked for later disposal. This fire took place in the hatch boards between the lower 'tween deck and the orlop deck. Below the orlop desk was the ice machine room, where two of us were stationed while the fire was being fought.

As described in a letter of June 9, 1944, from the captain to the chief of the Bureau of Ships, our fire fighting installations in the machinery spaces were:

Engine Room
    4 - 15 lb. CO_2 hand extinguishers
    1 - 1½-inch fire hose with fog nozzle
    2 - 1½-inch steam smothering lines

Ice Machine Room
    2 - 15 lb. CO_2 hand extinguishers

Fireroom
    2 - 15 lb. CO_2 hand extinguishers
    1 - 100 lb. CO_2 50-foot hose and horn
    1,300 lb. CO_2 piped to bilges and tank tops
    3,500 lb. CO_2 piped to bilges and tank tops (from refrigerant lines in ice machine room)
    1 - 1½-inch steam smothering pipe aft fireroom
    1 - 1½-inch steam smothering pipe forward fireroom
    10 cubic feet of sand
    1 - twin 20 lb. pressure proportioner

In addition, we always had a reserve supply of full carbon dioxide cylinders stored in the shaft alley, which could be used directly as local fire extinguishers or hooked up one at a time to the distribution system.

With the fire out, the ship got underway at 1312, escorted by HMNZS *Tui* to shift anchorages and piloted back to Tulagi Harbor, dropping the anchor there at 1521. At 1805, we commenced discharging cargo to boats alongside, with SeaBee personnel in the holds.

December 20: Anchored as before, with ship on Condition 4, on 30-minute standby notice, all boilers hot, and cargo being worked. At 0725, the ship got underway and moved to the Government Wharf, Tulagi Harbor. At 0908, we commenced unloading operations again, some to the small boats on the outboard side and some to the dock. A raid alert sounded from the shore at 1520, the ship went to general quarters, and the men working the cargo ceased all operations and took cover. At 1615, the all clear signal was given, and unloading resumed, with the ship again on Condition 4.

The fire in hold #3 and the saltwater from the fire hose damaged 10,700 pounds of frozen cargo, most in hold #3 and a small amount in hold #4. It was discharged into tank lighters alongside at 1830 for disposal.

December 21: Moored at Government Wharf as before, working

cargo around the clock. At 0450, a second class storekeeper was found intoxicated and was acting in a disorderly manner. He was placed in the brig, and a few minutes later, he forced the door open and broke out. I don't know where he thought he was going. Tulagi was not the best place to attempt to escape from the Navy's legal system. He was placed in the master-at-arms office and then, at 0750, transferred to the Naval base ashore for temporary confinement. This case was dealt with swiftly and surely, as follows:

0955: The storekeeper was brought back on board for captain's report mast and was sentenced to a deck court martial.
1030: A deck court was convened by the executive officer, the case was duly reviewed, and the deck court was adjourned at 1100, to decide the disposition.
1200: Sentence was announced; reduced to the next inferior rating. Busted!
1315: The storekeeper was transferred — bag, baggage, hammock, records, and transfer papers — to the commanding officer of the Naval base ashore for disciplinary action.

December 22: The day started as before, but at 0130, all cargo handling was stopped to shift berths with the help of a Navy tug; dropped anchor out in the harbor at 1131. We commenced working cargo at 1245, stopping at 1500. A convoy was being formed; so at 1410, the commander of the convoy, with his staff of an ensign and four enlisted men, came aboard — they were to be our guests for the coming convoy. It was a sorry day for our captain. The commanding officers of two of the Navy escorts and the masters of three of the merchant ships came aboard for a conference at 1645; they left the ship 30 minutes later. We were underway at 1802, at Condition 2 for the next three days.

As the convoy was finally formed, about 1900, it consisted of the *Octans,* as guide with convoy commander aboard, four merchant ships, a Navy ATF, and three AMs as escorts. We headed in a southerly direction, enroute to Noumea, New Caledonia, standard speed 10 knots, in two columns.

December 23: Convoy proceeding generally southeast, intermittently zigzagging on base course, and with intervals of steering a true course, and speed varying as required to maintain position in convoy. At 0622, changed order of convoy to three columns, and increased speed to 11 knots. About 2300, met and passed another convoy on approximate opposite and parallel course, to starboard.

December 24: Convoy steaming as before, with one of the escorts reporting a submarine contact at 0035. Nothing further came of it, so it was either too far away to be a danger, or it was a false contact. At 1513, passed Torres Island to starboard, 45 miles distant. Again, at 1825, one of the escorts reported a sound contact (possible submarine) five miles distant. Another escort dropped astern to investigate it, but it was not found. The escort resumed her place in the convoy, screening as before.

December 25, Christmas Day: No Santa Claus, no presents, just ships in the convoy and lots of ocean first part of the day. Three of the merchant ships, with one of our escorts, dropped out of the convoy to proceed to Espiritu Santo at 0909; the escort returned to our group at 1100, at which time, one of the other escorts left the convoy. At 1020, another UFC ship, the USS *Talamanca* (AF-15) passed abeam to port. She was noted for fast cargo handling, higher speeds, and generally better appointments in crew and passenger comforts. A sister ship to the *Talamanca*, but from a different yard, was the former SS *Quirigua*, now the USS *Mizar* (AF-12), which was also a part of the SFSF. Most of their World War II life was spent in the South Pacific on routes similar to ours. Each had a gross tonnage of 6,963, as compared to our 6,494.[30]

Another UFC ship taken over by the Navy, and running in nearly the same area as us, was the USS *Calamares* (AF-18), launched in 1913, with a gross tonnage of 7,782. The four of us crisscrossed the south, southwest, and central Pacific during the entire war period and were responsible for delivering thousands of tons of food to the ships and shore forces in the area.

Christmas dinner, 1943, was served on board the *Octans* while we were still in convoy, enroute to Noumea, New Caledonia. Our cooks and bakers did an excellent job of serving up a traditional feast, much more than some of us could eat.

With Malekula Island on the port beam, we entered Ambrym Channel at 1415, and another of the escorts left us. We exited the channel at 1630, and three hours later secured from Condition 2 and set Condition 3, the danger having abated somewhat. This was a great relief for the crew, who could now get a little more "sack time" between watches.

Down below in the ice machine room, we were just idling along, as the holds were nearly empty of cargo. Our work load did not follow the same pattern as those in the fireroom and engine room, which sometimes led to feelings of envy from the men in those departments. We in the ice machine gang were used to the digs and remarks and learned to take it good-naturedly. Our room was quite a lot cooler than either of the other two below-deck machinery spaces, and men from the engine room often came back to just chat for a while when things got too hot for them forward. As mentioned earlier, there were thermometers installed in the air ducts. These had to be read and the temperatures recorded once each watch that the holds were being used. One of us in the ice machine watch would leave the room and go up into the fan rooms (items 12 and 19 on page 30), record the temperatures, then come back to the ice machine room and enter the readings in the log sheet. We attempted to perform this task in the middle of each watch, but, in fact, there were times when this was impossible, so the readings sometimes got entered a little late. This was not a problem since the temperatures remained fairly steady most of the time.

Those on watch in the fireroom and the engine room had their own log sheets to keep up to date, which were much more complicated than our simple ones. They had to take readings every hour in most cases.

Back in the States, it was winter, but down here it was the middle of summer; so during the day the portholes were open, with air scoops in them to bring any breeze available into the crew's quarters. To some extent, it was the lazy days of summer, even in the war zone.

December 26, 27: Our little convoy followed a continuous routine of zigzagging along on base course, followed by a stretch, directly on base course, then resumption of zigzagging again. Our standard speed and course would be changed frequently, to keep the convoy together and headed in the right direction, always keeping the speed as high as possible for the remaining ships in the convoy to keep their assigned positions. Normally, the merchant ships in any convoy set the pace of the entire convoy, especially if any of them were single screw ships.

As the convoy steamed towards its destination, one of the merchant ships had considerable difficulty in maintaining its assigned station in the convoy. Repeated questions, threats, and comments by the commander made no effect on the wandering vessel's skipper. Finally, in desperation, the commander had Flags send a semaphore signal: "Relieve the officer of the deck with an intelligent person!"

No immediate answer. In vain, the commander waited for an answer, while doing a slow burn. Finally, after about an hour, it came: "There are no intelligent people on this ship!"

The commander went into a rage, which could only be relieved by another hefty helping of the captain's ice cream.

December 28: Convoy steaming as before, set Condition 1 for morning sunrise at 0410, convoy formed into single file for entering port. Ship went to Condition 3 at 0520, and at 0657, the convoy broke up, each ship proceeding on its way independently. The *Octans* anchored at the Great Roads anchorage, Noumea, New Caledonia, at 0845. Soon after, the commander of the convoy left the ship with his staff.

As the task unit commander and his staff left the ship, our captain heaved a huge sigh of relief. For the entire six days of his convoy operation, the task unit commander, following the standard Navy protocol, had lived as a guest of our captain, including use of his cabin and free food and beverage, paid for out of the captain's own personal account.

That would be a considerable imposition even if the commander had been an average-sized person. But he was huge, with a healthy appetite. Apparently, he had been months without his favorite food, ice cream, so when he discovered that his host had a private store of many gallons of ice cream, he insisted on living on it almost exclusively for the entire stay on board.

Two of our crew were transferred off, bound stateside for further assignment. One of them was the fireman who had contaminated the freshwater system on the trip south from San Francisco and who had served a stretch as my oiler in the ice machine gang. Shortly after noon, the last of the cargo was removed from the holds, and four officers were transferred from the ship for further duty elsewhere, two of them having been advanced in rank just prior to being transferred. Upward and outward — the road to advancement in the Navy.

Our mail clerk, Flags, was badgered about going after the mail as soon as we dropped anchor in any port, regardless of location or the passage of time since the last "Mail call!" Because of our constant moving around, the mail was usually slow in catching up to us. When it did, it was often months old and often in large quantities.

As we dropped anchor this stop in Noumea, Flags went ashore for his normal trip to the FPO (Fleet Post Office) and was gone for some time, with some of the crew getting fidgety over the delay. Finally, an LCT pulled alongside, with Flags in the bow, waiting to jump aboard the *Octans*. As he landed on board, he said to the crew members standing there, "Well, I hope you guys are happy this time! Look what I brought ya! Now don't let me hear any more complaints!"

The deck force quickly activated the closest cargo boom and lowered a cargo net over the side and in position for the boxes, crates, and bags to be placed in the net and then swung up and over the side onto the deck. The deck force eagerly lifted the contents out of the net and onto the deck. Soon they noticed that what they were handling was mostly the ship's allotment of miscellaneous materials and equipment which had missed the ship at Oakland. There were more than the usual number of bags of mail with the stacks of boxes and crates, which mollified the crew somewhat, especially since the Christmas mail was included.

There were still no spare parts or special tools in the lot for the many small refrigeration units on board, which meant I was practically helpless in my side job of keeping the scuttlebutts and other small refrigeration units and the geedunk stand in first-class condition.

The loss of eight officers with a gain of only one during this month of December left the ship rather shorthanded in the wardroom; so the captain applied to the 7th Fleet Force headquarters for replacements. There were none available. In fact, it was pointed out that, throughout the entire command, many of the service vessels were short of officers. So the captain returned to the ship, with nothing to show for his request but another hole punched in his TS (tough shit!) card.

December 29: At 0512, we got underway for Melbourne, Australia, alone, standard speed 13 knots, zigzagging on base course. At 1030, the captain held report mast and assigned punishment to a seaman first class who was disrespectful to his petty officer in performance of his duties. Result, he was bound over to a deck court martial.

December 30, 31: Steady steaming on course, zigzagging at times. Sighted several ships, two of which were never identified. At 1030 on December 31, the executive officer convened the deck court martial to try the case of the seaman first class from captain's report mast of December 29.

January 1, 1944: Steaming singly as before. At 1100, the sentence for the seaman first class was posted; busted to the next inferior rate, seaman second class. At 1150, the port engine was stopped for repairs because a gasket had blown out on the high-pressure cylinder drain. It was repaired; at 1204, the engine was started up again, and the ship resumed its regular steaming schedule. At 1212, the gasket again blew out, and the ship was again slowed by the loss of the engine. We were back at full speed at 1236. But our troubles were not over, for we had to stop the port engine at 2328 to tighten the port propeller shaft coupling bolts in the engine room.

January 2: More trouble, still from the port propeller shaft; at 1051, the same coupling bolts had to be tightened again. Then at 2013, the coupling bolts on the port tail shaft had to be tightened. This was the section of shaft that was furthest aft, and went through the tail shaft bearing and packing gland, with the propeller attached.

As if we were not having enough trouble, during this phase of the run into Melbourne, an apprentice navigator was practicing the art of guiding a ship by the stars. He was doing so under the watchful eye of the first lieutenant in the early morning watch. The novice was having trouble and could not get the plot right on the chart. According to him, we were lost. His complaint was that he could not find the North Star from which to take a position sight. The first lieutenant exploded, and said, "Well, if you find it, let me know! You damned dummy! Down here we steer by the Southern Cross!"

At about this time we crossed the line separating the South Pacific Area Command and entered the Southwest Pacific Area Command, under General Douglas MacArthur. We were still part of the 7th Fleet Service Force, which had been established by letter October 15, 1942, with headquarters in Hawaii.

January 3: Steaming as before, no further trouble from the port engine or propeller shaft. At 0835, the island of Tasmania came into view, the island that protects the entrance to Melbourne. It appears to have been at one time part of the mainland, but something happened to form a channel between it and the harbor at Melbourne. This happened, of course, eons ago, long before what the Australian aborigines call the "Dream Time."

A large number of the deck force had been going to general quarters without their gas masks, and on this day the boom was lowered on 17 of them at captain's report mast, held at 1030. The punishment for each was loss of two liberties.

January 4: Steaming alone as before. The crew were making preliminary preparations for entering this new port, with high anticipation.

January 5: Steaming alone as before on all four boilers. The pilot came aboard at 0850 to take us into Port Phillip, then South Channel, and then Port Melbourne Channel. At 1307, the harbor pilot came aboard to take us up the Yarra River and up to Victoria Dock, berth #17, where we moored at 1400. Both pilots left the ship, the gyrocompass was secured, and the engine room telegraph signalled "Finished with Engines." We had arrived in Australia, and liberty was announced commencing at 1600 for the starboard section.

No longer would we be having liberty in New Zealand. We were now in a new country, one which some of us felt would probably be similar to New Zealand. The founders of both came from the same Mother country therefore, logically, they should be very much alike. Not so, as we soon found out.

By now, it was possible to see a separation of the crew into different classes by liberty styles. These styles came about by the sailors following their own priorities, based on what they expected from a liberty port. This, in turn, depended upon what they chose as their immediate goal and excited their inner needs.

Without going any deeper into what motivated them, the first class of liberty goers consisted of a small group who placed the location of the sources of liquor as their first priority, with a second, and incidental, priority being the finding of women. Nothing else mattered, and these were the ones who were often AOL, sometimes being drunk and disorderly on board, who often tangled with the shore patrol, and who were not always too particular about the class of women they accidentally found.

The next class consisted of men who were more interested in finding agreeable women to help them enjoy the few hours granted them ashore. The use of beer and liquor was only incidental, and often didn't even enter into the quest. They were not in any great hurry and often ended up with a fairly good selection. To this class, quality was more important than quantity or immediacy. As a result, this class could, and sometimes, did, make permanent connections, even ending up taking a war bride back home or joining her in her native land. I have no firsthand proof of it, but I suspect that the officers usually fell into this class, as well as most of the enlisted men.

The third class was the tourist, the sailor who believed the enlistment poster slogan, "Join the Navy and see the world!" He spent his liberties visiting the better known tourist attractions for the younger set, such as the roller skating rinks, the beaches, the race courses, amusement parks, and so on. He utilized all of the local methods of transportation to see as much as he could in the short time allotted him. If he just by chance happened across a female companion, there was nothing wrong with that.

As you might expect, there was no hard dividing line between the two adjoining classes. Any sailor could, and often did, cross the borders from one into the next one. He didn't know it, of course, and if he did, it would not have made any difference. He was not going on liberty to satisfy some future budding author's hindsight.

Chapter 8

Supply Run #4: A Death at Sea

The Japanese bombed Darwin, Australia, on February 8, 1942,[31] and threw the entire Australian population into near panic. They were virtually powerless, most of her troops at that time were occupied in North Africa and other parts of the British Empire. General MacArthur had not yet been ordered to leave Bataan and establish headquarters in Australia.

The first load of American troops had been hastily assembled on the east coast, sent through the Panama Canal, south around Fiji, and into Melbourne, arriving February 17, 1942. They were enthusiastically welcomed by the local civilian and military personnel. They were the Signal Corps with the Army Air Corps, and they had just spent 37 days at sea, on the liner *Mariposa*.[32] Since that arrival, much had happened prior to our appearance up the Yarra River. The southward intrusion of the Yellow Peril had been stopped at the battle of the Coral Sea (actually fought partly in the Solomon Sea), and the Allied forces were beginning to throw them back on all South Pacific fronts. We did not expect to be received with quite the amount of exuberance exhibited the previous year, but we were determined to make the best of whatever the people of Melbourne had to offer.

No sooner had the mooring lines been doubled up than things began to happen in rapid order. For the next two days, holds #1 and #3 were busy with both reefer and frozen cargo being stuffed into them, until the ship dropped to its point of highest permissible draft for the river and harbor. This was a definite limitation, which meant we could not fill the holds to the ship's maximum capacity. This also meant that liberty in Melbourne would be short, one each for port and starboard watches, in fact. I rated liberty the first night but declined to take it for some reason which escapes me.

In New Zealand, liberty for visiting sailors ended at 0100. In Melbourne, liberty ended at 0730 the next morning. This meant, of course, that we visiting Yankees had more time in which to indulge our desires and whims. The 0800 muster the next morning was indicative of it; there were four men absent: two machinist's mates, an electrician's mate, and a seaman.

Liberty for the port watch commenced again at 1600, January 6, ending at 0730 the next morning. Evidently the port watch was more sanguine than the starboard watch, for at muster the next morning, there was only one man, a fireman, who was absent, and he came back aboard 2 hours and 40 minutes AOL. I do not recall hearing any stories from the crew regarding their activities ashore, but at least some of them must have enjoyed themselves. The effect on the local citizens—especially the women—was probably surprising. There were quite a lot of Yanks stationed in the area, even though MacArthur had moved his staff north several months before. He wanted to be nearer the action at Darwin and Port Moresby. Another very good reason why General MacArthur wanted to be moved up closer to the action front was the lack of good communication facilities between Melbourne and points along the north coast of Australia and the lower tip of New Guinea.

Shortly after noon chow on January 7, the holds were buttoned up, only partially full, and preparations were made for getting underway. The pilot came aboard, the tug appeared alongside, and we were nudged away from the dock. We steamed down the Yarra River toward Hobson Bay, where the pilot was joined by another one. At 1907, both pilots left the ship, having taken us through Port Phillip Bay. We were now on our own, with a course set to take us around Wilson Promontory and up the east coast toward Sydney, our next stop.

Two white magnesium flares were dropped by unidentified aircraft off the starboard bow, distance about five miles, early on January 8. The remainder of this day was spent in rounding the southeast coast of Victoria, Australia, changing course as needed, and proceeding up the coast. In the late afternoon of January 9, we took on the pilot, near Outer North Head, just outside of Sydney Harbor, for entering Port Jackson. There we picked up two tugs, which took us under the Sydney Harbor Bridge at 1736, and moored at Central Wharf, Walsh Bay. All those off watch were lined up along the rail, eager to get a look at this new liberty port, anticipating, shouting, and counting what remained of their money. It was an awesome sight passing under the Harbor Bridge; we were hoping that we would see it many times in the future. The harbor, the wharfs, the parks, houses, and businesses facing the harbor were a beautiful sight to us. To top it all off, liberty was declared, commencing at 1800, for the starboard section — my section — all night, until 0730 the next morning.

Soon after the 7th Fleet Service Force* for the Southwest Pacific Area (SWPA) was established, Captain H.A. Paddock, USN, was assigned as commander of the new organization. He moved his headquarters into the Grace Building in Sydney in early November 1942. His responsibilities were:

(1) Supervision of all auxiliary vessels assigned to the SWPA;
(2) Establish and operate maintenance facilities for all ships operating in the SWPA;
(3) Administer all personnel in the SWPA, and related functions;
(4) Handle all financial accounts for his command;
(5) Establish and administer all necessary related functions.

The organizations grew at a fast rate, in keeping with developments on the fighting front. By the time of our first arrival at Sydney, there were elements of the command scattered over the entire southern portion of the SWPA. There had been several split-offs in grouping and new commands as a result.

That first night ashore in Sydney is just a blur in my memory. It was all so new, different, and exciting. As much as I can recall, I left the ship alone and teamed up later with another sailor from the ship. We took off together to explore this new sailor's heaven. We were hungry, having left the ship without supper, so we looked up the first likely restaurant, sat down, and ordered that old faithful we had learned to like in New Zealand, "styke and eyggs." It tasted the same, and we loved it. The money system was basically the same, just slightly different in value; but to a sailor, typical Yankees, that did not matter. We spent the remainder of the evening walking around; getting acquainted with the area, the street layout, and the local spots that looked inviting; and inspecting the products of the local pubs. My shipmate wanted to stay ashore as long as possible, but I had the 0800 to 1200 watch and so went back to the ship around midnight and hit the sack.

Occasionally, the bureaucratic military systems foul up in their placement and assignment procedures, with the result that a complete

---

*All references to the 7th Fleet Service Force herein were obtained from the History of the Seventh Fleet Force, by Captain M.R. Kelley, unpublished and undated.

8. Supply Run #4: A Death at Sea

misfit of an officer is placed in control of a contingent of enlisted men, be it a platoon, division, battalion, or a ship's crew. When this happens, the resulting tensions and low morale among the men can bring out both the best and the worst among them. Sooner or later, someone may decide that conditions have deteriorated far enough, and he is just not going to take it anymore. When this happens, there are several avenues of relief open.

He can ask to be transferred, and if enough such requests are filed, someone higher up eventually may notice that things are not right. He can write to his congressman or senator and complain. He can attempt to go over the officer's head and report conditions, in the slim hope that something will be done about it.

In the extreme case, he can resort to inciting mutiny or at least combined action. Or he can take unilateral action and attempt to murder the officer.

No matter which course of action is taken, the righter of wrongs is going to suffer personally for his attempt, even though he gets the desired results. Retribution from higher up will come, either immediately or at some point down the line, for he will forever be branded as a "whistle blower" and a threat to the officer corps.

We have already seen in Chapter 6 how one steward's mate intended to solve his problem with the executive officer, without success. On board the *Octans,* two first class petty officers, a bos'un's mate and a watertender, both regular Navy, whose escapades are reported elsewhere in this book, decided they could rectify the current situation involving the executive officer simply by going ashore in Sydney and requesting an audience with the commandant of the Naval base there, an admiral. The more they discussed it, the more they became convinced that it was the best thing to do, and the only way to solve an unhealthy problem on board.

With this as their mission for the day, as soon as liberty was announced, they prepared themselves in the usual manner, showering, shaving, and donning their best and neatest dress blues. With their hats on in the prescribed Navy tradition, they stepped off the gangway, after saluting the colors, of course. Down the pier they strode, full of purpose, through the gate and into the streets of King's Cross, bound for the Naval Base and Navy Headquarters.

But first, time out for a quick one at a pub, that just happened to be close by. And the mission was scratched.

The work of the ship went on as usual. The engine room and fireroom were on auxiliary watch, the ice machine gang was on strippeddown Condition 3 watch during the night, and the off-duty watch on working parties during the day. The ship took on fuel oil, and cargo was being loaded into the holds. The loading was not too different than the procedures we saw in Auckland, with one exception. True to what we had been told in Auckland, the Aussies were inveterate gamblers. During their breaks in working the holds (announced by the call "Tea-O!"), they not only fired up their billies for tea, but immediately set to with gusto at one of their favorite pastimes, penny pitching, known as "Two-Up."

The area chosen would be marked off on deck or on one of the hatches, and the game would commence, using the large copper pennies so familiar down there. It was interesting to watch them, as they were very good at it, some highly proficient in their mastery of the game. The game was a fast one, with fairly large sums of money often changing hands. To perform the pitch, a flat stick was provided, the two pennies were placed on one end of the stick, and then tossed up by a flip of the wrist. The bets were on the result when they landed.

It was always easy to tell when the game was in progress from their loud, enthusiastic comments, such as: "Bloody good toss, mite!" "Bad luck, mite!" "Don't throw 'em in the bloody scuppers, Jack-o, keep 'em in the game!"

In addition to tea breaks, one frequently heard the call "Smoke-O!" which called for another break from work.

The afternoon of January 10, the captain held report mast with the following punishments handed out: one warning, loss of one liberty (2), loss of two liberties (2), and deck court martials (3), to be tried later. The results of this wonderful liberty port were beginning to tell.

"Now hear this! The smoking lamp is out throughout the ship!" This came over the ship's loudspeaker system on the morning of January 11. That pronouncement was used whenever the ship was being refueled or was taking on ammunition; in this case, it was both. Fueling took about an hour, and we also received from the U.S. Navy Base Ammo and Ordnance Unit at Sydney, 1,080 rounds of 20mm ammo, 30 3-inch tracer shells, 25 common target projectiles, and 25 charges of 5-inch powder in tanks. We also took on $474,350 in cash, government funds, for transfer north. Probably as a result of that last night in Auckland, we transferred six men to the U.S. Navy Base Hospital for treatment of VD. There are times when life ashore can be more dangerous than life afloat. Or, depending, of course, on your priorities, much more satisfying.

The executive officer convened the deck court martial at 1300 to try the three cases remanded over from captain's report mast of January 10. After 30 minutes, the court was closed, the results to be determined and posted at a later date. No hurry about it — let the culprits worry about their future.

8. Supply Run #4: A Death at Sea

At 1615 this day, the chief signalman took a party of three men ashore for duty with the local Navy shore patrol, the only party supplied this stay at Sydney. Liberty started out by teaming up with another sailor, whose rating and name I do not recall. After going to the offices of the leading daily newspaper in Sydney and taking out a three-month's subscription to their paper, to be mailed to my sister in Maryland, we decided to have the usual supper of "styke and eyggs" and then see a movie. The Aussies, like the British, insist in naming many things different from the Yanks; our *movies* are their *cinema*. The features were usually American, with some British movies often shown.

When the ship was at Alameda being converted to the USS *Octans*, there was an application put in to Washington for a movie projector, complete with all accessories, such as screen, tools, and spare parts. The request was refused, advising our captain that he was to apply for one from the area headquarters when we arrived in the South Pacific. At one of our many stops in the South Pacific area, we picked up the projector and accessories and were treated to movies in the mess hall while out of liberty port. The film "library" was a circulating affair, covering about 8,000 miles in the circuit, with exchanges being made among other ships and the shore bases at our ports of call. Regardless of this, there were some sailors from the ship who were glad to see what was being offered in the movie houses "down under," myself included. It was interesting to hear the reactions of the crowd when patriotic scenes with John Wayne, or any current Hollywood hero, would appear on the screen, with some speech obviously sounding much like propaganda. There was usually good-natured laughing, with sly glances at any Yanks that happened to be around.

We had heard so many of the crew talking and raving about a club called Ziegfeld's in Sydney, that another sailor and I decided to check it out. It was fairly close to the wharf where we were tied up, within walking distance, and the cost was rather reasonable. It was one of the few places in the city where one could get something to eat after regular hours. Our liberties being so late and haphazard as they sometimes were, this was sure nice to know.

Entrance to the basement club was at street level, with a man at the door collecting the fare and frisking the men for knives, guns, and liquor, all of which were not allowed. They did not frisk the ladies or their handbags; that would not be gentlemanly. As might be expected, many of the women carried liquor into the place in their handbags. The fare was only three shillings and sixpence, which was about $.85 in U.S. currency. Not only was it cheap, but the admission fee also included a meal, which was usually adequate to satisfy us until breakfast on the ship.

There was a dance band, small but loud and good enough for some of the Yanks who wanted to dance or jitterbug with their dates, or with any of the other miscellaneous classifications of women that frequented the place. There were quite a few of the latter, who held some type of job during the day and came there to get some relaxation and probably have their evening meal. And, of course, some of them were exponents of the private enterprise system, always ready to make a few extra Yankee dollars if any unattached sailor was interested. The going rate was $20, and I was propositioned more than once, turning them down each time. You can believe that or not, but it is true. The place was open until the early morning hours, so it was often fairly well packed and noisy. As one would expect, Ziegfeld's was the center for many of the stories that circulated around the ship covering liberty exploits.

There was a light above the doorway at the foot of the stairs which would light up at about 0100, switched on by the man up on the street taking the fares. This indicated that the vice squad was on its way down. This started everyone straightening out their clothes and adopting their best cherubic manner. The vice squad were men, and they would stand at the foot of the stairs, look around for a few minutes, and then depart.

With the holds nearly full, hold #4 containing dry cargo, with the U.S. mail aboard, preparations for getting underway were commenced at 1000, January 12. The pilot came aboard, the tug was fast alongside, and we retraced our route out of the harbor, dropping the pilot at the exit of East Channel off Outer North Heads. From then, we were on our own, zigzagging north on the base course and standard speed of 13 knots. No sooner had we hit the open sea than the captain held report mast to handle the case of two men charged with drinking on duty, neglect of duty, and standing an improper watch. Punishment: deck court martial for both. The results of the three deck court martial cases held the previous day were posted; two were confined to the ship for periods of 15 and 20 days while in port and docked pay of $27 and $36, respectively. There was no decision posted on the third case. Captain's report mast was reconvened again in the afternoon, apparently in an attempt to finish off the books on recalcitrants; the cases were disposed of in rapid order. There were four of them, and they were all cleaned up by the end of the day. The results were published the following day.

At noon, January 13, the ship changed course to inspect a floating life raft, but there was no one on it, no identifying features, and it had evidently been afloat for a long time. Another of those mysteries of the sea, it probably had come from one of those numerous Merchant Marine cargo vessels which had been torpedoed early in the war. What happened to the poor souls it was supposed to save, we can only speculate, if, indeed, it had ever been called upon to serve its purpose.

8. Supply Run #4: A Death at Sea

On January 14, we were steaming as before, enroute to Brisbane, Australia, standard speed now 12 knots, zigzagging normally. In the afternoon, we entered the swept (checked for mines) channel, passed Cape Moreton, and picked up the pilot at 1800, who took us into Brisbane Roads, Moreton Bay, where we anchored. Underway again about midnight, we entered Brisbane River Channel, following the river up to our mooring at the Abattoir Dock, berth C, where we swung ship and tied up at 0140, January 15, 1944.

The first American troops arrived in Brisbane, almost completely by surprise to the local citizens, on December 23, 1941. They were originally destined for the Philippines but were rerouted to Brisbane, under escort by the USS *Pensacola* (CA-24). By the time we arrived, the buildup of Yankees in the area had reached approximately 325,000, over the prewar population of about 75,000.

Just 17 months prior to our arrival in Brisbane, General MacArthur had arrived, July 20, 1942, from Melbourne after a long train ride of about 1,200 miles, with two train changes. His family and staff were with him, and he moved his family into the Lennon Hotel. His office was established on the eighth floor of the building formerly containing an insurance firm, the Australian Mutual Provident Society, which had been evacuated south.[33]

There were several contingents of our forces there, including the U.S. Army, the new Air Force, a submarine flotilla, and various other miscellaneous establishments connected to our pouring of men and material into Australia. For that reason, there were plenty of our military police and shore patrol walking around and policing the area.

On January 14, 1944, while we were preparing to enter Brisbane Roads, the Australian troops were advancing steadily along the coast of lower New Guinea. They had already taken Saidor, and on that day, they secured Sio, New Guinea, which was about 75 miles northwest along the coast from Finschafen.[34]

For the U.S. troops in New Zealand and Australia, our Merchant Marine forces helped deliver the troops, war materiel, and other supplies. In the engine room of one of these vessels was a Merchant Marine Academy graduate by the name of Ken. He managed to get ashore several times and formed his own opinion of the Kiwis and the Aussies.

Ken survived the war and entered into civilian life with a will to attain the usual fruits of life according to the American Dream. He married, raised a family, and rose steadily in his career in various fields of engineering. When he retired, he and his wife settled down in a comfortable home east of Los Angeles and started enjoying themselves, their children, and grandchildren. They spent several weeks each year traveling in different parts of the world, and finally they decided to go down under and visit New Zealand and Australia on an extended tour.

They went first to New Zealand and spent several weeks there, exploring the country's main attractions. Ken managed to spend some leisure time in New Zealand pubs, talking to the customers and the barmen and bargirls. Most of those with whom he talked appeared appreciative of our efforts to save the area from the Japanese during the war. There were some ill feelings over the impact our troop concentrations had made on their country, and especially on their women. But for the most part, they recognized that some inconveniences had to be expected in such trying times.

Ken and his wife then moved on to Australia and continued their tourist routines, with Ken stopping at the local pubs to sample the local gossip and feelings as he had done in New Zealand. Mostly, he met the same responses. In Brisbane, after joining in with a group in a pub and after several rounds of warm Australian beer, one of the local characters whom we shall call "Bluey," after the perverse Aussie method of naming a person with red hair, became talkative and confidential. This is his story.

Right after Pearl Harbor Day, the Japanese started their advance southward into the Solomons and what the Aussies considered their home territory, some of which they had for years exercised active control. Their northern sections of the country were also very much at risk, and they were worried. The government of Australia hurried along plans for strengthening their defense installations on the northern tip and northeast shores of the country. The plans were completed, and bids were taken from contractors to rush the completion of the new defenses. That area is rather bleak, and when the successful contractor started assembling his crews for the move north, he met with demands from the subcontracting crews for increased pay, due to the bleakness of the job site.

The government entered the negotiations, pleading for the strikers to consider the gravity and urgency of the situation; an appeal to patriotism was even tried — all to no avail. The men held firm, time passed, and the union leaders were of no help, as their authority was at stake.

Bluey stated their philosophy very plainly. The government was worried, and many of the citizens were worried, but the working blokes were not worried in the least. They were quite confident that the Yanks would not let them fall and would come to their rescue; so there was no hurry to complete the new defense works in the north.

They held out and got their demands for higher pay; and we saved their necks in the battle of the Coral Sea. Bluey was right in his assumptions.

8. Supply Run #4: A Death at Sea

The first day in the new port, the dry cargo carried in hold #4 was unloaded, commencing at 0900, and continued into the following day. Three new ensigns reported aboard for duty.

The remaining space available in the holds was topped off, and hold #4 was filled during our brief stay in Brisbane. The stay was so brief that no liberty was granted. A very hard blow, all we could do was stand at the rail, look over the assortment of industrial buildings at the wharfside, and speculate on what was awaiting us in the city. And above all, there arose the stench from the dockside. The Abattoir Dock — (*abattoir* means "slaughterhouse") was aptly named.

January 16 was a great day for all those on board who had suffered from the deck court martials. The executive officer, whose duty it was to hold them, was directed to report to the commander, Service Force, 7th Fleet, for duty. Those who had faced him under unfavorable circumstances were generally the ones celebrating his removal, including his fellow officers. Most of us who had never been in that position took it as a routine occurrence. Personally, I had nothing against him. He had the job of maintaining order and directing the operation of a fairly large U.S. Naval vessel, with a staff of about 20 officers and 220 enlisted men, most of whom were reservists who had little, if any, peacetime training prior to enlisting in the Navy. That is not an easy job, and I would not envy anyone assigned to it. Let's face it — we were for the most part an odd assortment of raw recruits, fresh out of boot camp, and with no previous experience afloat.

Generally those regular Navy men aboard knew their job very well, but when it came to serving as role models, many of them left a lot to be desired. (The new executive officer was the lieutenant who had come aboard December 12.)

That afternoon, a lieutenant came aboard for temporary duty, and one of our warrant officers was transferred to the commander, Service Force, 7th Fleet, for duty. Finally, about midnight, the last of the cargo was loaded into the holds. The hatches were covered and battened down, a tug got into position, the mooring lines were singled up, and, when the pilot appeared on board, we got underway shortly after midnight, January 17, for Milne Bay, New Guinea. Two hours later, we left the Brisbane River Channel and entered Moreton Bay. Another four hours, and we dropped the pilot, leaving us alone to steam past Cape Moreton and into the open sea to start zigzagging, first in a northeasterly direction, then north.

Several days after leaving port, the assistant engineer came below with a gallon can of alcohol and injected some of it into the oil separator to absorb the moisture in the system. It worked, and after that we did not have nearly the problem that we had been having with the compressor stalling. He left the gallon can of alcohol in the locker in the room, with the warning that no one else was to touch it but me, overlooking the fact that the locker did not have a lock on it. A couple of days later, another MM2c on my gang became sick and ended up in sick bay. I cornered one of the chancre mechanics and quietly asked him what was wrong with my man. I was told he had gotten hold of some alcohol someplace and had not cut it enough when he mixed his drinks.

To avoid the embarrassment of "friendly fire" between ships and between ships and planes, there was a recognized system of signals to be passed between them. If the challenged ship or plane did not respond, presumably they were fair game for being fired upon. I bring this up because the failure of some of the U.S. Air Force pilots to answer our recognition signals in a prompt manner caused quite a commotion throughout the ship. It meant going to general quarters until identification had been established. The incident which brought this to mind was the challenging of our ship by a friendly plane, about 70 miles out of Brisbane. We must have satisfied its pilot, for he did not fire on us.

Since this was our first trip from Australia to the islands and New Guinea, I will detail the route. After passing Cape Moreton, we tended to follow the coast rather closely, inside the Great Barrier Reef, which brought us past Townsville, Halifax, Dunk Island, and Fitzroy Island. At that point, we picked up an escort because we were leaving the protection of the Great Barrier Reef and going into the open sea again. Our escort was HMAS *Warrega,* which took us through Grafton Passage through the Reef and headed for Milne Bay, New Guinea. During the long passage up the coast, zigzagging was out of the question, due to the confines and relative safety of the route. Now that we had crossed the Reef, we were fair game again for enemy submarines, so we resumed the normal zigzagging procedure on a general northeast bearing.

As it had now been over a week since the last defrosting, the brine coil banks in the after two holds were getting well clogged with ice. It was time to shut down the brine and the fan in the holds, wrestle the fire hose down the ladders into the fan rooms, and proceed to melt and wash the ice off the coils. When they were cleaned of ice, the fans were turned back on, and after waiting for a few minutes for the coils to dry off, we could then turn the brine back on for another week or ten days of cooling in the tropics. This procedure was to be followed often during the coming months.

About dawn, January 22, we sighted the southeast coast of New Guinea and went to morning general quarters for the sunrise until securing at 0707. We transmitted China Strait, then took the pilot aboard at 1000, and anchored in Gili anchorage, Milne Bay at 1055. Little time was lost as we opened the holds to supply the ships in the harbor. These included the cruisers USS *Boise* (CL-47) and USS *Phoenix* (CL-46) and the destroyers USS *Ammen* (DD-527), USS *Mullany* (DD-528), and USS *Bush* (DD-529).

The Navy Supply Depot ashore also came out for its share of frozen and reefer cargo.

The port engine was in need of repairs again, so the job was attacked while the opportunity was granted from the Naval Base, our anchorage being under their security. The repairs took three hours, and the engine room was then placed on 30-minute standby notice. We in the ice machine gang were kept fairly busy, tending the ice machine and changing the fan and air controls as the unloading procedures changed from hold to hold and deck to deck.

This routine continued until the morning of January 23 when, assisted by a Navy tug and the presence on board of the port director, we tied up at Gamadodo Dock in Milne Bay. Cargo unloading continued at a fair pace, and we took on freshwater from the dock, as our supply was rather low for some undisclosed reason. This was a surprise since we had a large tank capacity, 151,000 gallons, and a 12,000-gallon-a-day evaporator to supply the needs of the boilers and the crew.

In the morning of January 24, the ship shifted berths again, tying up to Pier 1 at Ahioma, Milne Bay, at 0813. Unloading continued throughout the day, interrupted once by one of those typical New Guinea rain showers. Also, there was an interruption in the #3 lower hold, when one of the Army privates was struck by a falling hatch plug, skinning his shoulder and bruising him on the head. He was treated by our sick bay chancre mechanics and went back to work.

On January 25, a seaman first class was transferred ashore to the hospital, for treatment of VD. Holds #2 and #4 were emptied, and then loaded with dry stores for further shipment up the coast. We apparently lost our priority on the pier, for at 1807 we cast off from the pier and steamed out into the harbor, dropped the anchor and continued with the unloading.

While closing up the holds on January 26, another seaman second class had an accident on #3 hatch, breaking his lower left arm. At 1500, we got underway for Buna, lying west along the north coast of New Guinea. We traveled east to leave Milne Bay, then rounded the tip of the bay, went into Condition 2 watches, ship darkened but navigation lights burning, and crept along the coast towards Buna. During the night, we slowed to half speed, due to torrential rain, with visibility greatly reduced. This condition continued until about dawn of the next day,

January 27, when we could again increase speed to full ahead. At noon, we anchored in Buna Roads channel, went to Condition 4 watches, then proceeded into anchorage at Buna. The following ships started taking provisions from us immediately: destroyers USS *Helm* (DD-388) and USS *Ralph Talbot* (DD-390); HMAS *Arunta*; and LSTs 206, 168, 171, and 68.

The men of the USS *Rigel* (AR-11), a Navy repair vessel, would be happy to know that on January 28 we transferred to their paymaster the sum of $424,350. Assuming that a good share of it was destined for payday disbursement, they might not have had much opportunity to spend it. A seaman second class, from the boat crew of LST 171 received a lower abdominal injury when he fell between the motor launch and the side of the *Octans*. The extent of his injuries and his treatment were not recorded in the deck log.

January 29 was a very eventful day. We shifted berths twice and continued to discharge cargo at every stop. To check the propellers for nicks and dents, a diver from the *Rigel* dove and inspected them but found only slight nicks on both, not sufficient to cause the vibration which we were experiencing and had thought to have caused the engine and shaft problems.

While getting under way for one of the shifts in berths, the #2 hatch was being covered temporarily, with covers off the lower hold hatchways. One of our seamen stepped on one of the hatch plugs, which slipped and he fell through three decks, landing on the orlop deck, about 26 feet below. He was smashed very badly on his right side and suffered internal injuries to his head. He was removed and transferred to the LST 464, which had hospital facilities. He was pronounced dead. There was a general feeling of sadness and shock throughout the ship.

It may sound as if we had an inordinate number of accidents this trip. When you consider that the opening and closing of the holds and related deck activities were being done mostly by relatively inexperienced men, some of whom were rather young to be engaged in this type of work, it is not too surprising that there would be more than the normal number of accidents. After all, ship's cargo working is considered to be one of the more dangerous occupations, even among those who are experienced in the job and its hazards. Add to this the age and condition of the ship, and our accident rate becomes more reasonable, although still to be deplored.

Provisioning ships continued as it had before January 30. Seventeen enlisted men came aboard as passengers, bound for Mobile Hospital Unit #9, for treatment of VD. They were from the LST 464 and USS *Rigel*.

At 1430 on January 31, the flag was lowered to half mast while burial services ashore were being held for the unfortunate seaman. Six men from

8. Supply Run #4: A Death at Sea

the ship went ashore, at Buna Mission, as pallbearers. The burial was in a small military cemetery in a clearing in the jungle. An officer read the brief eulogy and then suggested that perhaps those present would contact the seaman's relatives when they got back to the states.

> THOMAS D. ANDREWS, S2c, #576-78-06, from Burlington, Texas. Died accidently, 1055, 29 January 1944, in Buna Roads, New Guinea.

And that was all there was to it. Burial ashore for one lone, young man who was attempting to do his duty to the best of his ability. Felled, not by enemy action, but by fickle fate, administered by a defective element of an overage banana boat, brought back into service to serve its last days in the service of our country. He joined the ranks of the many who were "killed in the line of duty," such duty not always being in direct contact with the enemy. I do not wish to sound harsh, merely sad. In the case of wartime activities, such accidents are a part of the wastage of war. That does not make the loss any more acceptable to the survivors. The deceased did his very best, which is all anyone can expect of a person.

The entry in the deck log for this accident was short and gave very little explanation, other than one of the hatch plugs upon which the sailor was standing slipped out from under him. There is another angle to the accident, which I was told in preparation for writing this book.

A bos'un's mate first class, a regular Navy man who had seen service on merchant type ships previous to this one, had worked out what he considered to be the proper and safe procedure for opening and closing the hatches. His method worked and had worked for some months without accidents. On that particular day, for some unknown reason, the executive officer decided the method was wrong; so he took charge from the forward walk on the promenade deck by dismissing the bos'un and directing the hatch crew personally. He reversed the order of installing the hatch plugs. The accident took place, and it is impossible at this late date to firmly place responsibility for it. One can only speculate.

At 1725, we commenced preparations for getting underway, taking aboard two pilots, only to be forced to go to general quarters because of a red alert ashore. The all clear sent us on our way, late evening, for Oro Bay, New Guinea.

We spent February 1 anchored in Oro Bay, off-loading cargo to Army lighters alongside, destined for cold storage warehouses ashore. All four boilers were hot and on the line, ready for departure on two hours notice. That condition continued throughout the day and through the next.

At that time, there appeared on board the first issue of the ship's newspaper, *The* Octans *Scuttlebutt*. It gave several of the crew opportunity to exercise their literary and artistic capabilities, as well as could be done with the mimeograph copy equipment on board. It came out monthly and included items of interest to most of the crew, with such straight dope as:

> Stateside news, such as tunes on the Hit Parade;
> New arrivals on board and names of those leaving the ship;
> Current jokes from the home front and war front;
> Advancements in ratings;
> Poems and gems of wisdom;
> Cartoons;
> Gossip and scuttlebutt of the crew and officers.

The latter items had to be covered with some degree of circumspection and common sense. I do not know if each issue was subjected to official review, but I imagine it was, as some copies probably found their way into the stateside mail. The result reminded me a lot of the high school paper in my school a few years previous, in which the student writers attempted to take pot shots at the teachers and the administration without inciting the wrath of officialdom.

Very few of the stories going the rounds about the men on liberty, and none of those appearing here, ever found their way into the *Scuttlebutt*. The result was pure pablum, but we ate it up.

Our outgoing mail was censored, of course, by several officers assigned to the task. There were cases of men being given a lecture after attempting to pass on too much "classified" information, often in an attempt to push the policy to its limit.

One of the jokes which appeared in, as I recall, the *Reader's Digest*, related the story of the serviceman's girlfriend back in the States who opened her letter from the boyfriend to find only a note which read:

> Your boyfriend still loves you, but he talks too much!
> [signed] The Censor

There was also published, probably by the same budding editors, a weekly newsletter called the *USS* Octans *Press News*. It gave short items of interest from around the world and helped to keep us up to date on what was happening on the war front elsewhere than our own theatre. It also gave choice bits of gossip from some of the noted columnists of the time, as well as other journalistic tidbits.

8. Supply Run #4: A Death at Sea

By this time in our cruise, some members of the crew had begun to refer to the ship as *The Mighty O*. It appeared in *The* Octans *Scuttlebutt* quite often in the ensuing months.

On February 3, engines were placed on 30-minute standby notice, and all cargo was discharged from the holds. That called for a little sigh of relief from those of us in the ice machine gang. The machinery was secured, the compressor suction and discharge valves were closed, and we went on daytime maintenance. This consisted mostly of reworking the main bearings on the crankshaft, with general cleaning in the ice machine room and in the fan rooms taking some of the time. About three days before we were due in port, the compressor had to be back in working order, started up and the holds ready to take on another load of cargo when we docked.

We got underway at 0732, enroute to Buna Roads again, retracing our wake back up the coast. The sole purpose was to pick up a large draft of U.S. Navy personnel bound for various posts and duties. There were even three lucky individuals who were going to a Navy Beach Party, Ping-Wo, whatever or wherever that was. These were taken aboard at about 1050 while anchored in Liberty Ship anchorage, Buna Roads.

At 1318, underway again, bound for Milne Bay, the gyrocompass failed as soon as we got up to speed, which meant that until it was repaired, all navigating had to be down by the standard magnetic compass. The Navy Standard Magnetic compass was nothing more than an enlarged, upgraded version of the typical Boy Scout camping compass. It is based on the magnetized needle principle, known for centuries, which always points towards magnetic north, providing there is no iron in the vicinity, or any other disturbing influence, such as a ship's hull with a mass of electrical gear aboard in full operation. The influence of the ship can be negated somewhat by adjusting the steel spheres attached to the compass stand, or binnacle.

The gyrocompass, on the other hand, is an electrically driven gyroscope, very similar to the ordinary toy gyroscope, except that the mounting is designed to transfer any shift in the axis into a compass reading. In practice, both compasses are used, with the gyrocompass serving as the main one and the standard being the backup. The variation between the two is continually noted, and when the gyrocompass is out of order for any reason, such as an electrical failure, the magnetic compass can be used until the repair is made. That was probably the case in this instance because in about an hour, the electricians had the gyrocompass operating again. There was no loss in time or position as a result of the temporary disablement, merely a little inconvenience on the navigator's part.

Mike, electrician's mate, was the specialist on board who knew how to service the gyrocompass and keep it operating properly. The problems were mostly electrical because its motor and instrumentation were very delicate. All elements had to be kept adjusted and periodically cleaned. He often applied to the sick bay for alcohol to perform the cleaning tasks, which request was always granted, no questions asked. However, anyone passing by while the gyrocompass was being serviced would not doubt have noticed that the cleaning solution being used had a strong odor of carbon tetrachloride instead of alcohol. Resourceful people, those electrician's mates.

February 4 found us steaming as before for the first half of the day, anchoring at Gili anchorage in Milne Bay just before noon. Proof of the high state of morale of our fighting forces lay in the 403 sacks of mail taken aboard there for transportation to the next port, Sydney. At 1606, we were underway again, enroute to Sydney, joining a convoy of five ships in column, escorted by three Australian Navy ships, traveling towards China Strait. Leaving China Strait, the column turned south out of the Strait and formed into a rectangular convoy. The convoy took the form as shown on page 231, with the escorts ranging around the perimeter. The other ships in the convoy were all merchant ships, the *Andrew D. White,* the *Albert Hill,* the *John Nolan,* and the *Peter Rowe.* The next day, we were steaming in convoy as before, heading southwest towards the Great Barrier Reef along the northeast coast of Australia, retracing our wake made on the northbound trip.

We entered Grafton Passage through the Reef on February 6, and the convoy commander gave us permission to leave the convoy and proceed independently. We increased speed to full ahead and threaded our way along the coast, just as we had done on the way north a few weeks before. At 0921, we fell in with the HMAS *Lithgow,* which volunteered to escort us part way south.

February 7 was uneventful until the evening, when the forced draft fan in the fan room failed and the boilers had to operate on natural draft, causing a reduction in steam pressure. Both engines went to half speed ahead. The condition lasted for about 30 minutes; then the engine room telegraph jingled and rang up full ahead both engines. Our escort departed company shortly after noon on February 8, leaving us to make our way alone into Sydney.

At 1551 on February 9, it was necessary to reduce speed to half ahead while the fireroom worked to keep the boilers on the line, due to flame-outs from slugs of water coming through with the fuel oil. This trouble usually happens when taking suction from a fuel tank which has not been used very much, as the water in the oil then has time to settle out and enter the fuel pump suction. When it happens, the burners must be shut off, the lines purged of the water, then lit off again.

February 11 was another day of problems with water in the fuel oil. Three times it happened, causing a slowdown each time. It was aggravating, but fortunately we were almost into Sydney, which made our troubles less onerous, with the thought of liberty in that beautiful city.

It was always a pleasure to come into Sydney in the morning, to see the city and the harbor laid out before us. It was one of the most beautiful sights of the entire cruise in the South Pacific for me. When we stopped to pick up the pilot just outside the harbor, we lined the rail to watch the pilot boat come alongside and the pilot climb the sea ladder up to the deck. That pilot boat was a beauty. There was, at the time of this writing, a boat in the harbor at San Diego, California, used as a tourist attraction, which I believe could be a sister ship to the Sydney pilot boat. It was about 30 feet long, with a clipper bow, a small cabin forward, a steam engine and boiler amidships, and a distinctive stack. The one in San Diego was built in Scotland.

That morning of 11 February, the pilot boat pulled away, and the pilot climbed the ladder to the deck and then went up to take charge on the bridge. He took us into Port Jackson, then under the Harbor Bridge. The tug came alongside, and we tied up to Pyrmont Dock at 0918. The engine room telegraph jingled out "Finished with Engines."

By this time, the results of the shakedown cruises were beginning to bear fruit throughout the ship. The atmosphere of fear which had permeated officer's country was mitigated somewhat, due mostly to the change in the executive officer. The crew had been jostled and shook and turned over sufficiently to produce a force that was more efficient but still very rough in spots. Conditions in the engineering department were considerably better, but there were still problems with the leaky boilers; the main engines and their auxiliaries were still thumping too much and would for another six months through two more overhauls.

The ice machine was working better, with still some bearing problems, and moisture in the carbon dioxide lines, but we at least now knew how to work our way out of the intermittent glitches. Our gang, even through constant changes in oilers, had the department working relatively smoothly. This was fortunate, as the ice machine was the key element in the main purpose for the *Octans* being in existence.

Chapter 9

Supply Run #5: Aground!

"Now hear this! Liberty for the port section will commence at 1630!"

First, there were still a few passengers to discharge from the ship, some of whom were hospital patients. Next, we acquired five new crew members, two cox'suns, a seaman, and two radiomen.

As usual on the first day in port, the ice machine gang had a number of carbon dioxide cylinders to get up out of the shaft alley and onto the dock alongside for trucking to the local gas supply firm. The filled replacements would be back alongside about the day we were due to leave port.

A storekeeper and a seaman were a little late getting back on board after liberty on February 12, but they made it back in time to appear at 0800 muster. The holds were opened, and the dock crews commenced moving the food from the dock into the holds. One seaman was transferred, with bag, hammock, records, and transfer papers, to the local Navy Base Hospital for treatment of VD. At 1300, we took on board 150 gallons of ice cream for the general mess. Following normal procedure, any food brought aboard for the crew had to be inspected by the medical officer.

Liberty in Sydney began to work into a pattern, similar with that in seaports all over the world. It took anywhere from one to three liberties for a sailor to get oriented, and from then on his general behavior followed a set schedule and behavior, with a few variations from time to time.

After the crew knew the local scene well enough, the men would form into groups before they left the ship, depending on their goals. A certain small number of men would always head first for the nearest source of liquor and brag before they even left the ship about what they were going to do, once they were free of the ship. It was this group that gave the Navy a bad name in any port of call. Fortunately for the Navy—and the local population—the majority of the men on liberty were of the middle ground, circulating in groups of two or three, maybe going to a movie, to the amusement park, and finishing with a supper at a late-night restaurant. And, if by chance, they should happen to meet with one or two girls who were willing to join this group, happy day.

At one of these early stops in Sydney, a situation developed which caused the crew some problems. Sometimes when a sailor would wend his wavy way back to the ship, perhaps slightly intoxicated, the path often led through one of the many parks abounding in Sydney. Hiding in the bushes would be two or three Aussie men who would jump out and beat up the sailor, and then remove his wallet. Later, this would be known as "mugging" back home in the States.

Rather than call in the Marines or the shore patrol, three of the *Octans'* crew decided to teach those Aussies a lesson. Jim, an electrician's mate, and two machinist's mates, Moe and Joe laid their plans carefully. One night, after a tour of the liberty spots, Moe and Joe left and took up their vigil in the bushes of the park where the muggings had taken place. After a respectable interval, Jim, feigning drunkenness (which was probably not hard for him to do) came staggering along the path, inviting trouble.

Two Aussies jumped out and started to work Jim over. Moe and Joe came running from their hiding place and proceeded to give the two Aussies the working over of their lives. That stopped the muggings, for awhile, at least.

On another early liberty in Sydney, a fellow sailor and I stopped in at Ziegfeld's late for our "styke and eyggs" before going back to the ship. Seating arrangements were always haphazard, as there was a lot of moving around due to tablehopping, dancing, and so on. That night, I found myself sitting in the corner of a booth, eating my supper, when I looked up to see two girls sitting opposite me. Finishing my meal, we all started talking, but the girls did most of it, mostly between themselves. I noticed that the one sitting opposite me was one of the most beautiful girls I have ever seen. (I had not been drinking.) I looked at her, and after a few minutes, I motioned with my finger for her to lean over toward me. We met in the middle, with a kiss; than I asked her if I could walk her home. She agreed; some time later we got together, and I walked with her for several blocks, talking and enjoying ourselves. Soon she told me this was as far as I could go. She gave me a short kiss, then hurried off. I called after her, asking for her phone number, but she merely waved back and continued on, walking fast. Just another one that got away. I never saw her again.

Meanwhile, back at the ship, loading of the holds continued around the clock, stopping only for the rain and for the inevitable Tea-O, Smoke-O, and penny-pitching breaks for the stevedores.

The master-at-arms was patrolling around the ship early one morning, and found a seaman sleeping on watch. That evening, the seaman made a "fantail liberty" and got caught coming back aboard early the next morning. A cox'sun was with him, and they were both put through the captain's report mast, deck court martial, and sentencing. Before we left Sydney, the seaman and another troublemaker were transferred off the ship to the Navy base ashore. Several other men were transferred, also, not necessarily as troublemakers, and several officers came aboard for duty, including two ensigns who were apparently newly commissioned.

The two new ensigns were what was known as "90-day wonders" because of their speedy transition from college students to Naval officers. One of these, who shall be known as Ensign Fraser, was to prove a constant problem to his fellow officers. He had an apparent thirst for knowledge and was forever wandering around the ship, below decks as well as above. The bridge or wardroom seldom knew where he was—until, that is, he fouled up at some distant portion of the ship. We saw him down in the ice machine room a couple of times, and we never knew how to behave in his presence; so we generally just went about our business and endeavored to answer any questions he had. Personally, I felt a little sorry for him, as he appeared to be so out of his element, and I knew what the rest of the ship thought of him. For one thing, as I mention elsewhere in this narrative, we seldom saw any of the deck officers down below, and his appearance was odd in that respect. To the officers on the bridge and in the wardroom he was a nuisance. To the ship's crew he was a joke and actually gave our morale a boost at times.

There is an axiom in the Navy to the effect that the real backbone of the Navy is the chief petty officers. I noticed that no matter how many enlisted men were transferred off the ship, their replacements made very little difference in the operation of the ship or the morale of the crew, at least in the level of the engineering division. From what I saw, the CPO position was a very stable and desirable one, and, on board our ship, CPOs enjoyed the respect of the men under them. I know of no enlisted man ever making a complaint about any of them. Any complaints usually were directed to the officer level, correct or not.

Another liberty for me began on February 16 along with the other hundred or more on the same liberty section. It started out in the usual manner, with a few of us gathering at a local pub to discuss the evening's entertainment search over a warm glass of beer or ale. The conversation was taking a turn I did not care for, so I joined up with another petty officer, who was I believe, a radioman named Ralph, and we struck out for one of the local cinemas, as they call them down under. We were standing in a short queue, or line, waiting to get our tickets, when we noticed a couple of girls in military uniform ahead of us, so we struck up a conversation with them. They proved to be members of the Women's Australian Air Force Auxiliary, or some such organization similar to it. At any rate, one thing led to another, and we wound up taking them to the movie and to dinner afterward. They were young, fairly beautiful, and very talkative, which made for an interesting time. My shipmate ended up with the blonde, whose name I recall as Jean, while I took to the sandy haired, freckle faced one, whose name was Betty. They had to get back to their base fairly early, so we saw them off on the train, with their telephone numbers in our pocket.

A couple of men, AOL, were returned to the ship the next morning by the local shore patrol. All together, it was a good liberty stop, judging by the cases of "fantail liberties," AOL men brought back by the shore patrol while we were here, and the comments of the crew — not to mention my own experiences.

All good things must come to an end, so goes the old saying, and so, too, must liberty in a port as fantastic as Sydney. At 1515, February 17, we were underway from the harbor, bound for Milne Bay, New Guinea, with the pilot and a harbor tug helping us out of the harbor. Our outbound passage retraced the track upon which we entered, taking us under the Harbor Bridge and just off Outer North Heads, where we dropped off the pilot. By 1700, we were free of the harbor approaches and steaming at 13½ knots toward our new destination at New Guinea. Our route north along the coast was the same we had taken before, and we made good time until the afternoon of February 18, when the forced draft fan for the boilers decided to rebel three times, forcing a temporary slowdown of the main engines each time the steam pressure dropped during the fan outages.

Soon after clearing the harbor, with the ice machine working fairly well and steaming routine in force, I took the time to check the geedunk stand refrigeration system. It had been operating sporadically, due to moisture in the gas cycle which I could not get out, the same problem we were having with the ship's ice machine. We had been unable to obtain a replacement dehydrator cartridge for it, so we were forced to work with it as best we could. It was fortunate that it was working fairly well, as we had just taken on a storage chest full of ice cream. Some of the crew were sitting at the tables, enjoying coke and ice cream, and telling of their escapades ashore. I joined them, always more than willing to listen to their exploits, such as the following:

One of the deck force had gone ashore the first night in port and had been fortunate enough to make the willing acquaintance of a nice looking girl. They had a lot of fun that first night, and he managed to get a date for the next liberty. When he went ashore that second night, planning ahead, he stopped off to rent a room at a local hotel/pub for the night, not bothering to inspect the room but taking it on faith based on what was common back home in the States. When he met the girl, she was dressed in a wild fashion, which told him a lot; the evening bore out his expectations.

They ended up in the hotel room he had rented, and after a few minutes of playful bantering, she undressed and got into bed. He proceeded to do likewise. Then right after he had turned out the lights and was getting into bed, she let out a scream! "EEEEK! Turn on the bloody lights! Somethin's crawling on me back!"

He hastened to turn on the lights, then turned back the bedding, and searched. Bedbugs! Several of them. She was squirming and insisted that he help her search for any more bugs on her, which he was only too happy to oblige, chivalrous Yank that he was. He found one more, inside her thigh, crawling upwards.

She got dressed, thoroughly disillusioned, and he saw her off at the train station, the end of what had started to be an enjoyable evening.

The word got around the ship in the usual rapid order, and from then on, the order of the day when renting a room was to inspect the beds before putting your money down to the landlord.

That escapade brings out one of the shortcomings in Australia's law which required pubs to be operated with a hotel service offering at least four rooms for rental to the public. Obviously, the most income was from the pub and the private lounges, and not from the room rental. It was only natural that the innkeeper was not going to spend much time in keeping his meager rooms up to anything approaching tourist class service. As a result, the crew found it was much better to rent rooms from one of the many rooming houses available, which did not bother to inquire of the sailor as to his use of the room. These houses were soon spotted and were patronized constantly.

For the next few days the trip was routine, blacked out at night, with the navigation lights burning, dodging numerous small islands, sighting and challenging several ships and planes, and exchanging recognition signals. This portion of our passage must have been excellent practice for any neophyte navigators on the bridge, for it was a constant procedure of sighting landmarks, taking bearings with the peloruses, plotting them on the chart, calculating distances from them to the ship, and making the

9. Supply Run #5: Aground!

many course alterations necessary to keep us free of obstacles. It was fortunate that the Australian coastal authorities had provided plenty of lighthouses and beacons on the coast, with good charts for wandering mariners like us. Ours was a very popular route; we must have sighted or passed at least 25 ships along the coast, inside the Great Barrier Reef.

At 2200 on February 20, we were beset with a heavy rain squall, which reduced our visibility to about 400 yards, and required sounding the eerie wail of the fog horn at prescribed intervals. This lasted for about 30 minutes, when visibility increased sufficiently to permit securing the fog horn. Following this interruption, we resumed normal steaming northward until late afternoon on February 21 when we entered Grafton Passage through the reef and passed into the open sea, headed northeast towards Milne Bay on standard zigzagging procedure. This time we were alone, without an escort, steaming at 13 knots. We passed through fields of torn trees the next day, obvious debris from some violent storm in the area. On the morning of February 23, we entered China Strait and rounded the tip of Milne Bay, anchoring in Gili anchorage just before noon — chow time.

It was always a pleasure to stand at the rail and watch as we transited the China Strait approach to Milne Bay, then steamed westward into the bay. As long as we were on the ship, we could enjoy the lush tropical shore and the jungle, knowing that we did not have to fight that mass of undergrowth. Some of the most beautiful sunrises I have ever seen were while we were anchored in Milne Bay, even though within a couple of hours the heat would be almost unbearable. This was true of a large number of islands we passed, some containing neat rows of coconut palms which were still in fairly good condition, without having been adequately maintained since the start of hostilities in the area. Those neat rows of palm trees, surrounded by lush jungle, were very attractive to look at from the ship as we passed by. Some on board may have even wished they could be there, living out their lives in tropical splendor, eating coconuts, fishing and swimming, and waited on by Dorothy Lamour clones.

The coconut trees and their fruit were probably swarming with red army ants, whose sting, though not fatal, could drive a person close to insanity. Often, resting on the coconuts would be a small, deadly snake, the black death adder, for which there was no known antidote. These were so much of a menace that the local natives, hired to harvest the crop, would use long poles to knock the coconuts down to the ground, where they could brush the nuts with sticks before picking them up and tossing them into the carts.[35]

Aside from the coconut palms, the beaches and the seas were often home to sharks, sting rays, several forms of poisonous fish, Portuguese men-of-war (described in an earlier chapter), and numerous other vile life forms waiting to pounce on the intruder to their domain. The coral beaches also could give a person cancerous chancres, as evidenced by the sores and bleeding on the legs of many of the natives. Paradise is not always as it appears.

We on the ship could be thankful that we were not on those islands, fighting not only the enemy, but the jungle also. Our hats were off to the U.S. Marines, SeaBees, and Army men on those jungle hot spots. I did not envy them one bit, nor did I begrudge them the pensions, bonuses, and life insurance paid to their survivors.

With the hook in the mud of Gili anchorage, all holds were opened, and the cargo started moving into the lighters alongside and into the various ships and the cold storage sheds ashore. After a couple of hours, we lifted anchor, steamed alongside the Gamadodo dock, and resumed the discharge of cargo. During the 24 hours we were at Milne Bay, we took aboard two new crew members for duty.

Afternoon of February 24, the mooring lines were cast off from the dock, and we got underway for Buna, up the coast of New Guinea. Our route was the same as followed on the previous run from Milne Bay to Buna, going east out of the bay, rounding the cape, then northwest up the coast. We anchored in Liberty Ship Anchorage, Buna Roads, February 25, and the holds were opened as required to service LCTs 380 and 389 and army lighters alongside. By 2200 that day, enough provisions had been dispensed to keep the local forces from starving for awhile; so we cast off early the next morning and proceeded to Oro Bay, dropping the anchor there at mid-morning. The lighters again swarmed around with their requisitions, and all holds were open to fill their needs, both reefer and frozen cargo.

Within a few hours after arriving there and opening up shop for the floating customers, our radio shack picked up a broadcast from that ubiquitous laughing stock of the Pacific, Tokyo Rose. This time, however, it was really no laughing matter, as her message was: "Hello there, all you boys on the USS *Octans* in Oro Bay, New Guinea. We just wanted you to know that we have our eye on you." As Japanese submarines continually patrolled the coast of New Guinea, and as we often sailed alone, this wasn't a very welcome message.

Standing at the rail and watching the loaded cargo nets being moved out of the holds, swung over the side and lowered into lighters for emptying before they were raised back aboard and dropped into the holds for the next load reminded one of fishing off a boat for hungry sharks in the water — with the "sharks" stealing the bait and spitting out the hooks, of course. The "sharks" in this case were deserving of anything we could give them.

9. Supply Run #5: Aground! 127

By midnight, with the hungry maws of the "sharks" alongside satisfied, we could close up the holds and speed up the ice machine to get the hold temperatures down again, ready for the next customer delivery. So early on February 28, it was up anchor again and back to Buna, where we got rid of our Navy passengers and more provisions. A slight accident happened while there that broke the boat boom that was rigged out the side to which the ship's boats were tied when not in use. A boat from the amphibious force flagship, the USS *Blue Ridge* (AGC-2), in the harbor came alongside to approach the starboard gangway and got fouled up in the Jacob's ladder suspended from the boom. In attempting to get clear, the strain on the boom broke it off. No one was hurt, just the pride of a few chagrined boat handlers.

Our next stop was to be Finschafen, further up the New Guinea coast. We were to join a convoy for that portion of the passage because there was some possibility of air attack from the enemy on New Britain in the Bismarck Archipelago and because enemy submarines were still active in the area.

We anchored in Cape Sudest anchorage over night, then joined the convoy early on February 29, forming a single column with the convoy commander, LST 171, in the lead, followed by LSTs 454 and 458, with the *Octans* bringing up the rear, with the deepest draft of 22 feet forward and 25 feet aft. Our escorts were the USS *Long* (DMS-12), minesweeper, and the USS *PC-1134*, subchaser. The minesweeper had a draft of 11 feet, the subchaser a draft of 7 feet, and all of the LSTs, including the convoy commander's vessel, had a draft of 11 feet. Standard speed was 10 knots.

What happened next will be described using a combination of the deck log entries, what we received by the bridge personnel passing on information to us down on the main deck, and our own perception during the ordeal.

One of the major hazards of steaming around in the South Pacific, other than danger from the enemy, was the lack of reliable navigation charts, which are the basic necessity for keeping out of trouble. Many in use were adapted from charts made in the 1800s, when the techniques of pinpointing true locations on the surface of the oceans were far from developed. As a result, many underwater hazards were often shown on charts far from their true locations. What happened to us next was probably a result of this situation and was not an uncommon event.

Like all good navigators, ours was watching the progress very carefully and became alarmed at the route being followed. The captain sent a message to the convoy commander, reminding him that we drew 25 feet. The return message was something to this effect: "Acknowledged. Follow me." Which we did, for he, not our captain, was the convoy commander.

The crew was mustered on stations at 0800, and we were getting ready to carry out our daily duties when, at 0810, the ship stopped dead, with a shudder that went through the entire ship, causing many of us on board to grab fast onto anything at hand. I was in the crew's berthing area and so grabbed a nearby bunk.

Both engines went immediately into full astern. The ship shuddered and vibrated but did not budge. We were aground, about half a mile southwest of the charted position of Margaret Shoal, off Holnicote Bay, just out of Buna Roads, with 3 fathoms (18 feet) of water forward and 12 ½ fathoms (75 feet) aft. For the next two days, we attempted various tricks and procedures to free ourselves.

In other chapters, I described how a ship reacts to the forces of the wind and the waves, as the ship rolls and pitches, rises and falls, to a definite rhythm. However, when the ship runs aground, the reaction to the wind and the waves is entirely different. The motion is far from smooth but consists of short, jerky motions, giving an eerie sensation to which it is very difficult to become accustomed. The history of maritime travel is full of stories of ships running aground and being pounded to pieces by the seas and the winds. A ship on the rocks is just another stationery obstacle to the waves, which proceed to pound away at it, with the ship unable to give way, to move so as to adjust to the force and movement of the water around it. Fortunately for us, the weather remained relatively mild, with only a slight sea running to constantly remind us of our plight.

Within minutes of becoming stranded on the reef, the fantail of the ship became crowded with erstwhile fishermen, dangling their lines over the railing and chatting about the possibilities of the ship having to go back to the States for repair and survivor's leave. Fishing was only incidental to this subject. However, many fish were caught, of different sizes and types, many of which were unknown to those on the fantail. One prize catch was a stingray with a wingspan of about four feet, which was hung up for all to see.

The convoy merely paused briefly and then proceeded on its way. That was the usual procedure so as not to endanger the remaining ships in the convoy, which had to keep moving to maintain their safety and schedule.

I shall describe the various efforts taken to free the ship, keeping in mind that, in addition, every few hours the main engines were operated full astern for about five minutes at a time, after the initial flurry of attempts to get off the shoal. At about 1100, three hours after running aground, minesweepers USS *YMS-52* and *336* appeared on the scene to lend a hand.

A prize catch (author's collection).

February 29:
1. The first major step taken was to pump all freshwater from the forward ballast tanks to tanks aft.
2. Both anchors were let go and dropped beside the #2 hold. This removed a lot of weight from the forward part of the ship.
3. Both minesweepers took a towline aboard astern and attempted

to pull us off with the main engines assisting. When one towline parted, this approach was stopped, and the minesweepers departed to complete their assigned duty elsewhere.
4. The deck hands paid out a total of 45 fathoms of chain to each anchor and moved the anchors further aft in the water with the cargo booms.
5. LST 68 and 184 appeared; LST 68 took a towline and attempted to pull us off, until the towline parted.
6. We discharged some of the cargo from holds #1 and #2 into LST 68 and LCT 184.

March 1:
1. Both assisting vessels, one on each side abeam of the ship, took breast lines and pulled aft, with our engines straining and strain on both anchors with the anchor windlass. No results, except that both towlines parted.
2. In casting off the towline, it fouled in the propeller of LCT 184. After getting free of the towline, it departed for Buna.
3. LST 68 transferred its cargo taken from our forward holds into #4 hold.
4. LST 456 appeared to aid. Both LSTs tied up abeam and attempted to pull the ship off the shoal. No results.
5. Commenced discharging more cargo from holds #1 and #2 into the LSTs, but stopped temporarily due to rain.
6. LST 68 departed and anchored at Cape Sudest.

March 2, 0400: Ship is swinging slightly, showing signs of coming off the shoal. Worked ship with both engines slow astern, easing her off the shoal, and heaved in the anchors when free. Underway at 0759 for Buna, where we anchored at Cape Sudest and LST 68 reloaded our cargo back into the two forward holds. Divers from the USS *Rigel* inspected the hull and found no damage. We then discharged provisions to high-speed transports USS *Humphreys* (APD-12), USS *Sands* (APD-13), and USS *Brooks* (APD-10).

Morning, March 3: Underway again for Finschafen, for which we had been bound when the unfortunate grounding took place, interrupting our schedule. We joined a convoy again, but we were now in the lead as convoy commander and guide. The convoy was formed in single column, with *Octans* followed by SS *John Alden,* SS *Sibigo,* LSTs 467 and 170. The escorts were two subchasers, *SC-737* and *746.* Our destination lay almost due north from Buna, but we followed the coast up for some distance, into Huon Bay, where LST 170 was forced to drop back to repair her engines and the SS *Sibigo* left the convoy to stop off at Lae. LST 170 rejoined the convoy after an absence of four hours, and the course was changed to northeast out of Huon Bay. On the morning of March 4, both LSTs left the convoy to go their separate ways. Soon after, the *Octans* received orders to heave to and await further orders, while the SS *John Alden* was detached from the convoy, leaving the *Octans* to proceed alone to our destination, Dreger Harbor, Finschafen, mooring to the dock at noon.

During the 30 hours we were in Finschafen, the rest of our cargo was discharged to the dock, destined for cold-storage warehouses ashore and for the Naval forces in the area. The port was being used as a base of operations, having been declared secured five months previous to this, our first stop there. At that time, there was military action taking place about 1,200 miles to the north, at Los Negros and Manus in the Admiralties. Both islands were declared secure by General MacArthur about this time.[36]

Evening, March 5: "Now hear this! Set Condition 2 watches throughout the ship! Set Condition, affirm!" We were underway again, from Dreger Harbor to join a convoy south toward Milne Bay. We took our position in the convoy and found ourselves with the merchant ships *Cape Cleare, James Rolph, Japara,* and *Admiral Halstead*. Also in the convoy were LSTs 18, 459, 470, and 475. Escorts were subchaser PC-1134 and minesweeper YMS-72. Our course south was a retrace of the trip north just a few days before, with the ship in Condition 3 again. This convoy was of short duration, being ordered to disperse at noon, March 6, all ships to proceed to their destinations. So it was full ahead both engines for the *Octans* at 13½ knots.

Word was received that we would be stopping off at Brisbane for a few days, then on to Sydney for some much-needed work on the ship. This meant that we would not be taking on refrigerated cargo for several weeks, so it was turn-to time in the ice machine department, overhauling, cleaning, painting, and so on.

In Chapter 8, I reported on the ship's newspaper, *The* Octans *Scuttlebutt,* and gave a short list of typical items to be found in it. The following items will further indicate what type of talent could be found in a crew of about 250 officers and enlisted men. They were taken from issue #3, March 5, 1944.

WHAT'S THE USE?

I have a son, in forty-one,
A great to-do, in forty-two,
Across the sea, in forty-three,
A lively war, in forty-four,

Still alive, in forty-five,
Tojo kicks in, in forty-six,
Close to heaven, in forty-seven,
Golden Gate, in forty-eight,
That home of mine, in forty-nine,
The world's nifty, in nineteen-fifty,
Nothing to do, in sixty-two,
My son's at war, in sixty-four!

Then there was a parody of one of Rudyard Kipling's poems, contributed by the captain. It represents the feelings of a man who worked in the dockyards and watched the sailors going to sea.

THE VAMPIRE SEA*

A fool there was and he went to sea
  (Even as you and I)
And he chose a life of misery
  (The poets call it brave and free).
Yet a fool he was and a fool he'll be,
For only a fool will follow the sea
  (Even as you and I).

Oh the years we waste have a bitter taste
When we turn again to the land,
And the land regrets we derelicts
  (With our withered minds as mental wrecks)
With a cold disdainful hand.

A fool there was and his life he spent
  (Even as you and I)
In a vile hole that was never meant
For a thing that God His image lent.
But we go to sea by our own consent,
For only a fool knows a fool's content
  (Even as you and I).

Oh the love we lost and the joy we lost,
And the light of the home we planned,
Was won by the man who stayed ashore,
Who had brains and sense and a whole lot more
Of the things we don't understand.

All he owns is his foolish hide
  (Even as you and I).

That's carefully fleeced and flung aside
To sink or float on that deep sea tide
Where some of him lived but the most of him died.
But still he would go — whether or no —
   (Even as you and I).

*With apologies to Rudyard Kipling.

There was about a page and a half covering the estimates of the various crew members as to when the war would end and a plea for all interested men who would like to join the ship's softball teams, as the turnover in the crew roster was causing problems in maintaining the program. A boxing program was being formed, trainers were available, and an attempt was being made to start an orchestra.

The propeller shafts had a tendency to gather a coating of rust if they were not periodically cleaned and oiled. The only time this could be done was when the shafts were turning, with the men leaning on them with a sheet of emery cloth until the surface was clean, at which time they were oiled. So the shafts got the full treatment during this run down to Brisbane and Sydney, all 125 feet of them. They would be sitting idle for almost a month and would gather rust. This work was done by the oilers on the gang, while we three machinist's mates scraped away at the bearings on the ice machine. At times, we wondered which task was the more futile of the two.

It was on one of those quiet nights in the ice machine room while on "dead watch," with the machinery shut down, that one of the firemen from forward wandered in, sat down, and felt like talking. This is the gist of what he had to say.

At one of the recent stops in Sydney, he and one of the machinist's mates had teamed up for a night of fun and games by double dating with two very agreeable girls. He and his buddy had started the evening by taking a night's rental of a bedroom with two beds in it, in preparation for the good times coming. They met the girls at the train station and went to the nearest private lounge for a couple of quick short drinks and then out for dinner. After that, it was getting late, so they started to walk to the rooming house. It was during this walk that the machinist's mate and his date wandered off, saying they would meet at the room later. The fireman and his date agreed and continued to saunter around the park, until he deemed it time to go to the room.

They walked up the stair, down the hall, and saw that there was no light showing in the transom over the door. He opened the door and turned on the light. It was a mistake. "Shut the damned light off!" was the demand from the two nude bodies on the bed.

The flustered fireman complied, muttering and stammering his apologies, backed out of the room, and closed the door. His date said this wasn't going to work because she and the other girl were very good friends, and she did not want to do anything further to embarrass her. So the fireman walked her to the train station, kissed her goodbye, and that was the end for them. He walked back to the ship, depressed and dejected.

The ship continued its routine passage southeast along the coast of New Guinea, then rounded the tip of Milne Bay and anchored in Gili Anchorage the morning of March 7. At noon, all boilers were shut down, and the engine room auxiliary machinery was secured for two hours. During this time, the emergency electrical generator was given a good run-in and test, while some simple repairs were made in the fireroom and engine room.

Our stay in Milne Bay this stop was just six hours, and we were underway again for Brisbane, southeast out of the bay, into China Strait, south around the tip of New Guinea and a direct route towards northern Australia. A couple of hours were spent the afternoon of March 8 in practice firing the 20mm guns, a total of 694 rounds at two targets. This was followed by shooting off 300 rounds of .30 and .45 caliber ammunition. Right after that, we were slowed down again because of water in the fuel oil. This lasted for about ten minutes, just long enough for the fireroom crew to purge the lines, get rid of the water, and then light off again.

The morning of March 9, we passed through the Great Barrier Reef via Grafton Passage, then followed our old route down the coast of Australia, threading our way between the numerous islands and buoys, guided by the many beacons on the route, and dodging other ships. The bridge personnel on their watches must have had a full four hours of it during this portion of the trip for three full days. Finally, on the morning of March 12, we tied up at Borthwick Dock, Brisbane. Three enlisted men and two officers came aboard for duty. There was liberty ashore for one watch, the port section, which was not mine. We furnished several men for shore patrol for the evening, and there were no AOL cases when we left port about noon on March 13.

One hour after getting underway from the dock, the gyrocompass failed again, and it took four hours to repair it. This portion of the trip simply retraced our previous route again, broken up on the morning of March 14 by a change in course to avoid a waterspout sighted off the starboard bow. No use in taking any chances, those things can be dangerous. That same afternoon, it was decided on the bridge that the crew were

9. Supply Run #5: Aground! 135

getting rusty in their emergency drills. This was corrected by holding a fire drill and then an abandon ship drill, each drill taking about 12 minutes. It took two minutes from the first sound of the fire drill until water was turned on at the announced scene of the fire.

March 15 was another great day of anticipation — twenty-one days of overhaul time in Sydney. At 0713, we stopped just outside Port Jackson to take on the pilot from that sleek pilot boat described earlier. Then it was only a matter of two hours slow steaming until we tied up at Woolloomooloo dock, berth 8.

"Now hear this! Liberty will commence at 1430 for the starboard watch, until 0730 tomorrow morning!" That included me, and about a hundred more excited men; enlisted men, of course, as officers suppressed their exuberance. Actually, many of the Navy officers were so financially bound up that they could not afford to squander much money ashore. When they become officers at the entry level of ensign, they are saddled with so many financial responsibilities that there is very little left for fun and games, especially if they are married. Traditionally, the married officer in the services has a hard time maintaining his status as an officer on service pay alone. This in the past has been one of the perennial scandals connected with military life. As an officer advances in rank, the situation slowly becomes better, or the officer learns to adjust.

And so ended another eventful supply run. No survivor's leave stateside, but 21 days in Sydney. Not exactly home, but we would make the best of it.

Chapter 10

Overhaul in Sydney in the Fall

The climate of Sydney is similar to that of San Francisco, except, of course, that the seasons are reversed. Sydney is south of the equator at about 35 degrees south latitude, whereas San Francisco is about 40 degrees north latitude. In truth, it makes little difference what the climate is to a sailor on liberty. If it's raining, you wear your raincoat and stay out of the parks and amusement centers. There is plenty of time when summer comes to loll around with the girls in the parks. And there is always another liberty or two when the seasons change.

We just got moored to the dock when the ship's mailman left the ship to pick up our mail, and we received notice to supply our regular shore patrol contingent, who left the ship just prior to the liberty party, at 1630. Our repairs were to be performed by the Navy repair facilities on the dock and by two private contractors ashore. The deck log contains practically no data on the work performed during this overhaul, and there is very little data in the correspondence between Washington and the ship. Consequently, I can only approximate what work was done on the ship.

The boilers were a constant source of trouble, due to their age and condition, so it is safe to assume that more attempts were made at this time to renew leaky stay bolts and a few rivets. There was always the necessity to clean tubes in the boiler, overhaul the main steam stop valves, blowdown valves, and the numerous smaller items on the boiler trim. The forced draft fan and drivers which had caused several slowdowns at sea had to be overhauled, and the fuel oil pumping and heating systems cleaned and repaired.

Most of the repair work on the boilers was confined to boiler #3, as

10. Overhaul in Sydney in the Fall

that was the one causing most of the trouble. All boilers did have general corrosion along the bottom of the shell, inside, which is common with that style of boiler. There is no record of anything being done about it, other than a letter from the BuShips recommending that all boilers be tested at the earliest opportunity. I am sure that it was done several times in our various overhaul periods. This style of boiler contains a tremendous amount of stored energy in the shell full of high temperature water blanketed with steam. Consequently, if the bottom of the shell became weak enough to burst, the entire boiler could be propelled upward, through the skylight, taking everything in its way with it. The entire fireroom staff would be killed instantly. Submarine commanders loved to torpedo older merchant ships with Scotch marine style boilers. If the torpedo hit anywhere close to the fireroom, the boilers would explode, with a spectacular display much larger than the torpedo explosion itself. Usually, the ship was broken into two parts when that happened.

In the engine room, there were always routine cleaning jobs, such as condenser tubes to be cleaned and replacing or plugging those which leaked. The main engine bearings could be overhauled; gland packings, gaskets, lubricating lines, piston drain valves, and miscellaneous other minor items could always be checked, cleaned, or replaced. The numerous auxiliaries, such as boiler feedwater pumps, the condenser air and condensate pumps, the electrical generators, bilge pumps and manifolds, freshwater pumps, fire pumps, and all attached valving required periodic maintenance.

In the ice machine room, we had our work cut out for us. We three machinist's mates were drafted for part-time night watch in the engine room, whereas the firemen/oilers were often drafted for work parties, usually during the day. Overhauling of the ice machine consisted mostly of resumption of our regular exercise in scraping and spotting-in the two main flywheel bearings, that never-ending search for the ultimate in perfection, which we never actually reached. The lubricating pumps and reservoirs for the compressor rods were overhauled, which didn't help too much. The brine circulating pumps were repacked, as was the air pump on the condenser. The carbon dioxide condensers were cleaned out on the seawater side, nearly flooding the ice machine compartment in the process. This was the result of my trusting the ancient seawater shut-off valves to perform their designed function over night. The bilges needed flushing out anyway, but that did not stop me from getting thoroughly chastised by the assistant engineer.

The ship was tied up at berth #8 at the Woolloomooloo dock. From there, it was an easy walk to King's Cross, the Greenwich Village of Sydney, and, therefore, a favorite hangout for sailors with only a few hours to spend or, as was the case this time in port, an overnight stay— alone or otherwise. There is a railway station at King's Cross from which one can travel to almost any of the more desirable areas of Sydney. Hyde Park lies just to the west of King's Cross, and there are three more railway stations in Hyde Park, one of which is a central transfer point for lines going throughout the area. It did not take long for a young sailor to get acquainted with the layout. It is almost as if the districts of Woolloomooloo and King's Cross were laid out with the interests of transient merchant and Naval sailors in mind. This may have been the case, of course, as the layout of the harbor was such as to cause a natural spreading inland from the more favorable docking points for incoming ships. This is the norm in most seaports which have been in use for centuries and has led to the reputation often accorded to any seaport in the world, regardless of any validity to the prejudicial taint applied to it.

Muster at 0800 the morning of March 16 disclosed that three men were AOL, reporting aboard from one to three hours late. The captain held mast at 1300 with the following results:

One deck court martial for sleeping on watch
One loss of ten liberties for dozing while on watch
Two cases, loss of one liberty for being AOL one hour
One loss of ten liberties for being AOL over three hours

Another and more telling indication of the effects of the previous liberties came on March 17 when three men were transferred to the U.S. Naval Base Hospital #10 for treatment of VD. One of these cases was an officer, the only one on record for the entire cruise. In all fairness to the many liberty stops we made at various ports, it is not possible to accurately place the blame for VD cases on any one port more than others. According to the medical books, the visible effects of gonorrhea can appear any time between two and eight days after contact, and the effects of syphilis can appear two to eight weeks after contact. This makes it difficult to determine any variation in infection rate between ports. It must be remembered that at any one night while the ship was in port, there were over 100 men from the ship ashore.

On March 18, we secured the electrical service from the dock and went on our own generators, #2 and #3. We continued the hookup to the dock for freshwater and telephone service. At 1455, the executive officer held a deck court martial to try the case of the man sleeping on watch. The sentence was announced the next day: confined to the ship for 20 days and loss of pay of $30.

Two men reported aboard 45 minutes AOL on March 21. At 1008,

10. Overhaul in Sydney in the Fall

we secured the ship's generators and resumed electrical service from the dock. Commencing this date, we ate our meals for several days at the general mess at the Naval maintenance repair facilities on the dock while the galley range was being overhauled.

March 23, we topped off our diesel oil tank from a fuel lighter tied alongside. We lost our executive officer this day, his services apparently required elsewhere. We had another lieutenant ready to fill the spot.

Australia, like the United States and many other countries, had adopted the same system of switching time twice annually to take advantage of the increased hours of daylight as it became available. On March 26, at 0200, it was time to set the clock back one hour, as local time went off war time to standard time. The *Octans* followed suit; we had to be in tune with the local facilities.

I do not know how many men ashore were aware of the fact that they had an extra hour of liberty available when they left the ship at 1630 on the 25th. I wasn't, I know; but then, I often came back aboard early anyway. There were quite a number of the men who were shocked and hurt when they reported aboard and found they were an hour earlier than necessary. After all, one extra hour liberty time was golden time to those who were shacked up with a girl.

Also on the 26th, down below it was time to work on the freshwater supply pumps, even though it was Sunday. This meant that for the two hours it took to repair the pumps, there was no freshwater pressure on board. Fortunately, there was very little activity on board, and many of the crew got in extra sack time. Liberty commenced at 1300, ending at 0730 the next morning. At 0800 muster on Monday, two men were AOL; one of them came back aboard about an hour AOL, and the other one was brought back aboard, drunk, by the shore patrol at 1300.

Another member of the crew was transferred to the hospital for treatment of VD on the 27th. A chief bos'un's mate came aboard for transportation. I hope he enjoyed our hospitality, which he probably expected would be better than what he had ashore. We were not due to leave Sydney for another two weeks.

The next several days were rather quiet on board. The ship's electrical generators were finally able to take the load and were put in service; service from the dock was secured. The anchor chains were payed out and examined, all 130 fathoms for each anchor, and repairs were made as necessary. We lost ten men from the medical staff, transferred to the base hospital ashore for duty there. I hadn't realized we had that many chancre mechanics on board.

Liberty continued of course, but the crew were behaving a little better in regards to getting back aboard on time. Ralph and I managed to get another date with Betty and Jean, and this time they were more friendly and relaxed, which made for a much better time. Betty expressed a desire to open a line of communication with my friends or relatives back in the States, so I gave her my sister's name and address. I could not think of anyone else to whom she would be interested in writing, except, possibly, a recent girl friend, but I decided that would not be appropriate. So then our date consisted of the old favorite, dinner and a movie. They both enjoyed the cinema. Anything they wanted to do, we were happy to oblige, if possible. The evening ended as before, and we saw them off on the train at an early hour. Ralph and I ended up at Ziegfeld's for a late supper, then back to the ship.

The liberty routine for Sunday, April 2, was changed from the usual one, as liberty was announced for the port section, commencing at 1000, to end at 2400. The ship was moved forward along the dock this day, which meant the dockside services had to be disconnected, then reconnected from a different set of facilities on the dock. It also meant both anchors had to be brought up to the hawsepipes.

During this overhaul period, those in ship's service felt it was time to have another ship's dance to let the crew shed some of that excess energy, what was left over from liberty, that is. By now, since it was the second one organized, the plans were better made and carried out. The dates were April 4 and 5, 1944, at the Paddington Town Hall in Sydney. Invitations were printed and issued to all on board who wanted them, and all preparations were made, including the inevitable punch. This was, as usual, liberally laced with alcohol from the private hiding places.

It was the usual wild affair, with a dance band playing a combination of Australian round dances and American jazz. Rumor had it that some members of the band were from Artie Shaw's band, which was reported to be touring the area at the time. I dropped in to see what was going on, sat down at a table where there was an empty seat, and started up a conversation with the others at the table, a mixture of our crew and local girls. One of the girls, slightly looped, moved over by me, and started up a conversation. She had come with one of the other men from the ship, who had abandoned her. She grabbed me and pulled me over to have our picture taken. I accepted.

When it was time for the dance to close, she asked me to walk her to the train station, which I did, seeing her off on the right train. I then went back aboard the ship. Later, in listening to all of the stories about the dance, it was evident that what had occurred to me was fairly common. The men did not always go home with the girls they brought. It appeared to be an acceptable practice down there, possibly a result of the surplus of women. It was a sailor's market.

10. Overhaul in Sydney in the Fall

> *You are cordially invited to attend a Dance sponsored by the Officers and Crew of a vessel of the U. S. Navy the night of April 4, 1944, at the Paddington Town Hall*
>
> DANCING, 8 – 12 MIDNIGHT

Invitation to the ship's dance (R. Mielandt, Lt.).

During these dances, the officers usually sat by themselves with their dates. Some even had their own private stock of liquor or concoctions made for the occasion. The captain, for instance, at one of these dances, had his own bottle, sitting on the floor at his feet. There was a local rationing system in operation, limiting weekly amounts of beer, wine, liqueur, and other liquor to all American servicemen. Those stationed in the area naturally got the first choice, as they knew when and where to be when it was available. Those of us who were in and out had to take what was left, usually wine or liqueur. The base of the alcoholic concoctions made for these special occasions was fruit juice in large cans from the general mess stores, supplied by the duty cooks in the galley on request. Some, of course, was filched from the cargo in the holds at any time it was available or desired by the thirsty men off watch.

The men in the fireroom often had a jug of brew working on top of the boilers. The brew did not always behave as planned. Explosions were common, when the jug was capped too tightly, for instance. There were remains of the various fruit mixtures splattered all over in the fireroom, and anyone entering the fireroom from the main deck access platform and ladder was often struck immediately by the conspicuous odor.

During this quiet time, one more man was shipped off to the Naval hospital for treatment of VD. One seaman second class decided the ship was not granting enough time for a red-blooded man to enjoy life ashore, so he overstayed his liberty by two days. At a later deck court martial, he was given three days on P & P and fined $18, the sentence to be carried out immediately. Presumably he had time then to ponder whether or not the two days extra freedom was worth it. All life is a trade-off. Sometimes the result is good, sometimes bad; the luck of the draw.

The captain held report mast for the case of the man brought aboard by the shore patrol and given a deck court martial. He was charged with being drunk and disorderly in public, in addition to being AOL. His sentence was five days on P & P and reduced one rating. Naval regulations stipulated that a man cannot be kept on bread and water for more than three days without getting a full ration every third day; we have to keep his strength up so he can perform his full duties after being released. Otherwise, he might write his congressman, and then there would be hell to pay.

A favorite gathering place for men off watch in the evenings was the mess hall, where letters were often written and stories exchanged. These stories were of prewar life, what plans had been made for postwar life, if it existed, and of course, liberty experiences. One evening, while tied up at the Woolloomooloo dock, we were sitting at a table in the mess hall after supper, and one of the men, whose name and rating I do not r᠎ 'l, told of his last overnight liberty. He had met a girl a couple of nights previous, and he had made arrangements to meet her again for an all-night stay. He rented a room in a local rooming house, and they spent the night there. In the early morning hours, it was almost time to get dressed and return to the ship, so she got up first and started dressing, while he lay in bed and watched her. Beside the bed was a small nightstand, and she had placed some of the miscellaneous items from her purse on it. Among them was another sailor's ID card. My shipmate mentioned to the girl that this ID card's loss cost that poor gob at least two liberties. She stopped adjusting her bra, looked at him, and said, "Don't feel too sorry for the bloke. I'm quite sure he felt it was bloody well worth it." When you stop to ponder for a moment, those few words contained a mass of sailor's philosophy.

On Saturday, April 8, another man was packed off to the base hospital for treatment of VD. All repairs were completed that could be completed this stay in the repair docks, so at 1130, the dock trials were commenced for the main engines repaired while the ship was moored to the dock. The engines were put through their paces to determine the result of the repairs and to spot any bugs which might remain. Following this, the pilot came aboard, the tug made fast to the port quarter, and we got underway about noon for Walsh Bay. This took us west past Mrs. Macquaries' Point and under the Harbor Bridge. It was then a turn to port and into berth #8 at Central Wharf, Walsh Bay, at 1400.

Down below in the ice machine room, we had already started the compressor, the brine circulating pumps, and the fans in the holds; the hold temperatures were starting to come down. The rest of the ship was on Condition 4, but we were on modified Condition 3 again.

Monday morning, April 10, the ship was due for the degaussing and compass adjustment ranges, both of which took place in the harbor, in the Man-of-War anchorage. We were assisted by specialists taken on board before leaving the wharf at Walsh Bay and by two tugs which helped position the ship and guide it through the necessary changes in heading. When finished, we proceeded back to Walsh Bay, tying up at berth #9 this time.

Two men who went ashore on liberty on Sunday, while the ship was still at berth #8, did not get back to the ship until after it returned to berth #9, and therefore missed muster at 0800 Monday morning. They reported aboard soon after the ship docked but were given only a warning at captain's report mast, held Tuesday, April 11.

So ended another happy time in Sydney. Now it was back to reality and the war and our part in it.

Chapter 11

Supply Run #6: To the Admiralty Islands

The first cargo came aboard into #2 hold at 1015, April 11, and the holds were prepared for it. By the end of this day, cargo was flowing into all holds, assisted by large gulps of Australian tea prepared by the stevedores in their billies during the tea breaks. Also this day, that old devil, VD, caught up with two more men who were shipped off, bag and baggage, to the hospital for treatment. However, two more came back from their stint in the hospital, treatment complete, and roaring to have another bloody go at liberty.

    Several times during this chronicle I have mentioned the use of fantail liberties for those men who felt that they just had to go ashore, regardless of whether or not they rated liberty. To do so was to take the risk that during one's absence, his presence would be requested for some purpose or that the officer of the day would call for a surprise muster at quarters in the evening or night. One of these surprise musters at quarters was held at 2030 on April 12, and one man was missing. He was a bos'un's mate first class, who came back aboard at 0455 the next morning. Boats, being an old Navy hand, decided to get back aboard the ship that morning by climbing, apelike, up one of the forward mooring lines. As he reached the foc'sle deck, he paused and peered through the railing. He was looking right down the muzzle of a Colt .45 service automatic, cocked and ready. The steady hand holding it belonged to Brooklyn, a seaman who just happened to have guard duty that watch.

    Several days previous to this, Boats had marched Brooklyn to the ship's barber shop and stood there while the barber removed long, beautiful blond hair from Brooklyn's head, ending with the regulation Navy haircut. Boats for weeks had been riding Brooklyn, not only about that hair, but also about other minor things, to the extent that it was obvious Boats was out to make a real Navy man of Brooklyn, who vowed to be patient and get his revenge, as he knew that Boats had at least one weakness.

When the AWOL Boats entered the wharf, Brooklyn knew he had his chance. He removed the automatic from its holster, cocked it, took his position, and waited. When Boats saw the gun, he paused, and Brooklyn said, "Welcome aboard, Boats," or something to that effect. What Boats said has not been recorded. He was charged with being AWOL for eight hours and, at captain's report mast held the next afternoon, was busted back down to second class.

On the morning of April 13, someone noticed that some of the cargo being loaded into #1 hold was in very bad condition; in fact, it was rotting. The 7th Fleet liaison officer ashore was notified; he came aboard, inspected the questionable produce—turnips—and rejected the lot. They were off-loaded onto the wharf, and loading of good cargo was resumed. This did not happen very often. Generally, our suppliers (provenders, they were called) were usually honest in their dealings. The Navy had its own supply staff at each loading point who handled procurement, including inspection and policing.

The fall rains came in intermittent bursts, causing interruptions in loading cargo. When this happened, if the rain was of any consequence, the hatches had to be covered over until it was considered permissible to resume loading operations.

There was still some question as to the condition of the port main engine drive train, as it had caused considerable trouble in the past. We noticed it down in the ice machine compartment because the spring bearings on the port shafting often heated up. While the ship was moored to the dock and being loaded, it was decided to perform another dock trial on the port engine. The deck log does not give the results.

Our function as a passenger liner was called upon again; on April 14, we took on a large draft of passengers for transportation. This included two enlisted men brought on board by the shore patrol and confined to the ship's brig. They were released soon after we left Port Jackson, heading north to Brisbane, April 15.

The run north of Brisbane was along the coast, much the same route as we had followed on the previous trips. We went to morning general quarters at sunrise, met or passed other ships, and challenged aircraft overhead. The morning of April 17, the gyrocompass started acting up, so it was necessary to switch to the old standby, the Navy standard compass. This, with the pilot, guided us into the various channels leading into

Brisbane where we swung ship and moored to the Abattoir Wharf at 0940. Two hours later, cargo was being loaded into the holds, and this continued around the clock.

Just before docking, the two enlisted men who had been brought aboard by the shore patrol in Sydney were placed back in the brig for safekeeping. They appeared not to like our brand of hospitality; they sawed the hasp from the door and disappeared. The shore patrol was notified, they were soon apprehended, and a letter was sent to the COMSERVFOR7THFLT (Commander Service Fleet Seventh Fleet) reporting the incident. Just what they had in mind is hard to determine; the ship was a mile and half from the closest suburb of Brisbane, and the land adjoining the wharf was mostly pasture. I doubt that they had any large amount of money on them. Perhaps they were just desperate.

There was only one liberty this time in Brisbane, and I did not go ashore. To get into Brisbane proper, it was necessary to take a taxi or the one train which came by the wharf area and ride a winding track into the city. Many venturous souls did make the trip, and when talking to one of the firemen who made it, he said his group was primarily intent on locating a source of liquor. It took them about an hour to obtain help from one of the local citizens, who directed them to a certain address in the residential district. They engaged a taxi, gave him the address, and off they went. The house was on a corner lot, and there was a board fence along the walk. The instructions were to ring the doorbell twice, go to the side fence, find the loose board, and push an arm through the fence with a twenty dollar bill in the hand. One of the more adventurous members of the group volunteered to be the one to risk his arm. He followed the prescribed procedure, not knowing what to expect. To his surprise, the twenty dollar bill was snatched from his hand, and a bottle was thrust into it. He withdrew his hand with the bottle and ran back to the waiting group. They took it over under a streetlight and, to their astonishment and glee, found that it was a quart of a well-known local gin. They were set for an evening's drinking and made it back to the ship in plenty of time.

There was an exchange of men while in Brisbane, six leaving and six new ones reporting aboard. Among those leaving was Boats, busted from first class the second day in Sydney. One warrant officer was transferred to start him on his way back to the States for further duty.

The holds were finally full, the refrigeration system working as well as was expected and the temperatures beginning to stabilize in the holds. Early on April 19, we were underway for Milne Bay again. First, it was necessary to stop outside the harbor and take on a compass adjuster so we could swing the ship in Brisbane Roads and make the needed adjustments to the magnetic compasses on board. When this was done, the pilot and the compass adjuster were let off the ship, and it was northbound for us. Instead of hugging the coast most of the way, we headed out for the open sea, clear of the shallows along the coast and bypassing the Great Barrier Reef. At 2000, all major caliber guns, meaning the four 3-inch guns and the 5-inch gun were manned on special Condition 3. This did not effect the ice machine gang, as those guns were manned mostly by the gunner's mates and the deck force.

The next three days saw fast steaming, alternating between base course and zigzagging. Fire and abandon ship drills were held, and the line-throwing cannon and various pyrotechnics were test fired. During this run, in the early morning watch, the lookouts spotted an American submarine dead ahead, running on the surface, probably charging its batteries. There was no collision, so we can assume that either it or us changed course, although there is no mention of it in the deck log. It was probably one of those operating out of Brisbane at the time. Down below in the ice machine room, we were watching the ice build up on the coils in the holds. About the time we entered Milne Bay, it was time again to apply the fire hose to the coil banks and remove the ice buildup.

During one of these many stops in Australia, we took on board a passenger as guest of the wardroom for passage north. He was Sir Herbert Gepp, a highly distinguished member of the Australian government. Sir Herbert was educated as a chemical engineer, and his early career was in that and allied fields, all in support of the Commonwealth of Australia. He soon branched out into other fields and steadily became involved with the government. In 1933, King George V of England bestowed knighthood on him for his services. During World War II, he was chairman of the Central Cargo Control Committee, and it was probably pursuit of his duties that brought him on board the *Octans*. The officers in the wardroom enjoyed their conversations with him and wished him well as he left the ship, not having disclosed his mission. The deck log does not give the point of departure, but it was probably in the Papua, New Guinea, area, as that territory was under Australian mandate.[37]

As we approached China Strait, more and more ship traffic was encountered. About dawn, April 23, we entered the Strait and headed for Waga Waga anchorage, Milne Bay, where we dropped the hook into the mud. That afternoon, we discharged two trucks carried as deck cargo, some medical supplies, and 200 bags of U.S. mail.

Pranks and tricks among the crew were always a sign that morale was fairly high, and the *Octans* had its share of practical jokers. One, who became known as the Phantom Belcher, operated only at night while at sea. In port, the quarterdeck was amidships, with the officer of the deck

(OOD) stationed there. He had available a microphone for calling to personnel who were wanted on the quarterdeck and for various other announcements, known as "Passing the Word." At sea, when the OOD was on the bridge, this amidships station was not manned.

For several months, at sea at some early morning hour, some practical joker would flip the switch to the microphone, let loose a loud BUUUURRRP! into it, and then disappear. Some half-hearted attempts were made to catch the culprit, to no avail. If he is still alive and reads this, to him I offer my heartiest congratulations for lending some much-needed light entertainment to those crew members on watch during the deep, dark, lonely, and boring night watches.

Under orders from the commander of the Naval base at Milne Bay, we weighed anchor at noon on April 24 and proceeded down the coast of the bay, rounded the tip, and reversed direction northwest to Cape Sudest. The trip was without incident until 0027 the morning of April 25 when we passed a ship aground on or near Ham Reef, about 90 miles southeast of where we had run aground. Our orders were to proceed, so we wished them luck and kept on our way, at full speed when well clear of the reef area. The anchor was planted in the mud at Cape Sudest, Buna, about breakfast time. Shortly thereafter, the provisioning officer from the USS *Blue Ridge* came aboard to help supervise the unloading of the precious cargo we were carrying.

Cargo handling continued into April 26. The unloading was performed by 32 men from the ships being supplied, under the control of two cox'suns from the *Blue Ridge* and the *Rigel* plus two officers from the *Rigel,* all controlling the boats and lighters alongside. The unloading went continuously until night, when the ship resumed its assigned berth at Cape Sudest. On April 27, the crews unloaded reefer and frozen cargo until 1800, when the working parties and their supervisors all left the ship. Now that the holds were closed, the hatches all covered, and the cooling fans turned on again, we could speed up the ice machine and attempt to regain some of the temperatures required to prevent the remaining cargo from being deep-sixed at the next port.

The commander of the Naval base at Milne Bay directed us to proceed up the coast of New Guinea to Morobe, which we did by weighing anchor at dawn on April 28. No sooner were we up to standard speed and running along nicely than it was necessary to stop both engines to let a small boat pass across our bow. The cox'sun of that boat either did not know the rules of the road or was simply being careless or daring. Then it was full ahead both engines until 0940, when it was slow ahead, due to water in the fuel oil again.

11. Supply Run #6: To the Admiralty Islands

Top: One of the 20mm gun stations (author's collection). *Bottom:* One of the 3-inch gun tubs (author's collection).

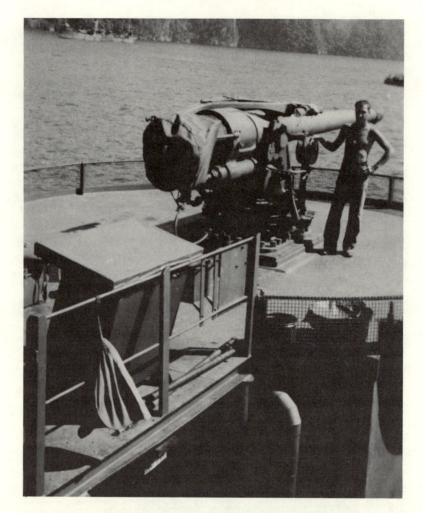

Five-inch gun over the poop (author's collection).

At 1046, the executive officer sounded "General quarters, all hands man your battle stations! Set Condition, affirm!" It was just a drill because ten minutes later, all stations went to modified Condition 1, with the guns manned, and the remainder of the crew at normal duties. The #1 3-inch gun was being fired when three friendly planes flew into the area, causing firing to be delayed for ten minutes until they were out of the area; then all 3-inch guns were given their chance to exercise their crews. Next, the 20mm crews got their chance. I do not know how many war bonds it took to pay for those rounds of ammunition fired that day, but from the results of an action which shall be described in a later

11. Supply Run #6: To the Admiralty Islands

chapter, I can assure the purchasers of the bonds that it was well worth it. At least it was to the lives of those who were on board the *Octans* at the time.

About noon that day, as we entered Morobe Harbor, a pilot and a supply officer came aboard, and we dropped anchor in the harbor at 1300. The holds were opened, and the cargo started flowing into the lighters alongside in the usual pattern, with the holds being worked by crews from ships in the harbor. It lasted for only a couple of hours because this was only a short stop to supply two ships. Then it was underway again, up the coast and into the next day, April 29, to our new destination, Finschafen, New Guinea. After several fits and stops, awaiting orders, we did not dock at Langamak Bay, Finschafen, until late afternoon, April 30. At 0800 that day, the flag had been lowered to half mast, in mourning for the Honorable Frank Knox, Secretary of the Navy. While anchored in the bay, awaiting docking instructions, we got rid of some more cargo. When we finally found our place at the dock, it was to open the holds to discharge more cargo and some of the U.S. mail we carried. The cargo was loaded into a Panamanian ship alongside and onto the dock, from which it was dispersed to the various facilities requiring it.

The morning of May 2, a short hour-and-a-half jaunt around the coast, to the south and then southwest, brought us to Cape Cretin to pick up another 72 bags of mail for passage to the Admiralty Islands. The next morning we retraced our track north to Langamak Bay, for a stop just long enough to pick up convoy instructions and three Royal Australian Navy signalmen. Then it was time to join the convoy. We were the only Navy ship in the seven ship group. Our escorts were subchaser PC-1134, HMAS *Cowra* and HMAS *Glenelg*. The convoy formed and then headed north towards the Admiralties, where the enemy had been declared contained just four weeks previous.[38] There were still isolated spots in the surrounding area from which enemy planes could sortie out and make themselves a nuisance, if they were desperate or brave enough. To declare an area secured from the enemy did not mean that there was no more resistance. To the Marines and GIs left to do the mopping up, the areas were often far from "contained" or "secured."

There was a fair amount of ship traffic on this trip, and we were on Condition 2 watches throughout the approximately 30 hours of the voyage. Partly to break the monotony, fire and boat station drills were held. At 1620, May 4, the convoy was broken up. After rounding Manus Island and entering Seeadler Harbor, we anchored. While unloading cargo on May 6, an air raid alert sounded ashore, so the ship went to general quarters. The stevedore crews climbed out of the holds in smart fashion and took cover as best they could until the all clear sounded, six minutes later. At 2200, we were boarded by a working party of 90 men from the cruisers *Phoenix, Boise,* and *Nashville,* who came aboard to work the holds. This proceeded immediately, with breaks during the nght, and resumed full force the next morning, continuing through the day.

That evening, one of the storekeepers discovered that some, lousy, no-good bum had tampered with the U.S. mail being carried in hold #1. Every sack of that mail was destined for the forces in the area, and only a low-lifer would dare mess with a fellow GI's mail. The captain and executive officer were notified, and the Fleet Post Office was also informed. Tampering with the U.S. mails is not to be tolerated, especially when it is destined for the troops in wartime.

The next afternoon, two lieutenants from Naval Intelligence came aboard to investigate the pilferage. With them were a number of extra men in dungarees. After consultation with the captain and the executive officer, all hands were directed to assemble on the forward-well deck. Those on watch were relieved by the men brought aboard so that the entire crew was finally assembled as directed. The two lieutenants then walked slowly down the length of the line, looking at each man in turn. They picked out a total of eight men, took them into one of the rooms, and interrogated them. The word leaked out that they all confessed to being a part of the pilferage. It was obvious that the two lieutenants were looking for certain known individuals who had been in trouble with the authorities before.

Right after noon on May 7, one of our seamen fell off a ladder and landed 12 feet below. The medical officer examined him and determined that he had not suffered any real injuries. He must have led a charmed life, or else his injuries were more severe than disclosed. I'll wager that he has been plagued ever since with those injuries and has been in constant contact with the Veteran's Hospital over them.

The morning of May 8, the ship was made host to two of the Navy's unwanteds, who were brought on board under guard and confined to the brig. By now, perhaps the carpenter had supplied a more sturdy hasp on the lock. The charges against the two men were for oral coition, and they were to be taken to Milne Bay for general court martial. The scuttlebutt had it that when in the brig, one would be inside, while the other was standing guard. Then every four hours they would exchange posts. I have no proof of this, but we only had one brig, and it surely does not make sense that they would be put in the brig together.

At noon, May 8, we were underway, north out of the harbor, to make a two-ship convoy, the other one being the USS *Sangay* (AE-10), with the USS *Stockton* (DD-646) as escort. We were in line ahead, with the *Sangay* in the lead for two hours, then in line abreast, 1,000 yards apart. I point this out, as the *Sangay* was an ammunition ship, and this led to a

11. Supply Run #6: To the Admiralty Islands 153

great deal of banter over our prospects should that ship get a torpedo. At sea, 1,000 yards is not a great distance, and an ammunition ship blowing up is not a minor affair. As a result of our discussion concerning the danger from the ammunition ship in the convoy, a number of us slept that night in the empty passenger bunks on the outboard side of the promenade deck. The ammunition ship was on the port side, so we slept on the starboard side. No sense in taking any chances.

When we joined the convoy it was considered safe enough to release our two prisoners, who were free to roam the ship, "at large." As far as I know, they did not contaminate the crew any more than we already were.

That night, our escort left and was replaced by the USS *Glendale* (PF-36), a new class of patrol ship called a frigate, copied after the ship of the same class in the British Navy. The convoy's route was the reverse of the one we took coming from Langamak Bay to Manus, and, about noon on May 9, we were detached from the convoy to heave to in Langamak Bay to pick up our next convoy and routing instructions. From there, it was around the coast to Cape Cretin, where we were to pick up passengers ready to leave; so we made haste to join up with the convoy, with the *Octans* as the guide and commodore over the remaining four ships, all merchant vessels. Our escorts were the PC-1120 and the HMAS *Goulburn*. The *Goulburn* had just taken up her position when she had a possible submarine contact and left the convoy to investigate. It proved false, and she regained her position.

In the evening, May 9, the convoy reduced speed to permit the USS *Porcupine* (IX-126) to join the convoy, which she did two hours later. She was a liberty ship, converted to a station tanker. Together we steamed south, disbanding about noon on May 10, each ship to proceed independently. Another round of fire and boat station drills were called that afternoon, just to keep us on our toes. Then it was southeast along the coast of New Guinea at standard speed most of the time, slowing when the traffic required it. In familiar seas, we entered Milne Bay the morning of May 11, anchoring at Waga Waga one hour later. The two Navy prisoners were taken off the ship under guard. Transferred to the Fleet Post Office ashore were 773 sacks of U.S. mail, and we took custody of 45,000 Australian pounds sterling, and $1,000 U.S. from the Naval Supply Depot ashore. An ensign reported aboard for duty with us, following which we weighed anchor and got underway for Brisbane, May 11.

When gathering material from former crew members for this book, several of them mentioned that on one trip down from New Guinea to Australia, we carried quite a large number of dead servicemen. None of the reports contained definite trip or date information, and their memories were very vague on that detail when I questioned them further. They were all of one mind on the fact that it did happen. Those bodies would have had to be carried in either #3 or #4 holds at freezing temperatures, which meant that the ice machine would have had to be working all the time on the return trip to Australia, where they were dropped off to the authorities ashore. There is a possibility that they were carried in the freezer boxes for the general mess, which was in operation all of the time. In that case, I would not have been aware of their presence on board. It all depended on how many of them were carried south, as the general mess freezer boxes were of limited capacity. I do not remember any time that the ice machine was in operation for the return trip from the islands.

Since the holds were emptied at Manus Island, we in the ice machine gang had little to do, except for the Condition 2 period out of Manus when the three oilers stood watch on the gun crews. After Condition 3 watches were resumed, the three of us machinist's mates stood round-the-clock watch, one at a time, in the ice machine room and took turns during the day scraping and fitting the flywheel bearings on the ice machine compressor, as usual. For the three oilers, there were the usual chores to be performed and maintenance tasks as well as cleaning and polishing to be done. Then on May 12 the compressor was started up, and the brine circulating pumps and the fans in the holds were turned on.

The trip down from Milne Bay to Brisbane was uneventful, broken only by the usual sunrise general quarters and one stint of fire and boat station drills. At 0115 on May 15, we picked up the pilot and proceeded at half speed into the Northwest Channel approach to Brisbane River Channel at 0408, swinging ship, and mooring to the Abattoir Dock at 0528. By now, the holds were down to working temperatures, having been steadily dropping for the previous three days.

"Now hear this! Liberty will commence at 1430 for the port watch!" We had arrived. End of Supply Run #7.

Chapter 12

Supply Run #7: Stormy Weather

My memory of Brisbane does not include anything of importance, but my impression of it was that it was dull in comparison to Auckland and Sydney. I am sure that some of the men from the *Octans* found entertainment there. If they did not find it, they could always make their own brand of excitement, which is why the ship had to furnish a contingent of shore patrol while in port. What I remember most of the place is the distinctive putrid odor from the meat packing district.

The first liberty started at 1630 and ended at 2400, and I did not rate it until the second night in port. A few of us went in together, followed our usual habit of going to a pub, sitting down to a glass of warm beer or ale, and discussing our prospects for the evening. Some sailors split off and went to search for those old standbys—liquor and girls. The rest of us just went sightseeing or to a movie. Just by walking the streets of the city and going into a restaurant for the usual "styke and eyggs," it did not take long to finish off the few hours of liberty allotted to us.

The stay in Brisbane was very brief; the only cargo we took aboard was meat in #3 and #4 holds and 714 bags of mail in hold #1. Each liberty section got one liberty for we were there only two days. During this time, we lost one officer transferred and took back one enlisted man returned from the hospital, cured of VD. There were no AOL cases from this stop-off, attesting to the military security and the general conditions in the city.

At 0130 on May 18, with a very light cargo, riding high in the bow and with a seven-foot drag aft, we left the dock with the pilot guiding us out of the channel. After the pilot left us, we rounded the northern tip of Moreton Island and then slowed down to adjust the compasses by swinging the ship on various headings, in the prescribed Navy manner. Next, the heading was southeast, with the crew being exercised at fire and boat station drills.

Standard procedure for ships at sea calls for a white light to be carried on the foremast while the ship is under way. In the case of the *Octans,* the yard at Alameda during conversion of the ship from commercial to Navy use had installed one at the very top of the foremast. By this time in the cruise, the light had failed, as all electric lights eventually do. The captain directed the executive officer to have it replaced before we hit the open sea. This was a function to be performed by the electrical department of E division. Therefore, the chief electrician's mate chose two of the men from his department to change the light as soon as the day's drills were over. Jim and Don were the lucky ones chosen.

With a minimum of drawings and instruction material to help them, they gathered their tools, a replacement bulb, and as much fortitude as they could muster and started gamely up the ladder to the crow's nest on the foremast. That part of the climb was fairly easy. However, while in the crow's nest, they looked up and found there was still some high climbing to do — the light to be replaced was some 95 feet above the deck. Undaunted, they commenced the last leg of the climb, with Jim in the lead and Don right behind with the bulb and moral support.

The ladder on the last portion of the climb was a narrow one, just wide enough for one foot, making the climb difficult, especially as the ship was then rolling and pitching. They got a good impression of the courage and skill those old time sailing vessel seamen had to possess and of how easy it was for the topmen in the old days to get thrown off, either into the sea or onto the deck below.

With the old sailor's adage of "one hand for yourself and one for the ship" in mind, Jim started removing the protective globe with one hand. During all of this, a storm was beginning to blow, increasing the corkscrew motion being experienced at their level. The executive officer shouted up at them to come down immediately, so Jim rapidly replaced the parts he had so painstakingly removed, and they both started down. Needless to say, the trip down was much faster than the one up. Instead of stooping down to kiss the deck, they hit the deck running and scooted into the shelter of the electrician's shack, shaking and shivering. The bulb was changed later, during one of the quiet times in port.

The following lines from *The Mikado,* an operetta by Gilbert and Sullivan written about one hundred years ago, are very appropriate here:

> To lay aloft in a howling breeze
> May tickle a landsman's taste,

> But the happiest hour a sailor sees
> Is when he's down in an inland town
> With his Nancy on his knees, yeo ho!
> And his arm around her waist!

The course then was almost due south, and, as we passed Cape Byron, we ran headlong into a storm. By 1800, the ship was pitching and working heavily, shipping heavy spray forward. The ship went to half speed to permit an inspection to be made of the weather decks, hatch coverings, and especially the forward-well deck and the fo'c'sle deck; these last were taking the brunt of the spray and water coming aboard. The ship appeared to be taking the waves very well, so the speed was increased to 10 knots, and we stayed on course.

Before going on watch below, I stood on the starboard promenade deck, just at dusk, watching the action of the waves and feeling the reaction of the ship. I walked forward to where I could see the bow angling into the waves, then rising to meet them, as the ship slid over the wave tops and the crests passed astern, causing the bow to dip then prepare to tackle the next wave. As the wave crests thinned to foam, the wailing wind snatched it and flung it astern, where it disappeared into the murky haze. It was probably a good thing that we were light in the bow, otherwise, there may have been more water coming over the bow and onto the forward-well deck. Looking out at the tops of the waves as they passed astern and then looking down at the side of the ship, I judged the waves to be about 35 feet from trough to tip, the tips coming considerably over my head as I stood there. The ship was groaning and creaking more than normal, as was to be expected.

When a ship meets the waves at close to head-on, as we were, the ship passes through first a sagging position and then a hogging position as the waves pass from bow to stern. There is a concentration of stresses at the midship sections, and, as the ship passes through successive cycles of hogging and sagging, these stresses reverse direction each time. With every groan and creak, I could feel the resistance of the rusty riveted joints as they complained of the load being forced upon them. The 27 years of almost constant working of the seams and joints, probably well permeated with rust, had no doubt increased the amount of sliding in the seams, thus increasing the groaning and creaking.

I watched the storm, the white-topped waves, and flying foam until it got too dark, and it was nearly time for me to go on watch at 2000. First, I went down into the crew's quarters and found the place was a shambles. The water in the troughs in the crew's head was sloshing back and forth from one end of the troughs to the other and was overflowing the ends at each pitch of the ship. The water, with all of its sewage, was flowing down the passageway and was inundating the deck in the crew's quarters. Soggy socks, shoes, and other personal gear were being sloshed all over the deck, so I gave up attempting to get anything out of my locker and went on watch. The ice machine room was pitching and rolling more than usual, but we managed to keep our footing and stay out of the compressor. By 2200, when it was time for me to go up on deck to enter the fan rooms to check the temperatures in the holds, the ship was riding much the same and there was still spray coming over the forward-well deck. My department did not suffer appreciably from the storm, except that the carbon dioxide cylinders stored in the center well in the shaft alley were rattling around and almost broke loose from their lashings.

At midnight, when I was relieved from watch, instead of going into my bunk, with all that mess sloshing around on the deck in the crew's quarters, I slept in my clothes in one of the bunks on the promenade deck, as provided for passengers. My Mae West jacket was my pillow, as it often was when sleeping on deck during the hot summer nights.

Reveille the next morning opened my eyes to the slightly different sea around me. During the night, we had slowed to eight knots and had either changed course or the storm had veered, for the waves were coming directly from dead ahead, and the ship was still pitching badly. Jumping out of my temporary bunk, I walked forward on the promenade deck and watched the waves attacking us over the bow. In spite of being light in the bow, we were now shipping water over the bow, onto the well deck, and then into the waterways and overboard through the scuppers. Lifelines had been rigged on the well deck, which was an excellent idea, not only as a lifesaver, but also to prevent any unfortunate sailor, such as myself, from getting swept off his feet and thrown into the bulwarks.

After breakfast, I went on watch to relieve my 0400–0800 MM2c and found that things were about the same as when I had left at midnight. The carbon dioxide cylinders were a little more disorganized in the shaft alley, but they were still holding their assigned positions fairly well. The port shaft spring bearings were running a little hotter than normal. The ice machine was still thumping and wheezing away at its regular beat, and it was a problem negotiating around the compressor without getting thrown into it. There was a guard around the flywheel end of the machine, but none around the compressor end. Running fore and aft along the outboard side of each stretch of floor plates from bulkhead to bulkhead was a substantial rail onto which we could hang while walking along the compartment. Getting across from side to side was more of a problem.

Soon after the change of the morning watch, the storm began to abate enough to permit resuming speed gradually from 8 knots to 10 knots. I do not know how the men in the fireroom and the engine room were managing, but I imagine they had a rougher time of it than we did in the ice machine room. I envied them not one bit, especially during a storm, as they were in a more dangerous environment.

One of the problems of a ship riding out a storm is the possibility of the stern rising and falling sufficiently to lift the screws out of the water, then thrusting them down into a solid mass of water. We in the ice machine room could feel the change in vibrations when the stern rose sufficiently for the screws to clear the surface and then the sudden shudder when the stern dropped or the wave passed by, submerging the screws as they grabbed a healthy chunk of the sea again. That throws a tremendous strain on the propeller shafts, which have been known to break under these conditions, but not, fortunately, on the *Octans*.

One of the reasons the officers were reluctant to show themselves in the crew's quarters was the musty stench permeating the area, even before the storm. The attempts at cleaning up after the storm had passed did not help much, and it took weeks before we really got used to the new stench.

With the storm behind us, we made it into Port Jackson after picking up the pilot. As a gray dawn broke, we passed by Woolloomooloo dock and moored to berth #4 at Circular Quay at 0740, May 20. It was a miserable day, probably from the storm through which we had just passed.

While entering Sydney harbor on one of these frequent stops, an accident happened that would become a favorite nightmare for ecologists in later years. It was particularly unfortunate in Sydney, with its many beaches, pleasure boats, and harbor installations.

The Oil King, one of the fireroom gang, was to transfer fuel oil between tanks. He started the transfer pump going, then sat back to watch the changing levels in the tanks. A roar from the bridge ended his reveries in short order. The fuel oil was being discharged directly into Sydney harbor and had been for some time before it was noticed. In lining up his valves, he overlooked an open one used to take on fuel oil from the dock or tankers alongside.

Naturally, a big uproar was made by the harbor authorities, for their shipping and recreational facilities were being contaminated. We were fined, the amount not disclosed, and proceeded with our duties for the war effort.

But life was not all bad, in spite of the weather. Liberty was declared for the starboard watch at 1300, ending at 2400. The rain had a dampening effect on liberty, but Ralph and I got to a telephone and made contact with Jean and Betty, who promised to meet us because they had important news to tell us. We met them as planned and immediately went to dinner. All through dinner, they refused to tell us their news, holding us in suspense like two little girls enjoying their secret. Finally, they told us that they were being transferred to a billet in Melbourne and were due to leave in two nights. They already had their travel vouchers and would be leaving while we were on liberty, which meant that we could see them off on the train. That sort of put a damper on the evening, but we decided to have fun regardless of the gloomy future. We saw them off at the train station that evening in plenty of time for them to get back to their barracks.

The next liberty was on a Sunday, but the gang had to stand our regular Condition 4 watches. We took advantage of the opportunity to straighten out the mess among the full cylinders as a result of the storm. The stevedores continued their work of loading our next cargo in between rain squalls, tea breaks, and penny pitching. Liberty that Sunday was declared at 1300 to end at 0730 the next morning. As Ralph and I were not due to meet the girls until around 1730, we did not leave the ship right away but got to the train station in plenty of time to meet them as they came up the stairs. The weather was miserable, and, after discussing the situation, we went to a restaurant to have a leisurely supper and sat and dawdled over it until it was time to saunter over to the station where they were to catch their train to Melbourne. They were to change trains at the border between New South Wales and Victoria because the rail gauge changed. That was something that General MacArthur had to contend with in evaluating conditions in regards to the defense of Australia. At least three different rail gauges throughout the country made it very difficult to plan on a quick movement of forces from one area to another. In fact, their were no rail connections at all to much of the country.

So we saw them off on the train, giving them a good, affectionate kiss first. It was not until many months later that I was told by my sister, who had been writing to Betty for some time, that Betty had a boyfriend in the North African desert forces, and there was an understanding between them that they would get married after he returned. However, he never returned. He was taken prisoner by the Germans, was confined to a camp in Tobruk, got sick, and died for lack of medical attention. She did not find this out until some time later, and it caused her to go into shock from which she never really recovered. She later got married, had a son, then became ill and gradually degenerated until she died prematurely. A sad situation it was indeed.

After seeing the girls off on the train, Ralph and I went to Ziegfeld's to see what was happening there and found the usual state of happy flux, with the band making its usual loud renditions of American songs and jazz. I was sitting at a table, with various others around me, when a tall civilian came over from another table, looked at me, and asked if I was Ken

Oliver. He looked familiar, but I had trouble placing him. When he identified himself, recognition came to me. Back in about the sixth grade in school, this man had spent the school year in my class, having been transferred for some reason or other from a school about 20 miles north of town. He was now in the Merchant Marine, and his ship was in the harbor being loaded. We talked for some time, then said good-bye, and that was the last I saw of him.

At muster the next morning, Monday, one man was AOL, turning up shortly after muster. At 1100, the captain held report mast, and the man was docked two liberties, which was a hard blow for a place like Sydney. Also at the same time, another man was given a deck court martial for returning aboard ship in a drunk and disorderly manner. The next day, the deck court was held, and he was fined $20 and assigned eight hours extra duty aboard ship. At the end of the day, one of the oilers on my gang came back from liberty in a U.S. Navy ambulance, having been treated for a leg injury while on liberty. I do not know what caused the injury, but I remember the banter among the engineering crew about it. He was able to stand his watches, once he managed the access ladder in the shaft alley.

One more liberty for the starboard watch section. One of the firemen from the auxiliary gang and I went ashore, went into one of the private lounges which was quite popular with the crew, and sat and discussed what to do for the evening. He got acquainted with a woman at nearby table and ended up asking her if she had a friend. She did not, so I told him to go ahead with her and I would find something else to do. She was rather plain, but neatly dressed, and more mature than most of the girls we met. As it turned out, they began rather a long-term relationship. More about them in a later chapter.

At muster the next morning, May 25, a CPO was missing, and he was still missing when we left port the next day. Soon after muster, the shore patrol brought two passengers aboard under guard, and they were placed in the brig. By 2100, all four holds were full and closed for sea, and the stevedores left the ship. The ship grew quiet for the night, waiting for the return of the liberty party at 0100, May 26, at which time the shore patrol contingent also returned. One seaman was 4 hours and 40 minutes late reporting aboard from liberty. At 0600, three more prisoners were brought aboard by the shore patrol for transportation, and they were confined to the brig for safekeeping. That brig must have been rather crowded. Add a traveling prison to the many other services offered by the *Octans*.

The pilot guided us out of the quay, east past Kiribili Point, then a turn to the north into Neutral Bay where the ship was to have its compasses adjusted. The harbor pilot disembarked, and with him went the service records, bag, hammock, and baggage of the CPO who had not returned from liberty, and also for a passenger who had been reported missing at the morning muster, all to be placed in the hands of the proper U.S. Naval authorities ashore. The compasses were all calibrated by 1100, and we then proceeded east, past Bradley Head, Outer North Heads, and then into the open sea on a northerly course towards New Guinea.

In the ice machine room, the gang was shaking out the kinks and creases left over from too much liberty (if there is such a thing), the compressor was thumping and wheezing its best, and the temperatures were stabilizing again. At 0840, May 27, the #3 boiler had to be shut down to caulk a leaking seam, which took about 45 minutes at reduced speed; then the boiler was put back on the line and the engines stepped up to full ahead. At 1300, the captain held report mast for the case of the seaman who was AOL for over four hours. He was given a deck court martial two days later and lost five liberties.

Our route up to New Guinea that time was a slight variation from the previous one, hugging the coast of Australia to just above Brisbane, then striking north directly to New Guinea. It was uneventful, with the usual shipboard activities, including another round of drills and small-arms firing drill. This included everything from .22 caliber up to .45 caliber pistol, with a few shotgun discharges. So the *Octans* was truly a versatile armed ship, everything from .22 caliber to 5 inches. We were equipped for almost anything, from rabbit hunting to sub hunting.

As we headed north, it was obvious that we were going from fall in Australia towards more temperate weather, as the days and nights were fairly balmy. When the nights were clear, as they often were, we could always look up and see that faithful old watchdog, the Southern Cross. We grew to recognize it and welcome its appearance, and many an hour was spent gathered by the rail in the early evening, talking and watching for the appearance of the Cross. When someone had to go on watch or the night turned chilly, the bull session would break up, to be resumed again at some undefined later time. If the night was too chilly for gathering out on deck, then the mess hall was the next choice, where we could always sit and write letters, read, play cards, or just swap stories.

At noon on May 31, we entered China Strait, at the extreme eastern tip of the mainland of New Guinea, turned north and started up the coast on a northwest course. The hook went splashing into the water at Sudest Bay, Buna, at 0730, June 1. This was the signal for Pappy, the master-at-arms, to confine our privileged prisoners to that famous *Octans* brig for safekeeping. This step was necessary, just in case the prisoners decided to forsake our palatial accommodations in a wild dash for freedom. Their stay in the brig was very short; they were taken ashore in the afternoon under guard and turned over to the Naval authorities.

12. Supply Run #7: Stormy Weather

Under the direction of a provision officer from the USS *Rigel* (AR-11) and a boat control officer from the USS *Henry T. Allen* (AP-30), the holds were opened and cargo was started into the lighters alongside by the working parties from the ships. Our rich disbursing officer this day handed over $300,000 to the disbursing officer of the *Henry T. Allen* and $100,000 to the disbursing officer of LST Group 19.

The cargo handling continued until dawn the next morning. After taking leave of the working parties and their officers, we got underway for Morobe, about 75 miles northwest along the coast, where we anchored about midafternoon. Working parties came aboard, and by 0100 the next morning, their reefer and frozen cargo requisitions had been filled. It was time to get underway again. This time it was for Dreger Harbor, Finschafen, mooring at a dock at 1400, where the same scene was repeated, with working parties coming aboard to get their share from this floating food market.

On board all Naval vessels, it is the standard duty of division officers to see that all personnel under their command take the initiative to study and prepare for advancement in rating. The Navy furnishes training manuals for this purpose, and often the enlisted men could be seen with their nose in one of them, cramming for future exams.

On June 1, 1944, the result of the first of these exams was posted, with many increases in rating assigned. Mine was included with several others from E division advancements. We lost no time in sewing the new badges on our jumpers. My new rating was MM1c, and it wasn't until April 13, 1945, that I was authorized to add refrigeration to my rating as a specialist.

Usually, when a group of advancements are announced, it is to be expected that soon thereafter would come a number of transfers to other ships or assignments ashore. The result is a continual turnover of personnel, as the drift is upward in rating. Incoming drafts of replacements of lower rating then take the place of those transferred. This is the path of advancement in the Navy, each ship attempting to maintain its assigned complement with the necessary experience and ratings. It has been in use for years, and it works very well, both to the advantage of the Navy and to the Naval personnel.

It was in Dreger Harbor that another unfortunate accident happened aboard the *Octans*, when at 1900 at seaman was removing one of the new vertical hatch liners in the trunk of #3 hold. He fell backward down the trunk to the next deck below, about seven feet. He was taken to the U.S.

Navy Advanced Base Dispensary ashore, and X-rays were taken. He came back aboard with his right forearm and right wrist encased in a plaster cast.

Our next step was to be the Admiralty Islands, almost due north from Dreger Harbor. We weighed anchor at dawn the morning of June 4 and joined up with a convoy being formed, with seven Merchant Marine ships, the *Octans*, plus USS *APC-11*, and USS *Cinnamon* (AN-50), with USS *PC-1121* and *PC-1122* screening on the flanks and HMAS *Strahan* screening ahead. Standard speed was 10 knots, and we did not zigzag. The trip was uneventful, and at 1800 on June 5, we dropped the anchor at Seeadler Harbor, on the north side of and between Manus Island and Los Negros Island. Manus had been declared secured from the enemy on March 25, and Los Negros on March 30.[39] The holds were opened almost immediately, the working parties came aboard, and the cargo started moving into the lighters, much the same procedure as at the previous stops on this run.

By midnight on June 7, we had supplied all the food requested at that stop and were ready for sea again. At 0705, we weighed anchor and rounded the western end of Manus Island, then turned south, where we were taken under escort by HMAS *Waga*. We were at Condition 2, all ahead full, at 13 knots for the remainder of that day and into the next. There then occurred an incident reported to the crew by the bridge enlisted men, but not recorded in the deck log.

At dawn the morning of June 8, while we were at morning general quarters, the escort reported a possible submarine contact to port and left to investigate, while we took a fast change of course and increased speed to 13½ knots. Fifteen minutes later, the escort reported "negative" on the contact, and we resumed our normal speed and course. Now this is the part reported via the scuttlebutt route to the crew. Shortly after resuming normal speed and course, the crow's nest lookout shouted, "Torpedo off the port bow!"

The captain looked at it and said to belay that word — it was only a fish. As the "fish" passed straight across the bow, several yards ahead, one of the forward gun tub lookouts was heard to say, "It can't be a torpedo; the Old Man says it isn't."

True or not, this is roughly the way it came down to the crew.

The rest of that portion of the trip was without further incident, except for another round of fire and boat station drills, followed by anchoring in Humboldt Bay, Hollandia, at 1803. The area had been invaded by our forces starting April 22 and had just been declared secured on June 6, two days before we dropped the hook in the bay.[40] However, it was not as dangerous as it sounds, as it had been a fairly easy victory, the enemy having been caught pretty well off guard. But we were not taking any chances, so the ship was kept on Condition 3 watches, and all boilers were simmering on the line, just in case.

While unloading cargo June 10, 1944, another issue of the *The* Octans *Scuttlebutt* was distributed to the crew. It contained the usual potshots at various members of the ship's roster, some with a grain of fact, some with nothing but the substitution of a crew member's name in one of the stories going the rounds on the home front or gleaned, along with a few jokes, from magazines or newspapers. "Bon Voyage" messages were given for departing crew members, and a couple of ditties were shared. A long letter from a "typical American family" back home to someone in the service, designed to boost morale, was reprinted, and congratulations were extended to a list of men who received advancement in rating.

As it was the first anniversary of the ship's commissioning, the birthday dinner was listed:

SHIP'S BIRTHDAY DINNER

	Beef Bouillon	
	Croutons	
Roast Chicken		Baked Spiced Ham
Sage Dressing		Cranberry Sauce
	Giblet Gravy	
Mashed Irish Potatoes		Candied Sweet Potatoes
Green Peas		Buttered Asparagus
Green Olives		Celery Hearts
	Assorted Pickles	
	Waldorf Salad	
Pound Cake	Strawberry Ice Cream	Berry Pie
Cigars		Cigarettes

The *Scuttlebutt* staff now consisted of:

Editor in chief	Terry L. Howard
Assistant editor	James T. Gray
Associate editors	Clifford E. Simmons and James D. Avey
Cartoonists	C.S. Simmons, P.T. Johnson, and E.A. Cowhey
Typists	C.A. Willis, C.A. Reynolds, and C.T. Mathews

During this stop, our disbursing officer received from the disbursing officer of the LCI(L), Flotilla 7, the sum of 4,174 Australian pounds sterling for transfer south. He gave in return $20,000 in American currency.

Our next orders were for a stop at Finschafen, down the coast to safer harbors, and we weighed anchor at 1611, June 13. This time we were escorted by two ships, the USS *Glendale* (PF-36) and USS *Orange* (PF-43), at standard speed 13½ knots and under Condition 2 watches. Another round of fire and boat station drills broke the monotony, and a signalman was taken before captain's report mast and reduced in rank for laying down on watch. The remainder of this leg was uneventful, and we anchored in Langamak Bay, Finschafen, June 15. A small amount of cargo was dropped off there, leaving very little remaining in the holds; so the ice machine load was very light, and the thumping and whooshing came at a much slower rate than usual.

Leaving Langamak Bay at dawn, June 17, we retraced familiar waters southeast along the coast of New Guinea, alone and at standard speed of 13 knots. Without incident, we entered Milne Bay at 1000, June 18, and dispatched a large number of bags of U.S. mail ashore to the Fleet Post Office.

The last of the refrigerated provisions were unloaded by evening, June 18, and the ice machine gasped and wheezed its last as the steam throttle valve was closed, and the brine pumps and fans were shut down. The gang went on our regular schedule of standby watches, while the rest of the engineering spaces were on regular steaming watches. During the day, there was the general shutdown routine in our department, consisting of repairs to the machinery, cylinder storage, cleaning the brine and fan rooms, and keeping the bilges dry. The bilges were usually cleaned by working parties from the enlisted passengers, a task which I did not relish assigning to them, but one which we thoroughly detested doing ourselves. The bilges of the *Octans* were usually sloshing with a mixture of water, oil, sludge, and bits and pieces of trash, such as peelings from the bitumastic coating which had been originally applied in the builder's yard, years before. It was absolutely forbidden to throw anything into the bilges, but it was impossible to enforce this policy completely when the civilian workmen were all over the ship during our several overhaul periods. Cigarette papers, wrappings, and butts could really cause havoc in the bilge suction screens. And, of course, urinating into the bilges was also strictly taboo.

The ship got underway at dawn, June 19, headed for Brisbane again. It was all ahead full, east out of the bay, turning south at the entrance to China Strait, through the Strait, then south into the open sea—open, that is, but for the usual heavy ship traffic to be encountered in this part of the run. The ships we met were of all types: destroyers, merchant ships, tugs with their tows, many unidentified types and nationalities, and even an occasional hospital ship or another reefer like ourselves. There were the usual fire and boat station drills to remind us of the ever-present dangers of life at sea.

There were many convoys, which had to be avoided by a change in course, always by us, as it was much easier for a lone ship to avoid collision than for an entire convoy to execute a change in course. There were standard procedures for convoy deployment under stated conditions, and the skipper of each ship in the convoy was expected to know those tactics. However, there was often one or more skippers in the group who could easily foul up the maneuver. When this happened, each skipper took full responsibility for the safety of his own ship, with sometimes complete confusion resulting.

At noon on June 20, the ship again came to a quick slow-down when a slug of water came through the fuel oil lines into the burners of all four boilers. It took just 15 minutes from the time of shutdown until we were back to standard speed again — a job well done.

East of the great Barrier Reef and south of the tip of Milne Bay, New Guinea, lies a group of many reefs, islets, and cays, and it was obvious from our many changes in course that we were avoiding these dangers to our passage south.

In the early morning of June 22, we started our approach to the channel into Brisbane, picking up the pilot shortly after noon and being guided past the intricate maze of buoys and lights, through various sections of dredged channel (termed "cuttings"), and up to Hamilton Wharf. Here a tug assisted us in swinging the ship around so as to moor to the dock on our port side, late evening. Our stay was to be only long enough to discharge passengers. We picked up one USN officer for transportation and one USN ensign for duty on board. At midnight we were underway again, out of the channel, then south toward Sydney.

The passage south to Sydney was uneventful, broken only by the usual fire and boat station drills, until at 2000, June 24, we were moored to berth #1, Circular Quay, just east of the Sydney Harbor Bridge. The first contingent of shore patrolmen left soon after docking.

End of the run. We had arrived.

Chapter 13

Supply Run #8: Fumigation

That stay in port got off to an entirely different start, as arrangements had been made to have the ship fumigated as soon as we arrived. This was an overdue operation, as the rats, cockroaches and other vermin were getting out of control. Every time we went into the fan rooms and turned on the lights, those cockroaches were all over the deck, scurrying for the corners to get out of the light. Without exaggeration, they were at least two and a half inches long, big, fat and healthy. Why shouldn't they be? They had their pick of food in the holds.

It is interesting to speculate as to how many rats were carried from New Zealand and Australia with each cargo to the islands and ships of the fleet. When tied up at a wharf, standard procedure was to install rat guards on each mooring line to the dock or wharf. However, with the cargo being foodstuff, sitting on the docks or in warehouses ashore and then being lifted by nets into the holds, it is certain that we gave free passage to many of the little varmints.

Incidentally, those same cargo nets have been known to furnish clandestine transportation to sailors on fantail liberty, both coming and going, while in liberty port. The general procedure was to bribe the stevedores with cigarettes to set the net beside the hold where the liberty hound could climb in. The net was then swung over onto the dock and lowered, all when the OOD was out of sight. Coming back aboard was just the reverse, hoping that the same stevedore crew was on duty.

As soon as the shore patrol contingent had left the ship, the remainder of the crew were sent ashore on liberty, with the exception of those involved in the fumigation. The ship was inspected to be sure no one was still on board, a security watch was posted, and the contract fumigators commenced getting the ship closed up for the job. The boilers had already been shut down before they commenced the fumigation. At 2130, the ship was opened for airing out the ship, and one hour later the assistant engineer and seven fireroom personnel went into the fireroom to start the boilers and get the ship up to auxiliary status again. By 0715 the next morning, the #1 and #2 boilers were on the line, and the ship's medical officer was able to inspect the ship and test for remaining gas. The returning liberty men were waiting on the dock, and as soon as the doctor declared the ship safe, we all trooped aboard. At 0900 muster, there were no absentees, but there were many happy sailors, after a full night ashore, and in Sydney, at that.

The ice machine gang immediately started up the compressor and got the fans circulating the air past the brine coils and into the holds, where the stevedores were waiting to load cargo. The two forward holds were started first, since they were the warmest holds and the quickest to cool down. Next, a major effort was placed on #4 hold to get it down in readiness for loading frozen cargo. Hold #3 was to be used for dry cargo this trip, as far as Brisbane. The cool winter temperatures helped, except for the interruptions from the rains, which made the stevedores take shelter around their billies of hot tea.

Liberty that Monday was declared at 1500, to end at 2400, for the port watch section. The rains put a slight damper on many of the liberty party, but they still had a good time and would not have stayed aboard even if they were flat broke. There were no absentees at muster the next morning, so the bad weather must have had a slight chilling effect on their behavior. In fact, that was evident throughout the stay in Sydney.

It was during one of these liberties in Sydney that for some reason or other, I found myself alone and hungry after the evening's activities, so I stopped into Ziegfeld's. I made the rounds of the booths, talking to the other men I knew from the ship, then sat down and ordered my meal. When it came, the waitress put it down in front of me. Just then, someone in the booth behind me called to me to ask what kind of a night I had so far. I made a brief report, then turned back, only to find my supper plate had disappeared. I looked around and saw that one of the girls at the booth, a regular at the joint, had it and was gobbling it up as fast as she could. Her comment was that it was getting cold, and she hadn't had her supper yet, so she decided to eat it. I started to make a fuss over it, when the waitress placed another meal in front of me. I asked her how much I owed for it, and she said, "He paid for it already," and pointed over to another sailor in the booth. It was an Australian sailor who had been a passenger on the *Octans* that last trip into Sydney. He refused to accept reimbursement, so I thanked him, ate the meal, and left, much chagrined.

The winter rains continued, intermittently delaying the loading of the ship. The degaussing expert came aboard to direct the demagnetizing of the ship. This step is one of the defenses against magnetic mines and torpedoes. It must have been effective because we never hit a mine and we never got torpedoed.

Liberty on Saturday, July 1, started as rather a sad affair, what with the miserable weather and the fact that I rather missed Betty. I joined up with another sailor from the ship. We sauntered up George Street and then looked for a dance hall we had heard was in the vicinity. I did not dance, but wherever there was action, I was prepared to go—you could never tell what might cross your path in the line of something pretty and available. We found our objective, went inside, and noticed that the women outnumbered the men considerably. The typical Australian round dance was in progress, with some sailors and Aussie men standing around or sitting at the tables around the outer edges. We circulated, and eventually I found myself next to a table containing a couple of girls. One of them appeared unescorted, so I sat down beside her and struck up a conversation. She was short and rather good looking, and with a freckled face and slightly red hair. Her name was Joyce, and she was Irish—a very good talker with a keen mind. I knew I did not have much time before her date showed up again, and I certainly did not want to get into any fight with another Yank; so I managed to get her name, address, and telephone number. I said I would be calling her, the next stay in port. She told me what time to call her, as she worked and lived at home with her parents. The more I talked to her, the more interested I became and resolved to pursue this contact as much as possible in the future.

It wasn't very often that we were able to get a girl's home address and telephone number in Australia. The usual procedure was to arrange to meet her at the train station. The reason for this was simply that many of the Australian mothers absolutely forbid their daughter to go out with a Yankee sailor. Many girls got around this restriction simply by telling their mother that she was going to the cinema with a girlfriend. However, there were quite a few girls living and working on their own who were free to go out with whomever they pleased. These were generally the girls we saw among the regulars at places like Ziegfeld's and were the party girls that some sailors just loved to meet.

What it all reduced to was that the Yankee serviceman was able to meet almost any type of Aussie girl he desired. The best selection was often made by those Yanks stationed there for some time, whereas we in-and-outers were under a severe time restriction. But it was still fun!

My oiler at that time was Don, from Seattle. He was a short, stocky, tough Dutchman with curly blond hair and a mild, pleasant disposition. He was a good and willing worker, never gave me any trouble, and was very cooperative. We got along beautifully. He had a fireman rating, and while with me he worked his way up steadily. We spent a lot of time talking and comparing notes about different things, including liberty. He did not drink much and did not smoke, but he sure loved the girls. They flocked to him readily, and he had no trouble taking his pick.

Sunday, July 2, another member of the crew was transferred to the base hospital for treatment of VD. Also, the CPO who was AOL since May 25 was brought aboard, having been apprehended on June 14, and was placed in the brig. At 0800 muster, a steward's mate was missing, AOL from liberty. The holds were closed up, the hatch covers in place, and the tarps battened down. The ship moved out into the Man-of-War anchorage to swing ship for compass and degaussing gear adjustment. Then, with the experts off the ship, at 1500 we left Port Jackson behind and entered the usual route north toward Brisbane. Soon we were bucking the waves from the storm which had brought the rain that had delayed our loading in Sydney. The wind was from the northeast, producing heavy seas and swells, with the ship pitching and rolling heavily at times, in a corkscrew pattern; our course was somewhat north of into the wind.

Just as the storm was building, one of the crew, a seaman first class, came down with an acute case of appendicitis; so the ship's Doctor, assisted by two passenger medical officers, performed the appendectomy in the surgery. It would be interesting to know what the patient was thinking when he went under the anesthetic, with the ship rolling and pitching, knowing that these three men were going to be working on him with sharp instruments in their hands. He really did not have much choice, regardless of what he thought. But, one hour later it was all over, he was doing fine, and he recovered in due course.

By the early morning hours of July 4, the seas were moderating slightly, and the ship was steaming along more smoothly, although still with some pitching and rolling. The weather did not delay captain's report mast, held in the morning to try the case of the missing CPO brought back from his "freedom" ashore in Sydney. He was given a summary court martial, to be held later.

As we approached the entrance to Brisbane Channel, the storm had abated so that the ship's motion was only moderately annoying. We stopped to pick up the pilot for the outer channel entrance but was told there were none available. So we entered the outer channel without a pilot and proceeded to the lighthouse marking the entrance to the inner channel. There we picked up the pilot who guided us into the inner channel and up to the Hamilton cold storage warehouse. The tug swung us around in the narrow channel, and we tied up at the dock.

Four hours after docking, dry cargo began moving out of #3 hold onto the dock, and frozen provisions were loaded into #4 hold, which continued around the clock into both after holds. We lost six members of the crew, all transferred to other ships or duty. The executive officer convened the summary court martial on July 6 to handle the case of the CPO who was AOL several weeks. The next day, a carpenter's mate was taken to the Naval dispensary to have his left arm and elbow X-rayed, having injured himself while on liberty. He was returned aboard after two hours; no explanation in the deck log how he injured himself. It was never known if his exuberance ashore exceeded his common sense or if it was an accident.

While in port and loading cargo, one boiler was usually all that was needed on the line, watched over by one man. That night, a second boiler was on the line, at low fire, simmering as a standby. All boilers were provided with a last-ditch safety device, called a fuseable plug, to guard against the danger of the water level dropping too far in the boiler, which could cause a disastrous explosion. The fuseable plug was to be put to the test that night, for the water level dropped to the danger point for some reason. The noise emitted by the blowing plug alerted the fireman on watch, who immediately shut the boiler down as he had been trained to do. The standby boiler was then brought up to full service within a few minutes, and the ship's operation continued, almost unnoticed.

As we were scheduled to pull out the next morning, it was imperative that the down boiler be put back into service, which meant that the boiler had to be entered and the blown plug replaced. The two men who could perform the task were on liberty, a watertender and a fireman. The shore patrol were notified, and they, cognizant of the habits and hangouts of the two, hunted them down and brought them back aboard — the end of what had promised to be a perfectly good liberty. They reluctantly, naturally, replaced the blown plug, and the ship was ready when we pulled out at midmorning.

On July 8, shortly after midnight, the last of the liberty party and the shore patrol contingent reported aboard. The holds were topped off with frozen goodies, and by 1000 the ship was getting ready for sea. At 1112, we pulled away from the dock, started down the long channel out to the sea, on our way to Milne Bay, New Guinea, again. The weather was moderate as we passed from winter in Australia toward the equatorial latitudes where it was always hot; but around New Guinea, it felt like spring. There was only one incident to mar this leg of the passage north.

Maintenance work on the #3 deck winches (author's collection).

It was normal procedure on board Navy vessels that any enlisted military passengers riding free were subject to being drafted for working parties. Of course, this meant that they usually got the worst possible assignments when drafted for work. Also, as was to be expected, the working parties were drafted first from the prisoners, and that is what happened on board the *Octans* that trip. We were assigned a couple of prisoners for bilge cleaning in the ice machine room, and we got our share of griping from them. I did not particularly like sending them into the bilges to work, but our bilges were probably the best and the cleanest on the ship. To make matters worse, the passengers were not allowed to take freshwater showers. On the after-well deck, saltwater showers had been rigged for their use, and there was a special type of soap furnished for cleaning or showering with saltwater. It worked, but just barely, and was not nearly as good as taking a shower in freshwater. The result was a slimy feeling, and you did not feel at all clean after taking a saltwater shower.

Out of the 25 prisoners drafted for work, six of them refused to work. Naturally, this could not be allowed to go unpunished, so the captain held report mast on July 11, and all six were confined to the brig for five days on P & P. That did not help their service record when they were delivered to their final place of confinement.

On the morning of July 12, we passed through China Strait, made the sharp turn to the west, and tied up at Gamadodo Dock, Milne Bay. The first activity was to get rid of 243 sacks of mail, which I'm sure made many GIs happy later. One new lieutenant reported aboard for duty, and we got rid of one of our prisoners there.

Ever since our arrival the morning of July 12, cargo had been moving out of the hold and onto barges alongside, the working parties from the shore base performing this task around the clock. Then on July 13, in the early morning hours, their appetite for our produce finally satisfied for this stop, the holds were buttoned up, the tarps stretched over the hatch covers and battened down, and we got underway again, this time for Finschafen. Shortly after leaving the harbor, it was again necessary for the captain to hold report mast for another rebellious prisoner, with the same result as for his other prison mates — five days on P & P. Meanwhile, the ship continued on up the coast, past Tufi Harbor, toward our immediate destination.

It was on one of these nightly jaunts up the coast of New Guinea, alone and blacked out, that an incident happened that caused Pandemonium on the bridge during the early morning hours. Suddenly, the entire forward deck of the ship was flooded in lights. The officer of the deck

13. Supply Run #8: Fumigation

was horrified, but soon recovered his senses and sounded general quarters. Enemy submarines had been known to operate in these waters recently, and we were now vulnerable.

The lights went out as mysteriously as they had come on. A search was started immediately for the culprit. He soon came forward, sheepishly. It was Ensign Fraser who had been on the prowl again and had attempted to turn on the lights inside the fo'c'sle; in his groping for the switch, he had turned on the wrong lights. What he was doing there at that time of the night, when all other self-respecting officers were in their cabins or in the wardroom drinking coffee, has not been determined. Only he knew for sure.

If there were any enemy submarines in the vicinity, they were probably too astonished to be able to react in time to launch an attack. In view of the blunder made by me that first night out of San Francisco, I could sympathize with Ensign Fraser.

The afternoon of July 14, we sidled up to the dock at Finschafen, and about 30 minutes later, the merchant vessel SS *Michael Casey* came alongside to tie up to us on our starboard side. Her captain miscalculated some way, and she crashed into our rigging and life raft on the forward well deck, starboard side. The raft and supporting rack were damaged. She finally managed to extricate herself, then worked alongside, and tied up to us. Just another one of those little accidents that happen between ships at sea and in harbor. It is not surprising when you consider how difficult it is to maneuver a large ship, especially when there is no tug available, such as in that situation.

Just before docking, the master-at-arms rounded up as many of the passenger prisoners as possible, 17 of them, and they were herded into our meager brig for safekeeping.

At this point in our narrative, there is a minor glitch. The deck log for the ship's travels from July 15 through July 31 is missing. However, I was able to obtain, through the help of a former shipmate, a schedule of the ship's travels, from which the following is taken for the missing period.

Destination	*Arrival*	*Departure*
Finschafen, New Guinea	July 14, 1944	July 15, 1944
Alexischafen, N.G.	July 16	July 17
Hollandia, N.G.	July 19	July 22
Finschafen, N.G.	July 24	July 24
Milne Bay, N.G.	July 25	July 26
Brisbane, Australia	July 29	August 4

There are no details of the ship's operations at those stops, with one exception.

Issue #8 of *The* Octans *Scuttlebutt* appeared July 15, available "on the newsstand," which meant various stacks placed throughout the ship. It contained a good-bye ditty to seven of the more well-known members of the crew. There was a dialogue concerning the sexploits of three machinist's mates, wherein one of them assisted in getting the other two slightly inebriated at a pub, then sneaked off to take over the girlfriend of one of those left behind in the pub. A complaint was published about the monotonous regularity of the same Sunday evening supper, not having been altered for 56 consecutive weeks. A list of promotions was published, with congratulations.

The sports section announced that during one of the recent trips there were four famous sports personalities among the passengers. They were: Don W. Padgett, formerly with the St. Louis Cardinals; Phil Rizzuto, of the New York Yankees; A. Christoforddis, former lightheavyweight boxing champion of the United States; Andrew E. Goss, former featherweight wrestling champion of the Navy.

A plea for help in finding Pappy Carter's fountain pen, which he claimed had sentimental value, appeared. There was a humorous "Essay on Man, the Woman's Angle," and a counterpoint poem, "The Men's Angle to Women." R.C. Wilson, one of the staff members, published one of his poems, entitled, "Memories," a nostalgic poem to his wife.

On July 21, 1944, while unloading our stock in trade at Hollandia, we were notified that we were now in Squadron Eight of the 7th Fleet Service Force. What difference that made is difficult to determine.

While out of liberty port, the electricians, who were in charge of the movie projector and the performances, would set up their equipment and the screen in the mess hall in the evenings. There were times when the pickings of available films were scarce, and it was then necessary to run a movie for more than the normal two times. In fact, during one "dry" period, for about a month, the only worthwhile film on board was that old faithful John Wayne movie, *Stagecoach*. Evening after evening it was run off, until the crew knew it almost word for word, scene for scene, crisis for crisis. It got so bad that, finally, the electrician who was the night's chosen projectionist, as a last ditch effort to get a rise out of the few crew members present, decided to mix up the several reels constituting the movie. The result was hilarious, and the crew were showing happy faces as the final, but not the ending, reel was run off.

We were bothered quite frequently with planes flying over that did not respond to our recognition challenges. When this happened, we were

13. Supply Run #8: Fumigation

immediately sent to general quarters and were not released until the plane had finally made the proper response. The executive officer finally blew his cool. Many members of the crew saw and heard him standing on the forward-well deck, shaking his fist at one of the disappearing planes and shouting, "You dirty bastards! I know what your game is! I've heard you young smart asses in the officer's clubs, bragging and laughing about not answering the challenge, just to make us go to GQ! Wait until I hear that again. You'll get a piece of my mind!"

That reaction may have been a little hard on the fly-boys. After all, it no doubt got boring cooped up in a plane for hours with nothing to do. They couldn't play marbles or roll a hoop in a plane. And they couldn't kill time by drinking some of that liquor they were ferrying, which was a common practice.

We left Hollandia with empty cargo holds on July 22, bound for Finschafen. The stop at Finschafen was brief, only a few hours, to make an exchange in passengers and mail. Then up anchor again, steaming alone down to Milne Bay, arriving July 25.

This jaunt down the coast of New Guinea was an easy time for the ice machine gang; we were on down-time maintenance in the department, with one man on watch during the off hours. Turn-to hours were spent in the usual manner, with the oilers on cleanup, some minor tasks, and at times helping we three machinist's mates on the machinery overhaul.

With a brief overnight stop at Milne Bay, during which time we discharged passengers and took on more for passage to Brisbane, we weighed and washed the anchor early on July 26. Heading southeast out of the bay, in the routine established by the previous trackings through this part of the trip, we turned south through China Strait, then took the open sea route south. This took us away from the Great Barrier Reef, until time to turn west into Brisbane. The passage was fairly routine, with the usual round of drills, temporary glitches in the ship's machinery, exchange of recognition signals with other ships and planes, and so on. On July 29, we took on the pilot near Caloundra Head, transitted Northwest Channel, then into the Main Channel, into Lytton Rocks Cutting, and into Eagle Farms Cutting. At that point, a tug swung the ship and nudged us up to the Hamilton cold storage docks, where we moored, secured from sea details, and set port routine. Finished with engines.

Brisbane did not seem to have the attraction that Sydney had for having fun on liberty, as I have mentioned before. I do not know why. It might have been the fact that Sydney was an older, established seaport, with more history behind it — a more cosmopolitan city. Brisbane, on the other hand, appeared to be more of a suburban city, with a slightly different attitude. Or it could have been the simple fact that Brisbane had a larger number of shore patrol and military police on the streets. There was a combined Army and Navy prison barracks and farm complex just outside the city. All those factors would no doubt dampen the atmosphere for the visiting sailor on liberty.

"Now hear this! Liberty for the port watch will commence at 1630 and end at 2400!"

Chapter 14

Supply Run #9: Scratch One Army Dock

On the very day that we pulled into Brisbane, there was a change in command for the Service Force, SWPA, when Rear Admiral Robert O. Glover took over. He immediately commenced plans for rolling up the southern installations of the Service Force facilities and relocating them further north to be more available to the advancing forces. The Force now consisted of 109,000 officers and men, 20 bases, and 77 ships of all auxiliary types. As a result, many of the established facilities were broken into smaller elements and scattered throughout the Hollandia, Woendi Island, and other areas. Many units were eliminated as no longer being needed. In effect, August 1944, was a month of drastic and far-reaching changes in the Service Force, of which we were a part.

Prior to that, the Navy's rebels and misfits were detained in any Navy brig which happened to be handy. There were several scattered throughout the SWPA, crowded and lacking in any facilities to rehabilitate the inmates or to use them to advance the war effort. Shortly after the change in command was effected, plans were made, and negotiations completed, to combine the Navy brig with the existing Army brig at Round Mountain, about 40 miles from Brisbane. It had ample capacity to drill, train, and rehabilitate the inmates, with farm land; hog ranch; chicken ranch; dairy; machine shops; shoe, radio, and carpenter's shops; chapel; infirmary; and medical staff. There were also 30 head of riding horses, presumably for the use of the Army officers of the 350 administrative and guard personnel.

And, oh, yes, there was the inevitable rock quarry, without which no military prison facility would ever be complete. Some men were just difficult to rehabilitate.

The weatherman in Brisbane cooperated with sailors from the *Octans,* and we encountered almost springlike weather. At least, there was no appreciable rain to mar our escapades ashore. The stevedores worked around the clock, as usual, to complete our load and get us out of their port. They lost no time in climbing down the hatch trunks and getting to work. But of course, this alacrity did not interfere with their Tea-O and Smoke-O breaks.

Another four men were transferred to the fleet hospital ashore, downed by that old familiar enemy VD. There was the usual exchange of personnel for various reasons; we lost four men and took on four. The shore patrol escorted one passenger-prisoner aboard for transportation, and he was immediately made acquainted with our confinement facilities.

At the request of our captain, a Navy lieutenant and a postal inspector came aboard to inspect our mail handling and shipping facilities. They found everything in order and departed. Our disbursing officer left the ship and returned with 100,000 Australian pounds sterling.

One of the firemen that we had taken aboard on a previous stop there apparently knew his way around Brisbane and had made a few female connections prior to coming with us. On one of our liberty stops in Brisbane, he made contact with some of them and arranged a party for the next liberty. Among those he chose from the ship was a MM2c from the engine room, who told about the party to a group of us gathered atop #4 hatch on our way out of port a couple of days later. The party was a lot of fun, and everyone was having a good time. It did get a little wild at times, but no one was complaining, and when it came time for the party to end, the girls, all of whom lived in the neighborhood, and the men paired up for the night. The fireman and his partner went to bed on the second floor of her house, and it was quite late. When morning came, he awoke to a call from an Aussie Digger, who had been sleeping on a balcony just outside the bedroom, with, "Hey, Yank! Yer mites are callin' yer!"

So he got up, called to his shipmates below the window, and said he would be down in a minute. It was time to get back to the ship, as liberty was over at 0730. He got dressed in a hurry, said good-bye to the girl, thanked the Digger for waking him, and then joined the other men in the street. They started back to the ship, and he asked the leader of the party, "Who was that Digger that woke me up?" He was told, "That's her brother, home on leave from the Burma area."

"Well," said the fireman, "Who is Allen? She kept mumbling about him all night."

"Oh, that's her husband. He's in North Africa." Ah, yes, it was quite a party!

14. Supply Run #9: Scratch One Army Dock

About this time I was reading one of the old issues of *Reader's Digest*, which was available in the ship's library. In that issue, there was a joke about a dialog between a Yank and an Aussie Digger over relations between the Yanks and the Aussie girls. The Yank had asked the Digger what he thought about our showing the Aussie girls a good time when we were in port and if the Digger minded it. His answer was, "Not at all, mite! Yer only sortin' em out fer us!"

Of course, the same process was taking place among us Yanks, although we were not aware of it at the time.

The stevedores were in the last stages of filling the holds, and gunner's mate Hugh was on guard duty at the gate, due to go off at 2400. The men on liberty were straggling back to the ship, reluctantly, but for the most part happy and satisfied. Hugh was watching for his relief to come walking down the wharf from the ship when he heard the noise of a jeep, coming full speed along the street, headed for the gate. It was an Air Force jeep, but driven by a sailor, with another one by his side. Hugh recognized them, so he motioned them through the gate. They drove along the wharf and parked beside #4 hold. One of the men hurried over to the gangplank, went up two steps at a time, saluted the colors aft, then ran back to #4 hold. In quick order, he had the boom rigged over the jeep, with two slings hanging from the hook. The sailor on the dock quickly placed the slings, then signaled for the lift. The deck winches whirred and clanged, and the jeep went up, over the bulwarks, inboard, and atop the hatch. Meanwhile, the man on the dock had come aboard, and raced aft, where an acetylene torch set had been previously positioned. The man was a shipfitter, and his accomplice was a bos'un's mate. They had just acquired a jeep for the ship's use and for the captain.

It took only a few minutes for the shipfitter to cut off both bumpers, bearing the Air Force identification, and a couple of deck hands were then ready to repaint the jeep in Navy gray. A few more minutes and the jeep was no longer identifiable, at first glance, at least.

The operation was a typical example of what I like to call the Military Covert Acquisition System. It is more commonly known as scrounging, or at times, thievery. It took about 45 minutes for the entire operation, starting with hopping into the jeep parked in a street close to the ship. The driver had parked it there, unattended, and had obviously been detained for some other duty. He now had the problem of explaining the loss.

That operation had been formulated several months before, and the two men were constantly on the watch for the opportunity to grab a jeep for the use of the ship. In fact, there was some scuttlebutt on the ship that an attempt had been made several months earlier in the New Caledonia area, but without success.

The jeep was normally carried on the top of #3 hatch while at sea. The officers, the crew, and, occasionally, the captain had the use of it. The mailman used it often to go after the mail. It received much use and was still on board when the ship pulled into San Francisco May 15, 1945.

The last hold had been topped off, the hatch covers were in place, the tarps stretched over them and battened down, and the ship was ready for sea.

On the morning of August 4, guided by a tug and a pilot, the ship threaded its way out of the channel and to the open ocean. The route was getting to be quite familiar. Down in the ice machine room, we were lashing down the last of the carbon dioxide cylinders brought aboard, the compressor was noisily performing its task, and the temperatures in the holds were beginning to stabilize. By evening, we were on our course toward Milne Bay, New Guinea, alone, steaming free, and at standard speed of 12½ knots. By that time in the cruise, things were going along fairly smoothly in the ice machine room. Our problems had either been mitigated somewhat, or we had resigned ourselves to living with them.

Soon after leaving Brisbane, fire broke out in the medical storeroom aft, caused by burning out of old piping in the port passageway outside the medical storeroom. I believe in that area the only piping containing high-temperature fluid would be a steam line. The hottest steam on board the ship was 388 degrees, and I know that a fire could not have started at that temperature. I believe it started from some other source. The loss damage was placed at $25. As fires go, it wasn't much of a fire, but small fires can soon become big fires and destroy a ship.

Approaching Milne Bay, we came into the area of islands and towns with names which were foreign sounding. They were often a mixture of the influences in the past from the British, French, Australians, New Zealanders, local natives, and, lately, Americans. The maps of that period are covered with variations of that mixture, sometimes with more than one name for a location. Just as an example, here are a few of the odd ones:

Gili Gili	Blupblup Island
Mei-Mei Ara Island	Liki Island
Gagidu Hook	Ham Reef
Bam Island	Isu Bobo Island
Karkar Island	Waga

14. Supply Run #9: Scratch One Army Dock

Examples of the Dutch influence are seen in Finschafen, which is Dutch for Finsch Harbor, and Hollandia, which, of course, means Little Holland, or something similar.

We dropped the hook into the mud at Waga anchorage, Milne Bay, mid-morning, August 8, and the two men left off at the base hospital there on the last stop were ready and anxious to come back aboard, presumably cured of VD. Some air freight cargo loaded on board at Brisbane was discharged. I do not know what portion of that cargo's voyage was actually by air, but the leg from Brisbane to Milne Bay was by ship at 12½ knots. Once the air freight cargo was out of the hold, into it went another lot of 502 bags of first class mail and 9 bags of registered mail.

Shortly after noon, August 8, we lifted the hook to the hawsepipe, hosed it down, and headed out of the bay, north around the tip, then northwest up the coast towards our next stop, Finschafen. The trip was fast and uneventful, and we tied up to the side of the USS *Triangulum* (AK-102) the evening of August 9. Hold #1 was opened, and 263 bags of mail were taken out and transferred ashore for the FPO. That completed, it was time to start up the coast for our next stop, Hollandia. Well on our way northwest, as we entered the danger zone, the ship went into Condition 2 watches. Fortunately, the brine coil banks had been defrosted before we had to strip the ice machine gang for service on the guns. Otherwise, we machinist's mates would have had to do it.

After passing two convoys, we entered Hollandia Bay, anchored, and opened the holds to all who were hungry and could provide requisitions and working parties to work the holds.

Our next stop was to be Woendi Island, taking from morning, August 13, to morning, August 14, on Condition 2 watches again, and tying up to the dock at Mios Woendi. That island is part of a group of small islands, comprising an atoll just off the southwestern tip of Biak, Schouten Islands, the whole of which forms a natural harbor, with only one entrance. Inside this ring of reefs there is enough room to anchor the entire Pacific fleet of that time. The reef was exposed at low tide, so that it was then possible to walk completely around the atoll, from one end of the entrance to the opposite end—between tides, of course.

Visible from the ship at anchor, was one very prominent feature on one of the larger islands, a gleaming white cone-shaped mound which appeared to be about 100 feet high. One of the officers inquired of a local Naval officer stationed at the base concerning the purpose and composition of the mound. He was told that it consisted of the skeletal remains of fish, clams, and other sea life, which had formed the major item of food for the natives for hundreds of years.

Another bit of local interest was the presence of a whore house on one of the islands. Its existence was a well-kept secret from the men on the ships anchored in the lagoon, thus reserving its use for the base personnel. That could also have helped to reduce the introduction of VD into the atoll or to keep it under control to some extent. The women were native to the atoll.

The invasion of Biak took place May 27, 1944,[41] and it was considered fairly well under control by July 22, with sporadic enemy actions for several months after that. Woendi Island is just a pin prick on most maps of this area and is not even shown on many maps. Its protected position, out of the way, but near to the larger bases and airfields on Biak, made it ideal as a supply concentration area, which is why we were there. Our forces were hungry, after the fast actions that year as a result of General MacArthur's rapid advances towards the Philippines.

The stop was to be another fast action one, with the working parties from the shore coming aboard and working like mad to get their share of the fresh and frozen goodies. It was all over by afternoon the next day, August 15, and we joined two merchant ships in a convoy escorted by the USS *Thomason* (DE-203), heading back towards Hollandia, on Condition 2 watches, at 7½ knots.

On August 15, 1944, issue #9 of *The Octans Scuttlebutt* was out and in the hands of the crew. On the front page was the following:

ADVICE

Do not become a nun, dear,
    while I'm far away,
Just have a lot of fun, dear,
    slip out each night and play.
The lads I left behind, dear,
    must also have their fling,
Be sure to treat them kindly, dear,
    and dance and laugh and sing.
Be everything you will, dear,
    just pet or flirt or park
With Jack or Joe, dear,
    Be careful after dark,
The years are all too few, dear,
    your happiness to wreck.
But if these things you do, dear,
    I'll break your damned neck!

Some helpful letter-writing suggestions were given to the crew: To be sure to put their name and rating on each page, as required. It appeared that some letters had been known to be put back into the wrong envelopes when the censor was through reading them. That could be very embarrassing.

Other poems in issue #9 received full honors but are too long to repeat here. They were: "Woes of a Civilian, Those Damned Old Corns of Mine"; "Tribute to the Boys of '17"; and "To the Marines Who Died on Tarawa."

In sports, the ship's team clobbered the team from Navy base 134, 11 to 2. In softball, the ship's CPOs beat the officers, 10 to 8, leaving them tied at one game each.

The men being transferred and those receiving promotions came in for the usual well-deserved accolades and or good-byes.

The staff now consisted of:

Editor in chief	Terry L. Howard
Assistant editor	James T. Gray
Associate editors	Leon G. Fuller and Clifford E. Simmons
Cartoonists	C.S. Simmons, P.T. Johnson, E.A. Cowhey, and Bill Woodard
Typists	C.A. Willis, C.A. Reynolds, R.C. Wilson, and C.T. Mathews

At mid-morning, August 16, the escort sent a signal requesting that we send medical aid; they had a casualty on board as a result of a fight between two crew members. One of the engineering staff had been attacked with a wrench. We sent over our doctor, the chief pharmacist's mate, and a first class pharmacist's mate, and then resumed our position in the convoy. About noon, we took them aboard after they had given first aid to the victim. The report from our medical staff after they arrived back on board was that the destroyer escort crew had not had liberty for over 20 months. They were all getting a little edgy, and the fight was the result. The transfers took place by means of the typical Navy highline between ships (see page 227). We then went to full ahead both engines and caught up to the convoy.

Another stopover was made at Hollandia, anchoring in the bay the afternoon of August 17. We signed on one new crew member from the base ashore and took aboard 26 boxes of captured enemy ordnance (souvenirs to grace veterans' future dens or family rooms?). Our disbursing officer received into his safe-keeping 6,832 Australian pounds sterling from the disbursing officer ashore. While all this activity was taking place above decks, reefer and frozen cargo were being moved from the holds to lighters and trucks alongside the ship for ships in the harbor and cold storage boxes ashore.

All food requirements had been met by the night of August 18, the holds closed up, the hatch plugs in place, the tarps on top and battened down, and ready for sea. The *Octans* raised the anchor in late evening and proceeded out of the bay to join with our escort, HMAS *Gascoyne* (K-354), for the run down the coast to Madang, our first call at that port.

The Australian Army had captured Madang and Alexischafen areas the last half of April 1944.[42]

Steaming at 12½ knots, the *Octans* and her escort made good time down the coast, without incident, and anchored in Alexischafen Harbor, the morning of August 20. The working parties from the ships in the harbor came aboard and commenced unloading our cargo one hour after we dropped the hook into the mud. Several hours later, one of the men from LST 474 missed his footing and fell from the lower 'tween deck to the orlop deck in #4 hold, a distance of about seven feet. Our medical staff diagnosed the damage as contusion of the scalp. He was given first aid and returned to his job.

At midnight, the holds were closed up, the hatches were covered, and the ship was getting ready to leave again. One hour later, we were underway for Langamak Bay, Finschafen, alone, under Condition 3, at 13 knots. The trip was routine and uneventful until we approached the dock at Langamak Bay, late afternoon, August 22. There was no tug available — there seldom is at these forward bases — so we were attempting to maneuver into our mooring by use of the twin screws on the ship. This can be a very tricky business, as there are two throttles, two reversing gear levers, and the engine room telegraph to be answered on orders from the bridge. This takes a great deal of coordination and practice. One slip in the chain of command and control, and disaster can be the result. In this case, it happened.

When approaching the dock from our port bow position, something happened in the engine room, and the ship tore into the dock about 90 feet from the end, doing considerable damage to the dock. The ship suffered only a slight dent in the side just abaft the bow, and the removal of some paint. So we backed off and tried again closer to shore, making it up to the dock this time. As a result of the mishap, one of the machinist's mates in the engine room was removed from his throttle station and given other tasks. It did not appear to affect his promotion in rating at a later date, however. There were no injuries to personnel, and a report was duly made in accordance with Navy regulations.

According to later information which I received, the report of that incident blamed it on low steam pressure at the steering engine, caused by excess activity on the deck winches which were in use at the same

14. Supply Run #9: Scratch One Army Dock

time. One steam line served all the winches and the steering engine. I wondered why, then, was a machinist's mate second class relieved of his station on the throttles and made to feel responsible for the mishap?

Working parties came aboard, the crew opened up the holds, the fans were secured to those holds being worked, and portions of our cargo were consigned to those having requisitions. At noon on August 23, we were underway again, this time for Milne Bay. Our course was southeast along the coast, tying up in the afternoon of August 24. This was our usual last stop before heading south for another load. The working parties swarmed aboard and dove into the holds with a will to help us get rid of the rest of the food that was sorely needed by both the local base personnel and the ships in the harbor.

Fresh water at sea is always a worry of the officers in the wardroom, and the consumption was watched very closely. The situation was aggravated by the unpredictable passenger load often carried, which made it difficult to maintain an adequate water supply at times. This meant that the use of the crew's shower and washroom had to be regulated, with penalties applied to those who violated the restrictions. On the trip down the coast from Finschafen, four men were caught taking showers at an unauthorized time, so the captain held report mast to hear their cases. The result was one warning, one loss of three liberties, and two loss of one liberty each.

Finally, August 25, all cargo was out of the holds, and it was time to shut down the ice machine and all cooling systems to the holds and to go into our down-time routine. At 1058, the last spring line was taken aboard. The ship backed away from the dock, swung around, and headed east out of the bay, south into China Strait, then out of the Strait and south towards Brisbane. The ship was on Condition 3, standard speed was 13 ½ knots. Right after midnight, it was necessary for the ship to stop for about three minutes and then alter course to avoid hitting two unidentified ships off the port bow.

Down below in the ice machine room, we had but one day to perform any maintenance tasks required, so we rushed to get them done. This required shutting off the compressor valves, both suction and discharge sides. Finally, when we were ready to start the machine up again, the chief opened the steam throttle, the engine started moving, and immediately a gasket blew out on the discharge line from the port compressor, spewing carbon dioxide into the room. The chief closed the steam throttle valve and announced "Everyone out of the compartment!" We all rushed into the shaft alley; then the chief looked around at me and suggested we go back in to see what had happened. We both rushed back, checked to see where the gas was coming from, and found that we had neglected to open the discharge valve on the line from the port compressor. The copper gasket could not stand the high pressure. There was nothing we could do until the gas had all blown out of the system. So we started the exhaust fan and joined the rest of the gang on deck to wait for the compartment to clear out. We had lost the entire charge in the port compressor, but we had sufficient reserve in the shaft alley to give the system another charge. We soon had the machine working again, and the holds started coming down to the required temperatures in time for loading at Brisbane.

The remainder of the trip south to Brisbane was without further incident, and we tied up to the Hamilton cold storage docks the morning of August 29. As we tied up, the captain gave orders to have "his" jeep put over on the dock. Our old friend Ensign Fraser came up to him and said, "Oh, captain, guess what I just did!"

"No. What did you do?" asked the captain.

"I painted the jeep!" was Ensign Fraser's reply. It was still wet, and did not dry for several hours. The captain went ashore without it, and the crew's mail was late that day.

Set Condition 4 watches. Finished with engines. Secure boilers #3 and #4.

Chapter 15

Supply Run #10: To the Pits

"Now hear this! Liberty for the port section will commence at 1630, ending at 0730 tomorrow morning!" This announcement came over the loudspeakers shortly after noon. But first, we disembarked our military passengers, a mixed lot of American, Australian, and Netherlands East Indian servicemen. The deck force must have been happy to see them leave because that contingent was more than the normal complement of the ship's personnel. They made quite a difference in the work of running the ship. Even though the enlisted passengers were restricted to certain areas on the ship, they were still a problem for some of the ship's crew. Down below, we didn't notice it too much; they were not allowed below deck, except when on working parties.

Within two hours after docking, the deck force opened the holds, and the dock stevedores started loading all four holds. Brisbane was the port of export for the meat and reefer produce grown in the Queensland area to the west of the city. The Hamilton cold storage warehouses were the repository for the food until the ships were available to carry it away. The Hamilton docks were about two miles from the meat processing plants and the Abattoir Dock, so the odor this time in port was not as noticeable as when we tied up at the Abattoir Dock.

The second day in port, August 30, six members of the crew transferred to the receiving barracks ashore for duty elsewhere. They were all from the engineering division, most of whom had just recently been promoted in rating. At 1400, the captain held report mast and reduced by one rating a seaman who had struck a petty officer. Another man, a fireman who was charged with insubordination for failing to carry out his duties and to relieve the watch properly, was also reduced in rank.

Liberty for the starboard section started at 1630 to end at 0730 the next morning. I went ashore and followed my usual routine of walking around, stopping into a restaurant for the usual "styke and eyggs," then going to a movie. There were very few stories going around the ship about anyone having a roaring time in Brisbane. Usually, after leaving a liberty port, there would be bull sessions among the crew, telling their stories of what a glorious time they had ashore. But very seldom did this happen in the case of Brisbane. This time in port, there was only one case of a member of the crew being brought back aboard by the shore patrol, charged with fighting with the shore patrol.

On August 31, a CPO was transferred to the fleet hospital ashore for treatment of VD. Also, the CPO who had overstayed his liberty by over 20 days in June was reduced to first class petty officer. That day, one of the deck force, while opening up the hatch for #3 hold, injured his wrist and was taken to the hospital ashore for an X-ray. The wrist was only strained, and he was returned aboard ship for duty.

A letter from home, received a few days earlier up north, told of another man from my hometown who was in the Naval hospital at Brisbane, recovering from an operation. I requested a few hours leave to go ashore and visit him, and the request was granted. I got directions from the OOD and was soon at the hospital and in the ward with him. He was about a year younger than I was and was serving on another former banana boat from the United Fruit Company, mentioned earlier. We had a pleasant time, comparing duties on the two ships and news from home regarding other servicemen and those left behind. I then returned to the ship, happy over the visit.

On Friday, September 1, four men were transferred off the ship, including the CPO who had been reduced to first class petty officer status. One man was sent to the hospital as a VD patient. We transferred one officer and took on another one. The ship's safe was made richer by $322,800 brought aboard by the disbursing officer.

On Saturday, September 2, the ship was filling up on all counts and getting ready for another run up north. Deck cargo was loaded on both well decks and on the hatches, and three more men were transferred off the ship. Another man was found to be drunk and disorderly while on duty and was confined to the brig. We took on another mixed bag of passengers, and one last liberty was granted for the port section.

During the afternoon, a number of RAAF enlisted men carried aboard about 15 large wooden boxes, closely resembling coffins. Each box was so heavy that it had to be carried by six men, using the six handles firmly attached to the sides of the boxes. They were all labeled clearly, in large letters, "Delicate Instruments," and they were deposited in the forward battle dressing station in the fo'c'sle. The door was locked with three locks, each requiring a different key, and each key was placed in the care of one of the officers of the ship. Clearly, the cargo was valuable, and this was bound to excite the curiosity of the ship's crew, giving birth to any number of rumors and suggestions.

A couple of nights after leaving for points north, one of the electricians decided to take a look. He gathered several tools, including a couple of files, and placed them in his belt kit. The night was dark; he went out onto the forward-well deck and proceeded to the fo'c'sle. As he approached his destination, he heard the sound of filing. Could it be that someone else had the same idea?

It was one of the carpenters, filing away at the lower portion of one of the hinge pins on the locked room. Together they filed off the lugs on the bottom of each pin, then pushed out the pins, freeing the door, which could then be opened from the hinge side. The electrician had brought with him four sea bags, and the carpenter had a crow bar, so it took only a few minutes to open some of the boxes. Their efforts were not in vain; the "Delicate Instruments" turned out to be bottles of high-proof brandy, destined for an officer's club being built at Woendi Island. They filled the four sea bags with as much loot as they could carry, about 80 bottles, took them all the way back to the poop deck house, and down the ladder to the shaft alley. Here they lifted up a couple of floor plates, suspended the bags from the floorings, and replaced the floor plates.

Before leaving the fo'c'sle with their loot, they replaced the box covers, closed the door, and replaced the hinge pins. A few nights later, the two men decided to make another raid on the cache, only to find that the locks had been removed, possibly indicating that the officers had also helped themselves. No one knows how many others had raided the store. When the boxes were removed at Woendi Island, they were obviously much lighter.

This was not the only such raid carried on against alcoholic cargo carried on board, consigned to our ally's bases up front in the islands. There were several such incidents during this cruise. Some of the favorite places for hiding the loot were in the empty fuel tanks, inside the hollow firebricks stacked in the fireroom, and similar spots. The officers, of course, could store it in their lockers in their staterooms without fear of being subjected to locker inspection. Obviously, rank hath its privileges, as the old Army saying goes.

During one of the many runs up north, one of the other machinist's mates in my gang went into the brine cooling room while on watch and saw a gallon glass jug snuggling up to one of the coolers. The contents were white in color. Thinking that it was milk, he took a healthy swig. It wasn't. It was liquid soap, which had turned white from the low temperature. That put him in the sick bay for a couple of days.

On September 3, the pilot came aboard at 0745, and soon the ship was swung in the channel, without a tug, and headed for the sea. That was some feat. The ship was 440 feet long, and the channel at that point had a maximum width of 500 feet. But it was accomplished without mishap, and the ship proceeded out of the channel. The pilot was dropped off about noon, and we headed north towards Milne Bay. The trip was without incident, other than taking care of the few breaches of regulations which occurred in Brisbane. A test was made of the ship's electric steering controls and found satisfactory, so the controls were switched back to the hand telemotor system.

We entered China Strait the morning of September 7, exited it 40 minutes later, and headed northwest up Milne Bay, anchoring at Waga anchorage about noon. Almost immediately, 24 new members of the crew were signed aboard, one officer was added to the ship's company, one officer was transferred ashore, and that ended the stop at Milne Bay. The anchor was weighed and washed, and we were underway for Langamak Bay, Finschafen, New Guinea.

At 13½ knots, we steamed past now familiar checkpoints and hove to just inside Langamak Bay the evening of September 8. The base there had been developed into quite a large distribution center for the forces in the area. The supplies included spare parts for equipment to be found on the ships and mobile equipment for operations on the way up to the Philippines. While there, we took aboard a spare crankshaft for the refrigeration compressor for the crew's mess storage boxes. When we unwrapped the "weatherproof" covering, we found the shaft in such bad shape from rust that it could only be used as a last-ditch replacement for a broken original. We gave it some cursory polishing, then rewrapped it and placed it in storage.

No one at the location requested any of our produce, so they must have been recently visited by one of the other reefer vessels on the same run. Two hours after dropping the hook, it was weighed and washed again, and we steamed out of the harbor heading northwest towards Woendi Island for our second visit to that tiny atoll in the Schouten Group. By then, the brine coils in the after holds needed defrosting again.

About two hours out of Finschafen, a steward's mate came down with a recurring hernia problem, so the ship's medical officer, assisted by one of the passengers who was also a medical officer, washed up, donned their robes, took scalpels in hand, and repaired the damaged sailor. This put him out of action for at least one month, possibly longer.

15. Supply Run #10: To the Pits

About noon, Sunday, September 10, the ship veered out of its course to inspect an unidentified floating object, which proved to be nothing but a knarled tree trunk, probably disgorged from one of the rivers on New Guinea as a result of a storm. We resumed course and anchored in Woendi anchorage, Padaido Island atoll, around 1000 on September 11. That morning, the results of three summary court martials held several days previous were posted. There were two reductions in rate and one fine with extra duty hours to be performed.

When we had first made the acquaintance of the forces at Woendi Island, just one month before, we had supplied provender to a Motor Torpedo Boat Squadron, which was headquartered there. Since that time, Ensign Fraser had been thinking very hard and came to the conclusion that those torpedo boats were just what he wanted for his ultimate duty. Now the question was how to finagle a transfer. The answer was in his locker—a quart of whiskey which he had been hoarding for just such an opportunity. As he did not drink such vile stuff, this was an excellent way to put it to use. No sooner thought than done. He went ashore, whiskey bottle in hand, and obtained an audience with the squadron commander. With the aid of the whiskey and his urgent pleas to become a member of the squadron, his wish was granted, providing that the captain of the *Octans* and commander of the 7th Fleet Service Force were agreeable. Ensign Fraser returned to the ship, hopeful of results.

Permission of the captain was no problem—good riddance. Approval from the 7th Fleet Service Force headquarters would take a little more time, so the captain put the official request in motion. Our Ensign Fraser remained on the ship, waiting patiently for the wheels of the bureaucratic machinery to produce, which, eventually it did.

At last we found a demand for our produce which we had cared for so tenderly all the way from Brisbane. The holds were opened, the working parties from the ships in the harbor entered them, and things started to happen with a will. While this was going on, we discharged passengers and took on more, and two were brought aboard under guard, their transgressions not stated. (Perhaps they had just discovered the existence of the clandestine whore house ashore.) While we were taking on oil, the hungry YP's (patrol vessels) were attached to our sides like leeches, taking on all the cargo they could hold.

By now, the thought of all that high-proof brandy swaying from side to side in sea bags in the shaft alley bilges had produced a knowing feeling in those who were in the know. To satisfy the longing, a poker party was organized one night, and the location chosen was in one of the lower fan rooms in a forward hold. There were eight of the thirsty crew, crowded into the tight confines of the fan room, and 12 bottles of the brandy were recovered for the occasion. The holds were still being cooled, at about 45 degrees, which meant that both fans in the room were running. In addition, there could very well have been rats and cockroaches scurrying about.

As the poker game and brandy swilling progressed, the game got wilder and wilder, so they were probably ignorant of their cold, vermin infested surroundings. Ultimately, the party ended with one of the men who was not quite so looped, carrying the others up two flights of ladders, along the deck, into the crew's quarters, and into their bunks. The next morning, one of the men discovered that in addition to a hangover, he had an ugly gash in his scalp where it had gotten banged against the ladder when he was being carried out of the fan rooms.

On September 15, the crew picked up issue #10 of *The* Octans *Scuttlebutt* to read about the idiosyncrasies of some of the crew, ashore and afloat. The poets were given much play in that issue with the following: "The Navy Blue" (author not given); "Memories" by Henry Reed (not to be confused with the poem mentioned in Chapter 13); "The Happy Warrior" by Wordsworth.

Another example of the store of talent and literary material available on the ship is the following:

CENSORED

I've got a gob so far away
And he is hearty and hale—
But how can I send my love to him
When the censor reads the mail?

This gob is, oh, so very grand,
His letters make me thrilly.
But how can I tell him of my love,
When in print it looks so silly?

I hate the thought of tender words,
Read by stranger's eyes,
The soulful words for him alone,
The mush and alibis.

15. Supply Run #10: To the Pits

So, read my letters gently, sir,
They are not meant for you,
But for a gob so far away,
I scrawl this silly goo.

And when you read this letter, sir,
And laugh with wild delight,
Remember that another censor
Reads every word you write.

There were hellos, good-byes, and congratulations for all changes in the crew. There was also a long dialogue in a tongue-in-cheek manner between two Army non-coms, regarding a bleak life in civies and relations with the females whose lives had been changed from working in factories on the home front. The final decision was that life for returning men in uniform was not going to be the same. Possibly, the old order of men and women in the family would be reversed, which would be hard to take.

In sports, the CPOs beat the officers in softball, 10 to 9, and the ship's crew walloped the team from MTB Squadron #12 at softball, 7 to 2.

By late afternoon on September 14, the hungry patrol craft alongside were all satiated, so we closed up shop, raised the hook to the hawsepipe, and headed south out of the anchorage, towards Alexischafen, New Guinea. No sooner had we gotten underway than there was trouble in the engine room. The steam line to the starboard engine had sprung a leak, and it took about an hour to repair it, while we sat still in the water. Then it was full ahead both engines until dropping the anchor in the harbor at Alexischafen about dawn on September 17. Another short stop, just enough time to discharge a few tons of produce out of all four holds. In the middle of the afternoon, it was underway again, for Langamak Bay, Finschafen, arriving there about 0800 the next morning.

Another few tons of food were dropped off there, and some dry stores and miscellaneous cargo were taken on for transportation south. By now, it was getting quite apparent that the center of action in this theatre was moving steadily north, as the stops along the coast of New Guinea were very well provided with our produce. With the seizure of Sansapor, New Guinea, and surrounding areas in early August 1944, MacArthur's left flank was fairly well secured, and he could then start his northern approach to the Philippines. His plans were well underway while we were making our slow, steady hops along this part of the New Guinea coast on this run.

On the morning of September 19, we were underway from the dock at Langamak Bay and headed southeast toward Milne Bay, with still some fresh and frozen cargo to dispense to any takers. Shortly, after passing Ham Reef and Tufi Harbor, at about 0300 the next morning, the weather thickened, and we were hit with a tropical downpour of rain and strong winds. The visibility decreased to about 200 yards, and we slowed to half speed for about 45 minutes. Then the storm abated to a visibility of about one mile, at which time we resumed standard speed. The anchor was dropped at Waga Anchorage, Milne Bay, about noon, and then raised so we could proceed to the dock. The cargo started flowing from the holds onto the dock, the last of our offering on that run.

It was at Milne Bay that a lieutenant commander came aboard as a relief for our present captain. The change in command was not due to take place until later, as the relief had to take time to become acquainted with the ship and its personnel.

At dawn on September 22, we were underway again, for Townsville, Australia, heading east out of Milne Bay, south through China Strait, then southwest towards our destination. Again, soon after hitting the open sea, we had to slow down as one of the seawater circulating pumps had failed, causing the engines to lose part of their power from loss of exhaust vacuum. It only took 30 minutes to make the necessary repairs, and we were back up to full speed again. On September 23, we passed through the outer fringes of the Great Barrier Reef and started south inside the reef, along the coast, past Fitzroy Island and Russell Island, to anchor in Cleveland Bay at Townsville. During the few hours we were anchored there, the captain and his relief-to-be held material inspection of the ship.

The normal population of Townsville was about 10,000 prior to the war. It lies inside Cleveland Bay, with Cape Cleveland protecting the harbor from the northeast and Magnetic Island protecting it from the north. The bay is rather shallow, and entrance to the city's wharves is only through Platypus Channel. The pilot came aboard, the *Octans* entered this channel, then turned to port into the swinging basin and up to the Overseas Cargo Shed on the Eastern Breakwater, where we moored. The city lies on the edge of a shallow, swampy plain, with several hills rising from the plain. The city itself is dominated by, and surrounds, Castle Hill, which is about 940 feet elevation.

Townsville is one of the export ports for agricultural and meat products which are produced to the west and which could not readily be shipped to larger ports farther south, such as Brisbane. The problem was the narrow-gauge railroads prevalent in Queensland. Melbourne, Victoria, was well served by numerous wide-gauge rail systems, and Sydney, New South Wales, was served by a fairly large network of "standard" gauge railroads. It was a logistic and transportation nightmare. The Townsville cargo-shed area was not too conveniently placed with respect to the center

15. Supply Run #10: To the Pits   197

of the city, and the transportation for liberty men was rather poor, from what some of the returning men told me.

In fact, relative to Sydney, Townsville was, for those on liberty, the pits. The reason for this was simply that there was a shortage of girls, a shortage of beer, and an overabundance of Army military police. The MPs were there because Townsville was the area headquarters for the U.S. Army Base Section II, Services of Supply, along with our 5th Air Force. Garbutt Field outside of Townsville saw a great deal of activity in former months as B-17s took off and landed during the early stages of our northward movement of the war. At the peak of the activity, the total population was approximately 100,000. Normally, Townsville in peacetime had the appearance of one of our country's western cattle towns of the 1890s.

The activity for the Army and Air Force bases had decreased somewhat when we first arrived, as the general movement for our forces had commenced its northward deployment out of Australia. Because our Navy had an ammunition dump in the area, there were a few of our shore patrol stationed there also.

Our forces also operated a POW camp there, as three of our E Division men discovered the first night ashore.

End of another run. Finished with engines. Secure sea detail. Liberty for the starboard section to commence at 1630, to end at 0730 the next morning. It didn't look like much of a liberty town, so I didn't go ashore. Many did, and a few managed to work up some excitement — at some cost to themselves, as we shall see in the next chapter.

Chapter 16

Supply Run #11: Change of Command

Soon after the liberty party had left the ship in Townsville, the remaining deck force opened holds #3 and #4, and the stevedores started transferring the frozen meat from the dock into the holds. At 0800 muster September 25, three men were missing but were returned to the ship by the shore patrol just before noon. They were made prisoners-at-large, pending charges from the shore patrol headquarters ashore. They had spent the night as "guests" of the local POW camp among the Japanese prisoners.

One of the civilian stevedores while working in #4 hold was pinned against a bulkhead by a swinging cargo net. He refused aid by our medical staff, and he was taken to the Townsville City Hospital by their ambulance. He was probably well covered by medical insurance and felt better about going to the local hospital. Australia had broad medical insurance coverage, but it no doubt had to be handled by their own facilities.

About dawn on September 26, a tug was made fast to the starboard bow, all spring lines were cast off and pulled aboard, the ship was swung in the channel, headed toward the sea through the channel, past Cape Cleveland, and southeast along the coast, inside the Great Barrier Reef. At 1600, the captain held report mast for the three "POWs." The shore patrol had charged one of them with assaulting a woman and the other two with forceful entry of a room and threatening the occupant. No charges had as yet been reported by the civil and military police at Townsville. The three men were continued on shipboard restriction pending further charges.

Soon after we left Townsville, with captain's report mast over, on our way south to Brisbane, the lieutenant commander who was destined to replace our captain, called one of the men, Jim, an electrician's mate restricted to the ship, into his cabin. The officer wished to have some improvements made in the lighting in his cabin. The changes were not "legal," but Jim and the lieutenant commander came to an agreement during the course of the conversation, and the changes were installed.

Our course was generally southeast until we passed Fraser Island, then we turned south along the coast, entered the channel leading into Brisbane, and tied up at Hamilton Wharf the evening of September 28.

At 0915 the morning of September 29, 1944, all hands not on watch were directed to assemble on the forward-well deck in dress blues. It was spring in Brisbane, the weather was hot, and the men were sweating in the sun while the captain gave a brief speech, handing over the ship to the new lieutenant commander. The new captain of the ship gave a brief speech of acceptance and then announced, "Now, get out of those damned dress blues!" With that, all hands were dismissed.

There no doubt were some alterations in atmosphere and policies noted among the officers in the wardroom and others working in officer's country, but from the main deck and below, we detected practically no difference in the day-to-day activities, which meant that the ship was fairly well run.

We took on no provisions at Brisbane this stop, so at 1500 on September 19, the tug swung us in the narrow channel and pointed us out toward the sea again, and without any liberty, yet. I am certain that some of the crew may have been a little upset about that, but I didn't mind too much.

Steady steaming south for two days without incident brought us into Sydney Harbor approaches, past Outer North Head, Bradley Head, Robertson Point, Fort Denison, Kiribilli Point, under the Harbor Bridge, then a swing to port, and into Berth #9, Central Wharf, Sydney, at mid-morning, October 1. Four hours later, the deck hands opened up holds #1 and #2, and the dock hands started loading reefer cargo into the holds.

"Now hear this! Liberty for the port section will commence at 1630 and end at 2400!" Our two-man contribution to the shore patrol forces left the ship about the same time.

This stay in Sydney I rated two liberties and took both of them. The first night ashore I called Joyce and made a date for the following liberty, two nights hence. It was spring in Australia, the weather was balmy, and the nights pleasant, with just an occasional light shower. Just walking through the parks, striking up conversations with girls, a fireman from the auxiliary gang and I managed to kill the first night and had a lot of fun doing it. We were both in the same situation; he had made a date with his "steady" from the last time in Sydney. It was the same type of game practiced back home before the war, walking around in groups on summer evenings, meeting girls, also in groups, sometimes stopping them to banter comments, compliments, and suggestions back and forth. The end result was always unpredictable. On this night in Sydney, we took up with two girls who were lively, interesting to talk to, but no nonsense. This was all right, as we were only interested in a little pleasant association. We met them outside of a cinema, and they were on their way to take the train from Hyde Park station. It took a long time to walk from the cinema to the station. By then, it had been a long time from our "styke and eyggs" after leaving the ship, so we stopped off at Ziegfeld's to see if there was anything new going on there. We had our midnight supper, then went back to the ship and turned in to get a good night's sleep. I had to go on watch the next morning.

The next afternoon, I happened to see one of the seamen on deck who had been at Ziegfeld's the night before. We got to talking about the joint, and I mentioned that I saw him dancing with one of the "regulars" there, and he told me about his experiences after that. He walked her to her flat, and she invited him to stay for awhile. When they got into the flat, he noticed it was very sparsely furnished, but there was a child's crib, with a crying child in it, a boy of about two years old. There was no sitter in sight, and the boy was hungry. She was the mother, and she said the father was in North Africa, and the last allotment check from the government was late. She started to fix a bottle for the boy, then discovered she was out of milk for him. There was no other food in the flat for him, either, and very little for her. At that time of night, there was no place open to buy food except at an all-night restaurant at King's Cross. So he walked to it, bought some milk for the boy and something for her breakfast, and then took the food back to her flat. She thanked him and fed the boy. He said good night, then left and came back to the ship, after leaving her all of his remaining cash. As you can see, we weren't all "Bloody Yanks."

The new captain decided that the three men on restriction were being punished too severely, especially as no charges had been received from the Townsville police or the U.S. MPs stationed there. He called Jim, the electrician's mate, up to his cabin, and told him that he and his two mates who were restricted were to get their liberty cards and go ashore. There was some opposition from the executive officer, but the captain overrode it. He told the men to be back by 2330, but they did not get back until 0700 the next morning. The executive officer marched them up to the captain as soon as they reported aboard. The captain was

16. Supply Run #11: Change of Command

roaring mad over the breech of faith on the part of the three men and insisted they explain their actions.

The electrician's mate said he understood that they had had until 0730 in the morning, not 2330. The captain shook his head, dismissing them. No further charges were made, as they were still under confinement from the previous captain's report mast, so more was to come. At 1100 on October 7, the new captain held his own report mast, and the three men were given two days each confinement for creating a disturbance ashore. The confinement consisted of being placed in the brig immediately, and released two days later as we left Brisbane. So they missed liberty in Brisbane this time in. In exchange, they got ashore in Sydney for one night.

My date with Joyce on the second liberty established a pattern. I met her at the train station, we walked around, talking and enjoying the spring evening until she made up her mind as to what she wanted to do and which cinema she wanted to attend. She was very interesting to talk to, had a very keen mind, but sensible, and we spent a lot of time just bantering back and forth about different subjects. Believe me, there were a lot of differences between the Aussies and the Yanks upon which to base a discussion. Yes, we smooched a little, but she made me keep my place, for which I respected her. She could not stay out too late, as she had to get up early to go to her job in a mustard factory. Just a common working girl, but she appeared to be somewhat above what one normally expects from factory workers. She still lived with her parents, so they kept a close watch on her hours. Consequently, I saw that she got to her train on time after each date.

The third day in Sydney, the Navy diving barge came alongside, and a diver went down to inspect the screws and the stern tubes where the shafts passed through the hull. Both stern tubes had been leaking badly for some time as evidenced by the amount of bilge pumping required in the shaft alley, aft of the ice machine room. On October 5, we steamed over to a drydock at Cockatoo Island at the mouth of the Parramatta River where two tugs nudged us into place gently, then left us inside. The ends of the dock were closed, the water pumps were started up and kept running until there were only a few feet of water left in the dock, with the keel resting on the blocks in the bottom of the dock and timber shoring along both sides of the ship to keep us in an upright position. As soon as the stern tubes were accessible, the dockyard workers commenced checking the propellers, stern tubes, tail shafts, and zinc anticorrosion plates. The propeller hubs and caps were in good condition. There was some pitting on the propellers but not enough to cause any worry. The clearance between the tail shafts and the lignum vitae wood bearings were barely acceptable. Both stern tube packing glands were repacked; the old packing was in poor condition and badly worn.

Boilers #1 and #2 were on the line to provide the ship's lifeblood, one circulating pump brought in seawater from the drydock, and this water was being discharged above the waterline, back into the dock. While the dockyard workers were working on the stern tubes, the engineering force overhauled nine valves on the seawater lines which discharged above the waterline.

The morning of October 6, the water was started into the drydock, and the ship became waterborne two hours later. A pilot and a tug nursed us out of the drydock and pushed our nose in the right direction. We headed under the Harbor Bridge, out of the harbor and into the open sea on our way to Brisbane. The first day out of Sydney, the captain disposed of three cases of AOL men. The remainder of the trip was routine, dodging the impediments to navigation along the coast, then, after being swung around by the tug, steaming up the channel to the Hamilton cold stores wharf at Brisbane, October 8. In two hours, cargo started flowing into the holds to fill the few voids left from our stop at Sydney. With the holds filled with fresh and frozen goodies for the forces up front, we cast off the last of the mooring lines, pulled away from the dock the afternoon of October 9, and carefully negotiated the dredged channel to the open sea. The course was almost due north, at a standard speed of 13 knots.

Friday morning, October 13, early, the captain and navigator were on the bridge. The chart showed shoal water ahead, so they rang up "Half Speed Both Engines." Forty minutes later, the lookouts spotted breakers dead ahead, so both engines were stopped, then put into "Full Astern, Both Engines" for four minutes, then stopped. In a few minutes, the engines were started again, "Slow Ahead," and the ship made a 90 degree turn to starboard, then straightened on a new course to eastward at 13 knots. We followed the barrier reef, which is the southern boundary of Cormorant Channel, until we found Jomard Passage into the channel. From there it was north around the D'Entrecasteau Islands, northwest along the coast of New Guinea, past Bam and Blupblup Islands, and into Hollandia Bay Monday morning, October 16. After lying to in the bay for four hours, we were directed to come into the dock to unload passengers and cargo. The USS *Arathusa* (IX-135) yard tanker came alongside and took aboard some of our offerings of food, then cast off. This transaction completed, we were sent out into the bay again to anchor and dispense more fresh and frozen produce to the ships in the harbor.

For another two days, the cargo kept flowing out of the holds and into the lighters alongside. Then, the morning of October 20, the pilot was taken aboard, the sea details were set, and we were underway for

16. Supply Run #11: Change of Command

Woendi Island in the Padaido Atoll, near Biak in the Schouten group, again.

Four hours out of harbor, general quarters was sounded to hold firing practice again. This time it was very short, four rounds of 3-inch and 21 rounds of 20mm — hardly worth fouling the gun bores for this exercise. Due to the salt sea air and the tendency of gunpowder to leave corrosive residue in the gun barrels after firing, they all had to be thoroughly cleaned after each firing, regardless of the number of rounds fired.

Right after one such drill, gunner's mate Hugh was up in the #1 20mm gun position cleaning the gun. To do so, it was necessary to remove the barrel and breech assembly, which weighed well over 100 pounds. In so doing, there was a catch to be released, which he did but did not follow the prescribed procedure correctly. The result was that a powerful spring ejected the entire barrel assembly out, which took a downward arc, landing muzzle first in the wood deck below, where it stuck in an upright position.

That deck space was one of the captain's favorite pacing stations, and he just happened to be there when the barrel stuck in the deck, some steps behind him. He did not look around but kept on his measured pacing, not even hesitating at the sound of the accident.

At 1900, one of the passengers was stricken with an attack of appendicitis, so the ship's doctor performed an appendectomy on him; the surgery went well. This was good for at least one month relief from duty.

It was just a short jaunt from Hollandia, and we tied up to the dock at Woendi Island the morning of October 21. The mail was sent ashore to the FPO, 136 sacks of it, and most of the passengers, including the hospital patient recuperating from the appendectomy, were put ashore here. The working parties came aboard to relieve us of more of our cargo of goodies.

Early on the morning of October 22, we anchored out in the bay to resume discharge of cargo. For two hours, the cargo handlers worked steadily and fast, hoisting the full nets up out of the hatches, swinging them over the side, and lowering them into the lighters alongside, where another crew unloaded them. By each hatch was a storekeeper, checking off each crate or box as it was transferred. Every parcel of food was accounted for, but I wonder how they listed the ones that showed signs of being opened.

Considering the availability of the food in the holds, it is surprising how little of it we actually consumed on watch. The ship fed us fairly well, and it was possible to scrounge from the night galley watch at times, as long as the requests were reasonable. Most of the use of the hot plate in the ice machine room was to keep the coffee pot hot. In fact, there was a standing joke in the gang that before we would accept any new replacement for our gang, he had to be able to make good coffee. The engine room and the fireroom each had their own setup for relieving their hunger pains on watch, but it was cooler in the ice machine room, so the assistant engineer often came in to help himself. Of course, he also had the responsibility for our department, so he had a valid reason for appearing any time he felt like it. We did not mind; he was pleasant to talk to and easy to get along with. Later he was promoted to chief engineer, and we did not see him quite as often, but we had a CPO over us then.

Whoever had produced the ship's equipment allotment had overlooked some of the other men on watch in the engineering division, with their long, lonely, and, at times, boring watches below decks. One of the traditional items needed by those poor souls on watch was a hot plate for brewing that old standby, Navy coffee — strong, so strong that at times you suspected that someone had put his old dirty socks in the brew with the coffee.

Food could always be scrounged, as I mentioned, but it was no good without means for cooking it, or at least warming it up. That was where the ingenuity of the electricians came in handy. They had access to the necessary materials, such as resistance heating wire, cords, switches, and connections, and the stacks of firebrick in the fireroom. The bricks were soft enough that they could be gouged and chiseled sufficiently to accommodate heating coils and switches and the electric leads to supply them. Result: ugly but serviceable and usable electric hot plates. The demand for them was great. It was so great that one night down below, the lights began to dim throughout the machinery spaces, and it was a few minutes before the culprit was traced to these same unauthorized hot plates. Needless to say, the word was soon passed around for the men to use more discretion, and there was no longer any problem from them.

All orders for our produce had been filled by 1600 on October 22, so the crew closed up the holds again, placed the hatch plugs in place, drew the tarps tight over them, and battened down the edges. Then we were underway for a stop at Seeadler Harbor at Manus Island in the Admiralties, almost due east from Woendi Island, alone, at standard speed of 13½ knots. The second day out of Woendi Island, the captain held report mast for minor infractions of discipline perpetrated by two members of the engineering division, with only a warning being issued in each case.

Issue #11 of *The* Octans *Scuttlebutt* was released to the crew on October 23. Two days before publication, a U.S. Army Air Force plane had buzzed the ship several times, causing some consternation among the

16. Supply Run #11: Change of Command

officers and crew. The *Scuttlebutt* explained that our own Feldman, SM1c, was aboard the plane, piloted by his brother, and they were just out joy-riding.

The following poem appeared:

GOVERNMENT ISSUE

Sitting on my G.I. bed,
My G.I. hat upon my head,
My G.I. pants and G.I. shoes,
Everything free and nothing to choose.
G.I. razor, G.I. comb,
G.I. wish I were home.

They issue everything I need,
Paper to write on and books to read,
They issue food to make us grow,
G.I. want a long leave.

My belt and shoes and G.I. tie,
Everything free and nothing to buy,
My food is served on G.I. trays,
My meals are served at G.I. rates.

It's G.I. this and G.I. that,
G.I. haircut and G.I. hat,
Everything here is Government Issue,
All but you, dear, G.I. miss you.

A biography of our new captain was given, with his long and varied Naval background. The list of new advances in rating was given, with congratulations proffered. Old hands recently transferred were listed and wished "Bon Voyage," while the new replacements were properly welcomed. The new hours for the geedunk stand were posted, and a long essay on the Statue of Liberty was printed. A two-page essay on what one could do with 40 acres of land offered several suggestions, with the most astute one being "sell it." Other suggestions were: take another job while farming it, buy an additional 80 acres and farm both lots, start a chicken ranch, and, last of all, put your wife to work on it since there aren't very many fat farm wives.

The final offering for that issue was a complete, two-page summary of the Servicemen's Readjustment Act of 1944, giving details of the "52-20 Club," veteran's educational benefits, and GI loans for buying homes and farms.

The morning of October 25, we eased into the dock at Seeadler Harbor and tied up fore and aft. The working parties came aboard to fill their orders from our larder. Then, early in the morning of October 27, all food commitments were completed for that stop, and it was out of the harbor, bound for Langamak Bay, Finschafen, alone again. We moored up to the dock there the morning of October 28. No sooner had the working parties started their task than one of them, a sergeant, got his hand caught between two pieces of frozen cargo and lost a fingernail. He was given immediate treatment by our doctor, and he went back to work. I knew that Army sergeants went on working parties, but didn't realize they actually pitched in. His loss of a fingernail didn't hold up the operation of unloading our cargo; by 1700 all demands for food had been satisfied, and the holds were closed up in the usual tight fashion by the crew.

When we pulled out of Seeadler Harbor at Manus the morning of October 27, we left behind a bustling wartime harbor with a large fleet supply center. We were not to know, of course, of the catastrophe which would hit the harbor about two weeks after our departure. It was one that seemed destined to occur frequently when there is a major war. Shortly after 0830, November 10, 1944, the USS *Mount Hood* (AE-11), an ammunition ship anchored in the harbor, suddenly blew up. The ship had been launched in 1943 and commissioned into the Navy in July 1944, from a standard C2-S-AJ1 hull, containing five holds; she was on her first productive run. Her cargo was primarily 3,800 tons of explosives for the fleet in the SWPA, consisting of ammunition for guns .30 caliber up to 14 inch, bombs from 100 pounds to 1,000 pounds, depth charges, rockets, pyrotechnics, and other miscellaneous sensitive explosives. The ship, along with 295 crew members on board, completely disappeared, with the exception of a piece of the hull found in the crater beneath the ship, such crater measuring about 300 feet long, 50 feet wide, and 40 feet deep. There were 43 other ships and numerous small boats either demolished or damaged, all within a radius of 2,200 yards from the *Mount Hood.* The only crew members who survived were 18 ashore on duty at the right time. In addition, there were 45 others known dead, 6 missing, and 360 injured.

A Board of Investigation was convened, and their report was issued in February 1945, containing over 1,000 pages of testimony, investigative reports, and the board's findings. Testimony disclosed that operating, cargo handling, and general safety measures on board were very lax, and that was determined to be the deciding factor for the accident, all other possibilities being ruled out.

Obviously, the concern shown when we were in a convoy beside an ammunition ship, described in an earlier chapter, was well founded.

The 7th Fleet Service Force at the time was having difficulty keeping the fleet supplied with ammunition, due to the rapid advances being

16. Supply Run #11: Change of Command

made northward toward the Philippines and Japan. They were forced to call upon shipments from wherever ammunition had been stored—from Australia, New Guinea, and the States. So it was difficult to determine the origin and age of some of the ammunition stored on board any ship at that time, as not only ammunition ships but also general cargo vessels were being pressed into service to keep the ammo flowing northward. The net result of those conditions was that much of the ammo being used by the fleet had been handled several times and stored at various locations, sometimes not under the best conditions, prior to being loaded into the magazines of the fleet.

Bright and early the morning of October 29, we were underway from Finschafen for Milne Bay, that last stop which had become so familiar to the crew that it was another routine passage, marred slightly by the gyrocompass failing again.

There is a distinctive landmark somewhere along the northern New Guinea coast, which could be seen for miles. It was an island almost wholly occupied by a cone-shaped volcanic mountain. There was always a slow, lazy whiff of smoke being emitted from the cutoff cone top, giving the impression of another sleeping volcano waiting to surprise the world by a violent eruption. It never erupted while we were in the South Pacific, and I don't recall ever reading anything about it in the news since then; so I would imagine that it is still there, the same as when we saw it, discharging its whiff of smoke.

About noon on October 30, Waga, Milne Bay, received our hook into its bed of muck and mud with the violent rattle of the anchor chain. Shortly thereafter, the anchor was brought up, washed down, and hoisted into the hawsepipe, and we proceeded into the dock, where we moored and opened shop. We did not have much left by then, having supplied all those hungry ships for the past four stops in two weeks. It only took about three hours for the work parties to clean us out, so we could shut the ice machine down with a last sigh, a whoosh, and a gasp from the driving steam pistons.

The spring lines were singled up at about 0730 on October 31, at 0800, the last line was cast off, and we were on our way to Brisbane again. East by southeast out of Milne Bay, south into China Strait, then past Isu Bobo Point, Manu Pisina Rocks, and Isu Mina Point, and we were out of China Strait, headed southwest toward our destination, alone and steaming free at 13 knots, down through the Coral Sea. We skirted the Great Barrier Reef until clear of it, then turned southwest to enter the Brisbane Channel shortly after midnight on November 4. At about 0700, the tug swung our ship and nudged us up to the Hamilton cold storage wharf for a temporary mooring. We took aboard two new crew members and transferred two. One of the latter was Ensign Fraser. The authorization for his transfer was waiting in Brisbane when we pulled in, and there was joy on the bridge and in the wardroom, which added immensely to the pleasures contemplated for the next four weeks in Sydney during another overhaul. He left the ship with his baggage, and a sigh of relief was heard on the upper decks. They were free of him at last — or so they thought.

On November 1, 1944, while on the run south from Milne Bay to Brisbane, the bridge was notified that another change had been made in the administration of the 7th Fleet Service Force, and we were now in Squadron Nine. This made no difference in our operations that was discernible outside of the bridge, and I doubt it made much difference there either.

Brisbane was another brief stopover. About eight hours after tying up to the wharf, we were on our way again, out of the channel, southbound for Sydney. It was a smooth and happy two-day trip, as the word went around that we were headed for a four-week overhaul in Sydney.

The sky was bright and clear, and the sea was sparkling brilliantly the morning of November 6 as we hove to just outside Sydney Harbor to take on the pilot. Those of us lucky enough to be off watch lined the railing to get a look at what was in store for us the next four weeks. The pilot boat pulled alongside, and the pilot swung deftly onto the sea ladder dropped for him and swiftly and nimbly climbed aboard to take over the conning of the ship into our mooring. As soon as he was over the rail, the engine room telegraph rang "Full Ahead Both Engines." We headed into the harbor, past Man-of-War Anchorage on our portside and Bradley's Head to starboard. We slowed to half speed to allow two tugs to make fast to our sides. They guided and worked us into our assigned berth at Woolloomooloo docks, at 1130, time for noon chow. The atmosphere aboard the *Octans* was one of happiness and expectations, as indicated by the loud and vociferous talking in the crew's berthing area and on the decks.

Then it came. "Now hear this! Liberty for the starboard section will commence at 1630 and end at 0730 tomorrow morning!" Summer in Sydney, money in our pockets, truly, all was right with our little world.

Chapter 17

Overhaul: Thirty Days in Sydney

At 1630, the liberty party was ready and left the ship with much shouting and laughing back and forth among the men. Leaving the dockyard, we split out into different routes into Sydney, each group in search of one or more of the three basic goals: entertainment, refreshments, and the telephones. I was among the latter and managed to reach Joyce right away, but, alas, she was tied up for the evening. Obviously, she had not known the *Octans* was due in port. I joined up with a small group, one I knew would probably not lead me into trouble. Temptation, yes; but trouble, no. As usual, our first stop was at one of the well-known watering spots in King's Cross, just a short walk from the Woolloomooloo docks. Our small group went for the private lounge, where we could sit and talk without being bombasted by a lot of loud-mouthed sailors.

We split up further, and I joined with a machinist's mate third class, formerly a fireman, with whom I had often gone on liberty before. He was the one who had attempted to remain faithful to his wife and had earned the sobriquet "Grandma," but he had decided he wanted a little "harmless" fun while away from home. In fact, this was the same private lounge where he and I had sat several months before when he had met the girl whom he had just talked to on the telephone and made a date for two nights hence. Joyce had agreed to meet me on my next liberty, also, and we would meet at the usual place and time, the Hyde Park station at about 1900. Grandma and I did not double date; we usually split up and went our own ways.

On my next liberty, Joyce and I spent some time talking over dinner, catching up on what had been going on since we had our last meeting. By now, I knew a lot about her family history. She related some of the family legends of the early days of Sydney. Her great-grandparents had left Ireland during the potato famine in the 1840s. She was planning to go further in her schooling, after working a little longer to save enough money to help pay for one of the special courses designed to help girls make their own way in the world. I do not recall what the course was called, as it was in the Australian system of education, which was totally foreign to me. After dinner, we walked around leisurely, talking and teasing each other good-naturedly; then we went to the cinema of her choice. There were mostly American movies showing. After the movie, we sat on a bench in Hyde Park, talked, giggled, and smooched a little, until it was time for her to catch the train home. Then it was a stopover at Ziegfeld's to see what the wilder portion of the ship's crew were up to. It was noisy, as it always was, with a lot of dancing, loud jazz music, table-hopping, joking, some loud talking, and once in awhile, a resounding slap.

At muster the next morning, the results of the first night's liberty were obvious when three men were brought back aboard at 0950, AOL two hours and twenty minutes. They were charged with being drunk, creating a disturbance, using obscene language, and molesting women. I can understand the first three charges as being in the very nature of some of the crew, but for the last charge, it was totally unnecessary in Sydney.

Right after muster, the assistant engineer came below and laid out the work to be done by the gang while we were undergoing the general overhaul. The things on the list were discussed, and the list was posted on the board over the watch desk, just aft of the compressor. The list was quite extensive and would keep us busy for the next four weeks.

I do not have the list of work to be done by the ship's crew in either the engine room, the fireroom, or by the auxiliary gang, but I do know they had their hands full. In addition to regular overhaul work, there was the regular maintenance and housekeeping chores to be performed—in between liberties, of course.

The main change in the ship's arrangement took place in the medical department. The number of ambulatory patients which we had been required to carry had increased dramatically recently, thoroughly taxing our original facilities. This trip into the Woolloomooloo docks was mainly for the purpose of increasing our ability to carry wounded and other hospital patients from the forward areas down to base hospitals for proper care. The result was a much larger medical facility with 30 beds, a pharmacy, and a modernized sick bay. So now we were to double as a hospital ship, without the usual protective identifying marks or designation. In short, we were still fair game for enemy submarines—not that they were known for observing the international conventions.

Arrangements had been made by the ship's service department for a dance to be given ashore, the nights of November 14 and 15. Announce-

17. Overhaul: Thirty Days in Sydney 211

ments were printed and distributed among the officers and crew as requested (see page 212). Two sets were printed, one for each night. This boosted the morale and the spirits of the crew, and the noise level in the crew's berthing area went up several decibels when the word got around.

Liberty the night of November 8 was a little different than usual. I met Joyce at the Hyde Park station, and we walked around for awhile, enjoying the spring climate in the park, and then went to dinner. After that, instead of going to the cinema, the night was so pleasant that we decided to go to the amusement park for the evening. There were quite a few other sailors there also, some in groups and some with their dates for the evening. Everyone, including us, was having a good time. It was spring, we were young, and there were only a few short hours in which to enjoy ourselves, so we made the most of it. It was no different than the average amusement park in the States, with the possible exception of the Aussie accents heard over the music, the loud shouting, and the thrilled whoops and yells of pleasure. When it was time to take Joyce to the station, we walked through Hyde Park, slowly, laughing and talking and delaying as long as possible the good night at the station. Then it was a stop at Ziegfeld's to check the action there. It was the same as every night, only this time I was not hungry, so I gave my meal ticket to one of the girls there, who thanked me gratefully. I gathered she was hungry. Then it was back to the ship and into the sack for a good night's rest of a few hours, and then breakfast and on duty below.

At muster the next morning, November 9, one man was absent, a watertender. In the afternoon, three tugs came alongside and worked us into drydock at Cockatoo Island. By 1900, the ship was entirely exposed, sitting on keel blocks, and shored up with timbers from the ship's sides to the drydock to keep us upright. With the ship exposed in this manner, it was then possible to do some of the maintenance and repair jobs on the lists which could not be done while the ship was waterborne. All services, including telephone, electricity, steam, and freshwater, were supplied by hookups to the dock.

Another man was AOL at morning muster, November 10, and the one AOL from the previous day was still missing. By 1400, both were back on board, the watertender having been arrested by the local constables for drunkenness and malicious damage. Liberty at 1630 found me again meeting Joyce at the station, but it was to be a short evening, as she was a little tired from lack of sleep. We had the usual leisurely dinner, then walked around through some of the local garden spots. I asked her if she would like to go to the ship's dance with me, and she readily accepted, although she knew I did not dance. I explained to her that it could be quite a mess. There was going to be plenty of beer and liquor

> *You are cordially invited to attend a Dance sponsored by the Officers and Crew of a vessel of the U. S. Navy the night of November 14th, 1944, at the Dungowan Ballroom*
>
> Dancing, 8—12 Midnight

Invitation to the ship's dance (author's collection).

around. She said she did not mind and would like to go anyway. Since she was of Irish heritage, and with the Aussie annual consumption of alcohol being one of the highest in the English-speaking world, it is not surprising that she wasn't shocked by my revelations. Their life expectancy at birth is also one of the highest in the civilized world, a fact which the Temperance Movement would do well to consider.

She asked that we not see each other quite so often; it was telling on her disposition at home and at work, due to the lack of sleep. I agreed, reluctantly, to limit my calls to her house for a date. She explained that by the time she got into bed it was well after midnight, and she had to get up at 6:00 in the morning in order to get to work on time. Her parents had suggested that we cool it, and that cinched it. She was old enough to make her own decisions, but she was still living under her parent's roof and her father held the traditional whip in the Irish household. So we said our good-byes at the station a little earlier than usual, and I went back to the ship to hit the sack.

When the word went around the ship that there would be another ship's dance in Sydney, someone started a movement in the crew's quarters to rent a flat (apartment) in Sydney for the week of the dances. The rent and the flat would be shared by about six men each from the starboard and port liberty sections. I went in on the arrangement, partly to satisfy my curiosity as to what was going on. I only used my share twice during the week; and the night of November 12, a Sunday, was the first

17. Overhaul: Thirty Days in Sydney

one. It was a fairly quiet night ashore. The Sunday laws were not conducive to sailors intent on raising hell.

Before liberty was announced, however, the ship left the drydock, assisted by three tugs again, and was pushed and pulled back to the docks at Woolloomooloo, mooring at about 1700. I joined a small group from the ship and we had dinner, then strolled around the streets and parks, much as we did back home on warm summer evenings during our young, carefree days as civilians — oh, so long ago and far away. The evening ended at Ziegfeld's again, for a late supper, then to the flat, where the bed reserved for me was waiting. There were several other sailors sitting around, drinking beer, and just talking and having a good time insulting each other and telling lies, while I turned into my bed and went to sleep.

Tuesday, November 14, was the day of the first dance, for the starboard section. Because of the dance, the ship was requested to furnish eight men for shore patrol, in anticipation of more than the normal rumpus to be expected. They left the ship at 1300 and came back aboard at 0900 the next morning, a total of 16 hours on duty.

Joyce had a quick supper at home, then got all dressed up for the dance. I met her a little after 2000, and we took our time strolling over to the dance at the Dungowan Ballroom. She was really dressed the best I had ever seen her, and it made me sorry that I had never learned to dance. There were no reserved seats that I could see, so we found a convenient table and joined in with those already sitting around, making merry and having a good time. There were refreshments, a buffet, and a fairly good band playing a mixture of American and Australian numbers, alternating between jazz and the local round dance. It was actually a larger version of Ziegfeld's. Joyce was asked to dance several times. I urged her to go ahead, but she refused, probably out of deference to me, which I appreciated. There was the usual table-hopping, eating, and drinking, and there was even a photo studio set up in one relatively quiet room. We had our pictures taken, both together and separately, which we exchanged. The dance lasted until midnight, but we left before that, and I saw her off on the train. She thanked me for taking her and seemed really pleased she had come.

I went to the flat expecting to get some sleep, but the place was in an uproar, with some of the crew trying to get extra beds for their girls. The flat consisted of a large two bedroom affair, in which the kitchenette was not expected to get much use, as the flat was almost exclusively let out to Yanks like us. The bedrooms and parlor were equipped with numerous single, portable beds, as many as could be reasonably accommodated.

The machinist's mate third class, Grandma, with whom I often went on liberty, and his "steady" were there. She had agreed to spend the night with him in the flat. He had been drinking more than he should have and was very loud in his attempts to "protect" her from the other men present. He insisted that her bed be placed against the wall and his next to it, so no one could get to her. She came over to me and quietly asked if I would help her move her bed out of the tight spot she was in after he fell asleep. She said she would come over and wake me up when the time was ripe, and we could then move her bed over next to mine. I agreed, then finally went to sleep.

Morning came and she had never shown up. She and her bed were still in the same spot, next to Grandma's.

I don't remember how we did it, but everyone on liberty for the dance beat the 0730 deadline. Some, I know, just made it with a few minutes to spare. There were dragged-out sailors on board that day, but beneath it all was a feeling of relief and satisfaction, at least for many of the starboard liberty section. There was very little work done the morning after. When my crew came down the shaft alley ladder to report for work, I could see that it would be useless to expect much to be done that day. By the afternoon work session, there was some improvement, and the day was not a total loss in tasks finally accomplished. The mood throughout the ship was relaxation, recovery, and reminiscing.

The eight members of the next shore patrol contingent went ashore at 1300, as before, to take up their posts after getting their assignment from the base headquarters. Right after that, the medical personnel had the captain sign the orders for sending two men to the hospital at the Naval base for treatment of VD. All pleasures carried to extreme carry definite inherent risks. Some people always get caught stepping over the line and have to ask themselves if it was it worth.

The port liberty section went ashore starting at 1630, straggling off the ship, prepared to kill time until the next dance started at about 1900, with the band scheduled for 2000. Judging from the results the next day, that dance was almost an exact duplicate of the previous one. It was another difficult day to get anything done, but it was sure interesting to listen to the many stories going around.

The morning of November 16, we lost our chief engineer, who was being transferred for assignment elsewhere. That meant some changes in the engineering department, which affected the ice machine gang. The assistant engineer was promoted to chief engineer, which left the CPO now in complete charge of my gang. He was a reasonable, levelheaded CPO who was easy to get along with, and there was no friction between us. In fact, he reminded me very much of my father in temperament.

Prior to the chief engineer leaving the ship, his fellow officers took the occasion to hold a farewell party for him in the wardroom. It was quite

17. Overhaul: Thirty Days in Sydney

an affair, with typed invitations to the women they had come to know in Sydney. There was music, dancing, food, and drink for all officers and their dates. The chief was probably unaware that he rated such a send-off, but he was one of the more stable and levelheaded members of the wardroom.

The two dances had the desired effect, for the crew was, for the most part, apparently satisfied and relatively quiet, except for the bull sessions in which the various escapades were related over and over to whomever would stop and listen. Unfortunately, I can only remember two of them. The shore patrol did its job very well, as there were no incidents of drunkenness, trouble making, or molested women reported to the ship as a result of the dances.

A seaman second class related the results of his attendance at the dance to a few of us gathered around the corner table in the geedunk stand one evening. He had met a girl at the dance who had come with another sailor, and he managed to get a date with her for two nights later. In preparation, he had purchased what was available in the line of alcoholic beverage for the evening. He had rented a room in a rooming house well known to the other sailors on the ship, stashed the liquor in the room, and then went to meet his date at the Hyde Park station.

Liquor was being rationed at the time, but those Yankees servicemen who were stationed in Sydney were always able to get the pick of what was available, regardless of the rationing allotment. When our sailor bought his allotment, all he could get were two bottles of peach liqueur, so he took them.

He met his date at the station, and, as soon as he saw her, he knew he was in for a ripsnorting evening. She came bounding up the stairs, dressed all in red, from her toenails to the earrings, purse, and hair ribbon. Immediately, she asked to be taken to a private lounge so they could have a drink, which he obliged. They sat in the private lounge, and she downed several glasses of beer. Finally, he got her out of the lounge, and they started walking over to King's Cross, where the rented room was located. On the way over, they went through the park area surrounding the bay, where there were a number of old concrete guard houses. They were installed at the beginning of the war to house the harbor guards but fortunately, had proved of no use. Right away, the beer began to take effect, and she had to stop off at one guard house after another, while he waited outside. Finally, he suggested she take off her panties and put them in her purse. She agreed it was a good idea, and she did just that.

They went upstairs to his room. As soon as she got inside, she took a drink of the liqueur and started getting sick. The window was open, so she stuck her head out and vomited. The landlady was walking down below and just missed getting hit. By now, our sailor realized he had a problem on his hands, and the only solution he could think of was to put her in the shower and see if he could sober her up. The shower was down the hall, so he got her undressed, guided her into the shower, and turned on the cold water first, then the hot. When the hot water came on, it produced a loud blowtorch noise.

As he was just getting her all wet and shuddering, the landlady came to the door of the shower and told him she wanted both of them out of there because they were upsetting the rest of her tenants. It was about 0100 by then, so the sailor attempted to talk the landlady into letting them stay there, as it was too late to get her home. During the discussion, the girl, thoroughly wilted and disgusted by now, told him to let it go, she would go home.

She got dressed, they walked down to the station, and he saw her off, after giving her a very affectionate kiss. She had a long walk at the end of the train run; the busses were no longer running at that late time. Before putting her on the train, he had made a date for two nights later.

I saw him a few days later and asked him about his second date with her. She was over a half hour late in coming up the station steps, the explanation being that her horse had escaped from its paddock, and she had to go hunt for him. "Great!" he thought. "Now I'm second fiddle to a horse! What next?"

She was more sedately dressed and more subdued. They walked around in the park and then went to dinner. This time, she didn't ask for any beer or liquor. After dinner, they strolled through Hyde Park for a while, then got down on the grass and started playing around.

The seaman paused at that point in his story and said, "I have a problem."

Oh, Oh, I thought; what's coming next? "How do I remove grass stains from the knees and elbows of my dress blues?"

A few days later, some of us were sitting on the #4 hatch, discussing things in general, and the dance in particular. A fireman third class, fairly new on board, was anxious to get into the discussion, and he finally made it. He had gone to the dance without a date but was mostly interested in being an observer, so he said. During the height of the festivities, while he was sitting at a table with some other sailors and their dates, a young girl, a little tipsy, came over and sat down beside him. She looked at him, then asked him if he would walk her to the train station after the dance and see that she made it. Being of a chivalrous nature, he agreed. She left him, and he noticed she continued having a good time out on the dance floor and table-hopping. Near the end of the dance she came over, sat down beside him and asked if they could leave now. She was considerably more intoxicated than at her previous stop.

As they were walking through the park to the station, she said she was tired and insisted on sitting down on a bench. He sat down beside her, and she put her head on his shoulder, sighed, and passed out.

He wondered what to do now. She couldn't be brought out of it, as hard as he tried. He didn't know her name or address or which train to put her on. She did not have a purse on her. He started to panic. Just then, a couple of shore patrolmen came along, so he asked for their help. They attempted to rouse her but had no success. So they told him to stay with her, and they would fetch the local constables to see if they could help. This they did, coming back with two constables who also tried their luck at waking the girl but also failed. They dismissed the shore patrolmen and the fireman, saying they would take care of her. This often happened, and they had a procedure to see that she was safely returned to her home. As far as her purse was concerned, she had probably left it at the dance, and it could be recovered later from the ballroom.

It was a great dance. Ask anyone who was there and stayed sober enough to remember it. The people of Sydney, I am sure, would remember it for a long time to come.

To those people back home in the States, this and similar shenanigans would probably cause considerable tongue-clicking. However, be that as it may, this was war time, and the boys from home needed a little release from the dangers and rigors of war.

As far as any thoughts about the effects on the people of Sydney is concerned, be assured that they were used to such blowouts and often looking forward to them, in peace as well as in war. In fact, during the later 1960s and 1970s, when the United States was in an uproar, the same thing was happening in Sydney, as well as other parts of the world. This resulted in Sydney earning the title "Swinging Sydney." If I remember correctly, the mini-skirts really got their start in Sydney, then spread to London, and thence to the United States. In Paris, of course, the girls there had always been known for revealing attire.

Regarding the effect on your hometown, rosy-cheeked boys, well, you can't hold them down forever, Mom! As mentioned earlier, in effect, we Bloody Yanks were getting sorted out.

Returning now to postdance Sydney, liberty the next time was a letdown for me, no doubt a result of the dances and the chilling effect of Joyce's parents clamping down on her extracurricular activities. I decided to test the atmosphere, so on my liberty on Thursday following the dance,

I called her house in the evening and asked if she could meet me Saturday evening. She readily agreed, so I guess things weren't so bad, after all. At the time, I rather resented their attitude. The years since then have caused me to shift my thinking, and I now have seen their point of view. This change was brought about by my being the father of two girls after the war. Fortunately, they both turned out beautifully, in spite of, rather than as a result of, my attempts at guiding them along life's tortuous highway, full of potholes.

Later that week, some of the 3-inch and 5-inch gun ammunition was replaced with different, more appropriate specifications to give the ship a more useful selection for conditions which were developing for our future runs.

Saturday night liberty started out earlier than usual, since Joyce had time to get ready for the date, so we had more time to stroll around the streets of Sydney, talking, and then having a leisurely dinner. There was a better than usual movie showing at one of the cinemas, so that was the major event of the evening. We then sat on a bench in Hyde Park, talking and smooching until time to walk her to the station for the last train to her home. Then it was the usual stop at Ziegfeld's for a last look at the action and back aboard the ship to hit the sack. A quiet liberty and one of which I'm sure her parents would approve, especially when you consider what could happen in Sydney when the ship was in!

The next day, Sunday, was a quiet one aboard the *Octans*. It was truly a day of rest. We were on the watch bill for standing part of the auxiliary watches in the engine room and the ice machine room combined. The port liberty section went ashore, as did also the regular contingent of shore patrolmen. The only thing of moment that happened that day was the return, voluntarily, of the seaman who had been missing for five and a half days. I wondered why he came back, knowing that he would be disciplined severely. There are several reasons why this could have happened, some of which have already been discussed. He may have run out of money; his girlfriend, if he was living with one, may have politely told him to get out, as she was unable to support both of them; or he may simply have gotten tired of dodging the shore patrol. Or it could have been a combination of those reasons. At any rate, and for whatever reason, he did come back of his own volition, which was a decided plus in his favor. At report mast the next morning, the captain had him assigned to a summary court martial. Also that Monday, one man was AOL two hours, and two watertenders were transferred off the ship, bound for training in the States — the lucky guys.

My next liberty, commencing at 1630, was spent first going to one of the better known book stores in Sydney to look for another book on refrigeration with which to improve my knowledge of the ancient system

17. Overhaul: Thirty Days in Sydney   219

we had been dealing with for these many months. I had no luck; the only one they had in stock was too recent in its coverage. What I needed was an old book on the subject, which they could not provide. I joined up with another man from the ship, and we ended up at the amusement park. After that we were hungry, since we had not stopped for dinner. We went to Ziegfeld's, rather earlier than usual for their late night supper and we were glad to get it. Things were just beginning to get exciting by then, so we stuck around until closing time and then went back to the ship — the end of liberty.

By Tuesday, November 21, the crew had settled down to a rather quiet routine of watch standing, liberty, working on the assigned machinery and space projects, eating, and sleeping, and always, of course, telling and retelling their experiences on liberty. Not all stories were about liberty here or on this cruise.

One man told of his time in San Francisco, or San Diego, I forget which, before he was assigned to the *Octans*. He had met a real cute girl at a dance given by the USO, and he made a date to meet her later in the week, at her house. They never left the house; she suggested they stay in, and she would provide the refreshments. He accepted the offer, thinking she must know what she was doing, and it would save him having to spend a lot of money on her. So they sat on the sofa in the living room, and the evening progressed along lines he had hoped, until things really got hot.

Just then, in walked a marine in shore patrol gear, complete with .45 service automatic on his hip. It was her father, coming off duty, and he stood at the door, legs akimbo, slowly sizing up the situation, while the girl attempted to straighten herself out to look more prim and presentable. The father simply stood aside, opened the door wide, and pointed his night stick at the sailor, then motioned for him to get out. The sailor did not waste any time following that gesture's intent. After he left, he stood outside for a few minutes to hear what was taking place inside the house. He learned a few additional words to add to his vocabulary, then hastened back to the base, lucky to be in one piece.

As a result of the ship's dances, Don, my oiler, had managed to get involved with a second girlfriend, and he started dating her on his off liberty nights. This meant that he would take a fantail liberty on his duty night, see his new girlfriend, and then manage to get back aboard just in time to stand his watch, which was 0400 to 0800. This went along for some time, and apparently all was fine, until the present stay in port. We often discussed what would happen if they caught on, as they were bound to do some day. That did not bother him in the least. He was the type which would have no problem attracting girls. I never met his "duty night" girlfriend, but I met his regular "liberty night" girl, and she was something to see—Irish, dark hair, blue eyes, dark, smooth complexion, well shaped, and a nurse. When I met her, I told myself that the guy was nuts to risk taking another one at the same time. I told him so, but it did not do any good. He enjoyed the thrill and the risk, and his two-timing life went on.

At one of the last liberties during this overhaul, he finally got himself in a tight spot and ended up with dates for both girls for his night aboard. He came to me for help, asking if I would keep his date with Ruby, his steady, while he took a fantail liberty and saw his new girlfriend. It was my liberty night, I had nothing else going for the night, so I agreed. That was a mistake.

I met her at a bench in the park where she was waiting for Don. As soon as I arrived, she knew what the score was and was really burning over it. I attempted to quiet her down and finally got her cooled off enough to see a movie with me. I doubt that she enjoyed it, since she was really steamed up over what Don had done. She knew he was seeing another girl. I was between the well-known rock and hard place, not wanting to lie for Don, when she obviously knew what the score was with him.

After the movie, we walked over to Hyde Park and sat and smooched, and she was giving me all kinds of body language which I knew was in retaliation for Don's two-timing her. I finally put a stop to the proceedings and walked her to the train station. Before she got on the train, she told me to tell Don they were through; she never wanted to see the bloody two-timing louse again.

On my way back to the ship, at first I was really mad at him, too. Then after calming down, I began to realize that it was my own fault for getting myself into that spot. When I saw him the next morning at turn-to time in the ice machine room, I told him what had happened and said I never wanted to be in that situation again. He apologized and seemed genuinely chagrined over the affair. He was transferred out of my gang soon after, then off the ship at Hollandia in February 1945. I had nothing to do with either move.

Wednesday, November 27, we took on 2,000 gallons of diesel oil for the motor boats and the emergency generator. A new ensign joined our ranks, fresh out of U.S. Navy Officer Training School. It was my liberty night, so I met another sailor from the ship, and we went to a restaurant for "styke and eyggs." Following that, I got to a telephone and made a date with Joyce for Friday night. I do not remember in what manner we spent the rest of the evening, but I probably ended up at Ziegfeld's; then it was back to the ship for a good night's rest.

17. Overhaul: Thirty Days in Sydney

By now, it was obvious that the prolonged stay in port was taking its toll in lack of money and sleep, and possibly in boredom. With a few exceptions, the liberty and duty routine was producing an undefinable quietness in the crew's quarters in making preparations for going on liberty. There was not the usual boisterous bustle starting at about 1600 every afternoon. Of course, most of the crew who had spent the first few liberties getting acquainted and attached to female companions were enjoying their conquests, so the exhilaration of pursuit was no longer present.

The repair and maintenance work below was coming along fairly well, with most of the work close to schedule. Some spare parts which had been on order for months finally caught up to us. Supplies were more plentiful now, and we even got a few more bundles of genuine rags for use in the engineering department, to replace the cotton waste previously furnished us. The new construction in the sick bay area was still in quite a mess, but coming along very well.

The last few days in the repair facilities saw another three men sent to the base hospital for treatment of VD and several returning from the same facilities, treatment completed. I only had a couple more dates with Joyce, not that I didn't try for more. Two more ensigns reported aboard for duty. There were a few cases of men AOL, and a couple returned to the ship by the shore patrol. There were enough cases of breach of regulations for the captain to hold report mast the morning of November 27, resulting in three deck court martials being assigned and three loss of liberties.

Also on November 27, it was time to start up the ice machine compressor and start bringing the holds down to carrying temperatures. Due to the length of time we had been shut down, it was necessary to recharge the compressors from the carbon dioxide cylinders in the shaft alley. The fans were started up, the brine pumps were turned on, and we watched the temperatures drop steadily throughout the holds. As we were still on regular liberty schedules, the night shifts were shorthanded, and only one man was on watch each night shift, which gave the oilers an opportunity to see what they could do on their own. There were no problems with this; they all proved out very well that stay in port. On my liberty nights after being ashore, I often stopped down to check on things before hitting the sack.

On November 28, a belated posting was made, giving the sentence in the case of the man tried by a summary court martial about six weeks ago. For being AOL for 81 days, he only got a reduction in rank and a fine of $100. There was something there that did not get into the deck log, something that warranted the weak sentence, for normally any sailor over

30 days AOL was counted as a deserter. Presumably the delay in sentencing was due to an investigation being made into his reason for being away so long.

All the major work had been finished by November 29, and it was time again to light off another boiler, move from the repair dock at Woolloomooloo, and tie up at Central Wharf. We didn't know it, but this next trip was to be a long one. We should have suspected it, considering the extensive changes in the medical department and the general machinery overhaul.

The month of November 1944 saw another change in the 7th Fleet Service Force, SWPA, when the ships under that command were divided into three squadrons, Squadrons 3, 4, and 9. The last, of which we were a part, was made up of all ammunition, cargo, and provision ships and tankers in the SWPA auxiliary fleet. This had no apparent effect on our operations, but no doubt there were some adjustments made on the bridge in the ship's administration.

Chapter 18

Supply Run #12: Into the Fray

November 30, 1944, the daily bulletin posted on the crew's notice board described the continuing battle on Leyte, Philippine Islands. We watched the changing fortunes being portrayed, wondering what, if any, those fortunes would have on our future runs. The *Octans* was being loaded with its next cargo of chilled and frozen food, and liberty commenced at 1630 for the starboard section. It was Thursday, so I knew I could not count on Joyce being available that night, but possibly Saturday night on my next liberty. I contacted Grandma, and he was in a similar fix, so we decided we would go ashore and see what we could work up in the line of entertainment.

To determine the effectiveness of the work that had been performed during this last overhaul, a dock trial was performed on Friday, December 1, while moored to the dock and while still loading cargo. For two hours, the ship was put through as many mechanical tests on the machinery as was possible without damaging the vessel, dock, or channel from the prop wash. Everything appeared to be working within reasonably acceptable tolerances, at least well enough that the ship could continue loading for the next run. Also on that day, we acquired four more crew members and transferred two officers for further assignment.

Liberty commenced at 1300 on Saturday, December 2, and ended at 1000 on Sunday, one of the longest ever for the ship. It was a day of hot sunshine and light rain, but that did not matter, as Joyce and I were flexible and could take the weather in good spirits. We went to the amusement park in the afternoon and then to a dinner. Joyce then picked a good movie to see. She continued to call it the cinema and I still referred to them as movies, but it was all in good fun. By then, we had learned to accept each other's language differences. She was a lot of fun to be with. I saw her to the train about midnight, then went to Ziegfeld's for a late supper and a check on the action there. I then went back to the ship, checked the ice machine operation, found it doing very well, and turned in for a few hour's sleep.

Monday morning came, as it has a habit of doing, and it was obvious that we would soon be leaving Sydney for our next run north. The holds were being topped off with cargo, and passengers were coming aboard. Two of the Navy passengers who were on the draft list did not show up when the draft came aboard. They were rounded up by the shore patrol and brought aboard at 1800, declared AOL four and a half hours, and put in the brig until we were clear of the harbor. The Navy looks after its men, as they found out.

Liberty Monday night was a solemn affair; we all knew we would be leaving the next day. Probably just as well, as many of the crew were reduced to borrowing money to go on liberty. There is such a thing as too much liberty.

Early Tuesday morning, the shore patrol brought one of the crew back aboard, charged with being drunk and causing malicious damage. The ship got underway for Brisbane at 0800, and the captain held report mast three hours later. The sentence was two days on P & P, plus no liberty in Sydney until the damages were paid.

The ship steamed north, following its usual route up the coast until we swung ship and moored at Hamilton Wharf, Brisbane, at noon, December 7, Pearl Harbor Day. In the Philippines that day, troops of the U.S. Army 77th Division landed just south of Ormoc, on the west coast of Leyte, and began an encirclement of the Japanese troops inland on the north end of Leyte.[43] Tacloban, on the coast at the north end of the island, had already been occupied by our forces.

Our stop at Brisbane was brief, just long enough to discharge one of the passengers of the hospital with acute appendicitis. Four prisoners were left off there, their transportation completed, destined for the combined-forces penal installation described earlier. At 1500, it was time to depart Brisbane, retracing the dredged channel out to sea, north into the China Strait, then west into Waga anchorage, Milne Bay, December 11. Our sole purpose for stopping there was to exchange passengers, to add one member to our crew, and to deliver $300,000 to the Navy Supply Depot #167.

This took about three hours, the anchor was weighed and washed, and then it was full ahead both engines east out of the bay. Our destination was Hollandia, on the coast of New Guinea, northwest from the lower tip of New Guinea. At 1330 on December 14, we moored to the

Navy Pier at Hollandia, and the first cargo to be unloaded was deck cargo from #2 hatch, followed by opening all holds to discharge both fresh and frozen cargo to the dock and to our ships in the harbor.

While we were cruising up the coast of New Guinea towards Hollandia, the Visayan, P.I. Task Force was making its way from Leyte Gulf to land on the southwest coast of Mindoro, December 15, as part of General MacArthur's plan to establish an air base utilizing the airfields on Mindoro.[44] The landing was virtually unopposed, but some lives were lost during the five days it took to secure the necessary airfields.

During this period, the *Octans* was busy at Hollandia, supplying food to the ships in the harbor and to the cold storage warehouses ashore. The FPO ashore got its share of our cargo when we sent them 398 sacks of mail, most of which was probably Christmas mail from the parents, girlfriends, and wives of the servicemen in the SWPA.

On December 17, while at Hollandia, among the notices posted on the crew's bulletin board was the disturbing news that a tropical storm was forming in the Philippines. It struck the next day, and Halsey's 3rd Fleet was hit very violently. Three destroyers were sunk; it damaged seven others of his fleet and wrecked about 200 planes, with a loss of about 800 men. Halsey was forced to withdraw his fleet to Ulithi for repairs.[45] Two of the three lost destroyers were of the "Farragut" class, known in the destroyer fleet for having an inherent stability problem and requiring close attention to ballasting. Wartime modifications made the condition worse, in that case producing a situation uncomfortably close to that which we were in during our first run down from Noumea to Auckland, described earlier.[46]

The typhoon notwithstanding, on December 19, we left the harbor to form a convoy heading northwest to our next stop, Leyte Gulf. We were the commodore and guide of the convoy, which consisted of, in addition to the *Octans,* an ammunition ship, a fleet tug, a hospital ship, a combat stores ship, 12 LSTs, and 10 merchant ships. Our escorts were USS *Riley* (DE-579), USS *PCE-848,* USS *McNulty* (DE-581), and USS *Metivier* (DE-582). The convoy was Task Unit 76.4.24. We gradually increased the convoy speed from 6 to 9 knots. On December 20, one of the crew was hit with a case of appendicitis, which required an emergency operation by our doctor, assisted by a doctor from the passengers. The operation was a success.

An LST dropped out of the convoy with engine trouble but rejoined the next day. A merchant ship joined us, and on December 21, we obtained two more escorts, the USS *Susquehanna* (AOG-5) and the USS *Leslie L.B. Knox* (DE-580). Shortly after that, we commenced zigzagging for a few hours and then resumed base course.

The convoy continued on its northwest course at a speed of 9 knots, and at noon on December 23, the convoy commodore commenced exercising the convoy at emergency turns, which was interesting to see with even a convoy as small as ours. Ours was nothing compared to those crossing the North Atlantic between the eastern seaboard and England or Russia. Herding one of those must have been quite a problem.

In the middle of the emergency-turn practice, the *McNulty* veered from the screen to explode a floating mine, which had evidently broken from its moorings and was now a menace to all ships, friend or foe. Not long after that, one of the merchant ships dropped back due to engine trouble, and the *McNulty* took over the job of escorting her until her engine trouble was solved, at which time they both resumed their place in the convoy. At 1550, the emergency-turn exercising was over, and we resumed our base course headed toward Leyte.

"Now hear this! Morning general quarters! All hands man your battle stations! Set Condition, affirm!" A call containing more than the usual urgency, which meant that we were approaching the danger area. This came at 0530 the morning of December 24 and lasted for two hours, which was unusual. At 1000, we resumed the zigzag pattern on base course, and soon after, the *Octans* left the convoy to go alongside the USS *McNulty* to receive (by highline) an ensign with a case of acute appendicitis. He was placed in the surgery, and our doctor took over his care. Also, about the same time, the USS *Appache* sighted another floating mine, left her position to explode it, then resumed her position in the screen. The *Octans* took position 51, off the forward starboard corner of the convoy, and we were back on our zigzagging course.

At 1403, the *Riley* signaled for an emergency turn to port for the convoy, as she had a submarine contact to starboard. She sped to the attack and dropped a series of depth charges. An oil slick and air bubbles appeared, so the *Riley* returned to the screen. Was it actually an enemy submarine or just an unlucky whale? Just to be safe, the *Octans* went to Battle Stations for 15 minutes, then secured from it to set Condition 3 again.

Down below in the ice machine room, whether on regular watch or general quarters station, the sound of distant depth charges or floating mines exploding gave us an eerie feeling, as the WHUMP! WHUMP! came through the water and battered our ship. In an attempt to take our minds off the sound, we gave the ice machine system extra good attention and did our best to appear nonchalant. When the ordeal was finally over, it was sure a relief to see the light of day again.

When there was little or no danger from enemy attack in the area being traversed, there was a certain comfortable feeling down below, especially if the weather topside was miserable. But when in the danger zone,

18. Supply Run #12: Into the Fray

Transferring a patient by highline (author's collection).

which meant Condition 2 watches or general quarters, the feeling changed to one of guarded apprehension. At one of the earlier morning general quarters, when there was only a minor danger from attack, the assistant engineer, who was stationed with us in the ice machine room, attempted to relieve our worries by making the observation, "What we need down here is a bucket of grease and a brush."

"What for?" I asked, going along with the gag.

"If a torpedo comes through the hull, we can grease it so it will go right on through without exploding!"

At 1500, the ship's doctor, with the same assistant from the passenger list as helped in the previous operation, performed another appendectomy, this time on the ensign from the *McNulty*. Postoperative condition was reported as being satisfactory. At 1600, the ship set Condition 2 and stayed in that condition until 1900. So ended the day, with the crew well aware that we were in the the danger zone.

December 25, Christmas Day, started off the same as the 24th, with morning general quarters at 0545, lasting until 0745. The rest of the morning and the early part of the afternoon were quiet, with everyone walking around about their jobs with a quiet feeling of expectation, wondering what was going to happen next. Our last hope of salvation from a watery grave, the Mae West jackets, were treated with a little more than the usual respect. Shortly after 1600, a Japanese bomber, apparently shore-based, approached the convoy off the port quarter, then vanished without taking any action. Obviously, a patrol plane checking out the location of the convoy. It gave us a queasy feeling, what with the Christmas dinner still digesting in our stomachs. This alarm started a series of emergency turns of the convoy, probably designed to throw off their sighting report, giving location and course. It did not help any, because at 1916 we were sent to general quarters when the convoy was approached again by a Japanese torpedo plane. He was either just checking our location, or else he simply wasn't the committed type, for there is no entrance in the log of a torpedo being dropped or of any other aggressive action on his part. We stayed in Condition 1 until 2016, then went to Condition 2 until midnight, at which time we went to Condition 3 again.

Just before midnight, we passed Desolation Point on the northern tip of Dinagat Island, on the south side of Leyte Gulf, at reduced speed, as we were in the process of opening up the convoy to 1,000 yards between columns from the normal 600 yards.

And so ended Christmas Day, 1944. The world was still at war, the enemy was on the defensive on all fronts, but not yet knocked out. Back in our own little world, we were surrounded on three sides by islands on many of which there were still enemy air bases with planes being readied to attack at any moment that appeared advantageous. Our forces held the major ports and coastal points, but there was no guarantee of safety from attack from the air.

In the early morning hours of December 26, we entered Leyte Gulf on the southern end, and the convoy was reformed into three columns for ease of maneuvering in the Gulf. We went to Condition 2, then at 0653, we hove to near Badung Badung Island, awaiting instructions for anchoring. At 0900, we were underway again, anchoring further into the bay. The remainder of the convoy had scattered and found their own designated anchorages in the bay. To the north and east of us was the island of Samar, the island of Leyte was to the west, and the Gulf was to the south. The harbor was crowded, an excellent target for any enemy planes in the area. It was very fortunate that there were very few of them left, and more fortunate still that their pilots were not of the caliber which raided Pearl Harbor.

Among the ships in the Gulf were the survivors of the recent typhoon just to the east, and ships from the battle of Surigao Strait, which had ended in a resounding victory for our fleet. Our forces were making headway against a surprised enemy garrison on Mindoro, after a virtually unopposed landing on December 15.[47]

It was the holiday season, the men in the fleet were hungry, and we were here, available, and with what it took to fill their stomachs.

About 1900, we went to general quarters when the air raid siren announced Condition Red, which was followed by a spectacular display of the antiaircraft batteries ashore firing skyward. Thirty minutes and it was all over, with the ship back on standard watches, Condition 3, then to standby status at 2030.

Like starving bees around a flower patch, at 0700 the morning of December 27, lighters and working crews from the Naval vessels in the harbor were flocking around us, waiting for the deck force to open up the holds for the day's business and to allow them to help themselves to our cornucopia of food. This was two days after General MacArthur optimistically announced that the battle for Leyte was now in its mopping up stages. This actually took another four months and resulted in many casualties yet to be suffered by our ground troops.[48]

Among the numerous small craft lining up for our provender were motor torpedo boats in all degrees of repair or disrepair, manned by rough, battleworn sailors in various conditions. Obviously, they had all been through a fair amount of action in the preceding weeks. As one of them nudged alongside, a young officer hailed our deck and identified himself.

It was Ensign Fraser, and he came on board, as enthusiastic as ever, seeking out his previous acquaintances and requesting his share of our cargo. He also had a list of other things he would like from our stores, which he knew we had available and were badly needed for his boat and crew. While this was happening, our men were talking over the railing with the crew of his boat and were told they would be happy if we would take Ensign Fraser back. After we had satisfied as much of his demands as we could, he thanked the officers involved, then left the ship. As his boat pulled away, he waved from the cockpit, and with a sputter and a roar, they were gone. This time for good.

Young Lochinvar and his trusty steed were off to smite the Oriental Dragon, which is how our country has fought and won our many wars and skirmishes.

At about 1800, another air raid warning was flashed from shore, which lasted about ten minutes, during which time we were at general quarters. During this entire day, our holds were open to all who came for a handout, as long as they were supplied with the necessary requisition from the supply officer of their ship or facility. This activity went along continuously until 2300 on the 28th. It resumed again early in the morning of the 29th and did not stop until 2130 on the 30th.

During the 79 hours of unloading time since our entry into the Gulf, we serviced 76 vessels, from small patrol craft, up to the largest carriers in that part of the Pacific. In between were the complete gamut of ships: yard oilers, repair ships, tenders, destroyers, cruisers, battleships, and all the various and sundry escort vessels in service at that time in our fight against Japan. They cleaned us out of our stock in trade, making us happy, too.

During December 30, there were four air raid warnings from shore, requiring us to go to general quarters each time, until the flash white signal came, announcing that all was clear. These interruptions were very unnerving, as each time the workers in the holds had to climb up the ladders out of the holds, then take shelter as best they could, and wait until the emergency was over. Then back to work until the next alarm went off, as signalled by our general quarters alarm.

One of the features of stopping at Leyte Gulf that we had not run into at any of our previous stops was the native boats crowding around the ship, attempting to trade with the crew. They were in dugouts for the most part and had fruit and vegetables and souvenirs for sale. The former were of doubtful quality, and the latter were of doubtful authenticity. In addition, there was the danger of a bomb being planted on the hull by an enemy disguised as a Filipino. The boats were made to stay off at a distance, which they did not like, as shown by their demeanor.

Sunday, December 31, with all holds empty, our usefulness was at an end; so at 1410, the anchor was hoisted out of the mud, run up to the hawsepipe, washed down, and secured. The engine room telegraph rang "Full Ahead Both Engines," and we steamed down the bay, into the Gulf, to join up with another convoy, a smaller one this time. Besides the *Octans,* as commodore and guide, there were nine merchant vessels,* with escorts USS *Willett* (DE-354), USS *Davis* (DE-357), USS *Mack* (DE-358), and the USS *PCE-854.* Our speed was 10 knots, and the course was southeast out of the Gulf. The ship was on Condition 2 from 1730 until 1930.

New Year's Day, 1945. At 0545, all hands were at Condition 2 until 0730. The day was warm and sunny and the convoy was steaming lazily at a steady 9 knots on course 097 degrees True. A quiet day to start, after noon chow, I went up on the 5-inch gun platform, took off my shirt and pants, and laid down on the steel decking for a sun bath. I was just snoozing off to sleep when I heard the sound of an airplane motor, which I knew was too close and sounded too rough and raspy to be one of ours. I jumped up and was just in time to see a Japanese plane drop two bombs in sequence on the Liberty ship on our port quarter. That ship had a deckload of servicemen, which is probably why it was the chosen target. Both bombs missed, but by then I had grabbed my clothes, was running down the ladder to the poop deck, shouting, "Air attack! General quarters!" At

---

*The deck log lists the following nine merchant ships in the convoy: SS Joseph Simon, SS N.J. Coleman, SS F.W. Spencer, SS P.C. Hewitt, SS A.D. White, SS J.C. Barbosa, SS W.V. Moody, SS F.B. Olson, and SS Mulcra. The Action Report filed by the captain on January 4, 1945, only shows eight merchant ships in the convoy action. It does not list the location code numbers for each one in the convoy, and neither does the deck log.

18. Supply Run #12: Into the Fray

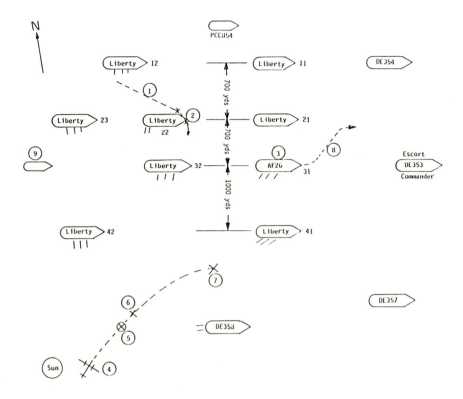

Air attack on the convoy, January 1, 1945. Legend: 1. Approximate attack of first action, at 1547; 2. Plane dropped two bombs, near misses; 3. USS *Octans*, convoy commodore and guide; 4. Japanese Kate torpedo-bomber approached, 1611; 5. Approximate point at which *Octans* opened fire; 6. Plane dropped what appeared to be a torpedo, result unknown; 7. Splashdown point for Kate; 8. *Octans* signalled emergency turn to port and executed, but no other ship in the convoy obeyed the signal; 9. Army small craft, name, type, or number unknown (two-digit numbers by each ship indicates position in the convoy by column number and position in the column).

about the time I had slid down the second ladder to the well deck, the ship's loud speaker blared out, "General quarters! This is not a drill! All hands man your battle stations! Set Condition, affirm!"

I was already on my way into the poop and down the ladder to my station in the ice machine room. There I was joined by the chief engineer and the other machinist's mate sharing this station during GQ.

We waited, with the chief engineer on the telephone, listening to any message which might be passed to those of us below decks.

I do not know how the others in the compartment felt, but I was just a little scared. We had often discussed what effect an air attack would have on our station here below. As long as there was cargo in the holds above us, we would be fairly safe from the small bombs carried by the average "Zero." However, a torpedo or a large bomb from one of their bombers was an entirely different matter. The thought of the magazine for the 5-inch and the two after 3-inch guns being just above the shaft alley did not make our situation any more enjoyable.

We had about 20 minutes of waiting when we heard the guns commence firing, with muffled POPs and some slight concussion coming down through the escape/ventilation shaft. The shooting was all over in about one minute. The chief engineer reported what he was hearing on the telephones. One low-flying plane was downed and several others were circling the convoy; but they apparently didn't like the idea of risking an attack and soon disappeared. We were secured from Condition 1 at 1707, went to Condition 2, and then at 1812 we were at sunset general quarters for an hour. End of the day.

I shall give some details from the ship's action report made out soon after the action took place. The first plane was a small single engine one, probably a Zero, from my observation just before I dashed below. The illustration on page 231 is made from the action report. From the same report, a Jap Kate bomber was picked up at a range of about 8,000 yards and was tracked by our starboard gunners (the two 3-inch guns and the four 20mm guns) until they opened fire at about 2,000 yards. Fourteen rounds of 3-inch and 61 rounds of 20mm ammunition were expended, with two-second fuses on the 3-inch rounds. The plane came in low and slow, and what was taken to be a torpedo was dropped at a range of approximately 1,500 yards. Then the plane banked and hit the water. The plane appeared to be undamaged as it went down.

With so many ships firing at once, how can anyone be sure that it was the *Octans* which did the final deed? It is highly probable that we were given credit for it simply because our ship was the convoy commodore and guide. One could discuss the numerous facets of the action for hours. In the final analysis, it was nothing but the swat of a gnat when taken in the perspective of the entire war.

Sunrise, January 2, 1945: We were zigzagging on base course, with the crew apprehensive and edgy, as evident from the strained and shaky conversation heard around the ship.

0855: Two unidentified aircraft were sighted, sending the crew to general quarters for 30 minutes.

1036: Same procedure as at 0855.

1203: A Japanese Sally was seen circling the convoy. The ship went to general quarters, the escorts put up a barrage, and the plane disappeared astern of us, undamaged. Fifteen minutes later, the secure from general quarters was sounded.

1228: Another unidentified plane passed overhead, another call to general quarters, until the plane was identified as a U.S. PBY patrol plane. The crew, tired and disgusted by now, were secured from battle stations at 1245. It was to be a day of constant irritation from the skies, obviously.

1817: General quarters again, another unidentified aircraft overflying the convoy. Secure from general quarters came a few minutes later when it was identified as a B-24 Liberator.

1843: Repeat performance. At general quarters for 15 minutes, until the plane was determined to be friendly.

End of a tired and hectic day. Those off watch were glad to hit the sack and attempt to restore their physical and mental reserves while expecting to be routed out of the sack any second to go to battle stations. But it didn't happen, and the night passed quietly. The sleeping crew hardly noticed the distant explosions at 0240 when one of the escorts depth-charged a possible submarine contact astern of the convoy. Down below, we both heard and felt the explosions, registered as THUMP, THUMP, THUMP, coming through the sides and bottom of the ship. It was then that we reviewed again the procedure of getting out of the ice machine compartment should a torpedo hit in the forward section of the ship. If it hit amidships or aft, there simply was nothing to worry about.

1422, January 3, 1945: The escort commander, DE-353, made contact with a possible submarine and alerted our bridge. The signal for emergency turn to starboard was made to the convoy, which obeyed the signal this time. Nothing further developed from the contact report.

1602: Another report of a contact by the escort commander, followed by another emergency turn to starboard. It was all over in five minutes; the contact turned out to be false.

The remainder of the day was quiet. The convoy continued on its plodding path, southeast toward Hollandia, New Guinea.

At 0520 in the morning of January 4, the escort commander reported another submarine contact, the convoy did another emergency turn to port, the escort dropped depth charges with no discernible effect, and the convoy resumed its course. The only things happening to break up our routine that day were another sighting of an unidentified plane, sending us to general quarters again for an hour, and the escort commander reporting what appeared to be a floating mine, which did not prove out.

That floating mine report was to be the last incident to plague us that trip, and at 0830 on January 6, the captain signaled to the convoy to proceed individually to their destinations. We entered Hollandia Bay, and eight crew members were put off the ship, all assigned to specific duty elsewhere. Eleven other crew members were transferred to the Naval Receiving Barracks ashore for further assignment. Two of the latter were former oilers from my ice machine gang, both good workers, but who had some minor troubles after being shifted to other duties. We then took aboard six firemen as replacements, permanent status, and another six motor machinist's as temporary crew. One of the new firemen was assigned as my oiler, although he was actually considered to be an electrician striker. He was an older man from Denver, quiet, efficient, and a willing worker. I believe he was a late draftee; he was about forty years old and had a business he left behind.

On January 6, we hoisted the anchor to the hawsepipe again, and at 1557, we were on our way to Townsville, Australia. Our course was almost an exact retrace of the northbound voyage a couple of weeks previous, with one exception: We bypassed Milne Bay and proceeded further east to pass south into Cormorant Channel, through Jomard Strait and into the Coral Sea. Down below in the ice machine room, we were getting the compressor and steam driver back into operating condition, after a several days shutdown and working over. The steam cylinders were warmed up and allowed to drain, then the steam throttle valve was opened to start the compressor. It wheezed, whooshed, and whumped, and the pressures throughout the system soon stabilized at normal operating conditions. The brine circulating pumps were started, the fans in the holds were started, and we were in business again, ready for another run.

After exiting Jomard Strait, we changed course to southwest, passed through Grafton Passage on January 10, and we were then inside the Great Barrier Reef, heading south towards Townsville. At about 1100 on January 11, we anchored briefly in Cleveland Bay, just outside of Townsville, to take on the pilot, who then guided us into Platypus Channel, and up to Berth #2 in Townsville.

End of Run #12. Such a run. Such a relief.

Chapter 19

Supply Run #13: Tempting Fate

"Now hear this! Liberty for the port section will commence at 1630, and end at 0730 tomorrow!" In Townsville? Well, yes, some of the crew were always anxious to go ashore any place the ship stopped, to see what entertainment or mischief they could cook up, and this time was no exception. The shore patrol contingent of only two men left the ship just ahead of the liberty party, in accordance with the usual requirement. At 0800 muster the next morning, four men were AOL. At 0930, the local U.S. Army military police brought them all back aboard, under arrest.

Commencing at 2130 the evening of January 11, right after docking, the #3 and #4 holds were opened up, the local stevedores pitched in, and the frozen meat began to flow into the holds, carton and carcasses, net by net. The starboard section was released on liberty at 1630 on January 12, to end at 2400. Also, our shore patrol allotment consisted of six men, instead of two. It had the desired effect; there were no more AOL cases this brief stop in Townsville. A few men went ashore and just walked around, stopped in to a local pub for a quick look, then returned to the ship, thoroughly unimpressed. Our shore patrol men returned aboard right after midnight to report a quiet evening. The reputation of the U.S. Navy had already been established in that port.

By 0500, we had all of the frozen meat in our holds that was available or on order, so the deck force closed up the hatches and made ready for sea. The pilot came aboard at 0800, the tug came alongside soon after that, and we were soon retracing our course out of the harbor. It was January 13, 1945, summer, and we were headed toward Sydney. The standard speed was increased to 80 rpm, which should have given us a 13-knot speed, but we seldom made good on the higher expectations. We went inside the Great Barrier Reef, threaded our way through the various straits and channels, as we had done before on this portion of the run south. On January 15, the captain held report mast, and sentenced two of the AOL cases from Townsville to two days on P & P, to commence immediately. We were in a relatively clear sea, so we commenced following a zigzag pattern for several hours each day, until entering Sydney Harbor approaches. Just before picking up the Sydney pilot, we ran into another of those sudden tropical rainstorms, forcing us to go to half ahead both engines for about 30 minutes. Then it was the usual entrance into Sydney Harbor, under the Harbor Bridge and up to Pyrmont docks, late afternoon, January 16. The distance from Townsville to Sydney by the path we took, including allowances for zigzagging, is about 1,040 nautical miles, and took us just about 80 hours. So we averaged almost exactly a 13-knot speed during that leg of the run, which wasn't bad, considering the age and condition of the *Octans*. All of the overhauls we had been given were paying off and showing some results. This was evident from the lack of slowdowns due to boiler or engine trouble that we had been having only a few weeks before. We were light in the bow during this passage, with about a seven-foot drag aft, which was not normal loading conditions.

"Now hear this! Liberty for the port section will commence at 1630 and end at 0730 tomorrow!" First, however, the two men confined to the brig were released, just in time for one of them to go on shore patrol duty. No doubt he was fed a good meal first, after being on P & P for two days.

Holds #1 and #2 were opened and the dock hands commenced loading the fresh provisions into them, continuing around the clock again. At 0800 muster the morning of January 18, one man was AOL, arriving back aboard two hours later.

My turn at liberty came that day at 1630. Several of us walked up the street to our usual haunts right off the ship, followed by the lineups at the telephone, to see if we were still remembered by those we had been thinking of for the past six weeks. Joyce was available for a Saturday night date, and we made the usual arrangements to meet at the Hyde Park station. Then another sailor and I headed further up into King's Cross for "styke and eyggs" at our usual restaurant, where we were well known by then. Then it was to a movie, one of those patriotic American wartime movies, the name of which escapes me now, but which were quite common for the period. After that, it was time to stroll around the streets and the byways in the parks, then to Ziegfeld's to top off the evening with another late supper. It was there that we first began to notice the changes taking place in Sydney. There were more strange uniforms walking the streets, and we saw several in Ziegfeld's. Obviously, they, too, had no trouble in locating the favorite hot spots so dear to a sailor's heart. Who were these strangers in our midst? British sailors. Limeys! (Pommies, to the Aussies.) Competition!

There had been some remarks made as we entered the harbor about the sighting of a couple of British warships moored to one of the docks we passed on the way in, and this started the speculation about what effect it would have on our "territory," as we then considered it. We felt that we had squatter's rights. Besides, we had more money, and in general, the Yanks were liked more than the British.

The resentment which the Aussies held against the British was primarily aimed at the British government. For years, in the many wars in which the British were engaged, starting with the Crimean War, Australia and New Zealand had supplied troops to aid in the Mother Country's battles, often taking the brunt of the enemy's forces. This was due in part to the renowned fighting ability of the ANZACS, as they were called. But when Australian home territory was right in the path of the rampaging Yellow Peril in 1941 and 1942, the British government could not see their way clear to release enough of the Aussie Diggers from North Africa to help their own countrymen. Instead, a former British colony, now free, had to go all out in saving one of the largest members of the British Commonwealth from invasion.

The term "Pommie" had nothing to do with the current war situation. It was applied to the English immigrants who had populated Australia for years prior to World War II. It is well known that the Limeys got their sobriquet from the efforts of the British Admiralty in the 1700s to defeat the prevalence of scurvy in the British Navy by issuing rations of lime juice and other citrus juices to the British tars.

At 0800 the next morning, January 19, there were three men AOL. One of them was brought back aboard by the shore patrol, having been AOL since 1900 the night before. That was an odd time, so obviously he had gone ashore on a fantail liberty about that time. For some reason, our shore patrol contingent that day was four men instead of the two we had been sending. Could that have been due to the increased number of British sailors in port? Whatever the reason, it did not help much, because at 0800 muster the morning of January 20, there were three additional men AOL, one of which straggled back aboard about 0930.

Liberty for the starboard section that Saturday commenced at 1300, ending at 2400. Several of us decided to take advantage of the beautiful summer day and go to one of the beaches. That required a trip on a ferryboat, a pleasant experience. The beaches of Sydney, as well as many others on the Australian coast, are known worldwide for their beauty, and that renown is well deserved. After the few hours enjoying the beach, I had to get back to the Hyde Park station to meet Joyce, so I took the ferry alone and got back in plenty of time to greet her as she came up the stairs from the train. She was dressed in her usual neat fashion, but she was a little more sedate in her manner this time. We did have a pleasant dinner, then walked around in the summer evening, talked a lot, laughed some more, smooched some, and then it was time to take her to the station again and the usual good-bye kiss, for which her attitude was just a little more reserved than it had been in the past. I skipped Ziegfeld's this time and went back to the ship just before the midnight deadline, stopped down to see how the lone night watch in the ice machine room was doing, then into the sack.

By 0800 the next morning, January 21, all AOL men had returned aboard, the holds were almost full, and we were loading special deck cargo, so special that it was accompanied by an armed guard of one man. Then it was time to make the ship ready for sea. At 1800, we left the dock, passed under the Harbor Bridge 30 minutes later, and headed for the open sea and north to Brisbane at full throttle all the way. The executive officer held a deck court martial to try the fantail liberty seaman who was caught ashore out of uniform and returned to the ship by the shore patrol. He was given five days on P & P. His sentence was commenced three hours later, just before we pulled into Brisbane. The pilot and the tug took us into the channel and swung us so we could tie up at the Hamilton cold stores wharf late afternoon on January 23. Almost immediately, #4 hold was opened, and some of the cargo taken aboard at Sydney was unloaded there. Our holds were then topped off with fresh and frozen provisions, which took until 2100, January 24.

Liberty for the port section commenced at 1630, to end at 2400. It was an apparently quiet liberty stop, for all hands were back aboard on time, with no repercussions from either the civilian authorities or the shore patrol. At 0800 the morning of January 25, the tug and the pilot were on hand to retrace our inbound trip through the channel and out to the sea. After getting rid of both of them, it was full ahead both engines again, north towards Hollandia. About 1800, while attempting to close up his port for Darken Ship, one of the officer passengers dropped the blackout port on his foot, fracturing two toes. He was admitted to the sick bay. Just one of those little, unfortunate accidents designed to make life more miserable for those who are only trying to do their duty to God and country.

There were still several cases of AOL liberty goers to dispose of, and the captain held report mast on January 26, resulting in two men assigned to summary court martial and two men given one day of confinement. After that, life went on as usual, with most of the crew not being aware of the fate of the four men. On the afternoon of January 27, the crew was sent to general quarters for practice at firing the guns. All guns, except the ship's small arms, were fired, then secure from general quarters was sounded. We went back to our regular routine, and the ship steamed on steadily northward. The next day, January 28, about noon, a discoloration in the water ahead was observed, and rather than take any chances, the ship was veered to starboard to go around the patch, then the course was resumed northwards. This event occurred at about the entrance to Jomard Passage, following which we entered Cormorant Channel, then rounded northwest up the coast of New Guinea.

The morning of January 29 was a busy one on board the *Octans*. The summary court martial was held for the two men assigned a few days earlier, and right after that, the ship was veered off course to investigate a strange object in the water, which turned out to be floating debris. The ship resumed course, then general quarters was sounded, for another session of practice with the guns. This time almost twice as much ammunition was discharged as on the exercise two days previous. The captain held report mast next to hear the case of a seaman who was charged with using obscene language and disobeying orders of a petty officer. The sentence: five days P & P. Obviously, the main charge was the latter one, which was legitimate. But as for the first charge, that was just thrown on as an extra to emphasize the seriousness of the situation. If every sailor that used obscene language was disciplined, the result would be pure chaos. The British Navy had attempted such a restriction, and it was all but laughed out of existence by both the Navy and the civilian population. The sentence was commenced immediately, at 1200.

The next morning, the lookout reported what looked like a submarine periscope about two miles off the port bow. General quarters sounded, and the ship turned slightly to starboard to bring the port guns to bear. The 5-inch gun and all port-side guns opened up, blasting away as fast as they could be served and sighted. The entire action took ten minutes, from sounding GQ to securing from it. The "periscope" obviously was not a submarine, and the speculation was rampant as to what it could have been. Personally, I suggest it was a South Pacific version of the Loch Ness monster. After all, in those waters, who knows?

Shortly after noon on January 31, we entered Hollandia Bay and moved to our assigned anchorage. The next day, I took the opportunity of requesting and receiving permission to go ashore to the base maintenance facilities for a short visit with the two men from my gang who had been my oilers at different times and who had been transferred ashore the last run. I went over with the mailman; it did not take long to look up the two men, and we had quite a good visit. They both appeared resigned to their fate. Of course, they missed the liberties they had been enjoying for so many months. One of them was Don, my former oiler who had two girls on the string at one time in Sydney. The climate here at Hollandia was not the best, being about three degrees below the equator, but by then the base was fairly well established, and living conditions were as good as was to be expected.

I then went to the FPO to see about my ride back to the ship, and, while there, I noticed a pile of stinking trash on the floor of the post office receiving department. It was about four feet high and consisted of miscellaneous junk, bits of smelly food, torn wrappings, books, magazines, you name it. It was all remnants of the Christmas mail which had not been properly wrapped or addressed and which had arrived at the post office in this sorry condition. I don't know what they were going to do with the mess, but I thought that they had better do something soon as it was getting to smell pretty ripe. We got back to the ship with the mail in good time, and it was soon distributed, with the usual assortment of comments, groans, curses, and joyous shouts.

The first anniversary issue of *The* Octans *Scuttlebutt* was distributed to the crew that day. The event was noted with an article giving the brief history of the ship. It included the statement that the *Octans* had the record among Navy reefer vessels in this area of carrying the most total tonnage of cargo.

The news flash concerning the disappearance of Glenn Miller in a flight from Paris to London was repeated. The members of the crew that were transferred since the previous issue were listed, along with good-bye wishes. New arrivals were welcomed aboard, also. The songs on the Hit Parade for Saturday, January 6, 1945 were given:

1. Don't Fence Me In
2. There Goes That Song Again
3. I'm Making Believe
4. I Dream of You
5. Trolley Song
6. Dance with a Dolly
7. Together
8. I Don't Wanta Love You
9. Sweet Dreams, Sweetheart

There were several examples of humor prevalent back home at the time, mostly moron jokes, which probably would not be considered in good taste today. A plea was printed for the crew to return their books to the library after reading them so someone else could use them. One of the lieutenants was holding classes for those on board who were interested in improving their use of the English language. The Hit Parade selections for the weeks of January 13 and 20 were published. The new ones were:

19. Supply Run #13: Tempting Fate

1. More and More
2. I'm Confessing
3. Accentuate the Positive
4. I Didn't Know About You
5. Always

The poem "The Land Down Under" appeared. An article describing the Smithsonian Institution was printed, and congratulations were extended to those crew members who were advanced in rating recently. The staff now consisted of:

Editor in chief	Terry L. Howard
Assistant editor	C.A. Willis
Associate editors	R.C. Wilson and Dave Pierce
Cartoonists	E.A. Cowhey, E.L. Noblitt, and T.J. Stage
Typists	R.C. Wilson, R.L. Norman, and R.E. Schmidt

On Saturday, February 3, we shipped one member of the crew to the hospital for treatment of VD. On Sunday, February 4, at 1442 the anchor was weighed, washed, and secured, and we left the bay to join a convoy. It was a large one, consisting of us as convoy commodore and guide, 31 merchant ships, some of which were towing other vessels, and three LSMs, AK-157, DD-681, and APC-10. The escorts were DEs numbers 345, 346, 420, and 421, and HMAS *Gascoyne*. There were also four British Navy ships in the convoy, the first time for us, another indication that they were beginning to be reassigned to the Pacific theatre. The speed of the convoy varied between 6 and 7 knots, and we steamed steadily, north towards our destination, Leyte Gulf in the Philippines. On February 6, four more merchant ships joined the convoy, and we steamed on, alternately zigzagging and steaming on base course in the prescribed pattern. Nothing exciting happened until the morning of February 7 when one of the escorts made what was felt was a positive submarine contact, as he went frothing to the attack, dropped several depth charges over a three-hour period, and then came back to his position in the escort screen. The next afternoon, another escort, the AGP-3, joined us and took screening position astern. Earlier that day, one of the forward escorts reported a submarine contact, but nothing came of it.

We did not know it at the time, but while we were enroute to Leyte Gulf from Hollandia, the USS *Wright* (AV-1), former seaplane tender, had already arrived at Leyte Gulf, carrying the entire staff of the Commander, Service Force. The entire command had grown to an extent never before imagined, but it was now in better condition to serve its function for the war effort. There were still isolated pockets of enemy resistance in the area, but only to the extent of becoming a nuisance to our forces.

About 1420, February 9, the ship was at general quarters for eight minutes because another one of our fly-boys was lax in answering the recognition challenge. We were again sent to Condition 2 stations at sunset for two hours. Later that night, one of the merchant ships towing another ship had to drop out of the convoy to repair the towline. Sunrise the next morning found us all at Condition 2 stations for two hours. The remainder of the morning was uneventful. Then right after lunch, another merchant ship dropped out to repair a towline, and an Army ship dropped out due to engine trouble. Then at sunset, it was back to Condition 2 stations again for two hours. The rest of the day was quiet.

It was obvious that the length of this portion of the trip north was beginning to tell on those vessels with tows, as the chafing of the towlines was taking its toll. With the dawning of February 11 came, all within a 30-minute time span, three more merchant ships dropping out of the formation to repair towlines. One ship left the convoy to strike out alone, as a result of the towing padeye tearing loose from the ship, its tow being taken over by another ship in the convoy. By noon, the other three ships had rejoined the convoy, repairs having been completed.

At 0938, the general quarters alarm sent us to our battle stations again, another unidentified plane approaching off the starboard bow. The plane was one of ours, a Mariner patrol bomber. Someone on the bridge was getting edgy by now, not that he could be blamed for it. In addition to our own valuable hides, there was the matter of the holds full of provisions for the fighting forces, plus a huge contingent of servicemen on board as passengers, just aching to get into action. Well, some of them were, at least. Also there was the matter of the remaining ships in the convoy which had to be considered, and we were in charge of it.

At about daybreak on February 12, two more ships suffered a loss of their tows, they left the convoy to retrieve them and proceed on their own to their destination, since we were practically at the end of the trip, being already in Leyte Gulf. Shortly, after noon, the convoy was broken up by a signal from our bridge, and all vessels proceeded independently to their ultimate berthings. We proceeded further into San Pedro Bay, and at 1537 the anchor rattled to the bottom between Leyte Island and Samar, near Tacloban, Philippine Islands.

At 1700, a brief ceremony was held, as our captain was detached from duty to take over command of the USS *Graffias* (AF-29), the former SS *Topa Topa,* another reefer launched in 1943 and acquired by the Navy just a year previous, in 1944. Our executive officer then took command of the *Octans* in the usual forward-well deck ceremony. Life went on aboard ship, and from the wardroom down there was practically no noticeable change in the operation of the ship, which is probably as it should be, that being a sign that everything was being run reasonably well.

Right after 0800 muster the morning of February 13, the disbursing officer left the ship, carrying $5,900 in old, worn U.S. currency, which had been through many, many sweating, dirty palms and many crap and poker games. A couple of hours later, he returned, with newer currency. At noon the anchor was weighed, washed, and hoisted to the hawsepipe, and we were underway again for an anchorage off the city of Dulag, just about 20 miles south of Tacloban on the eastern shore of Leyte Island. Two and a half hours later, it was underway again to join another convoy forming, heading for Mindoro Island on the northwest coast of the Philippines. It was a fairly large convoy, the actual size not given in the deck log; but from the positions held by the *Octans,* it was obvious that it was not a small one by South Pacific standards. The convoy commodore and guide was the LST 574, and we were assigned position number 15 to start. It was south out of Leyte Gulf, then into the Surigao Strait, southwest into the Mindanao Sea, and west into the Sulu Sea.

"Now hear this! Morning general quarters! Set Condition, affirm!" This came the morning of February 15 just before daylight began to show. It was over in 45 minutes, and we were back to regular Condition 3 watches. At 1500, there was a shake-up in the convoy, and the *Octans* was shifted to near the center of the convoy. The reason for the shift was not given in the log, but it could have been to place us in a more protected position.

By then, we were in the Sulu Sea, following almost the exact route that our invasion force had taken just two months before, when it went ashore at southwest Mindoro. The troops encountered very light opposition once on land, but the ships offshore suffered the loss of two LSTs and damage to one destroyer. Once ashore, our troops pushed rapidly inland to establish a foothold. There had been some minor attempts at impeding the invasion fleet on its passage north along this same route. Mindoro was considered secure by January 3, 1945, two days after our convoy was attacked in Leyte Gulf, as described in the previous chapter.[49]

After dispersal of the convoy the morning of February 16, the *Octans* dropped anchor in Mangarin Bay, near Dongon, on the west coast of Mindoro. Right after noon chow, the deck force opened all holds, and our provisions were lifted by cargo net out of the holds, swung over to the waiting boats alongside, where they were emptied, then brought back aboard for another net load. This went on steadily until 1050 the next morning, when all of the hungry vultures had been satisfied for the time being. In the bay we sat, waiting for our next assignment, which came that evening, directing us to proceed the next day, February 18, to Subic Bay, where our forces were in need of fresh food. This 48-hour delay with the holds closed gave us time to regain the temperatures in the cargo spaces.

Subic Bay had been considered secure on February 5, just 13 days before we sailed for that port. Elements of the XI Corps of MacArthur's forces had gone ashore January 29 at the San Felipe–San Antonia area, about 15 miles above Subic Bay and the town of Subic. The invasion forces had been transported there from Leyte by the 7th Fleet. Local guerrillas helped by giving guidance and some advice on the enemy forces, which were practically nonexistent. By February 5, it was all but over.[50]

We joined a convoy the afternoon of February 18, consisting of two ships. Our position was astern of the USS *Pecos* (AO-65), which was the guide, with the USS *Newman* (APD-59) as the escort. Standard speed was 12 knots, and the course was northwest along the coast of Mindoro, past Lubang Island, then north into Subic Bay, with the crew at Condition 2 most of the time. The morning of February 19, the anchor was dropped in Subic Bay, the engines were on standby, all the holds were opened, and the storeship *Octans* was in business again. The deck log does not list the ships which we serviced, but it must have been many, for we discharged cargo for four days, during the daylight hours.

There was no attempt at harassing us by the enemy while there, and the unloading went smoothly to completion. We had the old problem with native Filipinos coming alongside and trying to enter into barter with the crew. Some of the crew managed to take pictures of the canoes, and strangely, after leaving Subic Bay, a number of commercially available sets of pictures of native life were made available to the crew.

Another small convoy was formed the morning of February 24, with the *Octans* as commodore and guide, with escorts USS *Knox* (DE-580) and the USS *Potawatomi* (ATF-109). Our standard speed was 13 knots, and the route was the reverse of our inbound one just a week previous. There was only one incident to break the routine when on February 25, at 1655, one of the escorts reported a submarine contact, sending us to general quarters for about ten minutes, until the contact was lost.

Down below in the ice machine room, we were cleaning up after the long run we had just gone through. Things were going smoothly; the only thing to mar our operation was those two main flywheel bearings, as usual. We just could never get rid of the THUMP! THUMP! with every revolution, scrape and spot-in as we tried. We never did get them to sound like we felt they should. We got plenty of practice in scraping and fitting babbitt bearings, if we learned nothing else.

At midmorning on February 26, the convoy dispersed, with the *Octans* proceeding to its source of fuel oil in San Pedro Bay. We then dropped our anchor further up into the bay, only to shift berths early the next morning. On February 28, two seamen decided they could not get along, and the result was one of them being struck on the back of the head with a scrubber, sending him to the sick bay for six stitches. When considering the number of men on board, including the space and work involved in carrying fairly large numbers of passengers, it is not surprising that there would be occasional altercations between men. The many visits to liberty ports helped considerably in reducing these incidents to a minimum.

For several weeks, salvage operations had been underway in Manila Harbor, aided by experts recently deployed from similar operations in Europe. Much of the early work had been done while under harassment from enemy artillery and sniper fire. The harbor was swept clear of mines, and on March 1, there was sufficient clearance for shipping to commence activities in support of the coming actions further up the west coast. The harbor clearance continued for several more weeks, and some hulks were left in place to serve as moorings.

During this period, the USS *Arequipa* (AF-31), newly launched the previous December, joined the Service Force. In addition, it was also decided to utilize such space as was available in some of the various other reefer ships not previously under the control of the 7th Fleet, and arrangements were made to accomplish this.

Our operations in the Philippines were expanding at an enormous rate, in support of cleaning up the islands and for action in Borneo and surrounding areas. Some of the bases established at this time became fairly permanent, such as Cavite and Subic Bay, P.I.

The welfare and recreation facilities were expanded at an equal rate, with about two hundred 16mm movie projectors distributed to the fleet and a film-distribution circuit over 8,000 miles long to supply them. Numerous baseball and softball diamonds were built in the area, also. Freed prisoners from the Japanese camps were rehabilitated after classification, and the Navy established several brigs and disciplinary facilities in the area.

As the saying goes, the Navy takes care of its men.

In the evening of March 1, we were sent to general quarters for about an hour due to an air raid alarm ashore. At 0900 the next morning, the anchor was hoisted to the hawsepipe, and we were underway for

Hollandia, New Guinea. In the afternoon, at sea outside of Leyte Gulf, a convoy was formed of two ships and an escort, the USS *Lough* (DE-586). The other ship being convoyed was the HMS *Glenearn*, a British ship. Our trip to Hollandia was relatively calm as we retraced our route. On March 3, the captain held report mast for the men involved in the altercation four days previous. The man doing the striking with a scrubber received two days P & P, while the man getting the stitches in his scalp got five days P & P. Sounds somewhat like the father who spanked his son for letting the neighbor kid beat up on him.

A surprise occurred! A crew's locker inspection was held during that trip. What made it surprising was that it was the first mention in the log for the entire cruise of locker inspection being held. We had occasionally been visited by various officers walking through, ostensibly to look at some particular section or problem being encountered. After all, the enlisted area was noted for its stench, heat, grime, and oil spatters, not compatible with keeping one's uniform clean. They were probably looking for smuggled hooch. In the procedure, the executive officer, with the division officer for the crew section being examined and a yeoman recorder, would stand by the locker. The sailor would open it and stand back while the division officer went through it in a quick inspection. The yeoman would make a note of anything found out of regulation, as dictated by the executive officer. For anyone on duty, a shipmate would relieve him long enough for him to come up to the crew's quarters and open the locker for inspection.

This procedure continued from the forward section of the crew's quarters and aft into the last section, which was the engineering division area. In the process, a fireman was dispatched to the engine room to relieve Don, another fireman, who came running up the ladder, sweating, panting from the exertion, with a wiping rag in his hand, opened his locker, and stood back for the inspection. There was no hooch—just a pair of women's rayon panties, hanging on the inside of the door.

The *Octans* pulled out of the convoy just outside of Hollandia Bay about noon on March 8 and steamed to its assigned anchorage inside the bay, where the anchor was dropped. A few hours later, we got rid of one excess watertender, our medical officer, and a lieutenant, all three destined for other duties. Around dawn the next morning, the *Octans* was underway again, this time for Sydney. Our course was the familiar one we had steamed several times before, southeast along the New Guinea coast, through Cormorant Channel, then through Jomard Strait, and south into the Coral Sea.

The captain held report mast for three men who were before him under various charges, and each received the same punishment—loss of five liberties. This was more than we were destined to receive in Sydney, so the punishment was harsh, but probably not unduly so, considering their infractions of discipline. The next afternoon, the crew went to general quarters, and the gun crews got their chance to show what they could do, when all guns above decks were fired, then the secure from general quarters was announced.

A ship such as the *Octans* required more than one method of controlling the rudder in order to maneuver the ship, and the mechanisms employed were complicated and thus subject to getting out of order. Many times during the two-year cruise of the *Octans,* the bridge shifted methods of steering control to be sure that all was in order. The day before we were due in Sydney, another test was made by switching control methods for several hours, then returning to the most trusted method, the hydraulic system, on which we had relied for many months. All was declared in order, and we proceeded to Sydney.

The mood on the ship was different than on the previous approaches to Sydney. We knew that the British had been moving into the area, and there was some apprehension about what effect that would have on our former relations with the girls of Sydney. That was the main concern, naturally. Also, we had the feeling that our days in this part of the world were coming to an end, and this brought on many different attitudes and thoughts, some of relief, some of regrets, and some of satisfaction — satisfaction that we had tasted the best of life that Sydney had to offer and had still performed our duties to the war effort as best we knew how or were able to do. It was obvious that some of the crew were masking their thoughts with loud bravado, determined to get the last ounce of liberty pleasure that Sydney had to offer. Others in the crew knew it was time to slow down and to start to think of the future.

At 0816 on March 17, the ship passed under the Sydney Harbor Bridge and tied up at the wharf at Pyrmont, Sydney.

"Now hear this! Liberty will commence at 1300 for the port section, to end at 0730!"

Chapter 20

Supply Run #14: My Last Farewell

Soon after docking, two men were transferred to the base hospital ashore for medical treatment, type and cause not listed in the deck log. About noon, the shore patrol contingent left the ship, followed an hour later by the port liberty section, liberty to end at 0730 the next morning, March 18. There had been some difficulties with the ship's electrical system, so a few hours were devoted to repairing the trouble, while the ship was operating on the emergency generator until the normal service was restored about 1900.

Chronic troublemakers, of which we had a few on board the *Octans*, were of two types or philosophies. Some often fouled up ashore but managed to get back aboard after their liberty, although often AOL. These men recognized the ship as their temporary home far away from their real home. Not a perfect one, but a safe, reliable haven. One or two seemed to have no regard for the ship as a home and were constantly testing their ability to get off the ship at any price, to see if they could survive among the population without being grabbed and brought back aboard. They would stand out like sore thumbs, unable to get a job without a local ID card and having to live solely off some girl who was at the very best just able to support herself on the low wages being paid to the women. After about a week, if the girlfriend didn't report him to the local shore patrol, someone else probably would.

In the case of the *Octans*, there was a seaman who was constantly in trouble, apparently a typical chronic loser. He was usually confined to the ship or frequently in the brig for some infraction of the operating code. And as usual, when we pulled into Sydney, he was under shipboard confinement. At about 1700, he took a fantail liberty, going AWOL. Five and a half hours later, the shore patrol brought him back aboard. His freedom at an end, he was put in the brig for safekeeping, just to be sure. He was there just one day. At 2130 on March 18, a surprise muster was held of those who were supposed to be on board; and he, along with another chronic troublemaker, were both AWOL and remained AWOL for the remainder of our stay in Sydney. Just before sailing on March 23, their baggage, records, and hammocks were transferred to the Navy Receiving Barracks ashore. No further word was heard by the crew concerning their fate.

When the news of the defection of the two seaman reached the lower decks, there was a general flurry of speculations, mostly as to where they were and how long they could last before being apprehended. The name of one of them rang a bell in my mind, and I started to inquire of other crew members to see if my memory was correct. Referring back to Chapter 4, I mentioned the bull session held one evening on the fantail when a young seaman was expounding on patriotism and duty to his country. My hunch was correct. That young "patriot" was one of the men who were now AWOL. They would not be considered deserters until after 30 days AWOL. The speculation was that the shore patrol would pick them up soon or might wait and pick them up after 29 days, so they would not to be charged with desertion. The "patriot/ship jumper" was known to have a girlfriend in Sydney to whom he was very much attached.

Our next cargo load was ready for our holds, and on Sunday, March 18, the deck force opened the hatches. The Aussie stevedores pitched in, both to load the holds and to pitch pennies on their breaks. That was fascinating to watch, and it would probably be the last time to enjoy the spectacle. The amount of applause, jokes, and curses released over such a simple pastime was a cause for considerable comment from the crew. But then, the Aussies were noted the world over for being wild gamblers, probably as a result of their heritage in the founding and settlement of the country. In some respects, it was much like our own ancestors who developed and tamed this country, especially the West. It was easy to see now how right the New Zealanders were in their description of the typical Aussie sportsman; the actual sport did not appear to be as important to them as the joy and prestige of winning. The New Zealanders were more interested in the sport itself and its pleasures. It was no wonder that the New Zealanders did not like to enter into competitive sport with the Aussies.

"Now hear this! Liberty for the starboard section will commence at 1300 and end at 0730 tomorrow!" That meant me, among over one hundred others. I called Joyce as soon as I got off the ship, but since it was Sunday she was tied up with some family and church affairs. We made a date for Tuesday night, with the usual time and place of meeting. That left me free for the entire liberty, so I joined with a couple of others from the ship, and we made another trip by ferry over to one of the beaches. We took off our shoes, socks, jumpers, and skivvy shirts and relaxed and enjoyed the sun—enjoyed it a little too much, for we suffered some the next day from a mild case of sunburn. The evening was spent at the amusement park, which I remember was near the beach; then it was back to the city on the ferry and another dinner of "styke and eyggs." After that it was back to the ship, into the sack, and on watch again the next morning, while the holds were being loaded.

Monday was dull and slow, with the holds being worked, no new absences at the 0800 muster, and the general feeling around the ship that this was the last time to see Sydney. It was almost as if we were sorry to see the holds being filled. But the signs were obvious, there being several British ships in the harbor and quite a few British sailors walking around on "our" streets. We felt, too, that we were soon to be heading east across the Pacific to San Francisco.

Tuesday, March 20, and it was my liberty day again. In the morning, we took on more ammunition for the 3-inch and the 5-inch guns, topping off our storage space in the magazines. Then at 1630, I was one of the early ones to pick up my ID card, cross the quarterdeck, and proceed off the dock to join with a few of the others to have a quick one at the usual public lounge. We walked around, enjoying our last hours of Sydney; then it was time for me to meet Joyce at the Hyde Park station stairs. She was a little late and she apologized for it. We walked around for awhile, then went to dinner and dawdled over it. I noticed she was still much reserved and not her usual vibrant self. We went to a movie, then walked around in the park, talking. She suspected that the ship was leaving soon for good, but we did not dwell on it. I attempted to get her out of her reverie but was having no luck. She was cool to my approaches, and finally, she made the remark, "You know, most people think that the British sailors are slow, but they're not."

I got the message, loud and clear: the Bloody Yanks are out, the Limeys are in! C'est la guerre!

I kissed her good-bye, took her to the station, and she left. My last farewell.

Thursday, March 22, came and it was clear at the 1030 muster that some men were getting their last fling in before leaving Australia. There were four more men AOL in addition to the two that had been absent since the first day in port. Of those four, three were from the engineering division, and two of those were men who were often on report for being AOL or under shore patrol arrest. Two of the four did not come back aboard until 0700 the next morning, 21 hours AOL. Extra liberty time in Sydney was worth whatever the captain handed out at report mast — at least, to some.

There was a rumor going around in the E division quarters that Joe, one of the engine room machinist's mates, had requested to be transferred ashore here in Sydney — he had apparently become involved with an Australian woman and did not want to go back to the States. His request was denied at that time, and he stayed on board for the second cruise.

When the ship pulled into Brisbane for the second time during the second and last cruise, he was transferred to the Navy base for discharge from the service, so he apparently finally reached his goal. In attempting to locate former crew members in preparation for this book, the Veteran's Administration had a record of him and assisted me in trying to get in touch with him. He did not answer my letter sent through the Veteran's Administration.

I rated liberty that night, Thursday, March 22, the last one in Sydney. I wasn't going to go ashore, but, at about 2030, one of the machinist's mates in my gang that was on duty came to me and reported that his oiler, Armand, who also was on duty, had gone ashore on a fantail liberty. The machinist's mate felt that there was a danger Armand would not be back aboard in time for departure the next morning. Armand was one of two Mexican-Americans on my gang, both of them oilers and both very good workers while at sea; but they had a tendency to lose control of themselves when ashore and drinking. Armand was an easygoing, happy-go-lucky type, tall, with light skin and curly black hair, and obviously quite a lady's man. The other one, whose nickname was "Chili," was short, swarthy, tough, and a former lightweight Golden Gloves boxer. More than once, Chili had come back aboard from liberty, attended muster, and then disappeared, having crawled into some nook in the ship to sleep off his "great liberty" the night before. Because our gang was not subject to the constant presence of the engineering brass, we were able to cover for him. Fortunately, it did not happen too often.

I got into my dress blues, put on my shiny shoes, and went ashore about 2100, after finding out from Chili where Armand's normal hangouts were. The first was Sargeant's, an all-night restaurant and bar at King's Cross, frequented by some of the sailors. I also had the name of his girlfriend and was told that the man behind the cash register knew Armand and his girl and perhaps could tell me where to find them. The lead proved accurate, although I had to tell the cash register man that Armand was ashore AWOL and that his watch supervisor wanted him back aboard so as not to miss the sailing the next morning. Then he gave me the address and flat number and the directions for finding it. I located the building, entered the hall, and found the flat at the very end. It was dark, with no light shining at the transom. I knocked loudly on the door, twice, before a sleepy woman's voice called out, "Who is it?"

I identified myself, then asked if Armand was in there. She answered that he wasn't, so I told her that if he didn't get back to the ship right away he would be in trouble. This brought on a quiet discussion inside, followed by the light coming on, some rustling, and the door opening a crack. A small, dark-haired girl in a robe appeared at the door. I told her that his watch supervisor and I wanted him back aboard because he was AWOL and we did not want him to get into any further trouble. She closed the door. There was more discussion inside, and shortly the door opened, and Armand came out, slightly disheveled, but dressed. We took a taxi back to the wharf. As he was AWOL, I managed to escort him, still slightly drunk, around the piles of goods on the wharf, and, between appearances of the OOD at the gangway, I got him over the side of the ship and onto the after-well deck.

I then walked around the other side of the wharf and walked up toward King's Cross, determined to just walk around and see what was happening on my last night in Sydney. I was standing on a street corner at King's Cross, when a taxi stopped in front of me and the driver asked if I needed a lift. I decided to get in and ask him for some help in finding some clean excitement. There was a young lady sitting in the front seat beside him, a blonde, and apparently they were friends; so we all got to talking about how quiet the streets seemed. It now was past midnight. She asked if I would like to come home with her, as there was a birthday party going on for her little brother, who was eleven. I agreed. We got to the house, and the lights were on, but the party had broken up, with the remains all over the place. Her mother, a small, shriveled up old crone, and her brother were still up, talking over smokes and warm beer. Both were chain smokers, and the place reeked of cheap tobacco. Their main topic of discussion was the party we had missed, which was obviously a humdinger. Next, the conversation turned to the horse races. They were both avid horse racing fans, and I got a short course in horse racing, practically none of which I remember to this day.

It was getting close to dawn, so I decided I had better get back to the ship. First I gave the brother a pound note and told him to place it on a nag of his choice for me. The girl, who was a nurse, not bad looking, and with a rather pleasant personality, told me where to get a cab and walked me to the door. She kissed me good-bye, and I left.

That was my last night forever of liberty in Sydney.

20. Supply Run #14: My Last Farewell

By muster the next morning, all men who had been AOL were back on board, with the two exceptions of the ship-jumpers mentioned earlier, whose baggage had been transferred ashore and who were no longer on the roster. Soon after muster, the ship was being made ready for sea. As I was standing at the railing just aft of #3 hatch, watching the deck force getting the ship underway down on the after well deck, Armand appeared on the well deck, still slightly drunk, happy, and attempting to go over the side of the ship onto the dock. I ordered him to get below to the ice machine room; I knew he was supposed to be on watch. He ignored me, even after the second order to get below; so I got the master-at-arms and had Armand taken into custody. He was charged with being under the influence of intoxicating liquor and unable to perform his duties. At least he didn't miss the ship and was not caught AWOL.

At 1033 the morning of March 23, 1945, the *Octans* pulled away from the Pyrmont docks. At 1056, we passed under the Sydney Harbor Bridge on our way east towards the sea. Many of us were standing on deck, quietly watching the harbor, with a few of the crew waving and shouting at anyone they happened to see, or thought they saw, ashore. It was time to switch our thoughts from Sydney Harbor, fading away astern, to that other harbor bridge, the Golden Gate.

The ship was full of goodies, it was fall in Australia, and we were headed north into spring, along the same route we had traversed several times before.

The captain held report mast on March 26 to clean the slate of the nine cases of wrong-doers which had accumulated as a result of our last stay in Sydney. Armand was deprived of five liberties, as were three others. In addition, one was deprived of two liberties, two were deprived of three liberties, one was given ten hours extra duty, and one was assigned to a deck court martial. That was some liberty stop. The deck court martial held later ended with a reduction in rating.

And the *Octans* steamed on, north, through Jomard Strait, then Cormorant Channel, and then along the coast of New Guinea, without incident. At noon on March 31, we tied up alongside the USS *Villalobos* (IX-145) in the bay at Hollandia, New Guinea. The crew of that ship was thirsty, so we gave them 250 tons of freshwater. After that, we moved over to tie up alongside a merchant ship at the dock. There we unloaded some of our precious provisions from #1 hold and replaced the freshwater we had transferred earlier. Availability of freshwater was a problem in the entire Pacific campaign. There were several ships in service converted to carrying freshwater to the fleet, while the shore bases often had distilling plants to provide the barest essential requirements.

At mid-morning on April 2, we left the dock to join a convoy being formed outside the bay. It was a fairly large one, consisting of seven columns, with the USS *Blatchford* (AP-153) in the lead and escorts USS *Brazier* (DE-345), USS *Rutherford, PCE-874,* and HMAS *Barcoo*. Standard speed was 9 knots, course almost due north to start, then changing to northwest, toward Leyte again. The general route was similar to the one we had taken previously, but this time the convoy took many drastic alterations in course of 45 or 90 degrees, which could indicate that the convoy was being exercised to be prepared in case of emergency. Also, there are many islands and shoals between Hollandia and Leyte which would require changes in course, but when that happens, the course change is usually just enough to clear the danger.

On April 4, several other ships joined our convoy. The only thing that happened to mar the voyage was the #2 boiler had to be shut down for a short period for repairs. That boiler had not given too much trouble, and even then, due to our reduced speed, it did not slow the convoy. A day later, on April 9 in the early morning, the convoy split in two, with our portion going into Leyte Gulf in three columns, coming to anchor shortly after noon.

Bright and early on the morning of April 10, the holds were opened up, the many lighters swarmed alongside like a brunch of hungry sharks, and, with the aid of the work forces brought on board, the provisions commenced swinging over the side into the lighters. There is no record available of the names and numbers of the ships which we serviced, but it was considerable in number.

Another appendectomy was performed on one of our hospital attendants, in the ship's surgery, which was completed satisfactorily. The deed was done by our new medical officer, assisted by some of our own chancre mechanics.

On the morning of April 15, the announcement came over the ship's PA system telling of the death of President Franklin Roosevelt. All work stopped while memorial services were held over the PA system. The mood on board the remainder of this day was one of subdued thought and muted speculations. It was obvious that the war was coming to a close, and very little was known of the new president, Harry S Truman. The daily news bulletins posted on the crew's notice board gave encouraging news of the advance of the Allied troops in Europe. There had been rumors of plans being made to redeploy the European forces to the Pacific, so we were hopeful of a speedy end to our war out here in the Pacific. We knew that the Japanese forces were but a shadow of their former power, and, except for a few isolated pockets of die-hard resistors, there was nothing left but mopping up before the final push into the home islands of Japan. However, some of the remaining steps were to be the bloodiest of the whole Pacific war. We were completely unaware of the development of the atomic bomb, of course.

At 0355 on April 16, we received proof that there was still some fight left in those local enemy pockets when the shore base flashed red for an air raid alert, sending us to general quarters for about ten minutes, then securing.

That day saw the last of our cargo leaving the holds, the ice machine and the cooling system auxiliaries being shut down, and cleaning up before going into our standby watch schedule. On April 17, Yard Oiler YO-164 filled our fuel tanks and the disbursing officer went ashore with about 527 Australian pounds sterling, returning with $1,665 in good old American currency. On Thursday, April 19, the last of the passengers came aboard, and a happy bunch they were. The word was out, they knew their destination, had their orders, and this was the day they had been waiting for. We of the ship's crew, of course, shared their joy.

"Now hear this! Set special sea detail!"

It was 1000 on April 20, 1945, and for sure, there were no laggards this morning, for we were heading home, stateside, the Golden Gate Bridge, and all points east, north, and south from there for those who would be going on leave.

The special anchor detail was set, the anchor windlass was warming up, and in 15 minutes the steam was admitted to the port wildcat. It started to rotate, the whelps grabbing each link of the 45 fathoms of chain, one link at a time, straining, clanking, groaning, and steadily pulling in the chain. All the while, a hose stream of seawater was blasting the mud and marine growth off the chain as it came out of the hawsepipe. The muddy water which splashed on the sea detail in the vicinity brought forth no complaints that time.

Each link coming off the wildcat dropped down into the chain locker below the main deck, where it was being manhandled by a sturdy seaman, wielding his chain hook to guide the links into a neat pile, to prevent tangles and jams when it had to be payed out at the next stop in port.

The pull on the anchor chain eased the ship up close, until the anchor came free of the mud and was hanging plumb. The wildcat continued in its task of hoisting the anchor until its shank came up hard into the hawsepipe. The chain on deck was secured, the steam to the windlass was secured, and the ship was on its way!

At 1024, we were underway to join a convoy headed toward Eniwetok in the Marshall Islands. It was a five-column convoy, escorted by the USS *Parle* (DE-708), USS *PC-1131,* and USS *George A. Johnson* (DE-583). The course was east, and the standard speed was a meager 9 knots, but it was smooth sailing.

On April 23, we were detached from the convoy to proceed alone to Eniwetok, with standard speed 12 knots, zigzagging, just in case there were still some enemy submarines in the path. Many of them had been sunk by then or were held in home port from lack of fuel. Our luck held out, however, and at 1000 on April 30, we snuggled up to USS *YO-161* in the harbor at Eniwetok and refueled for the last leg home.

Our orders when we left Leyte Gulf were to proceed to San Francisco for repairs and alterations. During this first phase of the voyage home, lists were being prepared of those who wished to be transferred and those who wanted to stay on board for the next cruise. Those who stayed would have staggered leave, and those who left the ship for further duty would receive 30 days leave before being reassigned. I decided to take my chances on a new assignment, as did about 70 percent of the crew.

The refueling took just about four and a half hours. Then we were underway again, east toward San Francisco, at 12½ knots, zigzagging on our base course, with a happy crew aboard, and spring in the air. The second day out of Eniwetok, two electrician's mates were brought before captain's report mast for disobeying orders of the master-at-arms and were put in the brig, two days P & P.

The *Octans* crossed the international date line on Friday, May 4, thus giving us two Fridays, May 4. The second one was a bad one for a gunner's mate, who was caught leaving his gun station without a relief while on watch and was put in solitary confinement for two days on P & P. Well, the brig confinements were probably better than being restricted to the ship in San Francisco—if one had a choice, that is.

During this phase of the voyage home, there were a lot of bull sessions among the crew, discussing what their future was going to be like, making all types of plans, pledges, and preparations, as if they had much to say about the future. There were also some fond reminiscing about our liberties in New Zealand and Australia, with some of the stories being repeated and elaborated on several times, sailor fashion. There were a few regrets mentioned and some longing remembrances related to any who would listen. It was a time for reviewing and critiquing the past months, going over in our minds and in our discussions the things we did wrong, those times when we broke the rules without getting caught, and the positive accomplishments, also. There were many of the latter, but we did not dwell on them, taking what satisfaction we felt personally to ourselves.

For myself, I felt that my positive accomplishments outweighed the other two, in regard to my shipboard activities. In regard to my behavior on liberty, I felt that I had little cause for regret. Some of my shipmates went to extremes in their relations with the girls in port, as if they were simply trying to prove a point to themselves and their shipmates and to uphold the reputation assigned to Yanks abroad. Fortunately, we weren't all like that. My final assessment was simply: I tasted of the wine, but I didn't swallow it.

Still zigzagging at 12½ knots, we passed Makapuu Light just south of Hawaii and altered course to northeast, in a more direct line to San Francisco. We then ceased zigzagging and opened the throttle to 13 knots. On the morning of May 8 came the announcement over the PA system: "Now hear this! Germany has surrendered! The war in Europe is over!"

Details were then posted on the notice board for the crew to read. There was joy, backslapping, and happiness abounding all over the ship. Just how many men changed their future plans as a result of the announcement, it is hard to say. I didn't change mine. I had not formulated any definite plans, other than to make a side trip from San Francisco down to Los Angeles before taking the train to Minnesota. In January 1942, when my brother got married, I was the best man, and the bride's sister was bridesmaid. I happened to see her again in November while home on leave from boot camp. Since then, she had moved to Los Angeles and was working there; so I planned to go down and visit her before going on to finish my leave in Minnesota.

Day followed night and night followed day several more times, during which we came ever closer to the Golden Gate. Those crew members with sentences to serve got their brig hitches completed, with a full meal inside them again. Our speed had been reduced slightly, to permit us to enter the harbor at San Francisco at dawn. And this we did. On the morning of May 15, all hands not on watch were on deck, looking into the rising sun ahead of us, with the Golden Gate Bridge outlined against the sun. It was a beautiful spring morning, temperature just right, a light wind blowing as we passed under the bridge. We looked up as we passed under it and could see the cars driving along in both directions, carrying lucky civilians on their way to work. That, at least had not changed since our outward passage 23 long months ago.

At 0830, we anchored in San Francisco Bay near Yerba Buena Island, discharged our passengers, and took on two new ensigns for duty. It was underway again, to moor up to Pier #3, Hurley's Shipyard, at Oakland. While the yard workers commenced their survey of work to be done to our home of the past months, there was a general commotion on board. It was not until a full week had gone by that transfer orders and arrangements had been completed, and those men going on leave were able to walk off the ship and say good-bye to it and their shipmates. My turn came, along with many others, on May 23.

The regulation method for a sailor in the U.S. Navy to carry his gear was to have it all wrapped up so that it consisted of one kidney-shaped bundle, familiar to all who had seen the public relations picture of the typical American sailor on the move. By then, however, the hammock had been discarded by many of us on board the *Octans,* and in my case, I had packed everything into two seabags and a small satchel. The seabags I connected with a short double line, and slung the seabags over my shoulder, with one dangling ahead of me, bumping my knees with every step and the other one bouncing off my butt with every step. In my left hand I carried the satchel, containing loose items and my orders, and walked off the gangplank. My gear was carried by truck, and I joined the others in the Navy busses, which took us to the U.S. Navy Receiving Barracks at Treasure Island, where we all checked in, located our temporary bunks, and recovered our gear.

End of the cruise with the USS *Octans* for me. Start of another phase of my Navy life, and that of the ship.

Looking back at that day, after the intervening almost fifty years, several things are obvious in my mind. On that day, the ship was in the best condition it had been in for years. The constant efforts of the crew, coupled with all of the overhauls and changes which were made, produced a much better ship than when the Navy took her over in April 1943. It is really too bad that her owners, the United Fruit Company, did not see fit to retain her in service after the war, since she was better able to fulfill her previous job as a banana boat than when the War Shipping Administration took control of her. Economics apparently proved otherwise.

As for myself, I am convinced that when I left the ship that day in May 1945, I was in the best physical condition that I have ever been in my life. Score one point for the U.S. Navy.

Was the *Octans* a happy ship? Decidedly, yes. Oh, there were some bad times and a few bad misfits who were smoked out of the dark recesses of the ship, brought to light, identified, tried in some manner, and properly dealt with. But this process only made the final life for the rest of us that much happier and smoother. So taking everything into consideration, on balance, most members of the crew would agree that it was, indeed, a happy ship.

Did the *Octans* change our lives? It most certainly did, and for the most part, that change was for the better. It made men out of boys and started many of the crew on their future careers, where before they had just been drifting in their civilian lives. Score another point for the U.S. Navy.

Did we produce any heroes on board that cruise? Not that I am aware of. At least, none that would be paraded in the back seat of a convertible, driving slowly down Main Street of our larger cities. However, most of us were heroes in a small way to those left behind on the home front. That is about the most any of us expected, and we were thankful for that.

Let those who would be great heroes be so. We were on our way home to our loved ones, after having done our best and survived.

Chapter 21

The Final Months

From our return to San Francisco to the end of the ship's life, the records are very slim in detail. A member of the crew wrote an unofficial *History of USS Octans* around January 1, 1946, without signing his name. With apologies for using it without giving him full personal credit in writing, I shall borrow material from it. With additional data from the *Dictionary of U.S. Naval Fighting Ships,* published by the U.S. Government Printing Office, and with input from several members of the crew who were aboard during the cruise from the States, it is possible to give a fair account of the remaining months of service for the *Octans.*

As soon as the ship had entered Hurley Shipyard repair facilities, the work began in earnest. The assistant industrial manager, USN, located in the Ferry Building, San Francisco, had received a letter from the chief of the Bureau of Ships, listing the numerous alterations and improvements to be made to the *Octans,* should there be time and material available to make them. The list was quite extensive, and there is no confirming list checking off which ones had been accomplished. We do know that newer guns topside were installed, with all changes in equipment required to serve them, but the old fire control system was retained. The boilers came in for some extensive repair work, along with the fuel oil system. There were some repairs made in the engine room machinery. The past short stops for emergency repairs were showing their effect, and it was time to make more lasting repairs, within the short time available. The ventilation system had caused some concern in the past months, due to its inadequacy in the tropics, so it was improved to a considerable degree.

The first two weeks after the ship entered the yard, while large drafts of men were leaving the ship and before new replacements were due to arrive, there was a shortage of manpower on board. A chief watertender

Octans operations group (J.W. Williams, RdM).

was one of the first of the new men to come aboard, and he, with a fireman from the previous cruise, were alone in the fireroom. Fortunately, the duties were minor at that time. The only real problem came at the very beginning when the chief watertender was told to empty the fuel oil tanks to an oil barge alongside. There were no drawings on board showing the system, so he had to trace down the lines involved until he had the valves lined up properly and the pump started to perform the task. There were eight tanks which had to be emptied, which is quite a task.

While the ship was undergoing repair work at the Hurley Shipyards, the requisition placed two years previously for an SF radar was finally honored, and a new SF-2 was installed in and over the room which had been assigned in May 1943, but which had been occupied since then by one of the officers. One of the seamen, a radar striker, was sole man in charge until the ship arrived at Manila in August 1945. There, two radarmen were signed aboard, and three radarmen strikers, all seamen, were assigned to that duty, making up three, two-man watches on the radar system. Crash courses held by the two rated radarmen soon elevated the four strikers to radarmen third class, and the radar was then properly manned.

While the alterations were in progress in the shipyard, new replacements for crew transfers were taking place regularly, and some were going on leave, while others were returning from leave. For those remaining

U. S. S. Octans

Ship's Company Dance

2000 JUNE 26, 1945

PALACE HOTEL
(Gold Room)
MARKET AT MONTGOMERY
SAN FRANCSCO

INFORMAL

Music for Dancing Styled by
RAY HACKETT and His CBS Band

Announcement of ship's dance (W. Dowgiewicz, SC).

on the ship's roster as part of the 30 percent who chose to stay with the ship, liberty was an enjoyable experience in the San Francisco Bay area. There was even a ship's dance, given in the Palace Hotel, at the corner of Market and Montgomery Streets in San Francisco, the last week of June.

While available for this overhaul period, additional life rafts were supplied to the ship, which had been on order since before the commissioning in June 1943. Also, that very important item for the crew's comfort and enjoyment, the ice cream machine, was replaced with one of a larger capacity, but it almost took an act of Congress to get it. It meant

For Your Pleasure

THE KILGORE DANCERS
Princesses of Precision

DORIS DINELT
Song Stylist (Copacabana)

LO FON WA
Oriental Equilibrist

JACKIE DOLAN
Harmonica Wizard

THE THREE COPELANDS
Sensational Skaters

RAY HACKETT
Silhouettes in Music

Produced by
HAYMOND BOOKING AGENCY
Ships' Service

Dance entertainment program (W. Dowgiewicz, SC).

that the geedunk stand could remain open longer hours for the crew's refreshment breaks.

Some time around the first of July, the ship sailed again under the Golden Gate Bridge with a crew of 213 men, but that time for more repairs at Seattle. When those were over, the ship was loaded again with chilled and frozen cargo, and on July 18, she sailed for Supply Run #15.

The day before the ship was scheduled to leave Seattle, the chief watertender came back aboard from an all-night liberty and found that one of the boilers was out of service, due to a low-water condition which had happened during the night. The cause was unknown at first, only that the boiler had to be shut down when the fuseable plug, whose function was described in an earlier chapter, had blown. The chief called all of the firemen to the fireroom and asked them if anyone had been seen in the fireroom who was not authorized to be there. The only other person seen in the fireroom was the chief engineer, so the chief watertender went up to the chief engineer's office and confronted him. He was the only other one on the ship who knew how to let the water out of the boiler.

The chief engineer admitted he had done it because he wanted to stay in port for a few more days. It did not work—the captain was refused permission, and they sailed on schedule, on three boilers. It took about 36 hours to get the boiler back on the line. The chief watertender supervised giving the boiler the standard hydrotest on cold water, before lighting off and bringing the boiler up to full pressure on the line, after which the engine room telegraph rang "Full Ahead Both Engines."

The trip west to the Philippines was without major mechanical problems of any consequence, attesting to all the repair work which had been done. The new crew had to be broken in by those who were veterans of the first cruise. Their job was much easier, however, as the condition of the ship was much better than when we sailed outward bound under the Golden Gate Bridge about two years before.

The first stop was at Eniwetok, arriving approximately July 31, for refueling and victualing the numerous ships anchored in the atoll. When all orders had been filled, the ship sailed for Manila around August 1. The *Octans* was alone and zigzagging at a comfortable speed on a direct route to Leyte, almost due west along the 11 degrees north latitude line. This route was into an area which had become highly concentrated with heavy allied traffic converging upon Leyte Gulf, from whence the route into Manila was often taken. The enemy was well aware of this lucrative situation.[51]

On July 28, the cruiser USS *Indianapolis* (CA-35) left Guam, destination Leyte. She had delivered the vital material for the first atom bomb to Tinian. Her route was also direct, and she was cruising along in normal fashion. Just after midnight, July 30, the Japanese submarine I-58 sent two torpedoes into the *Indianapolis,* sinking her in about 15 minutes. Most of the crew managed to leave the sinking ship. The survivors were not spotted until August 2, and then only by accident.

When the first blobs of floating humanity were pulled from the sea and the oil cleaned off them, the word finally went out of the tragedy. Immediately, a warning was broadcast of enemy submarine activity in the area, which was received by the officers on the bridge of the *Octans,* fast approaching the area. Around August 6, she passed about 60 miles south of the site of the sinking, and all hands went to general quarters for several hours. The first atomic bomb was dropped on Hiroshima during this period, August 6, 1945, and was followed by another one dropped on Nagasaki three days later.

The *Octans* sailed into Manila Bay on August 13, past what was left of Corregidor, and anchored. The next day, while unloading to the many lighters alongside the ship, news spread around quickly that Japan had surrendered. There was great rejoicing throughout the ships in the harbor and the people and Allied forces in Manila. Around August 16, the *Octans* closed up shop and departed for a safe and enjoyable passage up the coast of Luzon and into Subic Bay. It did not take long to get rid of much of the remaining cargo on board.

"Now hear this! The recreational party will leave the ship at 1300!"

It was to be a beer and baseball game party on an island in Subic Bay, and the number signed up for it made a well-packed load for an LCM (see page 266) sent from the beach. The festivities got underway, with the beer allotment in hand, and the sides chosen for the game. The game commenced and the crew quickly worked up to their maximum enthusiasm. However, the game was not exciting enough to satisfy a couple of the men, so they decided to explore the jungle at the edge of the field. Very soon, they came upon an old enemy ammo dump, which immediately set their mischievous minds whirring. In no time at all, they had gathered enough material to start a fire. When it was burning brightly, they scrammed back to the game and waited to see what would happen.

The fireworks were spectacular, the noise deafening, and the flying debris was sufficient to cause the game to be called off, by unanimous consent. That ended the beach party, and the men returned to the ship, arguing over who would have won the game. It was never decided, naturally.

The mood throughout the ship reflected the relaxed sailing orders as the ship headed south to Hollandia, arriving about August 29. While en route, the ship passed over the equator, as she had many times before. This time there was a difference, however, as it was now peace time, and the ship could indulge in such a luxury as holding the traditional hijinks to initiate those who were crossing the line for the first time. It was August 28, and the old hands did themselves up proud in arranging the party.

The night before arriving at Hollandia, the captain, who had been on board since late December 1943, called the chief master-at-arms up to his cabin. He explained that there was a small clique of crew members on board which he wanted off the ship in the morning. He had a list of

En route to beer and baseball party, Subic Bay, P.I. (J.W. Williams, RdM).

seven men; they were rounded out of their bunks, told to pack their gear, and they were off the ship at 0700.

There were a number of ships of the fleet anchored at Hollandia, most of which were in need of food, and the *Octans* obliged, until it was all gone. Then it was up anchor, about September 8, course southeast along the coast of New Guinea, then south through the Cormorant Channel, through Jomard Strait, and southwest toward Brisbane.

The ship continued on its steady southerly course to tie up at Brisbane, ready for another load, Supply Run #16, around September 16. As might be expected, veterans of the first cruise knew their way around the city and its more enjoyable sailor hangouts, and they were not slow in teaching the new hands where to have the most fun. It was especially enjoyable now that peace had come to the world, and Australia had survived without being overrun by the enemy.

21. The Final Months

While in Brisbane to load for the next trip north, the first contingent of servicemen from the ship were put ashore at the Navy base. It was a happy 12 men who were told of their orders, who quickly packed their gear, and strode off the ship to board the bus for the Navy base, to start the first leg of their journey back to Uncle Sugar. This was only the beginning of the returning flood of Navy personnel, to be repeated at nearly every stop of the ship in the remaining months of her service.

When the *Octans* swung its last net load over the bulwarks and into the holds, the hatches were closed and battened down, and the ship steamed out of the channel to the open sea about September 24. This time it was a relaxed trip north to Manila Bay again, with no worry about enemy submarines and planes, arriving about October 4. The main talk on board was what a wonderful time they had had in Brisbane and what chances they had to get home by Christmas. The point system was in full operation, and the "old salts" among the crew were occupied in calculating their approximate date of returning home to the States.

While in Manila, another 16 men were transferred ashore, destination stateside for separation from the service. They were replaced by 28 men from the Navy base at Subic Bay assignment pool. As a result of the demobilization program, the demand for the fresh provisions was lighter, and it took longer than usual to get rid of the cargo. But the day finally came, October 12, when it was up anchor, out of the harbor, and south toward Brisbane again, for another load, arriving around October 23. The orders were to take on another full load of provisions and get back up to Manila.

Those orders were delayed, as there was a longshoremen's strike on. The ship went into a period of inaction, with the crew enjoying every minute of it. The following story is an example of the relaxed atmosphere on the ship.

It was a Sunday morning, the crew were in all stages of a typical morning-after awakening, a few fully dressed, but many in various stages of undress, when there appeared in the berthing quarters the ship's chief watertender with a woman friend. He had brought her down to the crew's quarters as a lark, to let her see the fun when she appeared. To them, it was hilariously funny; but to the crew, it was an entirely different matter. He had invited her aboard to have Sunday dinner with him, since he was the only CPO on board. They sat in the chief's quarters, having a few drinks, when the captain joined them, and asked if they minded. He was invited to stay, the chief put steaks on the grill, and the three of them had dinner.

As a result of the closure of the Navy base at Perth which took place about this time, a large draft of enlisted men were brought on board to be taken to the base at Subic Bay in the Philippines. There were approximately 200 "white hats" and 60 chiefs; the master-at-arms had some difficulty with a very small portion of the chiefs. The troublemakers were isolated and berthed in #4 hold, while the remainder were assigned berths on and above the main deck. All chiefs were fed in the crew's mess, having the privilege of being first in the chow line. The "white hats" were berthed in bunks provided for passengers in the upper decks, as described earlier in this book. Three of them objected to being assigned the task of painting the spaces above the engine room. Their objections vanished when the executive officer threatened them with a charge of open mutiny.

While the ship was waiting to load in Brisbane for Supply Run #17, another ship's dance was held at the Belle Vue Hotel on George Street in Brisbane, the nights of November 5 and 6, just to leave a wild and happy note as a remembrance among the citizens of Brisbane, as well as the crew itself. The arrangements were made by the following:

C.C. Frandsen	Machinist
R.E. Tygard	SK1c
L.A. Smith	BM1c
R.E. Schmidt	RM2c
F.K. Holcomb	CM2c
V.N. Haggard	MM2c
T. Dills	Cox

The strike over, it took several days to load the ship. During that time, two men were transferred ashore, one going to the station hospital for medical treatment, the other one for discharge. This last one was Joe, the machinist's mate from the engine room whose application for transfer ashore at Sydney had not been allowed, as mentioned in a previous chapter. He finally made it!

About November 9, the ship pulled out of the channel at Brisbane and turned north for an uneventful trip to Manila Bay, arriving around November 21. During the supply of the fleet and the bases ashore, a draft of 35 men were sent on their first leg of the trip home for separation from the Navy. They were replaced with 31 men from the assignment pool ashore.

In Manila Bay on that stop, it took longer than before to unload the fresh and frozen food, due to the scarcity of ships and armed forces remaining. In fact, while in Manila Bay, the demand was so low that the ship received orders to proceed to Shanghai, December 7. Perhaps they could get rid of the last of the cargo there.

It was worth a try, so they hoisted the anchor and sailed, arriving

God of peace statue, Shanghai (W. Dowgiewicz, SC).

in Shanghai Harbor about December 13. Liberty for part of the crew was declared the first night, and all of those who rated it hurried ashore to determine for themselves if the many lurid stories the old "Asiatic Hands" had been telling them were true. Many of these were about the fleshpots in the murky back alleys and behind beaded curtains. The men left behind on the ship were not to be forgotten, however. No sooner had the sun set than sampans began gliding alongside the ship. The men in the sampans were equipped with grappling hooks attached to knotted lines, which they swung unto the ship's bulwarks. As soon as a purchase had been achieved, a flood of girls clambered up the lines and established themselves on deck, ready for business.

When the captain came back aboard, he was furious and ordered them all off the ship. It was necessary for him to chase some of them off and to go on a hunt for every last one. The OOD was confined to his room for three days, and the bos'un's mate first class was restricted to the ship for one week.

With the liberty party ashore and the "party" on board that first night, there was a run on the sick bay and the duty chancre mechanics for prophylactics. During the remainder of the stay in Shanghai, a deck patrol guarded against any further such business enterprises.

When the ships in the harbor had been cajoled into taking as much of the cargo as they could handle, there was still about 600 tons left aboard. The USS *Calamares* was in port at the same time, and they agreed to take some of it, but there was still a few tons left. What to do with it? The decision was made to dump it in the harbor, that stinking sewer surrounding the ships at anchor. In some mysterious manner, the sampan owners in the harbor got wind of the intentions to deep-six the remaining cargo, mostly meat, and several were ready for the freebies with their own contrivances for recovering the meat as it sank. Before releasing a cargo net loaded with meat into the harbor, the crew would spray the sampans and their crew with the fire hose, in an attempt to force them away. But the sampan men would not be denied, and they crowded in to fight for the meat, as polluted as it must have been.

Christmas Day was observed on board with the traditional dinner, as follows:

CHRISTMAS DAY DINNER
December 25, 1945

Cream of Tomato Soup
Soda Crackers
Ripe Stuffed Olives   Sweet Mixed Pickles
Roast Young Tom Turkey
Giblet Gravy   Clam Dressing
Cranberry Sauce   Whipped Irish Potatoes
Baked Virginia Ham
Buttered Corn   Peas and Carrots
Cabbage and Pineapple Salad
with Sweet Mayonnaise

21. The Final Months

	Fruit Cake	Plum Pudding	
	Hard Candy	Mixed Salted Nuts	
	Bread	Butter	Coffee
	Cigars	Cigarettes	

Supply Officer,	Commissary Officer,	Commissary Steward,
Lt. H.H. Trice	J.R. Kuch, CPC	W.P. Dowgiewicz, SC1c

C.T. Fitzgerald,
Commanding

Before leaving Shanghai, there was an exchange of crew with the USS *Calamares*, they giving 60 replacements for 44 men the *Octans* sent to them. Most of the men from the *Calamares* were destined for stateside discharge.

Orders were received on December 29 to proceed to Pearl Harbor. There was a delay of several days before the ship actually sailed out of Shanghai Harbor and pointed her prow towards Pearl Harbor, due east. At Pearl Harbor, while taking on fuel, the orders were changed, directing the ship to proceed to Puerto Cortes, Costa Rica, where the ship was to take on a full cargo of bananas for the ship's owners, the United Fruit Company. Before leaving Pearl Harbor, there was another familiar exchange of crew, as those with high points to be discharged on the West Coast were put ashore, to be replaced with men destined for East Coast bases for separation.

At Puerto Cortes, about 62,000 bunches of bananas were loaded into the holds, through the hatches only, as the side ports were still welded shut. The next stop was at the city of Panama, to enter the canal and, thus, the Caribbean. The refrigeration machinist's mate had been discharged at Pearl Harbor, so it was necessary for the United Fruit Company to fly one of their banana specialists down to the Canal Zone to ensure the safety and treatment of the cargo. The bananas were watched over carefully by the expert, and most of them reached the port of unloading, Charleston, South Carolina, in salable condition. It took three days to unload them, due again to the uselessness of the side ports. The ship then proceeded to Norfolk, Virginia. There the ship was stripped of all excess Navy property, such as tools, instruments and spare parts, while tied up at the dock during the day. When evening came, a pilot took the ship out into the harbor for anchoring over night. The *Octans* had two anchors out, as the bottom there is soft. Shortly after the pilot left the ship, the OOD noticed that the ship was drifting, and position bearings taken with the pelorus confirmed it. The captain was called, and after cussing out the watch officers, started maneuvering the ship back into position for taking a new hold. This was done by riding forward while taking in the anchors, dropping the anchors into the new location, then backing down until the anchors took hold. Just then, one of the deck officers remembered that the motor whaleboat was tied up to the taffrail on the poop, so he sent the duty bos'un back to cut it adrift for retrieval later. Too late. The prop wash coming forward alongside the ship brought with it the obvious remains of the whaleboat.

A couple of evenings later, the *Octans* added to its already tarnished reputation while at Norfolk. The pilot left the ship, and the captain took over to get the ship to anchor. During the maneuvering, the ship crossed the bow of a destroyer escort (DE) at anchor, just a little too closely. As the ship crossed the DE's bow, the starboard wind scoops on the outside of the portholes were wiped off by the DE's bow, causing the crew of that ship to go to collision stations. As if that was not enough trouble, as the *Octans* continued past, the starboard screw ran afoul of the DE's anchor chains. A couple of tug boats in the harbor assisted the captain in clearing the area and finally dropping the anchors in the assigned location.

A couple of days later, the *Octans* took in the spring lines and pulled away from the dock, destined for Baltimore and decommissioning, arriving February 20, 1946. You can be sure that the Naval port authorities at Norfolk were happy to see her leave. On March 6, the ship was decommissioned at Baltimore, at which time the remaining 99 members of the crew were discharged to the Navy Receiving Station ashore, some for reassignment, but most of them destined for release from the Navy.

The United Fruit Company had no immediate use for the ship. Things had changed during the war years, and they had better ships and better methods in mind for carrying the bananas from the Caribbean to the United States market. Therefore, the ship went back into the James River in Virginia for layup, along with other ships whose services were no longer required or desired, until their owners could decide to what fate to relegate them. The final decision came the following year: sell her for scrap.

And so ended the life of the SS *Ulua*, then the USS *Octans*. Her life spanned just 30 years. She did her duty during two world wars, as did some other ships of her vintage. The ship is gone now, and her crew are scattered over the globe, both dead and alive.

And the scrap metal from the old hulk? Probably went back to Japan soon after the ship was cut up.

Epilogue

My transfer orders from the *Octans* bore the notation: Recommended for 30 days leave. The Naval authorities at Treasure Island issued my travel documents, authorizing me to travel anyplace in the USA for the next 30 days, plus three days travel time. I was to report to the U.S. Navy Receiving Station at Wold Chamberlin Field in Minneapolis, Minnesota, on June 27. With all of my records and accounts in hand, I left San Francisco, bound for Los Angeles, to pay a visit to the girl I mentioned in Chapter 20, whom I had met four years before in Minneapolis, when my brother married her sister.

To paraphrase a famous quotation from Julius Caeser: I came, I saw, she conquered.

We got along very well, so well, in fact that I ended up giving her an engagement ring, which she accepted, after attempting to talk me out of it. From there, I took the train to Minneapolis, went the round of the relatives, then settled down in my hometown, Walker, in north central Minnesota, on the south shore of Leech Lake, for a rest.

When my leave time was up, I reported into Wold Chamberlin Field as ordered, then left by train for Camp Shoemaker in California. The camp was in a hot, dry, wind-swept desert just inland from San Francisco. Fortunately, I wasn't there very long; I was soon transferred to the Outgoing Unit barracks at Goat Island in Oakland Harbor to await transportation out. On July 28, I boarded the USS *Warhawk* (AP-168) with a shipload of other sailors headed back to the Pacific. I was drafted to stand throttle watch, which lasted until we unloaded at Tacloban, on Samar, P.I.

My one remaining memory of the short stopover at Tacloban is of the Army-type latrine serving the base. It was an open air affair, no walls, no roof, just a row of seats on a deck over an open pit. This was not unusual in itself, but I just could not get over the idea of being approached, while sitting there in contemplation, by Filipino girls selling bananas. Even to this day, I am reminded of it whenever I bite into a banana.

I spent a few days in quonset huts there, then onto an LCM for a rough and wet trip to Buckner Bay, Okinawa. Three days ashore in a tent, eating boxed rations, and on September 14, I went aboard the USS *Mona Island* (ARG-9) to replace another machinist's mate who was due to go home on points soon. My billet there was as machinist's mate, refrigeration, in charge of the refrigeration system for the general mess. I bunked in the ice machine room and soon settled down into a routine of comparative ease. The ship was anchored in Buckner Bay, and life was easy: tender duty, in Navy lingo.

Tender, that is, until October 9, when a typhoon came roaring through the area, demolishing the Naval facilities ashore and tossing us up on a reef. The word was passed, "Prepare to abandon ship!" A quick examination soon disclosed that there was no appreciable damage to the hull, so the word was cancelled, and we sat on the reef and waited for the typhoon to pass over. While there, we rescued the crew of a patrol craft, which had been swamped just off our starboard bow.

Damage to the ship was slight but sufficient to prevent us from using the rudder or the engine, so we were towed to Guam for temporary repairs to the steering system, rudder, and screws. From there, we were able to steam under our own power, with a jury-rigged rudder control, first to Honolulu, for a liberty ashore, then to San Diego, arriving there December 11. There was enough time for a telephone call to Los Angeles to let my future wife know I was on my way home; then the ship sailed for the Panama Canal. We transited the canal just before Christmas, and steamed nonstop to the Brooklyn Navy Yard, entering January 3, 1946. Five days later, I was at the U.S. Naval Receiving Station, Wold Chamberlin Field, Minneapolis. My discharge, honorable, of course, from the U.S. Navy was effective on January 9.

My future wife was on hand to greet me, and together we made our wedding plans. End of one career; start of another one.

Notes

Preface

1. *Mister Roberts,* Heggen Thomas: Houghton Mifflin, Boston, 1946.

Chapter 1

2. *Audel's New Marine Engineer's Guide,* Theodore Audel & Co., 1937.
3. *Remember Pearl Harbor,* Don Reid and Sammy Kaye: Republic Music Corp., 1941.
4. *I'll Be Home for Christmas,* Kim Gannon and Walter Kent: G & K Music Co., 1943.
5. *I'm Dreaming of a White Christmas,* Irving Berlin: Irving Berlin Music Co., 1940 and 1943.

Chapter 2

6. Private correspondence with Cornelius Maher, retired UFC official.
7. Copyright 1987 by Cherry Lane Music Publishing Company/Lord Burgess Music Publishing Co.
8. *New Encyclopaedia Britannica,* Micropedia Edition, Vol. 12, pages 855 and 856.
9. C. Maher correspondence.
10. Ibid.

Chapter 3

11. *U.S. Warships of WWII,* Paul Silverstone, Naval Institute Press, pages 329 and 330.
12. U.S. Navy correspondence, Washington/Mare Island Navy Yard.

13. Ibid.
14. Ibid.

Chapter 4

15. *The Campaigns of MacArthur in the Pacific,* vol. 1, by his staff, Govt. Printing Office, 1966, pages 63 and 84.
16. Ibid., pages 117 and 118.
17. U.S. Navy correspondence, Washington/Mare Island Navy Yard.
18. Author's service records.
19. *History of WWII,* Francis Trevelyan Miller, Riverside Book and Bible House, 1948, page 469.
20. *Campaigns of MacArthur,* page 62.

Chapter 5

21. *History of WWII,* Miller, page 471.
22. *Campaigns of MacArthur,* page 118.
23. Ibid., page 125, Plate 37.

Chapter 6

24. Standard Reference Encyclopedia, Funk & Wagnalls, 1963 edition, Harper Collins, page 5569.
25. *The Pacific War,* by John Costello, Atlantic Communications, 1981, pages 422–425.
26. *Campaigns of MacArthur,* pages 125, 128, Plate 37.

Chapter 7

27. *Campaigns of MacArthur,* page 97.
28. *Ibid.,* pages 93 and 131.
29. *Ibid.,* pages 93 and 132, Plate 39.
30. *The Great White Fleet,* by John Melville, Vantage Press, Inc., 1976.

Chapter 8

31. *Jungle Fighters,* by Jules Archer, Julian Messner Div., Simon & Schuster, 1985, pages 19–22.
32. Ibid.
33. *Campaigns of MacArthur,* page 55. *American Caesar,* Wm. Manchester,

33. *Campaigns of MacArthur,* page 55. *American Caesar,* Wm. Manchester, paperback, Dell Publishing Co., 1978, page 342. *Brisbane Goes to War,* Brisbane City Council, brochure, ca. 1992.
34. *Campaigns of MacArthur,* page 132.

Chapter 9

35. *Jungle Fighters,* page 94.
36. *Campaigns of MacArthur,* pages 138-141.

Chapter 11

37. Correspondence, New Zealand Secretary of External Relations & Trade, 1/26/93.
38. *Campaigns of MacArthur,* pages 138-141.

Chapter 12

39. *Campaigns of MacArthur,* pages 138-141.
40. Ibid., pages 146-148.

Chapter 14

41. *Campaigns of MacArthur,* pages 152 and 153.
42. Ibid., page 142.

Chapter 18

43. *Campaigns of MacArthur,* pages 199 and 234.
44. Ibid., pages 250-252: The Visayan P.I. Task Force was the name assigned to the U.S. Forces in the Central Philippines.
45. *History of WWII,* page 887.
46. *Typhoon: The Other Enemy,* by Capt. C. Raymond Calhoun, 1981, U.S. Naval Institute, pages 178-181.
47. *Campaigns of MacArthur,* page 250.
48. Ibid., pages 236 and 237.

Chapter 19

49. *Campaigns of MacArthur,* pages 250-252.
50. Ibid., page 267.

Chapter 21

51. *All the Drowned Sailors,* by Raymond B. Lech, 1982, Military Heritage Press Division, Marboro Book Corp., various pages.

Appendix A

Manning Complement, USS *Octans*
As of June 25, 1943

Officers, commissioned and warrant		22
Chief Petty Officers (CPO)		18
AS	Seaman Apprentice	1
Bkr3c	Baker, third class	2
BM2c	Bos'un's Mate, second class	1
CM3c	Carpenter's Mate, third class	3
CM2c	Carpenter's Mate, second class	1
Ck3c	Cook, third class	1
Cox	Coxswain	3
EM3c	Electrician's Mate, third class	3
EM2c	Electrician's Mate, second class	2
F3c	Fireman, third class	14
F2c	Fireman, second class	2
F1c	Fireman, first class	17
GM3c	Gunner's Mate, third class	1
GM2c	Gunner's Mate, second class	1
HA2c	Hospital Apprentice, second class	1
MM2c	Machinist's Mate, second class	10
MM1c	Machinist's Mate, first class	2
OC1c	Officer's Cook, first class	1
Ptr1c	Painter, first class	1
PhM3c	Pharmacist's Mate, third class	1
PhM1c	Pharmacist's Mate, first class	1
QM3c	Quartermaster's Mate, third class	1
RM3c	Radioman, third class	1
RM2c	Radioman, second class	1
SC3c	Ship's Cook, third class	2
SC1c	Ship's Cook, first class	3
S2c	Seaman, second class	38
S1c	Seaman, first class	7
SF3c	Shipfitter, third class	3
SF1c	Shipfitter, first class	1
SM3c	Signalman, third class	2
SM2c	Signalman, second class	1
St2c	Steward, second class	1
StM2c	Steward's Mate, second class	11

SK3c	Storekeeper, third class	4	WT2c	Watertender, second class	3
SK2c	Storekeeper, second class	7	WT1c	Watertender, first class	1
SK1c	Storekeeper, first class	2	Y3c	Yeoman, third class	1
			Y1c	Yeoman, first class	1

Source: Administration Remarks, USS *Octans*, June 11, 1943 to June 26, 1943.

Note: The ratings above denotes a man's pay scale and basic specialty qualifications. Each one also had a job title describing his duties while on board.

Appendix B

Major Navy Abbreviations

The following list contains selected standard abbreviations used by the Navy.

ACE — Allied Command Europe
ADCOM — Administrative Command
ADSM — American Defense Service Medal
AEC — Atomic Energy Commission
AMG — Allied Military Government of Occupied Territory
AMPH — Amphibian, amphibious
ASW — Antisubmarine Warfare
BCD — Bad Conduct Discharge
BLT — Battalion Landing Team
BUDOCKS — Bureau of Yards and Docks
BUMED — Bureau of Medicine and Surgery
BUPERS — Bureau of Naval Personnel
BUSANDA — Bureau of Supplies and Accounts
BUSHIPS — Bureau of Ships
BUWEPS — Bureau of Naval Weapons
CAVU — Ceiling and visibility unlimited
CB — Construction Battalion
CEC — Civil Engineering Corps
CHC — Chaplain Corps
CINC — Commander-in-Chief
CINCFE — Commander-in-Chief Far East
CINCLANT — Commander-in-Chief Atlantic
CINCNE — Commander-in-Chief, U.S. Northeast Command
CINCNELM — Commander-in-Chief, U.S. Naval Forces, Eastern Atlantic and Mediterranean
CINCPAC — Commander-in-Chief Pacific
CHINFO — Chief of Information
CNO — Chief of Naval Operations
CONUS — Continental United States
CTF — Commander Task Force
CTG — Commander Task Group
CTU — Commander Task Unit
DCNO — Deputy Chief of Naval Operations
DC — Dental Corps
DFC — Distinguished Flying Cross
DNI — Director of Naval Intelligence
DSM — Distinguished Service Medal
ETA — Estimated time of arrival

Appendix B

ETC — Estimated time of completion
ETD — Estimated time of departure
ETR — Estimated time of return
FADM — Fleet Admiral
FAGU — Fleet Air Gunnery Unit
FAIR — Fleet Air
FLOGWING — Fleet Logistic Air Wing
FMCR — Fleet Marine Corps Reserve
FMF — Fleet Marine Force
FPO — Fleet Post Office
GCA — Ground controlled approach
GCM — General Court Martial
GD — General Discharge
HC — Hospital Corps
HYDRO — Hydrographic
IFR — Instrument Flight Rules
ILS — Instrument Landing System
JATO — Jet assisted take-off
JCS — Joint Chiefs of Staff
LSO — Landing Signal Officer
MATS — Military Air Transport Service
MAW — Marine Aircraft Wing
MC — Medical Corps
MSC — Medical Service Corps
MSTS — Military Sea Transportation Service
NAB — Naval Air Base
NAS — Naval Air Station
NATO — North Atlantic Treaty Organization
NAVFE — Naval Forces Far East
NC — Nurse Corps
NEL — Naval Electronics Laboratory
NRL — Naval Research Laboratory
NSD — Naval Supply Depot
NTC — Naval Training Center
NWC — National War College
OINC — Officer-in-Charge
ONI — Office of Naval Intelligence
ONR — Office of Naval Research
OOD — Officer of the Deck
OTC — Officer in Tactical Command
PIO — Public Information Officer
POA — Pacific Ocean Area
POW — Prisoner of War
PUC — Presidential Unit Citation
PWO — Public Works Officer
RDF — Radio direction finder
SANDA — Supplies and Accounts
SC — Supply Corps
SCM — Summary Court Martial
SECNAV — Secretary of the Navy
SDO — Special duty only
SP — Shore Patrol
SOP — Standing Operating Procedure
SUBASE — Submarine Base
UDT — Underwater Demolition Team
UHF — Ultra High Frequency
USNA — United States Naval Academy
USNFR — United States Naval Fleet Reserve
USNR — United States Naval Reserve
VHF — Very High Frequency
VIP — Very Important Person
VLF — Very Low Frequency
XO — Executive Officer

Source: The Navy Blue Book, Vol. 1, 1960, Bobbs-Merrill div., Macmillan Press, New York.

Appendix C

Refrigerated Stores Ships Operated by the U.S. Navy

Navy I.D.	Name	Former Name	Gross Tonnage	Life[1]
AF-1	Bridge[2]		5207	16/16/48
AF-7	Arctic	Yamhill	5976	18/21/47
AF-8	Boreas	Yaquina	6100	18/21/46
AF-9	Yukon	Mehanno	5970	19/21/46
AF-10	Aldebaran	Stag Hound	7169	39/40
AF-11	Polaris	Donald McKay	8222	39/41/57
*AF-12	Mizar	Quirigua	6982	32/41/46
*AF-13	Tarazed	Chiriqui	6963	31/41/46
AF-14	Uranus	Maria	1369	33/41/46
*AF-15	Talamanca		6963	31/42/45
*AF-16	Pastores		7241	12/41/47
*AF-18	Calamares		7782	13/41/47
AF-19	Roamer	African Reefer	1770	35/42/46
AF-20	Pontiac	Australian Reefer	2321	37/42/45
*AF-21	Merak	Veragua	6982	32/42/46
*AF-22	Ariel	USS Dione	6968	31/42/46
*AF-23	Cygnus	La Perla	3792	25/42/46
*AF-24	Delphinus	San Mateo	3289	15/42/46
*AF-25	Taurus	San Benito	3724	21/42/45
*AF-26	Octans	Ulua	6494	17/43/47
AF-28	Hyades	Iberville	6165	43/43
AF-29	Graffias	Topa Topa	6165	43/44
AF-30	Adria		3770	44/44/60
AF-31	Arequipa		3803	44/44/61
AF-32	Corduba		3803	44/44/60
AF-33	Karin		3803	44/45/61
AF-34	Kerstin		3804	44/45/49
AF-35	Latona		3804	44/45/49

Appendix C

Navy I.D.	Name	Former Name	Gross Tonnage	Life[1]
AF-36	*Lioba*		3804	44/45/60
AF-37	*Malabar*		3804	44/45/60
AF-38	*Merapi*		3804	44/45/60
AF-39	*Palisana*		3809	44/45/46
AF-41	*Athanasia*	*Stevedore Knot*	3803	44/45/46
AF-42	*Bondia*	*Flemish Bend*	3805	44/45/46
AF-43	*Gordonia*	*Whale Knot*	3770	44/45/46
AF-44	*Laurentia*	*Wall and Crown*	3805	44/45/46
AF-45	*Lucidor*		3809	45/45/46
AF-46	*Octavia*		3777	45/45/46
AF-47	*Valentine*		3777	45/45/46

*Indicates former United Fruit Company ships.
[1]Indicates year launched/acquired/dropped.
[2]Built for the Navy, and scrapped in 1948.

Sources: U.S. Warships of World War Two, by Silverstone; *The Great White Fleet,* by John Melville; data furnished by Cornelius Maher, former UFC official.

Appendix D

Ships of the U.S. Navy

AIRCRAFT CARRIERS

Designation	Type
CVA	Attack Aircraft Carrier
CVA(N)	Nuclear-Powered Attack Aircraft Carrier
CVE	Escort Aircraft Carrier
CVHE	Escort Helicopter Aircraft Carrier
CVL	Small Aircraft Carrier
CVS	ASW (Antisubmarine Warfare) Support Aircraft Carrier

See also Amphibious Warfare Ships and Auxiliary Ships

BATTLESHIPS

BB	Battleship
BBG	Guided Missile Capital Ship

CRUISERS

CA	Heavy Cruiser
CAG	Guided Missile Heavy Cruiser
CB	Large Cruiser
CL	Light Cruiser
CLAA	Anti-Aircraft Light Cruiser

See also Command Ships

COMMAND SHIPS

Designation	Type
CBC	Large Tactical Command Ship
CG	Guided Missile Cruiser
CG(N)	Nuclear Guided Missile Cruiser
CLC	Tactical Command Ship
CLG	Guided Missile Light Cruiser

See also Cruisers

DESTROYERS

DD	Destroyer
DDC	Corvette
DDE	Escort Destroyer
DDG	Guided Missile Destroyer
DDR	Radar Picket Destroyer
DL	Frigate
DLG	Guided Missile Frigate

See also Mine Warfare Ships

SUBMARINES

SS	Attack Submarine
SS(N)	Nuclear-Powered Submarine
SSB(N)	Fleet Ballistic Missile Submarine

285

Appendix D

Designation	Type
SSG	Guided Missile Submarine
SSG(N)	Nuclear-Powered Guided Missile Submarine
SSK	Antisubmarine Submarine
SSR	Radar Picket Submarine
SSR(N)	Nuclear-Powered Radar Picket Submarine

See also Amphibious Warfare Ships and Auxiliary Ships

AMPHIBIOUS WARFARE SHIPS

Designation	Type
AGC	Amphibious Force Flagship
AK(SS)	Cargo Submarine
AKA	Attack Cargo Ship
AP(SS)	Transport Submarine
APA	Attack Transport
APD	High Speed Transport
CVHA	Assault Helicopter Aircraft Carrier
IFS	Inshore Fire Support Ship
LCM	Landing Craft Medium
LCU	Landing Craft Utility
LPD	Amphibious Transport Dock
LPH	Amphibious Assault Ship (Aircraft Carrier)
LS(FF)	Flotilla Flagship Landing Ship
LSD	Docking Landing Ship
LSI(L)	Infantry Landing Ship (Large)
LSM	Medium Landing Ship
LSMR	Medium Landing Ship (Rocket)
LST	Tank Landing Ship

MINE WARFARE SHIPS

Designation	Type
DM	Minelayer, Destroyer
DMS	Minesweeper, Destroyer
MCS	Mine Warfare Command & Support Ship
MHC	Minehunter, Coastal
MMA	Minelayer, Auxiliary
MMC	Minelayer, Coastal
MMF	Minelayer, Fleet
MSA	Minesweeper, Auxiliary
MSC	Minesweeper, Coastal (Nonmagnetic)
MSC(O)	Minesweeper, Coastal (Old)
MSF	Minesweeper, Fleet (Steel Hulled)
MSO	Minesweeper, Ocean (Nonmagnetic)

PATROL SHIPS

Designation	Type
DE	Escort Vessel
DER	Radar Picket Escort Vessel
PC	Submarine Chaser (173')
PCE	Escort (180')
PCER	Rescue Escort (180')
PCH	Submarine Chaser (Hydrofoil)
PCS	Submarine Chaser (136')
PF	Patrol Escort
PGM	Motor Gunboat
PR	River Gunboat
PT	Motor Torpedo Boat
SC	Submarine Chaser (110')

AUXILIARY SHIPS

Designation	Type
AD	Destroyer Tender
ADG	Degaussing Vessel
AE	Ammunition Ship
AF	Store Ship
AG	Miscellaneous
AG(SS)	Auxiliary Submarine
AGB	Icebreaker
AGP	Motor Torpedo Boat Tender
AGS	Surveying Ship
AGSC	Coastal Surveying Ship
AH	Hospital Ship
AK	Cargo Ship
AKD	Cargo Ship, Dock
AKL	Light Cargo Ship
AKN	Net Cargo Ship
AKS	General Stores Issue Ship
AKV	Cargo Ships & Aircraft Ferry
AN	Netlaying Ship
AO	Oiler
AO(SS)	Submarine Oiler

Appendix D

Designation	Type
AOE	Logistics Support Vessel
AOG	Gasoline Tanker
AOR	Replenishment Fleet Tanker
AP	Transport
APB	Self-Propelled Barracks Ship
APC	Small Coastal Transport
AR	Repair Ship
ARB	Battle Damage Repair Ship
ARC	Cable Repairing or Laying Ship
ARG	Internal Combustion Engine Repair Ship
ARH	Heavy-Hull Repair Ship
ARL	Landing Craft Repair Ship
ARS	Salvage Ship
ARSD	Salvage Lifting Vessel
ARST	Salvage Craft Tender
ARV	Aircraft Repair Ship
ARVA	Aircraft Repair Ship (Aircraft)
ARVE	Aircraft Repair Ship (Engine)
AS	Submarine Tender
ASR	Submarine Rescue Vessel
ATA	Auxiliary Ocean Tug
ATF	Fleet Ocean Tug
ATR	Rescue Ocean Tug
AV	Seaplane Tender
AVB	Advanced Aviation Base Ship
AVM	Guided Missile Ship
AVP	Small Seaplane Tender
AVS	Aviation Supply Ship
AW	Distilling Ship
CVU	Utility Aircraft Carrier
IX	Unclassified Miscellaneous

SERVICE CRAFT

Designation	Type
AB	Crane Ship
AFDB	Large Auxiliary Floating Dry Dock
AFDL	Small Auxiliary Floating Dry Dock
AFDM	Medium Auxiliary Floating Dry Dock
APL	Barracks Ship (Non-Self-Propelled)
ARD	Auxiliary Floating Dry Dock
AVC	Large Catapult Lighter
LCU	Utility Landing Craft
MSB	Mine Sweeping Boat
SMI	Minesweeper, Inshore
PT	Motor Torpedo Boat
PYC	Coastal Yacht
SST	Target & Training Submarine
X	Submersible Craft
YAG	Miscellaneous Auxiliary
YAGR	Ocean Radar Station Ship
YC	Open Lighter
YCF	Car Float
YCK	Open Cargo Lighter
YCV	Aircraft Transportation Lighter
YD	Floating Derrick
YDT	Diving Tender
YF	Covered Lighter (Self-Propelled)
YFB	Ferryboat (or) Launch
YFD	Yard Floating Dry Dock
YFN	Covered Lighter (Non-Self-Propelled)
YFNB	Large Covered Lighter
YFND	Covered Lighter (For use with Dry Docks)
YFNG	Covered Lighter (Special Purpose)
YFNX	Lighter (Special Purpose)
YFP	Floating Power Barge
YFR	Refrigerated Covered Lighter (Self-Propelled)
YFRN	Refrigerated Covered Lighter (Non-Self-Propelled)
YFRT	Covered Lighter (Range Tender)
YFT	Torpedo Transportation Lighter
YG	Garbage Lighter (Self-Propelled)

Appendix D

Designation	Type
YGN	Garbage Lighter (Non-Self-Propelled)
YHB	House Boat
YM	Dredge
YMP	Motor Mine Planter
YMS	Auxiliary Motor Mine Sweeper
YNG	Gate Vessel
YO	Fuel Oil Barge (Self-Propelled)
YOG	Gasoline Barge (Self-Propelled)
YOGN	Gasoline Barge (Non-Self-Propelled)
YON	Fuel Oil Barge (Non-Self-Propelled)
YOS	Oil Storage Barge
YP	Patrol Vessel
YPD	Floating Pile Driver
YPK	Pontoon Stowage Barge
YR	Floating Workshop
YRB	Submarine Repair & Berthing Barge
YRBM	Submarine Repair, Berthing & Messing Barge
YRDH	Floating Dry Dock Workshop (Hull)
YRDM	Floating Dry Dock Workshop (Machinery)
YRL	Covered Lighter (Repair)
YSD	Seaplane Wrecking Derrick
YSR	Sludge Removal Barge
YTB	Large Harbor Tug
YTL	Small Harbor Tug
YTM	Medium Harbor Tug
YTT	Torpedo Testing Barge
YV	Drone Aircraft Catapult Control Craft
YVC	Catapult Lighter
YW	Water Barge (Self-Propelled)
YWN	Water Barge (Non-Self-Propelled)

Source: The Navy Blue Book, Vol. 1, 1960, Bobbs-Merrill div., Macmillan Press, New York.

Appendix E

Australian English

Back or Beyond	The Boondocks; *see also* Never-never land
Billabong	Pond or lake formed by a sharp bend in a river or creek
Billy	Open tin container for heating tea water
Birds	Young women or girls, usually under thirty
Bloke	A man
Bloody	An English swear word, used for emphasis
Bonzer	Great, terrific
Bore	Water well
Brumbies	Wild horses
Bush	Wild interior areas of Australia
Chrissy	Christmas
Cobber	Friend, close buddy
Contact points	Electrical outlets in the wall
Cove	A man, chap, or fellow
Crook	Not feeling very well
Damper	A type of unleavened bread
Digger	A gold miner, and term for the Aussie soldier
Dingo	A wild dog, lives on sheep and small varmints
Dinki-di	Real, factual
Dinkum, Fair dinkum	True, honest, genuine
Footy	Football
Fossicker	Prospector, miner, explorer
G'day	Good day
Give it a bloody go!	Apply your maximum effort
Give it a fair go!	Apply a good amount of effort
Good-Oh!	Fine, great, will do it
Good on ya, Yank!	Right on!
Gum tree	Australian name for the eucalyptus tree
Have a go	Give it a try
Humpies	Aboriginal huts

Appendix E

Joey	A young kangaroo
Jumbuck	Sheep
Karri	Common tree for building in Australia and New Zealand
Knock me up	Ring my doorbell, come and see me
Knocked up	Tired, pooped
Mite, mites	Friends, mates
Mozzies	Mosquitoes
Never-never land	Worst part of the outback region
Nuddy	In the nude, naked
Ocker	Heavily accented Aussie, solid type of bloke
Outback	Remote regions of Australia, in the bush
Paddocks	Fenced-in fields for livestock
Paddy dodgers	Cattle and sheep rustlers
Pline	Plain
Plonk	Cheap wine
Pokey	Slot machine
Pommies	Derogatory term for English immigrants
Rice Dies	Race days
Right-Oh!	Sure thing, absolutely correct, I will do it
Ringer	Station hand or worker
Roight	Correct, right
Screw (noun)	One's pay
Screwed (verb)	To get paid
Sheila	General term for a girl or woman
She'll be right, mite!	It will turn out fine, not to worry
Shout	Buy a round of drinks
Smoke-oh!	Break for a cigarette
Snags	Sausages
Station	Sheep or cattle ranch
Stretchers	Folding army style cots
Stubbies	Beer bottles, full or empty
Stuffed	Screwed in a sexual manner, also an insult; get stuffed!
Styke and eyggs	Steak and eggs, a favorite meal Down Under
Swag	Bedroll and belongings, with tucker
Swagman	A tramp, wanderer carrying a swag
Tall Poppy	Outstanding person in some field of endeavor
Tea-oh!	A break for tea
That'll be the Bloody Dye!	Don't bet on it happening
Too Roight	Definitely all right
Tucker	Food
Walkabout	A long wandering in the bush by aboriginals
Waltzing Matilda	Carrying a swag
Wogs	Bugs, European immigrants
Wrinklies	Middle-aged and older Aussie women
Veggies	Vegetables

Bibliography

Archer, Jules. *Jungle Fighters,* Julian Messner Div., New York: Simon & Schuster, 1985.
Bevan, Denys. *United States Forces in New Zealand, 1942–1945,* Alexandra, N.Z.: Macpherson, 1992.
Brisbane City Council. "Brisbane Goes to War," Brochure, 1992.
Bulkley, Capt. Robert J., Jr. "At Close Quarters," Naval History Division, U.S. Navy, Govt. Printing Office, 1962.
Calhoun, Capt. C. Raymond. *Typhoon: The Other Enemy,* Annapolis: U.S. Naval Institute Press, 1981.
Castillo, Cdr. Edmund L. *The Seabees of WW2,* New York: Random House, Landmark Books, 1963.
Christmas, Linda. *The Ribbon and the Ragged Square,* New York: Viking Penguin, 1986.
Costello, John. *The Pacific War,* New York: Rawson, Wade, Atlantic Communications, 1981.
Gunther, John. *Inside Australia,* New York: Harper & Row, 1972.
Kurzman, Dan. *Fatal Voyage,* Atheneum, New York: Macmillan, 1990.
Lech, Raymond B. *All the Drowned Sailors,* New York: Military Heritage Press, by Stein & Day, 1982.
Lord, Walter. *The Lonely Vigil,* New York: Viking, 1977.
MacArthur's Staff. *The Campaigns of MacArthur in the Pacific,* Vol. 1, Washington, DC: Govt. Printing Office, 1966.
McNally, Ward. *New Zealand,* South Brunswick, NJ: A.S. Barnes, 1966.
Manchester, Wm. *The American Caesar,* New York: Dell, 1979.
Melville, John. *The Great White Fleet,* New York: Vantage, 1976.
Miller, Francis Trevelyan. *History of WWII,* Iowa Falls, Iowa: Riverside Book and Bible House, 1945.
Morison, Samuel Eliot. *U.S. Naval Operations in World War Two,* vol. 12, New York: Little, Brown & Co. and Atlantic Monthly Press, 1974.
Noel, John V. and Beach, Edward L. *Naval Terms Dictionary,* Annapolis: Naval Institute Press, 1988.
Porter, Peter. *Sydney,* Amsterdam, Netherlands: Time/Life Books, 1980.

Schlessinger, Stephen C. and Stephen Kinzer. *Bitter Fruit,* Garden City, NY: Doubleday, 1989.
Silverstone, Paul. *U.S. Warships of World War II,* Annapolis: Naval Institue Press, 1989.
Sloan, Ethel. *Kangaroo in the Kitchen,* Indianapolis: Bobbs-Merrill, 1978.
U.S. Naval Institute. *Ship Organization and Personnel,* Annapolis: Naval Institute Press, 1972.
Withey, Lynne. *Voyages of Discovery,* William Morrow, 1987.
Wedertz, Bill. *Dictionary of Naval Abbreviations,* Annapolis: Naval Institute Press, 1984.

Index

aborigines of Australia 100
accidents 79, 80, 88, 91, 93, 113, 114, 127, 138, 139, 142, 152, 163, 175, 186, 187, 190, 198, 203, 206, 238, 271, 272
Admiralties 131, 151, 164, 204
advancements in rating 163
"Advice" (poem) 184
aground: off Buna, New Guinea 128–130
Ahioma, New Guinea 113
air raid alarms *see* general quarters
Alameda, CA 13, 77, 107, 156
Alcona, USS (AK-157, U.S. Navy) 241
Alexischafen, New Guinea 175, 186, 195
Aliiti Islands, Solomons 92
Ambrym Island, New Hebrides 90, 96
American Bureau of Shipping 22
Ammen, USS (DD-527, U.S. Navy) 113
Andrews, Thomas D.: death 91, 114, 115
Antics, crew's ashore: Armand, hunt for 251, 252; author's dates with girls 123, 159, 160, 209, 211–213, 218, 220, 238, 250; aviation gas filching 64; bedbugs discovered 124; "Brooklyn" gets even 144, 145; buzzed by Air Force plane 204; captain's jeep, acquisition of 181, 182, 188; CPOs win at softball 195; date gets sick 215, 216; dinner invite to workman's home 57; fights ashore 60; getting gin in Brisbane 146; girl passes out in park 216, 217; "Grandma" 209, 214; Hogan's great liberty 56; horse races 66; ID card, loss of 56, 60, 142; injuries on liberty 172; last liberty in Sydney 249–253; mission to see the admiral 105, 106; mugging problem solution 121; old salts and flowers 54; parties 68, 76, 180, 181, 265; POW camp, a night in a 198; pubs in Auckland, New Zealand 54; pubs in Australia 124; sailor's good deed 200; "Sharecropper" at Ma's place 61, 62; ship's dances 70, 71, 140, 141, 211–214, 262, 268; "Slygoggers" 55, 61, 72; USO date, stateside 219; Yanks vs. British sailors 236, 237; see also AOL; AWOL; Fantail Liberties
Antics, crew's on board: alcohol on board 80, 81, 111, 118, 193, 194; beer delivery to Guadalcanal 77; boxing lessons 60; brewing on board 141; cargo diverted while loading 37; CPO entertains woman on board 267; engine room drenching 65, 66; filching plane parts 83; gambling 10, 44, 61, 126, 193, 194; hot plates, jury-rigged 204; jumbo boom, unshipping of 92, 93; locker inspection 246; mast-head light change-out 156; MM requests transfer 251, 268;

MM sick on alcohol 111; MM swigs liquid soap 191, 192; movie *Stagecoach* 176; obscene language 239; "Phantom Belcher" 147, 148; prostitutes on board 269, 270; seamen fighting 245; steward's mate's wine 82; swimming parties 82, 83, 89; "Walking Pawnshop" 68
ANZACS 237
AOL (Absent Over Leave) cases 56, 60, 69, 71, 76, 87, 88, 100, 103, 123, 155, 161, 171, 172, 210, 211, 218, 221, 222, 224, 235–238, 251, 253
Apache, USS (ATF-67, U.S. Navy) 226
APC-10, USS (U.S. Navy) 241
APC-11, USS (U.S. Navy) 164
appendicitis cases 171, 203, 226, 227, 254
Arawe, New Britain 90
Arequipa, USS (AF-31, U.S. Navy) 245
Arethusa, USS (IX-135, U.S. Navy) 202
Armament, *Octans*: 23, 26, 260; *see also* gunnery practice
Artie Shaw's Band 67, 140
Arunta, HMAS (Australian Navy) 114
assistant engineer 43, 111, 137, 169, 204, 210, 214, 227; at ship's dances 70, 141
atomic bomb 255, 264, 265
Auckland, New Zealand 44, 47, 48–52, 55, 61, 63, 65, 66, 70, 71, 73, 83, 86, 92, 106, 155, 255
Australia 38, 46, 75, 99, 100, 102, 103, 109, 110, 112, 118, 134, 139, 147, 153, 160, 162, 168, 170, 172, 196, 197, 198, 210, 213, 237, 253, 265, 266
Australians 106, 107, 110
Australian Army troops 90, 109, 186
Australian English 289, 290
Australian government 147
Australian Naval ships *see* individual ship
AWOL (Absent Without Leave) cases 144, 145, 202, 249, 252

Badung Badung Island, Philippine Islands 228
Baltimore, MD 272
Bam Island, New Guinea 182, 202
bananas 14–16, 21, 271

Barcoo, HMAS (Australian Navy) 254
Bataan, Philippine Islands 102
battle stations *see* general quarters
Biak, Schouten Islands 183, 184, 203
Bismarck Archipelago 127
Blue Ridge, USS (AGC-2, U.S. Navy) 127, 148
Blupblup Island, New Guinea 182, 202
Bogacio Island, New Guinea 91
Boise, USS (CL-47, U.S. Navy) 113, 152
boot camp 5–8
Borneo 245
Bougainville 62, 79
Bradley's Head, Sydney 208
Breakdowns, troubles: brine coils freezing over 42, 43; cargo spoiled 43, 45, 145; engines and shafts 40, 47, 59, 99, 113, 145, 159, 195, 196, 201; fireroom 89, 90, 119, 123, 162, 172, 254; gyrocompass 117, 118, 134, 145, 207; ice machine 59, 72, 73, 137; water in fuel oil 90, 118, 119, 134, 148
brig, Navy 179, 245
brig, *Octans see* disciplinary actions
Brisbane, Australia 109, 110–112, 131, 134, 145, 146, 153–155, 162, 167, 169, 171, 172, 175, 177–180, 182, 187–193, 196, 199, 201, 202, 207, 208, 224, 238, 251, 266–268
British empire 102
British government 237
British Navy 153; ships and sailors 237, 246, 250
British wars, ANZACS in 237
Brooklyn Navy Yard 274
Brooks, USS (APD-10, U.S. Navy) 130
Buchner Bay, Okinawa 274
Buna, New Guinea 46, 90, 113, 114, 117, 126–128, 130, 148
burial services ashore 114, 115
Bush, USS (DD-529, U.S. Navy) 113
BuShps 22, 39, 94

Calamares, USS (AF-18, U.S. Navy) 96, 270, 271
Camp Shoemaker, CA 273
Cape Byron, Australia 157

Index

Cape Cleveland, Townsville, Australia 196, 198
Cape Cretin, New Guinea 151, 153
Cape Gloucester, New Britain 90
Cape Moreton, Australia 109, 111, 112
Cape Sudest, New Guinea 130, 148
captain's activities 69, 77, 89, 91, 98, 99, 100, 127, 141, 152, 193, 198, 203, 205, 233, 264, 265, 267, 270–272
cargo handling 46, 47, 79, 80, 106, 168, 198, 206
cargo officer 47
Cavite, Philippine Islands 245
"Censored" (poem) 194–195
change in command 199, 242
Charleston, SC 271
Chester T, O'Brien, USS (DE-421, U.S. Navy) 241
Chestnut, USS (AN-11, U.S. Navy) 92
chief engineer 42, 43, 81, 204, 214, 215, 231
China Straits, New Guinea 113, 118, 125, 134, 147, 162, 166, 174, 177, 187, 192, 196, 207, 224
Choiseul Islands, Solomons 62, 78
chow 8, 48, 203, 204
Christmas: *1942* 9; *1943* 96, 98; *1944* 227, 228; *1945* 270, 271
Cinnamon, USS (AN-50, U.S. Navy) 164
Cleveland Bay, Townsville, Australia 196, 234
Cockatoo drydock, Sydney 201, 211
conditions of readiness 34, 35
Constellations: Centaurus 2; Octantis 2, 3; Southern Cross (The Crux) 2, 3, 45, 99, 162
convoys and commodores 77, 78, 84, 85, 92, 95, 96–98, 118, 127, 128, 130, 131, 151–153, 225, 230, 232, 241, 242, 245, 246, 254, 255
Coral Sea, and battle of 102, 110, 207, 234, 246
Cormorant Channel 202, 234, 239, 246, 253, 266
Corregidor, Manila Bay, Philippine Islands 265
Cowra, HMAS (Australian Navy) 151
CPO's status on ship 35, 44, 122, 204, 214
Crater, USS (AK-70, U.S. Navy) 92

Crew's quarters 23, 25, 44, 59, 157–159
Crossing equator 43, 265

Daniels, Josephus 81
Daring, USS (AM-87, U.S. Navy) 90, 92
Darwin, Australia 102, 103
Degaussing system 26, 28, 75, 77, 79, 82, 89, 143, 170, 171
D'Entrecasteau Islands 202
Desolation Point, Philippine Islands 228
Dinagat Island, Philippine Islands 228
Disciplinary actions: bread and water (P & P) 49, 92, 141, 142, 224, 236, 238, 239, 246, 256; brig confinement 49, 92, 95, 141, 142, 145, 146, 152, 153, 162, 171, 174, 175, 190, 201, 224, 236, 238, 239, 246, 248, 256; deck court martial 89, 95, 99, 106, 108, 111, 122, 138, 141, 142, 161, 162, 221, 238, 253; desertion, definition 249; discharged from the Navy 69; general court martial 61, 152; report mast, captain's 40, 43, 48, 49, 60, 61, 69, 72, 74, 76, 89, 92, 95, 99, 106, 108, 122, 138, 142, 143, 145, 161, 162, 166, 171, 174, 187, 198, 202, 204, 221, 224, 236, 238, 246, 251, 253, 256; shipboard restriction 138, 198, 248; summary court martial 44, 56, 61, 69, 172, 221, 238, 239
discipline, USN versus Merchant Marine 49
doctor, medical 61, 69, 84, 91, 120, 152, 169, 171, 185, 186, 203, 214, 254
Dongon, Philippine Islands 243
Down Under, post-war visit 109, 110
Doyle C. Barnes, USS (DE-353, U.S. Navy) 233
Dreger Harbor, New Guinea 131, 163, 164
drills: fire and abandon ship 76, 135, 147, 151, 153, 154, 156, 162, 164
"dry" Navy 81
"Duffy's Tavern," Espiritu Santo 76
Dulag, Philippine Islands 243
Dunk Island, Australia 112

Early, Bert 57
Early, Stephen J., FDR's Secretary 57
"Ebbett's Field," Espiritu Santo 76
Edwin A. Howard, USS (DE-346, U.S. Navy) 241
Efate, New Hebrides 46, 90
Empress Augusta Bay, Bougainville 79
engine testing 28, 42, 142, 145
Eniwetok 256, 264
Ensign, C Division 91
Ensign, Engineering 43
Ensign Fraser 122, 174, 175, 188, 193, 208, 229
Espiritu Santo, New Hebrides 46, 47, 58, 75, 76, 84, 89, 91, 96
Europe, war in 254, 257
executive officer: activities 45, 46, 49, 52, 60, 65, 70, 80, 89, 91, 92, 93, 95, 99, 115, 152, 177, 200; complaints against 104, 105; duties 49, 111; stalked 82; transferred and replaced 111, 139

fantail liberties 122, 123, 144, 168, 219, 238, 251; *see also* AWOL
Fighting Free French 46
Fiji 43, 46, 102
Filipino bumboats 230, 244
financial limitations 135
Finschafen, New Guinea 90, 109, 127, 130, 131, 151, 163, 166, 177, 183, 186, 192, 195, 206
fire control for guns 26, 260
fire fighting equipment 94
fire on board 93, 94, 182
first lieutenant 55, 56, 99
Fitzroy Island, Australia 112, 196
fleet hospital, Brisbane 180
Fleet Post Office (FPO) 98, 152, 153, 203, 225, 240
Florida Island, Solomons 79, 82, 91, 92
foul-ups: boiler sabotaged by chief engineer 263, 264; cargo doors welded shut 21, 39; cargo, dropped 79, 80; dumping surplus cargo 270; fight on board escort 185; flashing light on deck 38, 174, 175; flooding bilges in ice machine room 137; flooding cargo spaces 39, 40; fresh water contamination 41; fuel oil contaminates harbor 159; mail tampering 152; novice navigator 99; spoiled cargo 43, 45, 145; stability test report 27, 48; unauthorized use of water 187; wrong ice machine oil 40, 43, 73; wrong turn by helmsman 84, 85
foul-ups, *Octans:* drags anchor 271, 272; rams into dock 186, 187; runs aground 127–130; tangles with Destroyer Escort 272; tangles with merchant ship 175
"fragging" 105
Fraser Island, Australia 199
fresh water evaporator 25, 41
fumigating the ship 168, 169

Gagidu Hook 182
Gamadodo, New Guinea 113, 174
gambling among stevedores 106, 249
Garbutt Field, Townsville, Australia 197
Gascogyne, HMAS (Australian Navy) 186, 241
Geedunk stand 25, 42, 44, 98, 123, 216, 262, 263
general quarters 76, 78, 79, 89, 94, 100, 112, 145, 150, 151, 154, 164, 175, 177, 203, 226, 228–233, 239, 242, 243, 245, 255, 264
Gen. R.M. Blatchford, USS (AP-153, U.S. Navy) 254
George A. Johnson, USS (DE-583, U.S. Navy) 255
George E. Davis, (DE-357, U.S. Navy) 230
George Street, Brisbane 268
George Street, Sydney 170
Gepp, Sir Herbert 147
Germany surrenders 257
Gili Gili, New Guinea 182
Gili, New Guinea 113, 118, 126, 134
Glendale, USS (PF-36, U.S. Navy) 153, 166
Glenelg, HMAS (Australian Navy) 151
Goat Island, Oakland 273

Index

Golden Gate, CA 37, 40, 253, 257, 263, 264
Gona, New Guinea 90
Goulburn, HMAS (Australian Navy) 153
"Government Issue" (poem) 205
Graffias, USS (AF-29, U.S. Navy) 242
Great Barrier Reef, Australia 112, 118, 125, 134, 147, 167, 177, 196, 198, 207, 234, 236
Great Britain 17, 18, 52
Great Lakes Naval Training Station 1, 6, 9
Great White Fleet, UFC 14, 18, 23
Guadalcanal 38, 77, 78, 79, 92
Guam 264, 274
gunnery practice 134, 147, 150, 162, 203, 239, 247

Halsey, Admiral 79, 225
Ham Reef, New Guinea 148, 182, 196
Hawaii 99, 257
Hawaikii 72
Helm, USS (DD-388, U.S. Navy) 114
Henry T. Allen, USS (AP-30, U.S. Navy) 163
hernia cases 192, 193
Hiroshima, Japan 265
hobbies 41, 83
Hobson Bay, Melbourne 103
Hobson Street, Auckland, New Zealand 51
Hollandia, New Guinea 175–177, 179, 183–185, 203, 220, 224, 225, 233, 234, 238, 239, 246, 265, 266
Holnicote Bay, New Guinea 128
homosexual prisoners 152, 153
Honolulu, Hawaii 274
Hopewell, USS (DD-681, U.S. Navy) 241
Horii, Lt. Gen. 46
hotels, Sydney 124
Huaraki Gulf, Auckland, New Zealand 48, 73, 74
Hugh, Gunner's Mate 181, 203
Humboldt Bay, Hollandia, New Guinea 164
Humphreys, USS (APD-12, U.S. Navy) 130

Huon Bay, New Guinea 130
Hurley's Shipyard, Oakland, CA 257, 260, 261
Hyde Park, Sydney 200, 209, 210, 216, 218, 236, 238, 250

ice machine: problems 40, 42, 43, 75, 85, 113, 187, 188; procedures 96, 97, 117, 120; repairs 59, 72, 73, 137; systems 28, 30–31
Infantry, 37th Div. 79
Indianapolis, USS (CA-35) torpedoed 264, 265
inspections 9, 246
islands, conditions on 125, 126
Isu Bobo Island, New Guinea 182, 207
Isu Mina Point, New Guinea 207

Jamestown, USS (AGP-3) 241
Japan 77, 207, 229, 255, 272; surrenders 265
Japanese aircraft 227, 228, 230, 232
Japanese Army 55, 90, 110, 224, 254
Japanese plane on board 83
Jarvis Island 43
Jesse Rutherford, USS (DE-347, U.S. Navy) 254
Jomard Passage 202, 234, 239, 246, 253, 266

Karangahape Road, Auckland, New Zealand 63
Karkar Island, New Guinea 182
Kenneth M. Willett, USS (DE-354, U.S. Navy) 230
Kenney, General 79
Kilombangara, New Georgia 62
King George V of England 16, 147
King's Cross, Sydney 105, 137, 200, 209, 215, 236, 251, 252
Kiribili Point, Sydney 161
Kiwi, HMNZS (New Zealand Navy) 93

Knox, Frank, Sec. of the Navy, dies 151
Koli Point, Guadalcanal 93

Lamour, Dorothy 125
Landing Craft: LCT 184 126, 130; LCT 380, 389 126; LCT 389 126; LST 18 131; LST 68 114, 130; LST 168 114; LST 170 130, 131; LST 171 114, 127; LST 206 114; LST 454 127; LST 456 130; LST 458 127; LST 459 131; LST 464 114; LST 467 130; LST 470 131; LST 475 131
Langamak Bay, New Guinea 151, 153, 166, 186, 192, 195, 206
LCI(L) Flotilla 7 166
Leland E. Thomas, USS (DE-420, U.S. Navy) 241
Lend-Lease Act 75
Leslie L.B. Knox, USS (DE-580, U.S. Navy) 225, 244
Leyte, Philippine Islands 223–225, 228–230, 241–244, 246, 254, 264
Liberty Ship anchorage, Buna 117, 126
library, ship's 44
lieutenant commander 199
lieutenant (jg) punished 69
life lines on board 158
Liki Island, New Guinea 182
Limies 237; *see also* British sailors
liquor rationing 141, 215
Lithgow, HMAS (Australian Navy) 118
locker inspection 246
Lonely Hearts Club, Auckland, New Zealand 52
Long, USS (DMS-12, U.S. Navy) 127
Los Angeles, CA 109, 257, 273
Los Negros, Admiralties 131, 164
Lough, USS (DE-586, U.S. Navy) 246
LST Group 19 163
Lubang Island, Philippine Islands 244
Lunga Point, Guadalcanal 93
Luzon, Philippine Islands 265

MacArthur, General Douglas 38, 90, 99, 102, 103, 109, 131, 184, 195, 229, 244

McConnell, USS (DE-163, U.S. Navy) 92
machine shop on board 25
machinist's mate school 9, 10, 11, 42
Mack, USS (DE-358, U.S. Navy) 230
McNulty, USS (DE-581, U.S. Navy) 225–227
magnetic mines, defense against *see* degaussing system
mail 89, 98, 118, 136, 152, 153, 240
Makapu Light 257
Malaulalo Island, Solomons 92
Malekula Island, New Hebrides 92, 96
Mangaron Bay, Philippine Islands 243
Manila, Philippine Islands 245, 261, 264, 265, 267
manning complement 23, 279, 280
Man-of-war anchorage, Sydney 143, 171, 208
Manus, Admiralties 131, 151, 153, 164, 204, 206
Maoris of New Zealand 56, 71, 72
Mare Island Navy Yard, CA 13, 39, 77, 90
Marshall Islands 255
"Ma's" place, Auckland 55, 61, 62, 72
master-at-arms 25, 35, 41, 44, 49, 68, 88, 95, 122, 162, 175, 253, 256, 265
Mei-Mei-Ara Island, New Guinea 182
Melbourne, Australia 99, 100–103, 109, 160, 196
merchant ships 92, 97, 102, 118, 130, 131, 175, 230, 242
Merrill, Admiral 78
Metivier, USS (DE-582, U.S. Navy) 225
Midway, battle of 46
military police 109, 197, 200
Milne Bay, New Guinea 113, 123, 125, 126, 131, 134, 146–148, 152–154, 166, 174, 175, 177, 182
Mindanao Sea, Philippine Islands 243
Mindoro, Philippine Islands 225, 228, 243
mines *see* convoys
Mios Woendi, Schoutens 183
Mississippi, USS (BB-41, U.S. Navy) 23
Mizar, USS (AF-12, U.S. Navy) 96
Mobile Hospital #9 114

Mona Island, USS (ARG-9, U.S. Navy) 274
Moresby, New Guinea 103
Moreton Island, Brisbane 155
Morobe, New Guinea 148, 151
Motor Torpedo Boats, USS 279
Mount Hood, USS (AE-11, U.S. Navy) 206
movies on board 107, 176, 245
Mrs. Macquaries' Point, Sydney 142
MTB squadron at Woendi 193, 195
Mullaney, USS (DD-528, U.S. Navy) 113
Munda, New Georgia 39, 62
mysteries: dead bodies on board 153, 154; the Phantom Belcher 147, 148; seaman falls from crow's nest 91; torpedo sighting 164

Nagasaki, Japan 265
Nashville, USS (CL-43, U.S. Navy) 152
naval reserve 5, 49
Naval Supply Center, Oakland, CA 33
navigator 89, 99, 127, 202
Navy Receiving Barracks 61, 69, 72
Navy Receiving Station, San Francisco, CA 13, 21
Navy ship routine 34, 35
Neutral Bay, Sydney 161
New Britain 90
New Caledonia 37, 45, 46, 85, 97, 181
New Georgia 62
New Guinea 39, 46, 103, 109, 111, 112, 115, 123, 126, 127, 134, 147, 148, 151, 153, 162, 166, 175, 177, 195, 203, 207, 224, 239, 246, 253
New Hebrides 46, 75, 91
New South Wales, Australia 160, 196
New Zealand 38, 46, 47, 51, 52, 54, 57, 64, 67, 71, 72, 75, 86, 103, 104, 109, 110, 168, 256
New Zealand Naval ships *see* individual ship
Newman, USS (APD-59, U.S. Navy) 244
Norfolk Island 48
Norfolk 48, 271, 272

Noumea, New Caledonia 44, 46, 95–98, 225

Oakland, CA 37, 74, 98, 257, 273
Oakland Bay bridge 37
Octans, USS (AF-26, U.S. Navy) 13, 24, 27, 29, 64, 70, 78, 80, 81, 88, 95, 96, 97, 98, 105, 114, 116, 117, 119, 121, 126, 127, 130, 131, 138, 147, 153, 155, 156, 161–163, 167, 169, 174, 180, 186, 193, 196, 208, 209, 218, 219, 223, 225, 226, 232, 244, 246, 247, 251, 253, 256, 258, 260, 264–267, 271–273
Octans, constellation 2, 3
Octans Press News 116
The *Octans Scuttlebutt* 116, 131–133, 165, 176, 184, 185, 194, 204, 205, 240, 241
Officer of the Deck (OOD) 69, 76, 144, 147, 148, 168, 174, 190; parties 62, 63, 65; Whore House at Woendi Island 183, 184
Orange, USS (PF-43, U.S. Navy) 166
Ormoc, New Guinea 224
Oro Bay, New Guinea 115, 126
overhauls: in New Zealand 50, 58–60, 71–73; in Oakland, CA 261–263; in Sydney 136, 137, 139, 142, 145, 210, 214, 221
overloading the ship 39

P & P *see* disciplinary actions, bread and water
Padaido Island Atoll 193, 203
Panama 102, 271, 274
Pappy, MAA 41, 45, 68, 88
Papua, New Guinea 147
Parle, USS (DE-708, U.S. Navy) 255
Parramatta River, Sydney 201
passengers 89, 147, 153, 171, 174, 177, 189, 267, 268
patriotic seaman 44, 249
PC-1120, USS (U.S. Navy) 153
PC-1122, USS (U.S. Navy) 164
PC-1134, USS (U.S. Navy) 127, 131, 151

PCE-848, USS (U.S. Navy) 225
PCE-854, USS (U.S. Navy) 230
PCE-874, USS (U.S. Navy) 254
Pearl Harbor 46, 224, 228, 271
Pecos, USS (AO-65, U.S. Navy) 244
Pensacola, USS (CA-24, U.S. Navy) 109
Perth, Australia 267
Philippine Islands 38, 90, 109, 184, 192, 195, 207, 224, 225, 241, 242, 245, 264, 273
Phoenix, USS (CL-46, U.S. Navy) 113, 152
Platypus Channel, Townsville, Australia 196, 234
poems 131–133, 184, 185, 194–195, 205; *see also* individual title
point system of discharge 267
pommies, derivation of term 238
Port Jackson, Sydney 159, 171
Port Moresby, New Guinea 46
Port Phillip Bay, Melbourne 103
Portuguese man-of-war 84, 125, 126
postal inspector comes aboard 180
Potawatomi, USS (ATF-109, U.S. Navy) 244
POW camp, Townsville, Australia 197
prison, military 178
"pro" stations 57, 270
provisioning: the ship 34, 36, 37; the submarine fleet 37, 45
Pubs Down Under 54, 124
Puerto Cortes, Costa Rica 271
Purvis Bay, Tulagi 82, 83, 92

"Q" ship in convoy 77, 78
Quay Street, Auckland, New Zealand 51
Queen Street, Auckland, New Zealand 52, 63, 64

Rabaul, New Britain 46, 79
radar on board 25, 261
railroad system, Australia 196
Ralph Talbot, USS (DD-390, U.S. Navy) 114
Rangitoto Channel, New Zealand 89

rats and cockroaches on board 168
recognition signals 112, 124, 177, 242
red alerts 79, 83, 94, 115, 228–230
refrigeration, crew's mess stores 36, 98
refrigeration school 10–13
refrigeration system, ship's holds *see* ice machine
Rendova Island, Solomons 39
report mast *see* disciplinary actions
Rigel, USS (AR-11, U.S. Navy) 114, 130, 148, 163
Riley, USS (DE-579, U.S. Navy) 225, 226
Robert Brazier, USS (DE-345, U.S. Navy) 241, 254
Roosevelt, Eleanor 66–67
Roosevelt, Franklin Delano, death 254
Royal Australian Air Force 190, 191
Royal New Zealand Air Force 88
Royal New Zealand Navy 62
Russell Island, Australia 196

Saidor, New Guinea 90, 109
salt water showers 174
Samoa 43
San Antonia, Philippine Islands 244
San Cristobal, Philippine Islands 92
San Diego, CA 119, 219, 274
San Felipe, Philippine Islands 244
San Francisco, CA 13, 20, 21, 39, 73, 91, 98, 136, 175, 182, 219, 250, 256, 257, 261, 262, 273
San Pedro Bay, Philippine Islands 242, 245
Sanananda, New Guinea 90
Sands, USS (APD-13, U.S. Navy) 130
Sangay, USS (AE-10, U.S. Navy) 152
Sansapor, New Guinea 195
SC-737, USS (U.S. Navy) 130
SC-746, USS (U.S. Navy) 130
Schouten Islands 192, 203
scuttlebutt, and derivation 87, 88
sea sickness 37, 48, 76
SeaBees 79, 81, 94, 126
Seattle, Washington 171, 263
Secretary of the Navy 81, 151
Seeadler Harbor, Manus 151, 164, 205, 206

Segund Channel, Espiritu Santo 47, 76, 77, 91
service school 5–10
Servicemen's Readjustment Act of 1944 205
Seventh Fleet Service Force (SFSF) 90, 99, 104, 222, 241, 245
shakedown cruises, tests and sea trials 28, 36, 48, 72, 73, 74
Shanghai 268–271
"Sharecropper" 51, 61
ship types, USN 285–288
ship's service 23, 70
shore patrol activities 56, 57, 63, 69, 70, 74, 87, 88, 100, 107, 136, 142, 145, 161, 168, 172, 178, 180, 190, 197, 198, 213, 214, 217–219, 221, 224, 235, 237, 238, 248, 251
sick bay 25
"Slap-Happy Road," Auckland, New Zealand 63
the "slot" 62
Slygroggers 55, 72
"Smoke-O!" 106, 180
Solomons 39, 46, 62, 84
songs 7, 9, 15, 55, 56, 156
Southern Cross (The Crux) 2, 3, 99
stability problems 26, 27, 225
Stockton, USS (DD-646, U.S. Navy) 152
storm at sea 156–159, 225
Strahan, HMAS (Australian Navy) 164
"styke and eyggs" 57, 66, 104
submarines 78, 96, 126, 137, 147, 153, 162, 175, 226, 233, 241, 244, 256, 264
Subic Bay, Philippine Islands 244, 265, 267
Sudest Bay, Buna, New Guinea 162
Sula Sea, Philippine Islands 243
summary court martial *see* disciplinary actions
supply officer 45, 55, 62, 63
Surigao Strait, Philippine Islands 228, 243
Susquehanna, USS (AOG-5, U.S. Navy) 225
SWPA, SWPAC 98, 222
Sydney, Australia 103–105, 118, 119, 120–123, 131, 133, 135, 136, 138, 140, 142, 143, 146, 155, 159, 167, 169, 171, 177, 196, 199, 201, 202, 208–210, 212, 215, 217, 218, 224, 235–237, 246–248, 251–253, 268

Tacloban, Philippine Islands 224, 242, 273
Taivu Point, Guadalcanal 92
Talamanca, USS (AF-15, U.S. Navy) 96
Tasman Sea 48
Tasmania, Australia 100
"Tea-O!" 106, 180
Thomason, USS (DE-203, U.S. Navy) 184
Tokyo Rose 126
torpedo juice 81
torpedoes 137, 164, 170, 227, 233, 264
Torres Islands, Solomons 84, 96
Townsville, Australia 112, 196–198, 200, 234–236
Treasure Island Naval Station 37, 258, 273
Treasury Islands Group 62, 78
Triangulum, USS (AK-102, U.S. Navy) 183
Truk 79
Tufi Harbor, New Guinea 174, 196
Tui, HMNZS (New Zealand Navy) 94
Tulagi 38, 79, 82, 92, 93–95
Tunney, Gene 76
"Two-Up" game 106
Typhoon 225, 228, 274

Ulithi 225
Ulua, SS 17, 18, 19, 20, 21, 23, 27, 272; conversion of 21–27
uniforms, Navy 35, 36
United Engineering Co.: Alameda, CA 13, 21
United Fruit Company (UFC) 16–19, 20, 21, 43, 44, 96, 190, 258, 272
U.S. Air Force 80, 109, 112, 197, 204
U.S. Army Forces 90, 109, 113, 126, 197, 224, 235, 243, 244
U.S. Marines 38, 52, 67, 78, 126, 151
U.S. Navy Hospital 105, 138, 141, 248
U.S. Navy Officer Training School 220

U.S. Navy Receiving Stations 5, 234, 248, 273
U.S. Navy Refrigerated Stores ships, list 283, 284
U.S. Navy Seventh Fleet 244
U.S. Navy ships *see* individual ship
U.S. Navy Supply Depot #167 224

"The Vampire Sea" (poem) 132–133
Vella Lavella, New Georgia 62, 78, 88
venereal diseases 8, 9, 57, 61, 62, 87, 106, 113, 114, 120, 138, 141, 142, 144, 155, 180, 183, 184, 190, 214, 221
Veteran's Administration 152, 251
Victoria, Australia 103, 160, 196
Villalobos, USS (IX-145, U.S. Navy) 253
Visayan, Philippine Islands task force 225

Waga anchorage, New Guinea 147, 153, 183, 192, 207, 224
Waga, HMAS (Australian Navy) 164
Waga Waga, New Guinea 153
Waitemata Harbor, Auckland, New Zealand 48, 61
Walsh Bay, Sydney 142, 143
War Hawk, USS (AP-168, U.S. Navy) 273
War Shipping Administration 19, 40, 258
Warrega, HMAS (Australian Navy) 112
warrant officers 44, 49, 65, 92, 93
water: fresh, for the fleet 253, 254; rationing 41

Water King 41
waterspout 134
"What's the Use?" (poem) 131–132
whistle blowers 105
Wilson, Woodrow, President 81
Wilson Promontory, Australia 103
Woendi Island, Schoutens 179, 183, 184, 192, 203, 204
Wold Chamberlin Field, Minnesota 5, 273
Women's Australian Air Force Auxiliary 123
Woolloomooloo, Sydney 137, 138, 142, 159, 208–210, 222
working parties from passengers 166, 174
Workman Clark & Co. 16–18
Wright, USS (AV-1, U.S. Navy) 76, 241

"Yankee Standium," Espiritu Santo 76
Yanks in Australia 107, 140, 198, 200, 217, 218, 257
Yanks in New Zealand 52, 53, 54, 67, 257
Yerba Buena Island, San Francisco 28, 257
YMCA, San Francisco 13, 22
YMS-52 (U.S. Navy) 128
YMS-72 (U.S. Navy) 131
YMS-336 (U.S. Navy) 128
YO-161 (U.S. Navy) 256
YO-164 (U.S. Navy) 255

Ziegfeld's Club, Sydney 107, 108, 121, 140, 160, 169, 170, 200, 210, 211, 213, 220, 224, 236

Military History of Kenneth G. Oliver

With a year and a half of engineering college behind him, Mr. Oliver was sworn into the USNR at the Naval Recruiting Station at Wold Chamberlin Field, Minneapolis, Minnesota, on October 13, 1942, at age 20. He was assigned to the Great Lakes Naval Training Station on October 15 for basic training, which he completed November 13 with a fireman third class rating. After a short leave home, he reported back on November 26 to attend the Machinist's Mate course. He graduated top of the class of 525 students on March 22, 1943, with a second class machinist's mate rating.

After another short leave, he reported into the Naval Training School at Carrier Corp., Syracuse, New York, for a four week course in refrigeration. Upon completion of the course, he was transferred to the receiving station at San Francisco on May 5, 1943, for commissioning and fitting-out duty of the ex–*Ulua,* refrigerated banana carrier of the United Fruit Company Great White Fleet, vintage of 1917, which was destined to be the USS *Octans* (AF-26).

The *Octans* was commissioned on June 11, and left Oakland on June 29, bound for the South Pacific Area, with Oliver as lead petty officer of the six-man ship's refrigeration crew. The cargo consisted of fresh and frozen food for the South Pacific fleet, as it was to be for the remainder of the ship's tour of duty.

Its service was performed with an excellent record, as shown by the following estimates:

    Number of ports visited, many more than once   38
    Total number of military passengers carried   5400

Total miles steamed	120,000
Total weight of provisions carried in long tons	36,000
Total number of ships provisioned	3500 or more

Oliver left the *Octans* on May 23, 1945 for a thirty day leave, reporting to the USNRS at Minneapolis on June 27, and from there he was transferred to the Naval Receiving Barracks at Shoemaker, California. From there he travelled by Navy ships to Tacloban, Philippine Islands, then to Buckner Bay, Okinawa, and finally, to duty on the USS *Mona Island* (ARG-9), on September 14, 1945, in sole charge of the ship's refrigeration systems.

The *Mona Island* survived a typhoon, was towed to Guam for emergency repairs, and then limped through the Panama Canal, and into Brooklyn Navy Yard. Oliver was discharged from the USNR at the Personnel Separation Center, at Minneapolis on January 11, 1946, with a good conduct award. He is eligible to wear American Theater, Asiatic-Pacific Theater and Philippine Liberation campaign bars. He served in the New Guinea area from January 1944 to April 1945, and in the Philippine area from December 1944 to April 1945.

He is now a retired mechanical engineer, living in Shoreview, Minnesota.